GENDER AND CRIME

GENDER AND CRIME

Edited by

R. EMERSON DOBASH, RUSSELL P. DOBASH
AND LESLEY NOAKS

CARDIFF
UNIVERSITY OF WALES PRESS
1995

British Library Cataloguing in Publication Data

A catalogue record for this book is available from the British Library.

ISBN 0-7083-1301-9

Published with the financial assistance of the
British Society of Criminology

Cover design by Pentan Design Practice

Typeset at the University of Wales Press
Printed in Wales by Dinefwr Press, Llandybïe

Contents

Acknowledgements

The editors would like to thank all of the contributors to this volume and all those who participated in the 1993 British Criminology Conference at Cardiff. We would also extend our thanks to the British Society of Criminology for their support both for the conference and the publication of this book.

Thanks are due also to the School of Social and Administrative Studies, University of Wales, Cardiff and the team of helpers at the 1993 conference, too numerous to mention individually but without whom neither the conference nor this publication would have been possible.

Editors and Contributors

John Beynon is a Reader in the School of Humanities and Social Sciences at the University of Glamorgan.

Kate Cavanagh is a Lecturer in the Department of Social Work, University of Glasgow.

Richard Collier is a Lecturer in Newcastle Law School, University of Newcastle.

Hazel Croall is a Principal Lecturer in the School of European and International Studies at Thames Valley University.

Russell P. Dobash is Senior Lecturer in the School of Social and Administrative Studies at University of Wales, Cardiff.

R. Emerson Dobash is Professor in the School of Social and Administrative Studies, University of Wales, Cardiff.

Ruth Frances is a researcher in the Department of Criminology, University of Melbourne.

Sylvie Frigon is Assistant Professor in the Department of Criminology, University of Ottawa.

Jo Goodey is a Lecturer in Law at the University of Sheffield.

Ruth Lewis is a Lecturer in Social Policy at the University of Newcastle.

A. Mark Liddle is a Research Fellow at the Institute of Criminology, University of Cambridge, and Research and Policy Development Officer at the London office of NACRO.

Lisa Maher is a Research Fellow at the University of New South Wales.

Rob Mawby is Principal Lecturer in Social Policy at the University of Plymouth.

Bronwyn Naylor is a Lecturer in the Faculty of Law at Monash University Victoria.

Lesley Noaks is a Lecturer in the School of Social and Administrative Studies, University of Wales, Cardiff.

Julie M. Owen is a Lecturer in Sociology at Barton Peveril College.

Margaret Shaw is Assistant Professor in Sociology in the Department of Sociology and Anthropology, Concordia University, Montreal.

Keith Soothill is Professor of Social Research in the Department of Applied Social Science, Lancaster University.

Richard Thurston was Leverhulme Research Fellow in the University of Glamorgan 1992–3 and is now Senior Researcher for Mid Glamorgan Probation Service.

Andromachi Tseloni is a researcher in Economics for the Greek Government.

Sandra Walklate is Reader in Criminology at the University of Keele.

Ania Wilczynski is Project Officer for the Child Deaths Review Committee, New South Wales Child Protection Council, Sydney, Australia.

Sam Wright is a researcher at the Centre for Research into Health and Substance Abuse, Manchester Metropolitan University.

Maggie Wykes is a Lecturer in Communication and Cultural Studies at Trinity College, Leeds University.

1

Thinking about gender and crime

R. EMERSON DOBASH, RUSSELL P. DOBASH
AND LESLEY NOAKS

Serious analysis of the relationship between gender, crime and
victimization did not begin until the 1970s when feminist scholars
focused on women as victims and criminals. The bulk of this early
feminist analysis centred on the physical and sexual victimization of
women, showing how historically and still today the hierarchical
gendered structures of society are intrinsically related to male
violence against women. Patriarchal relations loomed large in these
analyses, wherein it was argued, for example, that the privileged
position of men within the household led to violence against
partners. Other scholars focused on the much neglected role of
women in crime, revealing a glaring omission of this issue within
traditional criminologist discourse. Initial feminist work further
revealed that extant explanations of crimes of women were riddled
with unfounded assumptions about the motivations and backgrounds
of women who committed crime. In the last two decades an
extraordinary amount of work has been produced to provide more
valid knowledge of the victimization of women and the social and
cultural factors associated with their commission of crime. Gradually,
through the accumulation of this work the importance of gender
began to be more widely recognized. Recent theoretical and empirical
work on gender and crime has revealed the direct relationship
between masculinity and crime.

Despite the usual neglect of the issue of gender and crime, much
criminology in the post-war era, particularly, although not exclusively,
in the United States, was concerned about the relationship between
the attributes of males and the commission of crime. In the late 1950s
and early 1960s American theories of gang delinquency focused on
the way certain forms of maleness constituted functional adjustments

to status and achievement problems experienced in schools and wider society. In this type of analysis, patterns of working-class gang delinquency were seen as unique functional adaptations to the 'structural strains' and 'status frustrations' of school and neighbourhood. The implicit assumption of much of this work was that such functional adaptations were distinct cultural practices and patterns of young males from ethnic minorities and working-class backgrounds. Prison research of the same period focused on male subcultures of solidarity within institutions, identifying the 'male' values and patterns of behaviours associated with these cultures as means of functional adaptations to the pains of imprisonment. Another important focus of this work was patterns of sexually predacious behaviour of male inmates as a central feature of prison life. These studies provided important insights into patterns, values and actions that were linked to 'maleness'; the limitations of these early investigations involved a failure to link the 'functional adaptations' associated with delinquent gangs and inmate cultures to wider, hegemonic masculinities. Newer approaches emphasize hegemonic masculinity as a touchstone for a range of masculine ideals and practices. Emerging perspectives emphasize the social practices of young adult males – such as risk taking and defence of honour – as direct correlates of the commission of crime. Although masculinity is fractured and fragmented through social differentiation associated with, for example, class and ethnicity the core or at least central elements of risk taking, aggression and violence are central to an understanding of the crimes of males. Social practices associated with these factors were often apparent in criminology research but rarely foreground and explicitly analysed. The new scholarship on gender and crime seeks explicitly to explore these links.

Gender and Crime intends to contribute to this growing body of knowledge of gender, crime and victimization by bringing together the work of scholars from several countries. The papers included in this volume cover a range of issues: media representation of the crimes of women, violence and gender, masculinity and crime, victims and gender and criminal justice responses to violence against women. A variety of methods and concerns are represented, reflecting the new scholarship in this area. While there is a focus on the discourse of crime and victimization in many chapters, others consider gender issues more directly by analysing the actual patterns of behaviours and attitudes associated with crime and victimization.

In many papers, empirical analysis offers illuminating evidence, while in others theoretical discourses provide important insights.

The book begins with four papers examining media representations of gender and crime. In 'A Genealogy of Women's Madness', Sylvie Frigon begins the section on media representation of gender and crime with a deconstruction of the representation of the disorders, protests and struggles of women as 'madness' rather than actions denoting the civil disobedience of the citizen, the independent protests of community activists and/or the reactions of women against errant or violent husbands. She notes that in Britain 'while women constitute 4 per cent of the prison population, they represent 20 per cent of the patients in "special hospitals"'. Different 'regimes' of meanings ('regular patterns of occurrence of meanings or a mode of rule or management of different meanings') and images of women who transgress moral, cultural and legal boundaries are examined.

The genealogy of women as mad journeys through the representation of the witch, 'murderess', terrorist and political protester. The purpose is to consider the 'normal' and the 'pathological' meanings attached to the category 'woman' in order to 'demonstrate that these regimes of meanings pivot around womanhood'. Four theories of witchcraft are explored: the witch as mental patient, as healer, as scapegoat and as sexual deviant and the connection to modern psychiatric discourse is made. In both, the 'fallen woman', having stepped out of her 'proper place', is 'doomed to downfall'. The criminal woman is, by definition, a 'fallen woman', and the discourse of women criminals and prisoners, both past and present, is replete with such representations. Media commentary on the political actions of women, as exemplified by the lengthy protest of the Greenham Common women, follows similar patterns of discourse that disqualify the voices of women through criminalization of their demands, sexualization of their protests and psychiatrization of their voices as hysterical. 'The disciplinary matrix criminalization/ sexualization/psychiatrization is therefore an important way of disqualifying women's resistance and defiance to (white) masculine hegemonies.' Given the history of this type of representation of the protests of women, the narrative of the Greenham Common story was already written before the event occurred. The story of the Suffragettes illustrates the disqualification of political protest through the process of criminalizing militancy and the use of techniques of neutralization to confront disorder, with the vote occupying a central place of importance in defining women because without it women would not be 'complete citizens or complete reasonable people'. Frigon concludes that 'the representations of femininity in dissent are not totally dissociated from the representations of women who conform'.

Maggie Wykes follows with 'Passion, Marriage and Murder' in which she analyses the discourse used by the media in reporting cases of 'intimate' murders – killing of heterosexual lovers or spouses. The specific focus is on British press coverage of several cases during the 1990s. Going beyond anecdotal evidence and abstract theoretical discourse, Wykes applies rigorous empirical analysis to current notions about the gendered nature of media discourses about women and men who kill their intimate partners. The reader is treated to evidence rather than claims and suppositions; for no matter how developed or sophisticated the theory it cannot stand alone, does not convince and should not persuade simply through assertion alone.

'The norm of social power relations is composed partly of the dominance of men over women but also depends on the rule of law to control deviance . . . How can men who kill be accounted for in terms which castigated the illegality but continue the legitimation of male power . . .?' Investigating this and other issues is meant to 'inform a politics and praxis committed to resolving gender inequality'. An analysis of the discourses about men and women who kill their partners is set within and meant to add to the development of a wider analysis of gender within the broader social context, and Wykes asks:

> Without analysis of the discourse of violence as predominantly masculine how can the problem of violence in any arena be addressed; how can the mechanisms which allow it to continue be explained; how can women's place in that paradigm be considered and how can the continued social construction of subjects in unequal gendered relations, after thirty years of second wave feminism, be understood?

The answers formulated at both the level of the specific topic under consideration and the wider theoretical level are important and revealing. Submitting the 'data' of media representation to systematic analysis rather than creating another form of discourse, theoretical stance or ideological position strengthens the critical agenda and provides more subtle and sophisticated insights – 'The textual analysis indicates the active exercise of patriarchal power and in that very process reveals the possibility of a different reading and resistance.'

Bronwyn Naylor continues the analysis of media representation in her examination of the explanations of women's violence found in newspaper reporting. She maintains that explanations are central to labelling behaviour as criminal, attributing responsibility, deciding on disposition. 'Routine explanations' for women's crimes can be identified in criminal trials and reporting of crime in the media; they arise from 'discussions of intentionality and the use of various defences; in pleas in mitigation of sentence; and in sentencing decisions and judicial comments on sentence'. The media devote considerable space to violence and, according to Naylor, disproportionately report stories of women's violence. While only 6 per cent of crime involves personal violence, 'the main national UK newspapers devoted 64.5 per cent of crime reporting to stories of personal violence'. 'Violence by women is doubly fascinating; criminal women are titillating and at the same time horrifying in ways that violent men generally are not.' About one-third of violent crime stories in newspapers are about women offenders whilst their representation in the criminal statistics is much less. Violence incorporates drama, human emotion, and shattering of 'normal' expectations; violence by women offers up all of that as well as 'sexualized drama and emotion'. The expectations breached are not just those of normal human interaction but also gendered expectations. Love triangles and 'contract killings' are particularly newsworthy. Naylor proposes six 'common sense' stories used by the press in reporting about violent women; they are gendered in important ways. They include: madonna/whore; sexual passion/love as an 'excuse' for crime; reproduction and madness; the figure of evil – the witch – the monster; the criminal woman as 'not-woman'; and the female as devious and manipulative. These are discussed in detail using illustrations from both tabloid and broadsheet newspapers.

Completing this section is Keith Soothill's 'Sex Crime News from Abroad'. News coverage of sex murder and rape cases in Britain is compared primarily with those from the United States. Soothill notes that reports of rape are 'often titillating and more damaging to the victim' than reports of sex murder or serial killers. When concern at government level about the reporting of rape 'led to recommendations that the media should be banned from publishing the name of the raped woman and courts prohibited from enquiring into her previous sexual history (Sexual Offences (Amendment) Act 1976)' some believed that this might lead to a lessening of media interest in 'reporting rape in a [sensationalist] manner which could well deter rape victims from reporting the offence to the police'. Media interest, however, has increased rather than declined and might be seen 'as part of a soft-porn package to sell newspapers', with sex cases from abroad forming a significant part of this package and, importantly, falling outside the strictures of the 1976 Act. Soothill notes that while the overseas coverage of major events such as earthquakes, starvation and the overthrow of governments may be ignored, foreign sex stories are often highlighted, raising the question of whether 'the stories [are] potent symbols of what is of widespread concern throughout the world or is the choice of cases from abroad simply guided by the more prurient interests of newspapers [at home]?' Nine British newspapers for two sample years, 1985 and 1992, were examined to assess the nature and extent of the use of such material and to note shifts that might be occurring. The focus is on coercive sex, posing questions such as: Is such material from abroad used liberally by British newspapers? In which countries do stories originate? Do some British newspapers make greater use of this material than others? Is it on the increase? Is it changing? The infamous rape case of the American professional boxer Mike Tyson and the dominance of the American media provide some of the answers, but the question remains as to which British newspapers use 'this potential source of information and/or titillation' and what kind of material attracts most attention? Soothill concludes that some dramatic shifts are taking place with the themes of 'horror' and 'links with Britain' playing an important role in selection of material for presentation.

The section on criminal women and violence examines explanations of women offenders, women's violence, the killing of children by parents and women's agency in drug taking. This section opens with Shaw's 'Confronting Violence by Women'. She notes that in Canada, the current discourse about women and law centres on their 'low social and economic status . . . the extent of social controls over their behaviour, and . . . their position as victim'. One social label replaces another – 'the unfit mother or the fallen woman . . . becomes the helpless victim with low self-esteem'. A universal label seems to be applied to all women in the criminal justice system and 'oversimplifies explanations of their situation and behaviour'. 'At the level of the courts it has become "incorporated", particularly in terms of the Battered Woman Syndrome' in ways 'not always in the best interests of women' – to pathologize violence by women – or leading to 'counter-claims that women are just as violent in domestic situations as men'. While emphasizing that women who are violent to or kill men in a domestic relationship usually do so in the context of a history of male violence, Shaw wants to examine 'how many other women use violence apart from those who kill an abusive partner, and outside a domestic situation?' and how they and their violence might be contextualized and understood. What about the woman bank robber who kills, Canada's 'Machine-gun Molly' or Aileen Warnous, the first female 'serial killer' in the USA? The Canadian prison population of women charged with violent offences is small but apparently growing. They attract sensationalist reporting and 'there are a number of interrelated issues to be considered in confronting women as perpetrators of violence': media representations; oversimplification and single explanations; conceptualizing women's violent behaviour in masculine terms; the problem of what is meant by the word 'violent' in the criminal justice system and society in general; and the links between being victimized and using violence; and the problem of the appropriate and just response to women designated as violent. Each of these is examined in detail and Shaw puzzles over the complexities of human agency in women's acts of violence.

The issue of women's agency and intentionality in deciding to take illegal drugs and in the way they are consumed is addressed by Lisa Maher in 'In the Name of Love: Women and Initiation to Illicit Drugs'. Based on interviews with women drug users in New York, she examines the role of men in the drug taking of women. Do men lead women into taking drugs or do they find their own way into the world of drug taking and drug takers? Do men initiate women into drug taking? Do women just 'go along' with the activities of boyfriends and lovers or do they actively pursue these activities in their own right? Are there differences between women from various ethnic backgrounds in terms of whether men are involved in their initiation into drug use and/or the company they keep while consuming drugs? For Maher, the answers lie in the detailed accounts given by the women interviewed. While women's accounts of their own acts reveal a form of independence of action for some, they also provide insights into the wider contexts of poverty, racism and sexism which severely constrict the parameters within which individual choices might be made, leaving the reader with questions about wider issues and the limits of explanations solely based on interpretative accounts of human agency, whether applied to women or men, within the brutal, restricted and impoverished environments described by Maher.

Filicide, parental killing of a child, is a rare event and often assumed to be committed by 'someone who is either evil or mentally deranged'; it is also differentiated by the gender of the perpetrator. Ania Wilczynski examines forty-eight cases from files of the Director of Public Prosecutions (DPP) in England (28 female and 20 male offenders). She considers the role of social and gender issues on three dimensions of the cases: motivations, background features and the criminal justice response. Filicides are classified into eleven categories of motives ranging from jealousy to altruism and she notes gender differences in the nature of filicides committed by men and women. 'It is clear that men and women tend to kill their children for very different reasons', with men predominating in cases motivated by possessiveness, retaliation, jealousy, rejection by the victim, and discipline; and women tending to kill because they are psychotic, the child is unwanted or for altruistic reasons. 'This sex difference reflects an extreme version of traditional gender roles, in which men are socialized to be aggressive, dominant and sexually possessive, and women are taught to internalize stress and anger, and be passive, nurturing and self-sacrificing.' 'Risk' factors are classified according to demographic, social, psychiatric, situational and victim characteristics. 'Put simply, misery, isolation and instability are strongly correlated with filicide. Numerous social stresses [include] financial and housing problems, youthful parenthood, marital conflict, lack of preparation for parenthood and children who are difficult to care for . . . [offenders] usually have a lack of compensatory personal and social resources with which to cope with their problems.'

Wilczynski's study reveals that gender plays an important role in determining the nature of criminal justice response to those who kill: 'men are bad and normal' and to be treated in accordance with the 'legal/punishment' model while women are 'mad and abnormal' and in need of the 'welfare/treatment' model. And whilst criminal justice enforcement predicated on traditional gender stereotypes can be very oppressive to women (particularly young women), it would also appear that they can at times benefit from them. 'When a woman kills her own child, she offends not only against the criminal law, but against the sanctity of stereotypical femininity: it is therefore assumed that she must have been "mad".' It will not be lost on the reader that there are numerous points of correspondence with the chapters on media representations of criminal women and in a different way Wilczynski's chapter raises the question of women's agency in the commission of this particular crime.

As noted earlier, gender is no longer simply a 'code word' for women and femininity; but also refers to men and masculinity. The focus of the chapters in the section on Men, Masculinity and Crime and the final section on Criminal Justice Responses to Violence Against Women is on crimes committed by men. In 'Men, Violence and Masculinity', Richard Thurston and John Beynon report the findings of a study of the cultural context of men's everyday lives and their use of violence: '. . . what compels some men to use physical and/or symbolic violence?' Life history interviews, in-depth semi-structured interviews and participant observation were used over a number of weeks with thirty male offenders in prison and on probation. Thurston and Beynon comment on the cultural politics of identity using the life-history method of research. Both individual agency and cultural determination are considered in their attempt to 'make sense of connections between violence and masculinities'. They focus on gendered power relations at the institutional, cultural and symbolic levels in the formation of identities. Their primary interest is understanding how men construct their sense of masculinity through violence in various contexts; how violence is used to produce and sustain identity; and how this view of masculinity might be used politically to challenge men's violence. This forms part of their 'on-going attempt to explore the possibilities of critical life-history work with men for both theory, politics and practice'. The analysis gives 'clues as to how certain narrow definitions of "what it means to be a man" or "manly" are learned, discovered, expressed, and sustained (or reproduced) through violent acts and interactions'. 'The stories men tell about being violent, and the language and manner and context in which such stories are told, can provide insights into the gendered nature of some men's violence.' A biker, a wife-beater and a drinker tell their stories of developing a masculine identity.

In 'A Father's "Normal" Love?', Richard Collier notes, '. . . what we as a society understand "responsible" fathering to involve has moved to the centre of the political stage in Britain in relation to both the family and, in particular, to crime . . . Criminology is, at present, at something of a critical juncture with regard to what is being increasingly called the issue of the "masculinity of crime".' With a purported connection by politicians of a correlation between the absent father and criminality, dangerous male youth and single mothers have simultaneously been constructed as central to a 'law and order' agenda. Debates about the family and juvenile delinquency date back at least to the Victorians, but Collier is concerned with how criminology conceives of the 'masculine problematic' – the range of changes taking place around masculinity – in attempts to make sense of current social and political debates. An examination of the history of the concept of fatherhood in law is developed in order to explore 'what has to be at the heart of criminology's own project and [to] locate historically the emergence of specific discourses of masculinity'. Within the discourse of family law, masculinity has been constructed in terms of the respectable, caring, economically responsible, middle-class father in residence. Within criminology, the central project and discourse has been that of the wild, deviant, under-achieving, working-class young male. While both family law and criminology are largely based on models of masculinity, neither is truly aware of the model of the other and, more importantly, both are largely unaware of their own model. 'Criminology has, in short, failed to ask what it may be about men . . . not as working-class, not as immigrants, not as underprivileged individuals but *as men* that induced them to commit crime'.

Criminology needs to take seriously the central core of its intellectual project, the hitherto unarticulated problem of masculinity and crime. The work of feminist scholars has moved the agenda beyond previous positions of family law and criminology and problematized masculinity within both. Collier develops the history of the social construction of discourses of masculinity, particularly fatherhood, in relation to current political debates about crime, order and social stability as they are articulated in relation to single mothers and absent fathers, illustrated in the Child Support Act 1991 and embodied in the Child Support Agency. Collier notes that 'father absence' is problematized relative to crime among the 'underclass' and ultimately blamed upon lone mothers (with an eye to removing social benefits), while the absent father is, in fact, deemed both necessary and beneficial within the notions of the respectable, responsible father who is of necessity absent – sometimes to great excess – in the act of earning a living. Further, the discourse of the family man as a singularly positive image denies the physical and sexual crimes of violence men commit within the family and transforms legal reforms sought in order to help women into 'attacks' upon men. Imagining the family man as 'dangerous' remains profoundly difficult so long as he appears to be, a priori, the antithesis of that danger. Challenging the law's 'foreclosure of alternative subject positions involves fragmenting the purported unity of this heterosexual identity and revealing its sociality'.

The chapters included in the section on Victims and Gender address a variety of issues, including victims of physical violence, of child sexual abuse, of threatening behaviour and of white-collar crime as well as examinations of a victim oriented criminal justice system and self-conscious reflections upon feminist research on victims. In 'Target Women?', Croall examines while-collar crimes in which women are the sole or primary victims. Noting that the victimization of women through white-collar crime is largely unexplored, she provides an exploration of a whole range of issues. The realms of work, health, safety and wages may all be arenas in which women are victimized in a variety of ways. Sweat-shop conditions in the garment industry; the risk of miscarriage and respiratory ailments in 'high tech' industries such as silicone chip manufacture; dermatitis, asthma and bronchitis associated with working with high concentrations of food additives are examples. While all workers, male or female, may suffer the effects of poor and unsafe conditions at work, women may be particularly vulnerable to these conditions because of occupational segregation. Low pay and part-time status are problems in their own right and may contribute to women's vulnerability to the offences of employers. Additionally, sexual harassment at work either by employers or fellow employees occurs with some frequency and in a context of few protections either to prevent such behaviour or to respond effectively to those who perpetrate it. As consumers, women may be the target of fraud and deception under the Trades Descriptions Act for a host of consumer goods. Slimming products, cosmetics, and cosmetic surgery are specifically, if not exclusively, oriented to women and may be the subject of deception, over-pricing and misleading claims. Infamous cases include contraceptive scandals such as the Dalkon Shield intra-uterine device, first found unsafe in Western countries, then 'dumped' on the developing world; the thousands of birth defects associated with prescribing Thalidomide; and deaths and illness linked to consumption of certain 'chilled foods'. Forgery and fraud in the manufacture and/or sales of jewellery, perfumes, fashion goods and clothes involve substantial sums of money. The elderly woman or widow may be particularly vulnerable to bogus financial investors. Finally, women are also vulnerable to the crimes of physical and sexual violence which are discussed in this chapter and also considered in chapters by Owen and by Wright.

Julie Owen continues with a presentation of her research on victims which includes men as victims rather than in their more usual position as perpetrators. The premises of feminist research and method are examined in some detail, outlining the existing debates about qualitative and quantitative research methods and opting for the former. Focusing on the researcher as part of the research process allows for a self-conscious examination of the gendered roles of the researcher and respondent. Further insights are developed through the examination of the complexities and contradictions of a woman researcher interviewing men about their experiences of victimization. The usual positions of power and authority of the researcher and the abilities to empathize and relate as a 'fellow traveller' are made more transparent and problematized. Owen provides insight into the deeply gendered nature of experiences of violence and intimidation, willingness to discuss such experiences in the research context and differences in the willingness of men and women to be defined as victims. For some men it is possible to 'redefine the experience of violence in an almost positive light, and re-cast themselves as heroic moral victors and/or gallant losers'. In Owen's research men were more likely to relegate violent experiences to the past and see themselves as developing the skills to avoid further victimization. Men resisted acknowledging that they had been 'victims' as it seems inconsistent with notions of masculinity whereas no such contradiction exists between 'victim status' and traditional concepts of femininity. 'Significantly, when the men had become victims despite these skills, while being very traumatic and often having lasting effects, they could still be retrospectively mythologized in a way that violence experienced by women is not.'

As Owen's chapter shows, gender can have an important differential effect on responses to violent victimization. Andromachi Tseloni's chapter shows that gender is also an important determinant of the incidence of threats as revealed through an analysis of three years of the British Crime Survey. Using powerful statistical techniques – negative binomial regression analysis – her paper reveals the significant patterns associated with threats in a national sample.

As she points out, threats have been largely ignored by criminologists, although they can and do result in criminal prosecutions. The potential emotional and social consequences of these acts, as with school bullying, should not be ignored. Fear, anxiety and apprehension may be short- and long-term consequences of threats and if severe and/or repeated they may completely transform a person's sense of security and patterns of behaviour.

Tseloni examines the impact of a number of socio-demographic and life-style variables on the prevalence and repeat incidence of threats in the lives of men and women. Comparing rates of threats to an ideal typical statistical model of the type of individual who seems least likely to experience threats, she finds some clear and consistent patterns. Those most likely to be threatened live more outgoing lives in public settings and are likely to be poor unemployed inner-city males. Divorced women living on their own with children are also at considerable risk. Regional differences are also apparent; the risks of experiencing a threat are elevated for those living in the north-west, south-east and south-west. Tseloni notes that 'social vulnerability' is significantly linked to the risk of threats. Her evidence on active, young males mirrors existing research on risk of assaults; the novel finding concerns repeated threats directed at divorced women. Unfortunately, the data are not yet available to consider the specific relationship between those who engage in threatening behaviour and their victims, but as Tseloni notes 'divorced women . . . may be threatened by their present or former spouse', a pattern all too familiar to those who research violence in the home.

Jo Goodey's chapter 'Fear of Crime: Children and Gendered Socialization' considers another much-neglected issue. Very little research has investigated the nature and levels of fear among young people, whereas we apparently know a great deal about the way adults react to imagined and real incidents of crime. When young people appear in the literature of criminology it is usually as offenders not victims. Seeking to rectify this omission Goodey conducted research on the fears of girls and boys between the ages of eleven and sixteen. Goodey's study is located in a gendered analysis of the childhood development of males and females with a particular emphasis on the way puberty affects identity and attitudes. Using a primarily quantitative approach she shows that there is considerable fear among the young people she asked to fill out her questionnaire, and it seems children's fears are similar to but also distinct from those of adults. Like adults, children fear poorly lit areas and certain types of people, but they are also much concerned about other issues such as stray dogs. Levels of fear, Goodey shows, are strongly related to gender, but age is an additional factor and she demonstrates how the two interact in the creation of apprehension among the young.

Mark Liddle's chapter also focuses on children. He is primarily concerned to confront a number of libertarian arguments regarding sexual relations between adults and children. Libertarian arguments regarding sexual relations between children and adults, while certainly not in the ascendancy, are nevertheless still proffered. Representatives of paedophile groups and some libertarians – who are almost always male – point to historical evidence and cultural diversity in support of their views that sexual relations between adults and children are surely legitimate. They further argue that children are knowing sexual beings who can and do consent to such sex and that these relationships are rarely harmful to children. Harm, according to libertarians, primarily arises because of unwanted, obtrusive and aggressive intervention from the state. The state should withdraw from this arena except in those cases involving non-consensual relations and violence.

Liddle systematically and carefully 'deconstructs' these arguments. Historical and cross-cultural evidence, he shows, is often distorted and de-contextualized to support libertarian positions. As we now know, the world-wide historical record shows again and again a litany of abuse and exploitation of children. Children he argues do not consent to sexual relations with adults and it is impossible to speak of 'informed consent' when the differentials in power and emotional and psychological development are so great. Libertarians confuse consent with placid participation and acquiescence. The idea of genuine consent is 'demolished' when considered in light of these factors. For Liddle such sexual relations are always forms of injustice and violation of the rights of children who are deeply dependent on adults. Acknowledging that secondary harm does occur through state response, he rightly argues that this should not mean decriminalization and state withdrawal from this arena. Rather, intervention in the lives of children needs to be 'humanized' and he discusses the importance of recent criminal justice innovations for dealing with child witnesses.

Sandra Walklate and Rob Mawby shift attention away from the particular offences against victims to focus on the organizational responses to those who have been victimized. The notions of 'victims' rights' and the 'citizen's charter' reflect a concern to respond effectively to those affected by crime. Victims' rights, they argue, need strengthening in several areas: the right to play an active part in the criminal justice system, improved knowledge of the processing of their case, and financial help and advice and support. These issues are examined in detail by Walklate and Mawby who make positive suggestions and recommendations throughout. They examine victim/ offender reconciliation programmes and victim support schemes as means of responding to the rights and needs of victims while also aware of issues affecting offenders and of the priorities of organizations of the state. They also consider the process of 'going to court' and the need for information and support as victims weave through a system not designed with them in mind. Financial assistance and financial compensation are also examined in relation to the needs and 'rights' of those harmed by a criminal offence. The proposals for reform cover three main areas: 'change in the organizational structure through which victim services are provided'; 'the specification of services to which victims are entitled'; and 'identification of redress where services prove inadequate'. The third involves expansion of state provision and financial expenditure which some might argue is 'impossible in the current economic climate' but Walklate and Mawby claim that 'recognition of the victim as citizen requires that the cost of crime be borne by the community, not by crime victims who are frequently among the most disadvantaged . . . In a just system it is appropriate for the state . . . to take over that burden.'

The final section of the book – Criminal Justice Responses to Violence Against Women – includes three chapters exploring the methodologies used in and the results of research on criminal justice innovations on domestic violence in Britain, the United States and Australia. Russell Dobash, Rebecca Dobash, Kate Cavanagh and Ruth Lewis begin their primarily methodological chapter – Evaluating Programmes for Violent Men – by considering the range of innovations introduced in Britain and the United States. In both countries, improved police procedures, enhanced civil injunctions, and an emphasis on arrest and prosecution are only some of the more important innovations. An emphasis on arrest has been a particularly important element of innovations in the United States and Dobash and his colleagues review various evaluation studies in this arena.

This research has shown that on balance arrest is more likely to deter subsequent assaults on women than other types of police intervention. Whatever the efficacy of arrest, it is important to consider the impact of other reactions, such as civil injunctions and programmes for violent men.

Evidence from Britain and the United States indicates that injunctions (interdicts in Scotland) and orders of protection are defined as unhelpful by most women who attempt to use them. Women seeking to use these measures report that men ignore them and the police are often reluctant to enforce such measures even when provisions for arrest are attached. Less pessimistically, a minority of research reports indicate that injunctions can work when they are rigorously specified and enforced.

It is unlikely, however, that an emphasis on arrest and civil injunctions will curtail and eliminate the violence of men who have become habituated to its use in their relationships with intimate female partners. New sanctions and interventions are needed. In the last fifteen years hundreds of programmes for violent men have been created in North America, Australia and New Zealand. Many of these programmes are highly traditional, offering psychotherapeutic interventions; others are more educationally based and a few espouse pro-feminist ideals, stressing that violence is employed as a technique for dominating, controlling and punishing women. There are very few innovative programmes for violent men operating in Britain today and only a handful are criminal-justice based and dedicated to dealing with men who physically and sexually assault their partners. The first two dedicated criminal-justice-based programmes for violent men were established in Scotland in the late 1980s. CHANGE is an independent programme operating in Central Region, and the Lothian Domestic Violence Probation Project (LDVPP) is based in the Lothian social work department. Both are probation-based programmes offering forms of systematic group work over an extended period of time; CHANGE is also involved in community-wide education and training.

Dobash and his colleagues review evaluation studies conducted in North America on similar programmes and find them flawed in many respects. Although these evaluations indicate high rates of success, the research designs and procedures are often weak. Many of the studies are not comparative, are based on small samples, use only arrests as measures of success and do not routinely include the reports of women. These and other limitations are explored and a three-year evaluation of CHANGE and LDVPP is described. The Scottish Office and Home Office funded project employed a quasi-experimental design to compare men's programmes to other criminal justice sanctions such as a fine and probation. Employing newly developed measures of violence, injuries, controlling behaviours and quality of life, the research aimed to assess behaviours and attitudes at three points in time. At time one, immediately following a criminal justice sanction, men and women were interviewed as a means of establishing a comparative baseline, and at times two (three months after interview) and three (twelve months after interview) they were sent postal questionnaires in order to assess the impact of various sanctions. The chapter provides details of the methodological assumptions and techniques employed in the study and ends by outlining the mainly positive results observed.

In some Australian states, programmes for violent men are apparently an integral aspect of an over-arching approach to domestic violence. In Ruth Frances's chapter on community-based intervention programmes for men, she begins by outlining the development of group work for violent men, first introduced into the state of Victoria in 1985 'in response to initiatives in legal reform and following public meetings on what to do about family violence'. Few of these programmes are criminal-justice based; most are provided by health and welfare services and are operated by social workers and psychologists. Using a combination of educational and psychological strategies to facilitate attitude and behavioural change, men are apparently confronted about the criminality of their behaviour and encouraged to take full responsibility for their violence.

Frances reports that the group work draws from a range of sources, including psychology, sociology and feminist theory, but the principles of group dynamics and experiential learning are well to the fore. Re-creating and re-enacting 'problematic real-life situations' aimed at changing attitudes are important aspects of this work. Feminist perspectives are also important, providing, according to Frances, 'the central framework for understanding the nature of family violence'. However, as elsewhere, in Victoria women working with physically abused women express a certain amount of mistrust of the aims and techniques employed by these groups.

Other initiatives directed at violent men are described by Frances: on-going discussion 'support' groups; a men's telephone referral service; a 'Men's House'; and VICNET, a men's provider's network. Of particular note are the residential facilities for men who use violence against their female partners; two such houses are already in existence and more are being planned. They are based on the assumption that 'women and children should not have to move out of their own home, on account of men's violence'.

Frances and her colleagues have been involved in a primarily descriptive study of eight groups. They found that most participants are working-class men who failed to complete secondary education. Seventy-six per cent of these men admitted using violence against their partner and 84 per cent said they used other forms of abuse. The vast majority of men, 78 per cent, said they learned something about the roles of men and women in society and 59 per cent 'vividly remembered experiential learning experiences'. Significantly, three-quarters of the men told the researchers their attitudes and/or behaviours had been challenged or confronted by programme staff. Eight out of ten men believed the group had made a difference in their lives and nine out of ten believed the group had helped them change their behaviour. The reports of women, although positive, are rather less enthusiastic. Only 48 per cent of the women interviewed said the attendance of their partners at group sessions had made a real difference to their lives, while 64 per cent said attendance had been a worthwhile experience for their partner.

Provision of refuge and shelters, crisis telephone services and victim support will continue to provide the backbone of services for physically abused women. Programmes for violent men and other criminal justice interventions are, however, extremely important because women will continue to seek remedies through the use of the police and courts. Penal abolitionist and some feminist legal theorists who reject the use of criminal justice in this arena are out of touch with the realities of women's lives. Sam Wright's contribution to this volume – 'The Role of the Police in Combating Domestic Violence' – presents the results of research on police response to domestic violence. She is particularly concerned to assess developments subsequent to the issuing of new Home Office guidelines stressing the need for improved services to victims and more assertive responses to violent men.

Wright reviews existing research on police response to domestic violence which generally reveals a police reluctance to arrest and a tendency to underestimate the physical and emotional damage caused by men. She notes, however, that there has been a general improvement in police response, although reversion to traditional practices is always a threat. Women's attempts to obtain meaningful responses from the police continually confront a legacy of indifference and deflection. Wright provides an indication of the scope of domestic violence that comes to the attention of the police and explores the decisions regarding disposition of these cases.

The Nottinghamshire Constabulary where Wright carried out her research recently established a specially trained Family Support Unit to deal with cases involving the physical and sexual abuse of children and domestic violence. The statutory responsibility to deal with child abuse meant, however, that the bulk of the work of this unit involved cases of child abuse. Only the most serious cases of domestic violence are dealt with by the Family Support Unit and consequently Wright's research focused on the constabulary's usual responses to domestic violence as reflected in the newly created 'domestic violence registers'. The main purpose of the research was 'an assessment of the extent to which the official policy changes have been adopted by the police on the ground'. Wright's findings tend to show that changes have occurred in the policing of domestic violence but they do not represent a radical departure from practices that pre-dated recent changes in policy. The research reveals that police statistics derived from official registers of domestic 'incidents' seriously misrepresent the prevalence of domestic violence and the risk of arrest for perpetrators is still low. Wright concludes that an enhanced emphasis on domestic violence is important and the police need additional and improved training to act effectively in cases of domestic violence.

2

A genealogy of women's madness

SYLVIE FRIGON

Woman embodies madness. To be a woman is to be, somehow, mad. Madness serves to categorize, censure and disqualify. Madness serves as a signifier. It posits women as the 'other', as the outsider, as 'the second sex'. Within the dualistic systems of language and representation, women are situated on the side of irrationality, silence, nature and body, while men are positioned on the side of reason, discourse, culture and mind (see Lloyd 1984 for a fuller discussion of this). Hence, images of the female mind and body represent 'Woman' as madness. A deconstruction of madness does not take the discourses as isolated but rather as organized and regulated practices. A deconstruction of discursive practices, via a genealogy, is necessary in order to call into question underlying assumptions about the so-called madness of women. To label women mad and 'disorderly' is a strategy to disqualify women's protests, resistance and defiance. This paper is also about women's resistance.

While women constitute 4 per cent of the prison population, they represent 20 per cent of the patients in 'special hospitals'.[1] This evidence indicates that psychiatrists and agents of the criminal justice system see women as 'appropriate' patients for psychiatry which in turn is nourished by society's views on the proper feminine behaviour. Women are therefore seen as in need of psychiatric help more than men – they are 'mad' and not 'bad'. Let me briefly give a woman a voice.

K. Andrews is an ex-Broadmoor[2] and Rampton[3] patient who was committed to a special hospital for *fifteen years* for unlawful possession of drugs, criminal damage (a broken shop window) and burglary (a cigarette lighter). She was labelled a psychopath. She writes 'Possibly, my first mistake was being a female criminal.' She received drug therapy and electro-convulsive treatment. Her poetry sums up some of her experiences and encapsulates some of the fundamental issues surrounding the images of 'deviant' women. I want to let her speak her resistance.[4]

> She storms and steals her way through life
> Trying to overcome the toils and strife . . .
>
> Until she's spat out again, through those gates
> Into society she condemns and hates . . .
>
> Stereo-type women, wear blouses and skirts
> Trousered women are met with knowing smirks . . .
>
> If she breaks the law of the land
> She loses everything, whilst on remand . . .
>
> Women in prison, are life's failures
> A strange breed of mutant creatures . . .
>
> I wanted them to understand, or care, at least
> But yet again, they would lock up 'The Beast' . . .
>
> Frustration, coursing through my veins
> Please, listen, before I burst at the seams . . .
>
> . . . And they slam the door again, as I collapse . . .
>
> (K. Andrews, 1991)

I began to wonder what was behind the iconic image of the madwoman and what it revealed about some of the ways in which we look at women. I chose to examine the representations of some *disorderly* women. 'Disorderly' because of their evilness, as in the case of the witch in the Middle Ages. 'Disorderly' because criminal women deviate from appropriate gender norms. 'Disorderly' because of their political protests, as in the case of the suffragettes and the Greenham Common women in England. But also the entry of these 'disorderly' women defines what constitutes being a good woman. This good woman is, however, never quite 'ordinary' or 'normal'. In fact, being a woman is forever being deviant (Hutter and Williams 1981; Schur 1984).

Confining women through the label 'mad' is not a new

phenomenon. Through prison, psychiatry, the institution of marriage, medicine, tranquillizers, electro-convulsive therapy, 'premenstrual syndrome', gynaecological surgery and laws (e.g., abortion and new reproductive technologies), society pathologizes and criminalizes women's bodies and women's minds. Furthermore, the social regulation of women has also been modulated by race, culture, class, sexuality and ableism. These various interrelated 'technologies of gender'[5] reflect other historical manifestations and practices of the control of women at different times and places, such as the witch trials, Chinese footbinding, chastity belts, genital mutilations and Indian suttee, for example. In fact, these practices are analogous to more modern forms of regulation and control.

In order to understand and situate contemporary debates about the representations of women as mad, historical analyses must be undertaken through the prism of a genealogical gaze. This gaze will permit us to trace the continuities and discontinuities of the modern meaning of femininity and its transgression in diverse cultural, socio-political spaces and times.

In this paper, I will examine different *regimes* of meanings and images of women who are considered to transgress moral, cultural and legal boundaries. By 'regime' of meanings, I wish to convey the idea of a regular pattern of occurrence of meanings or a mode of rule or management of different meanings. To do this, I will locate this analysis in the discursive regimes of meanings of the witch, 'murderess', terrorist and political protesters in order to formulate, in the end, the links between the 'normal' and the 'pathological' meanings of the category 'woman'. I will try to demonstrate that these 'regimes of meanings' pivot around womanhood. They are at the heart of the various typifications.

To begin this genealogy, I will discuss and analyse the image, meaning and consequence of the 'witch', a very powerful representation in the portrayals of certain (deviant) women even in the twentieth century. Of course, their story has been told by their prosecutors and it is not *their* story. However, this representation is central to our analysis. As Heidensohn notes:

> Women are no longer hunted as witches in Scotland, nor indeed anywhere in the British Isles. The witch image, however, does remain, at least as a folk memory. It sits on top of a pyramid of related images of deviant women as especially evil, depraved and monstrous. (1985: 92)

The representation of women as witches

The image of the 'witch' is an interesting one for my overall argument because of at least seven related reasons. Firstly, in the Middle Ages, more than 85 per cent of the persons accused of witchcraft were women (MacFarlane 1970; Ben-Yehuda 1985; Sallman 1991). Secondly, witchcraft being predominantly considered to be the domain of women it was thus one of the first crimes for which women were accused in this period (Larner 1981:91). Thirdly, the image of the 'witch' and related ones provided a basis for some criminological theories as developed by Lombroso, Ferrero, Pollak and Thomas (Heidensohn 1985: 95) and representations of some criminalized women, as in the case of Lindy Chamberlain in 1980 (the 'dingo baby' case in Australia). Fourthly, the social control shifted from the religious (witchcraft) to the medical (mental illness) (Szasz 1961, 1971; Ussher 1991) and this is apparent in the case of women. Fifthly, the *social reaction* to witchcraft and mental illness is closely geared towards people who are in situations of poverty, lack of education and powerlessness: a situation more closely tied to women. Also, the witchcraze is a historical manifestation of violence against women. Finally, the image of the witch comes into discursive play in representations of 'deviant' women more generally.[6]

According to conservative estimates, from the early decades of the fifteenth century until 1650, between two and five hundred thousand witches were executed in Continental Europe, of whom more than 85 per cent were women. It appears that the witchcraze started in the fifteenth century because medieval society was eroding and a new social, political, economic, scientific and religious order was being founded. Although there were very positive reactions to these new social arrangements, there were also very violent, negative ones. Thus, the witch-hunt aimed at re-establishing the old social order was rooted in a search for collective identity.

But why were *women* the victims of this witchcraze? Were the witch-hunts *sex-related* or *sex-specific*. (Hester 1992)? In my view, they were not merely sex-related but rather were sex-specific. It has often been argued that certain kinds of women were the targets of this witch-hunt. However, as Ben-Yehuda notes, the major factor in the prosecution was the fact that they were women. In fact, he writes:

> At the beginning of the witchcraze, we often find that accused witches were widows, spinsters, or 'strange' old women. Later on, married women

and young girls were persecuted as well. Various historical sources reveal that neither social status nor age made any difference as the most crucial variable was the fact that most victims were women. (1985: 38–9)

However, hundred of thousands of lesbians and thousands of gay men were executed for heresy[7] during the Roman Catholic Inquisition of the fifteenth and sixteenth centuries in France (Pickard and Goldman 1992). Hence, the execution of gay men and lesbian women is thought to be an ancestor of a manifestation of heterosexist violence. Hence, 'queer-bashing' is argued to be a modern manifestation of this violence 'insofar as they are all aimed to intimidate and coerce lesbians and gay men into conformist, heterocentric lifestyles. And to eliminate those who resist' (Peterson in Pickard and Goldman 1992: 14).

Theories of witchcraft

In order to grasp the significance of the witchcraze, four theories of witchcraft are relevant: the witch as mental patient, the witch as healer, the witch as scapegoat and the witch as sexually deviant.[8] They are, however, intertwined. For the purpose of this exposé, I will examine one of the four theories of witchcraft, that is the witch as mental patient. In *The Manufacture of Madness*, Szasz parallels the practices of the Inquisition and those of modern institutional psychiatry.[9] He tries to show that the social controls of institutional psychiatry and its underlying concepts, rhetorical devices and applications resemble those of the Inquisition. Like the Inquisition, psychiatry as a modern method of manufacturing madness 'fulfils a basic human need – to validate the Self as good (normal), by invalidating the Other as evil (mentally ill)' (Szasz 1971: xxvii). [10] For example the *Malleus Maleficarum*, the most influential guide used by the Inquisitors, resembles textbooks in modern psychiatry. Szasz writes:

> . . . the *Malleus Maleficarum* might with a little editing serve as an excellent modern textbook of descriptive clinical psychiatry of the fifteenth century, if the word *witch* were substituted by the word *patient*, and the devil eliminated. (Zilboorg, 1935: 38; quoted in Szasz 1971: 68).

Philippe Pinel (1745–1826) believed that witches were mentally ill; Jean Etienne-Dominique Esquirol (1772–1840), Pinel's student, also believed this and even that most criminals were similarly afflicted.

Esquirol's views were dominant in the nineteenth century. For Jean-Martin Charcot (1825–1893), witchcraft became a problem of 'neuropathology' and in the hands of Freud, witchcraft became a problem of 'psychopathology' (Szasz 1971: 3). Zilboorg was the most important popularizer of the psychiatric interpretation of witchcraft. The results of this interpretation seem to be twofold. Firstly, witches were objects of psychological interest and 'their behaviour was regarded as proof of the transhistorical and transcultural 'reality' of mental illness' (Szasz 1971: 81). Secondly, the behaviour of prosecutors, inquisitors and judges was ignored. The politics of witchcraft are evident in Szasz's point that, 'what is called "mental illness" (or "psychopathology") emerges as the name of the product of a particular kind of relationship between oppressor and oppressed'(81). 'The end of one ideology is thus the beginning of another: where religious heresy ends, psychiatric heresy begins; where the persecution of the witch ends, the persecution of the madman begins' (110). However, before we enter the psychiatric heresy, let us see briefly how the ideology of witchcraft operated.

The social position of medieval women was a subject of constant debate between the Church and the aristocracy; however, their subordination seemed to be accepted. On the one hand, women were regarded as superior beings (e.g. the cult of the Virgin Mary) and, on the other hand, they were perceived as dangerous and seductive. Of course, women from different social positions were regarded differently. Lemay (1978) argues that in the thirteenth and fourteenth centuries, universities presented women as inferior and dangerous. Ben-Yehuda continues: 'the lecturers emphasized that menstruating women kill little children, that women insert chemicals in the vagina in order to wound the penis of a sexual partner, that they feign virginity and conceal pregnancy' (Ben-Yehuda 1985: 61).[11] As we can see, scientific and medical discourses provided the ideological basis for the persecution of certain women.

Moreover, serious demographical changes directly influenced the concentration of women as victims of witch-hunts. The Black Death devastated an important part of the population, but, after the end of the plague, women became more and more active in the economy and increased their economic power. Given the favourable conditions, it could have been expected that there would be an increase in the population, but this did not happen. Helleiner (1967) argues that there was no increase and even that a decrease in the population occurred in the second half of the fourteenth century due to increased use of contraception and infanticide. The limiting of offspring, the prevention of pregnancy and infanticide provoked serious demographic changes in the fifteenth and sixteenth centuries. This situation was also denounced by the Church as evil and thus linked to witchcraft. Trexler notes that '. . . child killing has been regarded almost exclusively as a female crime, the result of women's inherent tendency to lechery, passion and lack of responsibility . . . Infanticide was . . . the most common social crime imputed to . . . witches . . . by demonologists' (Trexler 1973: 98 and 103). Wet nurses (midwives) were thus sought to prevent this but they were soon to be seen as chief suspects of witchcraft, as the Dominicans suspected that they had knowledge and expertise (which they had) of birth control, and co-operated in infanticide.[12]

Interestingly, during this 'century of genius' many famous people believed in the reality of witchcraft, demonology and witches. As Ben-Yehuda notes, Newton, Bacon, Boyle, Locke and Hobbes all believed in demonology. As Russell puts it, 'ten of thousands of [witchcraft] trials continued throughout Europe generation after generation, while Leonardo painted, Palestrina composed and Shakespeare wrote' (Russell 1977: 79).

The witch: a regime of meanings
Thus, images of women as evil were reflected in a number of mirrors. For example, Shakespeare's Lady Macbeth illustrated 'both popular and élite concerns because his monarch James I (of England and VI of Scotland) was particularly interested in witches . . .' (Heidensohn 1985: 91). Lady Macbeth is 'linked in imagery, in a play full of witchcraft and dark images, with ravens, blood, smoke, illness, demons and infanticide'(ibid., p. 91). Again, as Heidensohn rightly argues, Lady Macbeth acknowledged her actions as transgressing accepted femininity as she conjures demons to

> 'unsex me here;
> And fill me, from the crown to the toe, top-full
> Of direst cruelty
>
> (*Macbeth*, Act I, sc. v 38–40).

But her downfall and end are terrible as she went mad and died. The message is, then, that when women transgress from accepted boundaries, their downfall is imminent. In fact, the 'fallen woman', having not kept her proper place, is thus doomed to downfall.[13] We will see that this idea is apparent in a number of cases related to the deviance of women even if women are no longer hunted as witches. I agree with Hester (1992) who argues that the English witch trials were historical examples of violence against women and help us understand male power in contemporary society. I will now examine some images of the fallen/criminal women which show the continuities of meanings between the historical definition of women as witches and contemporary examples of women's deviance.

The criminal woman as 'fallen woman'

The image of the witch is still an important one. In Australia, the demonization of Lindy Chamberlain and her stereotyping as a witch are clear from this quote:

> And all the time she was there behind me, staring. She just stares. She is, you know a witch. I could feel her eyes burning holes through my back. (Mrs Joy Kuhl quoted in Bryson 1985)

Also, consider the two following cases (see Heidensohn 1985: 92–3). In Italy in 1983, Carole Compton was convicted for arson and acquitted for attempted murder. She was referred to by the press as a *strega* – a witch – because of some allegedly bizarre and supernatural aspects of the case. Or consider the following headline: 'IRA's Evil Sisters Free' (*Evening Standard*, 30 August 1983) which was a 'report on the release of two politically motivated, highly organized women convicted of causing explosions and conspiracy to cause arson'. (Heidensohn 1985: 93).

As it was the case for the representation of the witches, psycho-biological and psychiatric interpretations also served and still serve to explain the deviance and criminality of women. According to Dobash, Dobash and Gutteridge (1986), ideas which dominated during the third quarter of the nineteenth century and into the twentieth focused on environment, physiognomy, physiology, psychology and psychiatry (p. 101). Discourses on criminal women and psycho-biological representations in the late nineteenth and early twentieth centuries affected the development of penal philosophies and institutions for women. Although historians such as Foucault and Ignatieff showed that the penitentiary was not a mere reaction to crime but was rather part of a strategy of reform to re-establish order, gender dimensions in social histories of punishment were not taken into account until recently.[14]

The eighteenth and nineteenth centuries witnessed a significant number of women convicted of crimes compared to today (Zedner 1991). Their crimes were determined rather more by socio-economic factors than by innate differences. Despite this, their crimes were translated into the language of 'moral degeneration', biological throwbacks and mental inadequacy. The nineteenth century approached female crime within the more general framework of Victorian morality (Dobash, Dobash and Gutteridge 1986; Zedner 1991). As Zedner argues: 'responses to female crime were deeply embedded in an even more complex value structure, at the heart of which was the highly artificial construct of ideal womanhood' (Zedner 1991: 320). Thus, the sinful women offended against the law but also against ascribed social and moral values and roles. Mid-nineteenth-century Britain was obsessed by crimes of morality (sexual offences, prostitution, drunkenness, vagrancy and illegal gambling). Women's criminality was thus translated in sexual deviance because women's transgressions were indicative of the 'increased demoralization' of society as a whole (Symons 1849: 25, in Zedner 1991: 328). Women's sexuality was thus regulated and prostitutes' behaviour closely controlled (see the Contagious Diseases Acts in 1883). Prostitution as well as alcoholism was a major preoccupation at this period with regard to women because of the serious consequences of alcoholism for women given their role in the family. The moral interpretations were transformed, to some extent, towards the end of the century by nascent scientific explanations. These scientific approaches to crime were, however, rooted in Victorian morality (Zedner 1991: 336).

Criminal women's biological constitution was viewed as pathological, a view which helped develop typologies of offenders (for both men and women) as well as penal institutions for women. According to Dobash et al. 1986, Maudsley appears to be the first British doctor to identify the 'normal functionings of women's bodies' as a cause of insanity and deviance, arguing that normal menstruation, pregnancy and lactation could form part of a pathological condition (Dobash 1986: 113–14). He then concluded that sexual deviations in women were the product of the '. . . irritation of the ovaries or uterus – a disease by which the chaste and modest woman is transformed into a raging fury of lust' (quoted in

Dobash, p. 114). Havelock Ellis (1890), for his part, argued that women found guilty of infanticide were 'endowed with excessive down in their faces, that female thieves went grey more quickly, were uglier, and exhibited more signs of degeneracy (especially of the sexual organs) than ordinary women' (quoted in Zedner 1991: 337). The female offenders, of course, were the antithesis of ideal femininity. Early-twentieth-century views of female crime were those of the 'eugenics' movement (Dobash *et al*. 1986: 111). The 'degenerate woman' was born. And this search for scientific proof provided criminology with a 'quasi-medical status' (Zedner 1991: 344). As a result, it appears that 'the basis of crime no longer lay in sin or in faulty reasoning but in an aberration or abnormality of the individual's constitution' (Garland 1985: 111). However, in the case of female criminality, this new medical and psychiatric interpretation was more intricately bound to moral reasoning (Zedner 1991).

The images of criminal women tend to be polarized between two extremes, the 'mad' and the 'bad' (Heidensohn 1985; Edwards 1984, 1986; Patullo 1983). In fact, for the woman who is viewed as good, her presence in the criminal justice system is seen as 'incongruous' (Worrall 1981: 90–1). Worrall warns that this fundamental incongruity may be seen as being to the advantage of women, 'but it serves, in fact, to define parameters of negotiation in a restrictive fashion and causes breaches of those parameters to be severely penalised' (p. 91). Heidensohn reiterates this point by arguing that 'there seems to be an added *factor of dissonance* in placing women in the dock . . .' (1985: 88, my emphasis). For Worrall, these women are 'nondescript'. The term refers to the

> product of the processes which subject particular female law-breakers to inappropriate and unsuccessful judicial and welfare needs to categorize them within the discourses of femininity – processes in which the women themselves play an active, if limited, part. (Worrall 1990: 178)

Moreover, women who commit crimes are dichotomized into 'good' and 'bad', 'madonnas' and 'whores' (Heidensohn 1985; Edwards 1984). As Heidensohn further argues, in the light of such cases as Florence Bravo, Constance Kent, Adelaide Bartlett and Lizzie Borden, what stands out over many decades 'is the way in which they are turned into moral fables about the lives of women involved' (1985: 88–9). Thus, two moral purposes are achieved: 1., appropriate gender roles are emphasized, and 2., more generally these cases with moral undertones serve as warnings 'to young women against dangers of reading or of flirtation or to older women against adultery or new ideas' (Heidensohn 1985: 89).[15]

In the following section I will explore some of the representations of women who kill their children, in order to juxtapose the historical and contemporary representations of the category *women*. In fact, the interest in women who kill, or in violent women in general, is not a new phenomenon. The case of the Pappin Sisters in Le Mans, France, is an illustration of this – not only of the interest of the public or the press but also of that of the French intelligentsia. Simone de Beauvoir, Jean-Paul Sartre, Lacan, the Surrealists and Genet in his play, *The Maids* (1946), all discussed the murder of the mistress and her daughter by those two young maids.

Maternal infant-killings

Let us consider now the discursive meanings of maternal infant-killing, a case where the virtues of femininity and motherhood are in deep contrast with the killing. In cases of infanticide, women are also depicted as 'bad' or 'mad'. Allen (1987) suggests that the Infanticide Act (1938) in England is an illustration, *par excellence*, of the psychiatrization of female infant-killing. It considers that

> where a woman by any wilful act or omission causes the death of her child, being a child under the age of twelve months, but at the time of the act or omission the balance of her mind was disturbed by reason of her not having fully recovered from the effect of giving birth to the child or by reason of the effect of lactation consequent upon the birth of the child, then, notwithstanding that the circumstances were such that for this Act the offence would have amounted to murder
>
> (Infanticide Act 1938, s1 quoted in Allen 1987: 27)

But it is important to trace how the Infanticide Act came into being and, more importantly, what were its consequences. Although the state did not regulate marriage, in 1623 unmarried mothers became subject to specific social and penal controls. Smart argues that this *woman* is perhaps one of the first to enter into statute specifically as *Woman*:

> her entry marks a number of associations which are implicit yet must be understood for the legislation to make any sense. Not only is she unmarried and hence without protection, she occupies a specific class

position (i.e. poor), she is deprived of the material conditions to raise a child, yet she is put to death for seeking to escape her plight – even if the child died of natural causes (or the effects of poverty on pregnancy and childbirth). (Smart 1992: 37)

The legislation was too severe, making it difficult for juries to convict. Hence, this strategy of inflicting harsh punishment on only a few women gave way to new legislation which aimed at disciplining and controlling the many (Smart: 38). As a result, the penalties became less tough and fewer women could evade the new legal categorization which made more women accountable for motherhood; strategies to avoid pregnancy and/or motherhood were penalized. For example, they became subject to new forms of discipline in the guise of philanthropy and mental health legislation and provision (Smart: 38). At the beginning of the twentieth century we witnessed the growth of surveillance with the introduction of health visitors and social workers (Donzelot 1979). Motherhood was thus constructed as 'natural' and a consequence of heterosex. As 'compulsory motherhood' was introduced, it meant more than the imposition of pregnancy and birth but also 'entry into the nexus of meanings and behaviours which are deemed to constitute proper mothering' (Smart 1992: 38). Moreover as Oakley (1981) and Greer (1984) suggest, the views expressed in the Infanticide Act of 1938 seem to be in congruence with the view that pregnancy and childbirth were already pathological and sick instances which required treatment and control.

In addition, Lord Hardwick's Marriage Act (1753) was the start of a process to regulate marriage and thus women were to be of married or unmarried status, in contrast with earlier versions of matrimony (Smart 1992: 38). Also, the Mental Deficiency Act (1913) made the incarceration of unmarried mothers easier, based on the grounds of imbecility or feeble-mindedness. Thus, the unmarried mother was seen not as a proper mother because she did not have a man. According to Smart,

the unmarried mother obviously served (and still serves) to reinforce our cultural understanding of what 'proper' motherhood means . . . She is the problem (supposedly) because she does not have a man. Therefore Man is the solution, he signifies the stability, legitimacy and mastery which is not only absent in her but inverted. (Smart 1992: 39)

This is relevant even in contemporary society because more women can be fitted into this enlarged category. The 'surrogate' mother and the woman seeking fertility treatment are illustrations of this. For example, the British press in 1991 publicized and problematized the case of 'virgin mothers', women seeking fertility treatment without ever having had sexual relations. This has been seen as a potential problem and reinforces the idea of 'compulsory heterosexuality' as research documented the fact that lesbian women and mothers have been denied access to their children because of the fact that they were not in heterosexual relationships (Smart and Sevenhuijsen 1989). In 1990 the British Parliament introduced the Human Fertilization and Embryology Act. The following passage of Section 13(5) reads:

> A woman shall not be provided with treatment services unless account has been taken of the welfare of any child who may be born as a result of the treatment (including *the need of that child for a father*). (Quoted in Smart 1992: 39; emphasis added).

This makes sense only when we know what the category 'woman' refers to and what it means to be an unmarried mother. As Smart suggests, these measures do not make sense '. . . unless you already know that the mother without a husband is a danger' (p. 39). Similarly society's perception of women who kill their children makes sense because it fits with certain representations of womanhood.

Intertwined with ideals of femininity and motherhood are issues of culture and race. To illustrate this briefly, let me use the case of Angélique Pilotte, an Ojibwa woman who was accused of infanticide in Chippawa, Upper Canada in 1817.[16] This case points, among other things, to a historical example of racism in relation to femininity and motherhood. Backhouse writes:

> One long, hot day in early August 1817, the body of a male infant was discovered in Chippawa, Upper Canada. It was unearthed from a very shallow grave near the home of Mary and John Ussher. The Usshers were white settlers in a racially mixed community. Peoples of the Algonquian-speaking Ojibwas, Ottawa, and Algonkian nations were confronted with an influx of Loyalist refugees who had begun to overrun their hunting grounds by the late eighteenth century. Despite the fact that infanticide was reportedly less common within the First Nations than in European cultures, suspicion settled upon twenty-year-old Angélique Pilotte, a First Nations' woman who was probably Ojibwa. (Backhouse 1991: 112).

Backhouse reports that those who were caught and accused of infanticide were usually married, working-class women. Like Angélique Pilotte, they were frequently domestic servants attempting to conceal pregnancy and childbirth because giving birth to an illegitimate child would bring the end to their employment. Hence, there were no real options.

Additionally, white criminal justice would have been unfamiliar to Angélique Pilotte. It was quite foreign to her and at odds with the First Nations justice system. She was found guilty and she was 'sentenced to be taken to the prison from whence she came, and from there to the place of execution and Thursday next, the 11th [of September], there to be hanged by the neck till she be dead, and her body to be delivered over for dissection' (quoted in Backhouse 1992: 118). Angélique Pilotte was finally granted a reprieve on 13 May 1818. With the help of ethnocentric bias her behaviour was excused by arguing that she had not yet been educated in Christian religion and European civilization. An important aspect to remember in order to understand this case is the fact that the experience of childbirth within Ojibwa culture was different from that of the Europeans. The Ojibwa system was perceived as problematic and thus, in need of supervision. Of course, this has not been acknowledged.[17]

Yet, another question about maternal infant-killings arises. Are these mothers 'mad' or 'bad'?

> In 1226, an inquiry was ordered to ascertain whether one Alice de la Lade had killed her baby 'from madness or maliciously and intentionally'; if from madness she was to be let go.
>
> (Kellum 1974: 373 quoted in Wilczynski 1991: 71)

> In May 1989, Mr Justice Owen of the Central Criminal Court, London said in the maternal filicide case of (*R v. Ricketts*: 'Should we treat you as a wicked person responsible for her actions . . . or as someone who was sick?' (Personal court observation quoted in Wilczynski 1991: 71)

Women who kill their children are viewed as mentally ill and this understanding fits very well with certain ideas about women, femininity and motherhood. Firstly, as a general point, the relationship of women to reason is not straightforward (Lloyd 1984). Thus, women are not seen as rational agents as men are.[18] Secondly, the label 'mentally abnormal' fits well onto women's criminal behaviour and particularly when they are accused of violence, because this is so much in contradiction with the 'appropriate' role of women (Naylor 1990; Patullo 1983; Millman 1982; Smart 1976). Thirdly, women's behaviour tends to be understood in terms of their hormones as the admissibility of the 'pre-menstrual syndrome' defence seems to indicate (Benn 1990). This is an important element in the construction of the 'disorderly' women. Fourthly, women who kill their children are in serious contradiction with the desired role of the loving and caring mother.

In these cases, although the women have killed their child, they are still viewed as loving their child, but they will be defined as mentally ill within the frame of the Infanticide Act in order to make some sense of the offence. Interestingly, although this mental illness would not be recognized by law in other contexts such as in the pleas of diminished responsibility (d'Orban 1979: 570) it is used in the case of infanticide. According to Wilczynski:

> virtually any type of perceived psychiatric, emotional, personal or mental problem whatsoever *can* be interpreted (if the psychiatrists, lawyers and/or judges so choose) as the severe mental illness (puerperal psychosis) *theoretically* required for the Infanticide Act. (Wilczynski 1991: 76)

Hence, personal turmoil can be reinterpreted in terms of mental illness: there seemed to be 'good reasons for the killing'; as the act was horrible she was not seen as responsible for her actions (Allen 1987: 95–6).

At the other end of the spectrum, the woman can be viewed as 'bad' (Sparrow 1970). In contrast with the category of women seen as 'mad', these 'bad' women are cold, selfish and are 'non-women' or masculine (Heidensohn 1985; Worrall 1981) or even monsters (Edwards 1986). The 'bad' woman is harshly punished. The 1980s case of Susan Poole illustrates this. Susan Poole and her common-law husband were convicted of the manslaughter of their ten-month-old son and the neglect of their other son. They both received custodial sentences. Poole was described by the popular press as 'evil', 'callous' and 'vile' and was said to refer to the child as 'it' (Roberts 1989: 10–11, quoted in Wilczynski 1991: 78). Moreover, the jury was informed that she went down to the pub with her common-law husband leaving the children alone and that 'she had severely neglected the housework, and that her son had starved to death whilst she was grossly overweight' (Roberts 1989: 10–11, Wilczynski: 78). Mr Justice Owen remarked: 'When one thinks of the extraordinary maternal sacrifice and care shown by lower animals one has to wonder at her apparent selfishness' (Roberts 1989: 10, quoted in Wilczynski 1991: 79). Although the evidence presented by four psychiatrists and one doctor pointed to her personality disorder and severe depression which would impair her responsibility, Mr Justice Owen accepted her plea of diminished responsibility but regarded her as fully guilty. Hence the 'seven-year sentence was more a reflection of the negative image he had created of Susan Poole as a mother than of the medical evidence presented (Roberts 1989: 11)'. (Wilczynski: 79).

Many types of non-conforming behaviour by women are tied to sexuality and this is also the case with regard to maternal infant killings. Resnick (1970) provides a classification of neonaticides in terms of sexuality. In this classification, there are, firstly, women who are passive and who submit to sexual relations and secondly, there are those who have 'strong instinctual drives and little ethical restraint . . .' (p. 1416). Moreover, 'their crime is usually premeditated and not out of keeping with their previous life style' (p. 1416).

Confining the explanations to the mad/bad dichotomy bypasses the possibility of seeing women's powerlessness and, in fact, locates the problem at an individual level and prevents us from looking at wider social and economic processes (Smart 1981; Edwards 1984, 1986; Heidensohn 1985).

Some of the ideas encapsulated in the discourses on women who kill their children (irrationality, madness and actions seen as in contradiction with ideals of femininity) are also echoed in cases of other, protesting women. Keeping this in mind, I now turn to women's political protests to examine the representations of women and to articulate a genealogy of the representations and social control of women.

Women's political protests: instances of similarity

Women who transgress penal norms are often transgressing or seen as transgressing appropriate gender roles and the norms of femininity. As an illustration of this, we can see how women defined as 'terrorists' have broken with the codes of womanhood and femininity. Four dimensions can be identified in relation to women terrorists (Jaccoub 1988): 1., physical traits – as being beautiful or ugly; 2., gender dimensions which are linked to the female nature and role: they are often viewed as being masculine, cruel, non-feminine, as rejecting appropriate female roles and even, sometimes, as being lesbians; 3., psychological problems and 4., the socio-political dimension. Hence, even if terrorism is defined as a strategy of violence of individual, collective or institutional force with the goal of changing social, political and economic structures, women's activities are reinterpreted in an analysis linked to their sexual roles. The meaning of their actions is individualized and pathologized and loses its political character. This is also the case of political protesters such as the Greenham Common women and the suffragettes. Various examples across time and space could be examined.[19]

There are many ways of neutralizing the political aspect in women's (political) protest. In the case of the Greenham Common women and the suffragettes[20] in England, three main techniques and processes can be identified in the disqualification of their demands: 1., the criminalization of women's demands; 2., the sexualization of women's protests; and 3., the psychiatrization of women's voices as hysterical. The disciplinary matrix criminalization/sexualization/psychiatrization is therefore an important way of disqualifying women's resistance and defiance to (white) masculine hegemonic order. Without further delay, I will explore briefly the discursive meanings of the Greenham women as 'other' and 'unrepresentative'.

Greenham Common women

The Greenham Common peace camp was a protest by women outside a cruise missile base in Berkshire, England. It began in 1981 and continued for a decade.[21] Their protest has been attacked and censured. One of the discursive tactics and modes of representation in relation to the Greenham Common women is the use of language and metaphor. This discursive tactic is very powerful in term of describing 'offending women'.[22] Young in *Femininity in Dissent* (1990) provides a good discussion of this. She contends that the media constructed a mythology which was elaborated on the protesters' womanhood and the information provided in the news stories was structured around the following dichotomies: 'criminal/law-abiding, mad/sane and good/evil in order to describe and evaluate social phenomena. The Greenham protest was represented through such oppositional constructs . . .' (Young 1990: 2–3). Using Sumner's notion of censure,[23] Young argues that the censure of the Greenham women was rooted around aspects of womanhood. The 'discursive violence' (Garland 1985) can be easily illustrated in the same context.

Blackwood (1984) testifies to this violence when writing that the Greenham women were portrayed as dirty, communists, Russian spies, lesbians, sex-starved, bad mothers and mad, to name a few. She writes:

> I was very curious to meet the *Greenham women*, for the press had decorated them with such loathsome and frightening adjectives, they had been made to sound almost mythical in their horror . . . They'd been described as 'a lot of silly women with nothing better to do', a merely contemptuous description. They'd been accused of being '*sex-starved*' which sounded a lot more deadly because it made them sound *so dangerous*. They were also described as being in the pay of the Soviet Union, and it was said that many of them were *Russian spies* . . . I found the charge that the Greenham women lived *like dogs and that they were smearing Newbury with their excrement* almost the most chilling one, although it had less political connotations. The claim of Auberon Waugh that the Greenham women *smelt of 'fish paste and bad oysters'* also haunted me for it had such distressing sexual associations . . . As these women had been attributed with almost every unsavoury characteristic, *I had become very curious to see why they aroused such violent hatred and to discover how evil-smelling and odious the Greenham women could be*.
>
> (Blackwood 1984: 1-2; emphasis added.)

In the case of 'offending women' who elude traditional criminological concepts and who are 'nondescripts', the task is to 'rehabilitate [them] within the discourses of femininity' (Worrall 1989: 32). In fact, Greenham Common women as an object of analysis is 'both a product of a particular historical moment and simultaneously a recent manifestation of a tendency to characterise women's political activity in various (censuring) ways' (Young 1990: 13). The descriptions of women's protests show that the censure of Greenham women was 'already written' (Grimshaw 1986: 27; Young 1990: 151), before the press coverage began, that there was a long history of representation. The censure operated under the disciplinary practices of the master-narratives of the law, sexuality and medicine. In studying the press coverage of the Greenham Common women, we can see that it has implications for the history of the portrayal of women political activists as insane, communist and sexually abnormal. The consequences of these associations led to negative attitudes to their demands (Doggett 1989).

Moreover, the political protest of the Greenham Common women, as well as various interrelated protests by women, could be described by analogy with the symbol of the web (Cook and Kirk 1983; Young 1990). Cook and Kirk describe the women's solidarity and strength in the following way:

> Each link in a web is fragile, but woven together creates a strong and coherent whole. A web with few links is weak and can be broken, but the more threads it is composed of, the greater its strength . . . By connections made through many diverse channels, a widespread network has grown up of women committed to working for peace.
>
> (Cook and Kirk 1983: 126)

This web of resistance is also present in the case of the political protests of the earlier suffragettes. Again, a genealogical enquiry into these practices of control means 'writing a history of the present' (Foucault 1977) for the past informs the present. As Young (1988) puts it in the case of the Women's Social and Political Union (WSPU):

> To examine specific discursive categories and practices relating to the WSPU's activities implicates an idealisation of womanhood, a normativity which continues to affect our en-gendered (power) relations today.
> (Foucault 1977: 280)

On censuring the suffragettes

The disciplinary matrix criminalization/sexualization/psychiatriza-tion is clearly in operation in the process of disqualification of women's political protest. As I will show, the demand for the vote is evacuated from the descriptions and representations of women. Their resistance and defiance to masculine hegemonic order is reinterpreted in different censuring ways.

The censure of these women points to wider conceptualizations of womanhood. It is a specific historic moment in which precise norma-tive prescriptions about women's role and place were in operation. Ideal-typical norms about women were not constructed at the particular moment of this group's campaign; rather norms had been constructed from the Victorian era into the 'votes for women' campaign. Hence, it could be argued that women's demand for the vote was surrounded by a certain kind of regime of meanings which precluded as well as framed their demands. This led to their demands being evacuated and dismissed.

The women's protest reached a significant phase when, in 1910, the

House of Commons announced that a bill for the enfranchisement for women was to be abandoned. This day was to be called 'Black Friday'. Groups of women marched to the House of Commons and many were injured by policemen; 135 statements of brutality were recorded. What is striking about those injuries is that they were often of a sexual nature. As one WSPU member recalled later:

> One policeman . . . put his arm around me and seized my left breast, nipping and wringing it very painfully, saying as he did so, 'You have been wanting this for a long time, haven't you?' (Brailsford and Murray 1911: 9, quoted in Young 1988: 281)

'Black Friday' was portrayed as disorder — disorder which stemmed from women themselves. Additionally, comparisons between the women's protest and communist activities were drawn. The *Daily Mail* reported that it was 'worse than anything witnessed in St Petersburg on Red Sunday', presenting the women as in contradiction with the ideals of 'our' liberal democracy. The *us* and *them* were thus created. Moreover, the images and metaphors used to describe women's protests were woven together so as to suggest the idea of a battlefield in a war between reason, democracy and order (the police, government and 'us') and unreason, communism and disorder (the women). If women's demands were presented as demands from the insane, their disqualification was legitimized as the insane do not constitute legal subjects; the mad cannot make legitimate protests and demands. This irrationality was epitomized in *The Times*:

> Mrs Pankhurst and her *maenads* have produced their answer . . . It takes the now stereotyped form of broken glass . . . None of its previous follies have been so thoroughly calculated to discredit the suffragist cause . . . No one can surely have imagined destruction on this scale in London as the work of a few unbalanced women whose only grievance lies in an insignificant point of Parliamentary procedure . . . For whatever may be thought of the . . . agitation its immediate evidence is simply *infantile* . . . An act of *wanton and hysterical self-advertisement*. (3 March 1912; my emphasis.)

The first control mechanism of this protest was the discourse of criminality and law and order. This was an important moment in the process of criminalizing militancy. Thus, techniques of neutralization emerged to confront disorder and these included the tightening of the law of public assembly, sentences of hard labour and the enactment of the 'Cat and Mouse' Act which broadened the legal powers of detention (Young 1988: 285). The tightening of the laws of public assembly had the effect of driving the women's campaign further underground. Nonetheless, these disciplinary powers were met with resistance.

Secondly, the suffragettes were sexualized. Their behaviour was not considered proper, ladylike or acceptable. The militancy was degrading womanhood. They were inversions of the ideal-type women, the good mother. They were described as either oversexed, or undersexed, unattractive and in need of a man. These discursive strategies converge with the social control of the Greenham Common women.

The third explanation of the suffragettes' behaviour was rooted in a medical/psychiatric model. These women were disorderly, unruly and hysterical. *The Times* wrote:

> the hysterical, the neurotic, the idle, the habitual imbibers of excitement . . . Some of them are out with their hammers and their bags full of stones because of dreary empty lives and high-strung, over-excitable natures: they are regrettable by-products of our civilisation. (16 March, 1913; quoted in Young 1988: 288)

Their militancy is thus seen as fuelled by mental disorder. Of course, these ideas were also used in controlling Victorian women. A condemnation of women was thus brought about and their demands trivialized. According to Young: 'Whether or not women should have the vote was only partially at issue: the fundamental question was the future of a particular idealisation of womanhood' (Young 1988: 292). In contrast with Young's position, I believe that the vote was a central issue in terms of defining women. Women without votes are not complete citizens, hence, in giving women the vote, we are reconstructing and reconceptualizing 'women'. This is, in my view, fundamental.

Through criminalization, sexualization and psychiatrization, the suffragettes, were 'disqualified' as was also the discursive category 'woman'. In articulating women's protests as a *genealogy* of women's representations and social control, it becomes clearer now how the discursive practices of discipline of women – the 'deviant' as well as the 'normal' – operate. This will be the subject of my concluding section.

Towards a conclusion: controlling women – the deviant and the normal

As Allen (1987) suggests, women appearing in courts are about twice as likely as men to be dealt with by psychiatric means rather than penal ones (p. xi). This kind of information invites the following question: Are women more mentally ill than men? If not, why and how are they represented in this way? Again, Allen's research shows that while the madness of the male offenders seems to be more severe, this is precisely what excludes them from psychiatric care. On the other hand, female offenders who are brought to court tend to be perceived as 'relatively normal women' and this is precisely what makes them suitable for psychiatric orders.

Let us consider a concrete example (Allen, 1987: 1). A man and a woman are jointly charged with a crime. They are both middle-aged, unemployed, black; both have considerable criminal records; both claim amnesia for the events and are remanded for psychiatric and social reports. In the case of the woman, who is found to have a disturbed background, a history of alcohol and drug abuse and other physical problems but no psychiatric illness, the psychiatric report notes: 'There is in my view no evidence of formal psychiatric illness'. (Psychiatric report, case 41, woman charged with robbery; quoted in Allen 1987: 1.) On the other hand, the man is found to suffer from major mental illness which dates back to 1968. The psychiatric report notes:

> The defendant has shown evidence of mental disorder for at least fifteen years with unequivocal evidence of schizophrenic illness . . . It is quite impossible here to categorically state whether or not he is/was responsible for his actions. In my mind there is a reasonable doubt.
> (Psychiatric report, case 123, male charged with robbery; quoted in Allen 1987: 1–2)

Both are convicted of the crime. The man is sentenced to two years' imprisonment. The woman is placed on probation, on condition she obtains psychiatric help. According to Allen, this illustrates the overall pattern which demonstrates that women are viewed as suitable subjects for psychiatric care. Furthermore, I would argue that, as women, they are perceived as irrational agents, whether or not they have committed crimes (Frigon 1989). For Hutter and Williams (1981) and Schur (1984), women are deviant because they are women.

The genealogy which I have tried to construct here points in this direction, that is to say, that the representations of femininity in dissent are not totally dissociated from representations of women who conform. For example, in the study by Broverman and his colleagues (1972), the discrepancy between (normal healthy) woman-hood and (normal healthy) adulthood is evident. In this study, the qualities necessary for a healthy adult are: the capacity for autonomous thinking, clear decision-making, responsible action, being independent, aggressive, competitive and objective. Attributes associated with masculinity are considered undesirable in female subjects. Hence, the equation is clear: being male is being a normal adult and being female is being pathological (passive, less aggressive, more emotional, dependent, for example). Even the 'normal' woman is 'deviant and 'pathological', and if you happen to be a black or native woman you are doubly deviant. In addition, if you are a native or a black woman offender you are triply deviant: you are native or black, a woman and a 'criminal'.

This genealogy of the representations of deviant/criminal women is an attempt to show some of continuities and discontinuities in how different actions of deviant women (witches, 'fallen' women, criminal women and women who kill their children) are translated into a discourse on madness – which also extends to political protesters. Moreover, as I have tried to argue in this chapter, it seems that it is not necessary to transgress penal boundaries to be transgressing: it suffices to be a woman. This argument is central to the analysis of women who deviate because the category *Woman* and its characteristics operate as the centre of the understanding (Frigon 1992, 1993). In fact, what is needed is to pivot the centre. The discursive meaning of *Woman* is pivotal to a genealogy of representations and social control of women and is central to the gendered nature of law and order.

Notes

[1] This percentage has been reported in the *Guardian*, 25 June 1991. These special hospitals, in terms of the 1959 Mental Health Act, existed to provide for people who 'require treatment under conditions of special security on account of their dangerous, violent or criminal propensities'. These special hospitals are administered through the Department of Health and not the NHS regional framework. It should be noted that under the Mental Health Act 1983, some of the functions of the 1959 Act changed. In the Mental Health Act 1983, '(3) Nothing in subsection (2)

above shall be construed as implying that a person may be dealt with under this act as suffering mental disorder, or from any form of mental disorder described in this section, by reason only of promiscuity or other immoral conduct, sexual deviance or dependence on alcohol or drugs' (Mental Health Act 1983, c.20). More importantly, however, the 'gender asymmetry' in definitions of madness is still prevalent in this Act. Women are defined, within the boundaries of the legal provisions, as more likely to be mad. See Thomas Szasz's *The Manufacture of Madness* (1971) and *The Myth of Mental Illness* (1961) for further discussion of the social construction of madness and mental illness.

[2] Broadmoor in Berkshire was the first state asylum built to cater for the mentally ill offender (Hutter and Williams 1981: 133).

[3] The largest institution of its kind. Two other 'special' hospitals are Moss Side and Park Lane (Hutter and Williams 1981: 133).

[4] Poetry made available at the conference 'Criminology into the Ethnic Minorities in the Criminal Justice System', London, 29 May 1991.

[5] Borrowed from T. De Lauretis (1987). 'Technology of gender' refers to how gender is represented and self-represented in various social technologies including institutional discourses and critical practices (De Lauretis 1987: ix).

[6] An example of this is the film *Fatal Attraction* where the dangerous, mad and over-sexualized woman is shown living near a meat market. We see her walking around bins; there is fire in them, smoke rising in the air. Her 'unruly' hair blows in the wind. She gets to her loft in a big garage-like lift. There is a sense of mystery and danger (see Faludi 1991).

[7] The majority of the victims were considered witches but lesbian woman and gay men were also executed. They were executed by burning at the stake and '[g]enerally, faggots (bundles of twigs used as kindling) were used to start the flames . . . it was common practice to save convicted gay males until the Inquisitors found a "witch" and then wrap them around the female to use them as faggots to fuel the flames. It was thus that the word "faggot" came to refer to gay men . . .' (Pickards and Goldman 1992: 34)

[8] The first three theories of witchcraft have been provided by Szasz 1971. See Frigon 1994 for a discussion of these theories and a more general discussion of the representation of witches.

[9] Szasz contrasts institutional psychiatry and contractual psychiatry. The former is imposed on the individual through private or public institutions whereas the latter is a contract negotiated between an individual and a therapist.

[10] Thomas Szasz's views have not been accepted by the established order of psychiatry and are viewed as the enemies of this order. Frederick G. Glaser (1965) asks the question of 'whether sanctions of some form ought to be taken against Dr Szasz, not only because of the content of his views but because of the manner in which he presents them. He has not chosen to limit his discussion to professional circles . . .' (Glaser 1965). Szasz writes

that this intolerance is understandable because 'doubt about the existence or dangerousness of mental patients would limit the methods permitted to institutional psychiatrists in combating mental illness, just as doubt about the existence or dangerousness of witches would have limited the methods permitted to inquisitors in combating witchcraft'(Szasz 1971: 19).

[11] See also Ussher 1991 and Hester 1992 for further discussions.

[12] It is perhaps interesting to note that there was a new statute to regulate and criminalize infanticide which thus became a crime in 1623 (see Smart 1992).

[13] A contemporary example of this can be found in the film *Thelma and Louise*. Having stepped out of place and knowing that they could not come back to their old lives, they choose to die. This ending is quite common in the feminist genre whether in novels or films.

[14] See Dobash, Dobash and Gutteridge (1986) and Zedner (1991) for notable exceptions.

[15] Hartman (1977) and Sullivan (1975) demonstrate that those women who were acquitted in the nineteenth century were so judged because of a strategy using conventional and appropriate stereotypes of femininity (Heidensohn 1985). In the 1980s and 1990s, Hollywood and the film industry have also exploited the image of the dangerous seductive mad sexual women in *Fatal Attraction, Thelma and Louise, The Hand that Rocks the Cradle, Basic Instinct, Single White Female*, for example.

[16] This case has been discussed by Constance Backhouse in *Petticoats and Prejudice* (1991). Ojibwas are one of the many groups of Aboriginal peoples. Faith (1993) notes that the term 'Aboriginal' was used by the Canadian legal system to 'designate people who were on what became Canadian land at the time of the first contact (invasion) by European explorers and settlers' (p. 186). In contrast, the term 'First Nations' flushes out the racism inherent in the Anglo concept of 'tribes'. The term signifies the literal truth that many diverse cultures shared this continent as its original occupants (Faith 1993: 187).

[17] Similarly, more than 150 years later through the Indian Act, Aboriginal experiences of child rearing, for example, were not respected. Hence, the Canadian government created 'residential schools'. Until the 1960s 'residential schools' had been imposed in order to 'educate' Indian children in white culture and silence their own cultural roots. Children were taken from their homes and were not allowed to speak their language.

[18] See Allen 1987 on the construction of the 'reasonable man' in law.

[19] For example, during the French Revolution in 1789, Théroigne de Méricourt was involved in the Revolution and was thus seen as transgressing appropriate gender norms. She was viewed as mad (see Roudinesco 1991).

[20] Young (1988) has discussed some of the techniques used in relation to the Suffragettes.

[21] To my knowledge, the peace camp no longer exists but the protests still

continue. It should be of no surprise that *women* should engage in a campaign for non-violence; feminism and non-violence share some common principles (Cook and Kirk 1983).

[22] I use the term 'offending women' coined by Worrall (1989), since I feel it illustrates the 'double deviancy' associated with female criminality. For an interesting and inspiring description and analysis on the dreams, nightmares and statements of the Greenham Common women, see Cook and Kirk (1983).

[23] For Summer (1983), the function of censure is to 'mark off the deviant, the pathological, the dangerous and the criminal from the normal and the good. As such they are clearly moral and political in character'(Sumner 1983: 195–6).

References

Allen, H. (1987). *Justice Unbalanced – Gender, Psychiatry and Judicial Decisions* (Milton Keynes, Open University Press).

Backhouse, C. (1991). *Petticoats and Prejudice* (Toronto Women's Press).

Benn, M. (1990). 'Every month a crisis', *New Statesman/Society* 7 December, 20–2.

Ben-Yehuda, N. (1985). *Deviance and Moral Boundaries* (Chicago, University of Chicago Press).

Blackwood, C. (1984). *On the Perimeter* (London, Fontana).

Broverman, I. *et al.* (1972), 'Sex-Roles and stereotypes: a current appraisal', *Journal of Social Issues*, 28, 59–78.

Brown, P. (1969). 'Society and the supernatural: a medieval change', *Daedalus*, 104, 133–51.

Bryson, J. (1985). *Evil Angels* (Victoria, Viking Press).

Cook, A. and Kirk, G. (1983). *Greenham Women Everywhere* (London, Routledge and Kegan Paul).

De Lauretis, T. (1987). *Technologies of Gender* (London, Macmillan).

Dobash, R. P., Dobash, R. E. and Gutteridge, S. (1986). *The Imprisonment of Women* (Oxford, Blackwell).

Doggett, M. (1989) 'Greenham Common and civil disobedience: making new meanings for women', *The Canadian Journal of Women and the Law/Revue juridique 'femmes et droit'*, 3/2, 395–419.

Donzelot, J. (1979), *The Policing of Families* (New York, Panther Books).

D'Orban, P. (1979). 'Women who kill their children', *British Journal of Psychiatry*, 134, 560–71.

Edwards, S. (1984). *Women on Trial: A Study of the Female Suspect, Defendant and Offender in the Criminal Law and Criminal Justice System* (Manchester, Manchester University Press).

Edwards, S. (1986). 'Neither bad nor mad: the female violent offender reassessed', *Women's Studies International Forum*, 9, 79–87.

Faith, K. (1993), *Unruly Women: The Politics of Confinement and Resistance* (Vancouver, BC:, Press Gang Publishers).

Foucault, M. (1977). *Discipline and Punish* (Harmondsworth, Penquin).

Foucault, M. (1980). *Power/Knowledge* (Gordon, C., ed., New York, Vintage).

Frigon, S. (1989). 'Femmes et héroines: bilan des connaissances, limites et perspectives nouvelles', *Criminologie*, 22/1, 85–110.

Frigon, S. (1992). 'Les femmes dites "violentes" ou un vrai discours de folles? Quelques enjeux', IInd World Congress on Violence and Human Coexistence. Montréal, Palais des Congrès, July 12–17.

Frigon, S. (1993). 'Unruly women – the social construction of deviant women', Joint Lecture at the Department of Philosophy and Centre of History and Philosophy of Science, University of Toronto, 31 March.

Frigon, S. (1994). 'Femmes, hérésies et contrôle social: des sorcières aux sages-femmes et au-delà', *Canadian Journal of Women and the Law/Revue jurididique 'femmes et droit'*, 7/1, 133–55.

Garland, D. (1985). *Punishment and Welfare* (London, Heinemann).

Glaser, F. (1965). 'The dichotomy game: A further consideration of the writings of Dr Thomas Szasz', *American Journal of Psychiatry*, May, 121: 1069-74.

Greer, G. (1984). *Sex and Destiny: The Politics of Human Fertility* (London, Picador).

Grimshaw, J. (1986). *Feminist Philosophers: Women's Perspectives on Philosophical Traditions* (London, Harvester Wheatsheaf).

Heidensohn, F. (1985). *Women and Crime* (New York, New York University Press).

Helleiner, K. (1967). 'The Population of Europe from the Black Death to the Eve of the Vital Revolution', in E.E. Rich and C.H. Wilson, eds., *The Cambridge Economic History of Europe*, Vol.4: *The Economy of Expanding Europe in the Sixteenth and Seventeenth Centuries* (Cambridge, Cambridge University Press).

Hester, M. (1992). *Lewd Women and Wicked Witches: A Study of the Dynamics of Male Domination* (London, Routledge).

Hutter, B. and Williams, G. (eds.) (1981). *Controlling Women: The Normal and the Pathological* (London, Croom Helm).

Jaccoub, M. (1988). 'Les femmes et le terrorisme', *Revue Beccaria*, 1/1, 31–45.

Larner, C. (1981). *Enemies of God*, (London, Chatto and Windus).

Lemay, R. H. (1978). 'Some thirteenth and fourteenth century lectures on female sexuality', *International Journal of Women's Studies*, 1, 391–400.

Lloyd, G. (1984). *The Man of Reason: 'Male' and 'Female' in Western Philosophy* (London, Methuen).

MacFarlane, A. (1970). *Witchcraft in Tudor and Stuart England: a Regional and Comparative Study* (London, Routledge and Kegan Paul).

Millman, M. (1982), 'Images of deviant men and women', in M. Evans, ed., *The Woman Question: Readings on the Subordination of Women* (London, Fontana).

Naylor, B. (1990). 'Media images of women who kill', *Legal Services Bulletin*, 15, 534–6.

Oakley, A. (1981). 'Normal motherhood: an exercise in self-control?', in B. Hutter and G. Williams eds., *Controlling Women: The Normal and the Pathological* (London, Croom Helm), 79–107.

Patullo, P. (1983). *Judging Women* (London, NCCC Rights for Women Unit).

Pickard, T. and Goldman, P. (1992). *Dimensions of Criminal Law* (Toronto, Emond Montgomery Publications).

Resnick, P.J. (1970). 'Murder of the newborn: a psychiatric review of filicide', *American Journal of Psychiatry*, 126, 325–34.

Roberts, Y. (1989). 'A bad mother', *New Statesman & Society*, 2/34, 10–11.

Roudinesco, E. (1991), *Madness and Revolution: The Lives and Legends of Theroigne de Mericourt* (London, Verso). Translation, Martin Thom, 1991.

Russell, J. B. (1977). *The Devil* (Ithaca; Cornell University Press).

Sallmann, J.-M. (1991). 'Sorcière', in G. Duby et M. Perrot, eds., *Histoire des femmes é XV – XVIII siècles* sous la direction de Natalie Zemon Davis et Arlette Parge (Paris, Plon), 455–67.

Schur, E. M. (1984). *Labelling Women Deviant: Gender, Stigma, and Social Control* (New York, Random House).

Smart, C. (1978). *Women, Crime and Criminology: A Feminist Critique* (London, Routledge & Kegan Paul).

Smart, C. (1992). 'The woman of legal discourse', *Social & Legal Studies*, 1, 29–44.

Smart, C. and Stevenhuijsen, S. (eds.)(1989). *Child Custody and the Politics of Gender* (London, Routledge).

Sparrow, G. (1970). *Women Who Murder* (London, Arthur Barker Ltd.).

Sumner, C. (1983). 'Rethinking deviance: towards a sociology of censures', in S. Spitzer, ed., *Research in Law, Deviance and Control* (London, J.A.I. Press).

Szasz, T. (1961). *The Myth of Mental Illness* (New York, Paul B. Hoeber Inc., Medical Division of Harper & Brothers).

Szasz, T. (1971). *The Manufacture of Madness* (London, Routledge & Kegan Paul).

Peterson, C. (1992). 'The prevalence of "queer-bashing"' in T. Pickard and P. Goldman eds, *Dimensions of Criminal Law* (Toronto, Emond Montgomery Publications), 9–14.

Trexler, R. (1973). 'Infanticide in Florence: new sources and first results', *History of Childhood Quarterly*, 1\1:98–116.

Ussher, J. (1991). *Women's Madness: Misogyny or Mental Illness* (Amherst, University of Massachusetts).

Wilczynski, A. (1991). 'Images of women who kill their infants: the mad and the bad', *Women and Criminal Justice*, 2, 71–88.

Worrall, A. (1981). 'Out of place: female offenders in court', *Probation Journal*, 28/3, 77–93.

Worrall, A. (1990). *Offending Women: Female Lawbreakers and the Criminal Justice System* (London, Routledge).

Young, A. (1988). '"Wild Women": the censure of the suffragette movement', *International Journal of the Sociology of Law*, 16/3, 279–93.

Young, A. (1990), *Femininity in Dissent* (London, Routledge).
Zedner, L. (1991). *Women, Crime and Custody in Victorian England* (Oxford, Oxford University Press).

3

Passion, marriage and murder: Analysing the press discourse

MAGGIE WYKES

This chapter addresses some issues identified by Sara Thornton, now serving life for killing the man who systematically beat and abused her. In a letter, addressed to the *Independent*, 23 August 1991, on the seventeenth day of her hunger strike, she wrote:

> Because I dared to fight I am being ignored . . . if Malcolm had killed me they would have used everything they are using against me now in his defence. I'd have been portrayed as a woman who nagged him over his drinking, who didn't always wear knickers, who went off to a conference and left him. Oh, I can just see the case they would build. And Malcolm, being the good upstanding citizen, despite his illness, oh yes, he would have walked free. Perhaps be advised to go for help or treatment.

My concerns are such accounts of men and women who commit *intimate* murders (that is who kill heterosexual lovers or spouses) as reported by the press. I consider how the kind of differences in such press accounts, noted by Sara Thornton, might relate to broader gender norms and roles. I argue that gender difference is maintained as inequality through discourse according to the exercise of power; a process dependent on violence – realized, institutionalized and symbolized. This paper supports the inclusion of discourse analysis in substantive research on issues of gender and violence as providing a valuable political resource.

Documenting women's deviance

Women's crime, minimal in quantity within the broad vista of a male-dominated activity, has recently attracted the attention of such feminist criminologists as Smart (1975, 1979, 1989), Heidensohn

(1985), Carlen (1983, 1985, 1987, 1988) and Allen (1987). In their work on women as criminals each has alluded to 'discourses of representation' specific to deviant women and routinely apparently denigratory beyond, between or beneath the condemnation of the crime itself.

In 1988 Alison Young described the *Censure of the Suffragette Movement* (as her book was partly titled) not as mere state repression but as more subtle constitutive discursive practice. Accounts at one level criminalized and so de-politicized the suffrage movement (discouraging similar revolutionary potential elsewhere in society); at a second level, accounts invoked the sexuality discourse, reinforcing norms of femininity by allying the suffragettes with 'perversity', either lesbianism or promiscuity (this discouraged 'normal' women from involvement); the third discourse of censure carried beyond the moment of the suffrage-struggles into the broader common sense of gender relations and acted also to reinforce traditional images of femininity as being commensurate with legitimate behaviour. In other words deviant women were not only criminal but deviant also in terms of their femininity. Deviant femininity was criminogenic.

In press accounts of the much more recent feminine political activity at Greenham Young found that news reports demonstrated, 'Through different manoeuvres how existence on the feminine edge of sexual difference becomes operationalised as a means to censure, condemn and control.' (Young, 1990:7). In the last few years that edge of difference can be identified less in accounts of politicized, public, women's movements and more often in accounts of change in female attitude and behaviour within the most traditional, essential social unit – heterosexual relations. Gender roles and relations were still on the media agenda in the early 1990s, but often presented in violent contexts.

Cosmopolitan magazine considers that such foci indicate profound conflicts between feminist and traditional gender values. Melissa Benn offers a serious warning:

> Finally women are achieving! We're really getting somewhere at work and gaining independence at home. But some men feel we're too close for comfort. If we believe the hype, equality is bad for us and freedom makes us unhappy. Only by recognising the propaganda can we fight it and then move forward.
>
> (Benn in *Cosmopolitan*, February 1992)

Melissa Benn's article discusses the 'bulletin of despair' which has subjected the career woman of the eighties to an 'onslaught of subtle disparaging images'. She describes how:

> Working women who have gone missing or been murdered – from estate agent Suzy Lamplugh to 17 year old Lynne Rogers – are often subtly implicated through their very enthusiasm for work and independence.
>
> (Ibid.)

Benn argues that both in the press and popular culture women are being represented as neurotic, unhappy and selfish. At its most extreme the message crosses into the violence discourse. In the film *Fatal Attraction* the single career women is not only all of these – she is also dangerous. She seduces happy husbands, tries to break up families and turns to violence. The resolution wherein the non-working wife and mother kills the pregnant *other* woman could not have a clearer moral message about family and sexual roles. When popular women's magazines are exploring such issues of representation it seems imperative that they are also placed on the academic agenda, particularly when feminists have become increasingly disturbed by violent events in real-life gender relations, (see Lees 1989, Edwards 1989).

The press

Violence committed against women by men, sometimes ending in death, seems to have assumed a particular salience for the press, as have those few cases where women kill men. Such acts of violence in an area of heterosexual relations normally assumed to be consenting, affectionate and stable (*intimate*) contain many of the requisite ingredients for the news, identified in Cohen and Young (1973), Chibnall (1977). Criminality slakes the thirst of journalists for the newsworthy event (see Galtung and Ruge 1965), that which seems 'to interrupt the unchanging consensual calm' (Hall *et al*. 1978: 66):

> Crime is news because its treatment [in the media] evokes threats to but also re-affirms the consensual morality of the society: a modern morality play takes place before us in which the devil both symbolically and physically is cast out from society by its guardians – the police and the judiciary.
>
> (Ibid.; my bracketed inclusion)

Not only do such murders satisfy 'news values' of the violent, the deviant and the sudden but they allow space for the sexual innuendo and romantic drama beloved of the British tabloid press. Chibnall (1977) quotes Young's (1974) statement that newspaper journalists '. . . hold their reader's attention by presenting material and sexual desiderata in an alluring though forbidden form. They fascinate, titillate, and then reassure by condemning (Young 1974: 31). Further work on the press is already justified by work, both theoretical and empirical, concerned with the ideological role of the media (Chibnall 1977, Curran 1977, Husband 1975, 1984, Van Dijk 1987, 1988, GUMG 1980, Mattelart 1986, Fowler 1991). In *Femininity in Dissent* (1990) Young explains her own commitment to press analysis:

> The discourse of the press is an important subject for analysis in the inquiry into the consideration of definitions of deviance and their representation because of its pervasive, non-specialist and everyday nature. The reading of a newspaper is an accepted part of the daily ritual of millions.
>
> (Young, 1990: viii)

Discourse analysis

Such discourse analysis is a complex matter both methodologically (it may consist of formal counting and labelling of a syntactic feature in a single text or interpretative, intertextual reading of a topic) and theoretically (meaning may be approached as systematically encoded in linguistic structures or only realized subjectively at any reading). Although much contemporary work on discourse has abandoned the structural project, Young 1990 advocates 'an adventure into the influence of structure' which 'recognises the interpenetration and essential inseparability of form and content' (Young 1990: 89). She also advocates sensitivity to the historical context of meaning, whereby conventionally shared meanings of Greenham depend on the 'established historical common-place' which equates 'statist strength with warmongering' (ibid.) (yet, as with structure, concepts of linearity, progression and collectivity have lost favour in contemporary approaches which emphasize the immediate, the experiential and the active individual as creating meaning).

The concerns for post-structuralism and post-modernism are agency and process, with the human actor, and moments of action, the valued focus for exploration. Harland (1987) explains the flaws of some such work:

> With the destruction of Objectivity and Truth, scientific knowledge becomes less valuable than literary or political activity; and detailed observational analysis and extended explicatory grids are discarded in favour of instantaneous flashes of paradoxical illumination.
>
> (Harland 1987: 3)

However, there seems no need to abandon the gains of contemporary post-structural and post-modern work in order to assert that there is a place for both structure and history in investigations of meaning. Whereas structuralism and post-structuralism appear to present theoretically, antithetically, as the immovable object and irresistible force, 'real' life seems (to me) to be both a collision and a syllogism of form and action. To advocate too strongly either theoretical position runs, therefore, the philosophical risk of burn-out in praxis. Post theory may be of limited value alone in the pursuance of political goals, concerned with evident long-term, systematic, collective oppression of one group by another, but neither could its structuralist and modernist predecessors account for the creative human action according to specific conditions necessary to achieve such goals. In this research I integrate approaches within media research in search of a resolution to the polarizing and excluding effect of a too-strong embrace of either pre or post epistemology. The result is, I hope, an analysis[1] of the press discourse which addresses Harland's criticisms by making explicit and siting interpretative *illuminations* of meaning (values, attributions and myths) within the systematic *explicatory grid* offered by content, stylistic, syntactic and narrative analysis.

Violence, discourse and power

News and popular culture, since the late eighties, have both mediated a stream of real and fictional instances of sexual violence and serial killing involving the dangerous stranger or the wicked woman. Statistics, however, indicate that the actual dysfunction leading to extreme violence in gender relations may not be the attacks of strangers but rather killing in 'intimate' partnerships. Specifically, a very great amount of violence of all kinds that is done to women is inflicted in their own homes by men with whom they have had affectional or/and sexual relationships. Women who are killed are as

killed by lovers as by strangers; by contrast in 1989
of men were killed by lovers (*Observer* 17.2.91).
show that, between 1982 and 1989, 785 men and
charged with killing their heterosexual partner.
have become concerned not only with the issue of 'femicide'
ford and Russell eds. 1993) but also with the apparently lenient
sentencing meted out to those men who have killed their sexual
partners (Lees 1989). Women who kill have often been severely
physically beaten and/or sexually abused over long periods of time by
their male victims, whereas men who kill generally claim to have been
provoked by *nagging* or *promiscuity*. Men regularly plea provocation
on these grounds, claiming to have acted in the *heat of the moment*,
whilst women killers may have to seek a weapon or wait for their
abusers to be asleep or drunk, signifying *premeditation*. The cases of
Sara Thornton and Joseph Mcgrail follow this pattern, resulting in a
life sentence for Thornton and probation for Mcgrail. Prompted by
such apparent inequity, this paper investigates the way society
accounts for these 'intimate' violences which demonstrate both the
ultimate collapse of gender relations and the ultimate exercise of
power, the taking of life.

Lukes (1986) describes power as operating in three fields: overtly in
the physical manifestation of force; covertly through institutionalized
rules and structures; and in the subjective unconscious, informing
attitudes and beliefs. In the case of men and women who kill, the act
is the overt level; the law provides the institutionalized context; and
the media institution represents these two levels at the level of
language for the subject-audience.

Alongside images and experience, language is vital to the process of
enculturement through which we become social subjects. It is also one
of the means through which we act on our world. Yet language bears
the representational burden of the exercise of power. It can be
understood as a site of symbolic struggle; an exercise in violence in
order to assume meaning. Gardiner offers Volosinov's Marxist view,
developed in 1929:

> Language constitutes the site of ideological phenomena *par excellence*. As
> such, the study of the word reveals the 'general ideological forms of
> semiotic communication' in sharp relief. It is the most sensitive possible
> index of wider social processes and antagonisms. (Gardiner 1991: 14)

For Foucault, social control depends on language. Discourses of sexuality, sanity and criminality are transformed into a technology of power 'always formulated in terms of law' (Foucault 1978: 87). Discourse, as a set of communicative practices either in a context or about a topic, provides the form for meaning and the context within which our 'subjectivity' is oriented, negotiated, constructed and reconstructed (Holloway 1989). Yet order of discourse can be identified as 'dimensions of the social order of institutions and societies' (Fairclough 1989: 43). If so, meaning is circumscribed by the power relations which sustain and are in turn sustained by the social world. Such relations support an understanding of meaning as won on behalf of the most powerful through the violent excision or obfuscation of the meanings concurrent with the lived experience of the least powerful. Preferred meaning equating to dominant perceptions becomes the most readily available meaning. Appearing to affix to form through use over time, meaning appears consensual, stable and natural. The violence of its selection is lost and alternatives are unexpressed. Subjects orient to meaning according to their differing places in social relations. Those outside dominance are always struggling for representation, forcing the continual re-exercise and reformation of power. So power, violence, institutions, language, change and social relations are held in an uneasy tension circumscribed as discourse. By examining the violent gendered phenomenon of men and women who kill *intimate* heterosexual partners there seems the possibility of making explicit that process which transforms the real exercise of violence, via the institutions of the law and media into the symbolic exercise of violence over meaning in language. Such a transformation may allow the symbolic reproduction of masculine control without the need for actual, physical violence, but may also, through the symbolic legitimation of masculine violence, culturally support male violence.

The norm of social power relations is composed partly of the dominance of men over women but also depends on the rule of law to control deviance. My exercise raised some curiosities: how could men who kill be accounted for in terms which castigate the illegality but continue the legitimation of male power; how would the aggression of female killers be accounted for when the feminine norm is passivity; how would the press deal with the inherent contradictions of the interplay of criminal violence (deviant) and heterosexual roles and relations (conforming) and could such representations of inter-personal relations in crisis relate to broader social trends and gender relations? Investigating such issues, it seemed, might inform a politics and praxis committed to resolving gender inequity.

Unless it can be made more explicit that the press *is* complicit with patriarchy then the power of the feminist argument becomes reduced to speculation that women's representation is different to and more castigatory than men's. So although my goal is to explore discourse in order to help explain the continuing and evident injustice to women in their own homes and in the courts, the means must address men – otherwise the project becomes too easily a study of victims.[2] Without analysis of the discourse of violence as predominantly masculine how can the problem of violence in any arena be addressed; how can the mechanisms which allow it to continue be explained; how can women's place in that paradigm be considered and how can the continued social construction of subjects in unequal gendered relations, after thirty years of second-wave feminism, be understood?

Press accounts of intimate murder

Despite the large numbers of women killed by men they know in contemporary Britain (averaging 120 every year) and the some thirty killings of male partners by women annually (*Observer* 17 February 1991, op. cit.), my research of the press could only identify twenty different cases reported in 1991 (six female and fourteen male killers; three of the male killers were Asian or Afro-Caribbean but all the women were white). As I was anxious to compare male and female case accounts (and to focus on dominant patriarchy),[3] I excluded the non-white male cases (although a comparison of accounts of white with non-white *intimate* killers would provide an interesting further study). I then limited my focus to cases in court during the last six months of 1991 (after the considerable interest raised by Sara Thornton's appeal which I feel may have affected the way the press reported such cases, mindful of Young's 1990 advice to be aware of the impact of the historical context of meaning). Anxious to be able to refer to the press as a whole (Fairclough 1992 advocates intertextual discourse analysis), I decided to look at press articles, both quality and tabloid, left- and right-wing, from the daily national papers (as most immediate to the court proceedings, most likely *steeped* in dominance through monopoly ownership and very widely read – some 15 m. are sold each day).

I constructed the framework for selections but the data also orchestrated the selection of cases. One man and one woman were co-defendants; one man had killed two women and several cases were not covered in each of the types of newspaper I wanted to include. Elimination and matching variables left me with Sara Thornton, Pamela Sainsbury, Linda Calvey, Joseph Mcgrail, John Perry and John Tanner and twenty-one articles consisting of 10,200 words.[4]

A brief review of some of the collected press reports illustrates the relevance of the *intimate* violence discourse to investigations of inequality in gender relations. It also highlights both the value and limitations of such *illuminative*, intuitive/interpretative readings.

Sara Thornton, a battered wife, killed her drunken alcoholic husband in June 1989. Sentenced for murder in February 1990 she appealed on the grounds of provocation. In late July 1991, her appeal was thrown out. Writing from prison Sara Thornton explained her decision to go on hunger strike in August 1991:

> 'All my life in one way or another I've allowed myself to be bullied. My father, my mother, my school, my grand-father and finally Malcolm. I've finally decided I won't be bullied any more.' Sara Thornton began to fast on hearing that 'a man who killed the bullying, alcoholic woman he was living with was given a two year suspended jail sentence' on 31 July 1991.
> (*Independent* 1.8.91)

Sara herself was clearly aware how she had been condemned as a bad wife on top of her sentence for murder. The case which provoked her hunger strike was that of Joseph Mcgrail, 'who killed his drunken wife' (*Daily Telegraph* 1.8.91) and was given a suspended sentence, on the grounds of provocation, two days after Thornton's appeal was denied. Mcgrail finally:

> cracked on Feb. 27 when he came home from work to find her drunk and demanding yet more drink. He refused, dragged her into a bedroom and kicked her as she lay on a bed. She died from internal bleeding soon afterwards.(*Independent* 1.8.91)

Mcgrail's reaction was described by prosecution counsel as a 'sudden, temporary loss of control caused by provocation' (ibid.). The judge commented that the murdered woman 'would have tried the patience of a saint'. He supplemented Mcgrail's suspended sentence by twelve months supervision to help him 'overcome his feelings of remorse'. Mcgrail's common-law wife never attacked him, resorting instead to alcoholic, verbal abuse and *nagging*.

The basis of the difference in sentencing was that Thornton's trip to the kitchen to collect a knife signified premeditation whilst Mcgrail's dragging of his wife to the bedroom before kicking her to death was signified as sudden loss of control. The *Daily Telegraph* (17.8.91) stated that resistance to allowing the provocation plea for Sara Thornton arose from the 'fear that sympathetic treatment of women who strike back at violent husbands could be seen as a licence for revenge'. Yet the converse argument does not, it seems, apply to men.

The descriptions of the murder of Rachel Mclean by John Tanner in April 1991 offer different explanatory grids for male violence, the evil stranger or/and female promiscuity/infidelity. Early accounts at the time of Rachel's disappearance show how readily the press assume the 'dangerous stranger' model of accounting for violence against women. At the start of the Oxford summer term the *Telegraph* highlighted, 'The danger beneath the dreaming spires', and succeeded in making some tenuous links between the state education system, homeless winos and 'bikers and heavy metal' with an Oxford where 'women undergraduates are nowadays loathe to walk alone at night across sinister Magdalen bridge' (28.4.91). The principal of Rachel's college is quoted as saying, 'There is no such thing as safety for young women.' All the assumptions are that Rachel has been the victim of a stranger in a dangerous city; that a woman should not go out on her own. Three days after this article, Rachel's body was found in her own home. In December 1991 her boyfriend was sentenced to life for her murder.

The *Daily Telegraph* headline after the trial was, 'Lover strangled student in jealous rage' (3.12.91) immediately connoting a crime of passion brought on by the infidelity of the student, so blaming the victim. Although the use of lover and student as the nouns disguises the sex of the perpetrator and victim it would be quite difficult to read other than the preferred interpretation. 'Girl lover strangles man student in jealous rage' is somehow not an acceptable alternative as it seems to contradict common-sense assumptions about gender difference both physical and cultural. The following text concentrates heavily on Tanner's claim that Rachel had confessed her infidelity. He states 'I lost control. It was as if something snapped inside my mind' (ibid.). Less space is afforded to the fact that he regained control sufficiently to spend the night next to the body; hide her under the floor; write to his dead girlfriend from the station; telephone and ask for her on returning to Nottingham and write again. His defence attempted a plea of provocation, albeit unsuccessfully.

In contrast to the quality press, the tabloids seem to emphasize less the court proceedings and more the detail of the crime and the background context to events. The tabloids provide fictional models of explanation for such terrible 'real' violence. The *Daily Mirror* front-page headline is simply, 'My Dearest Rachel', and the report begins, 'Jealous John Tanner strangled his unfaithful girlfriend' (3.12.91). The inside story again supplies a way out of attributing Tanner completely with blame. Tanner is, 'jailed for life for murdering the girl he loved while locked in the grip of a fatal obsession' (ibid.).

Having inappropriately connoted the film *Fatal Attraction* and its violent female protagonist, the *Mirror* continues by labelling Rachel 'unfaithful' (even though Tanner admitted he lied about her confession to provide himself with a reason for provocation). The story places the explanation for Tanner's crime outside of himself, something or someone after all locked him in his obsession. The *Daily Mirror* account is explicit on this, recounting Tanner's fellow inmate as saying, 'Now he blames her for provoking him into killing her. He has convinced himself it was her fault' (ibid.). The same account compares the detective work in the case to the TV series *Inspector Morse*. Curiously, the *Sun* displays a photo of Tanner clutching a teddy bear alongside one of a bejewelled Rachel in a strapless evening gown, looking as if she has stepped from a Gothic novel.[5] The *Gothic* is common in these accounts. Much is made of Rachel's preference for wearing black and Tanner's nickname for her, 'Black Rose'. More explicitly Gothic is his comment that 'she sapped his life-blood'.

Today, in reports of the trial of John Perry, offered gruesome but curiously domestically softened descriptions of his crime. Perry spent:

> Three days dissecting her carcass and cooking her flesh in their double oven. Police found cube-sized pieces of cooked flesh and bone stored in plastic bags in the kitchen and the garage.
>
> (*Today* 27.11.91)

The dead woman's sister and the killer's two ex-wives are interviewed in depth. Their reports of Perry's violence and cruelty make grim reading but again there is a softening when it comes to blame. Like the 'Yorkshire Ripper' as described by Jouve (1986)[6] he is a 'very moral man . . . who was never able to control his temper and that landed him in trouble' (ibid.), suggesting that somehow his violence was something for which he was not responsible. Culpability is further diminished by the hint at victim precipitation. The reader is told the tiny woman 'loved a jealous, sadistic, possessive monster' and there is discussion of her sexual history and her work as a 'go-go dancer in a night club'. Underlying these overtly descriptive phrases is the inference that she either sought death through her choice of sexual partner, or deserved it for her sexual activity. Either implies that she was somehow responsible for her own fate. There is also some discussion on his obsession with housekeeping, with both ex-wives citing their failure as cooks and housekeepers as causal of his violent outbreaks. In this way the story of the Perrys is likened to the film *Sleeping with the Enemy* 1991, even though in that story it is the obsessive husband who is eventually killed. My interpretation for the offering of such comment is that the victim Arminda Perry is being depicted as to some extent to blame for her own death; either by making a wrong choice in her husband; by being sexually promiscuous; by being foreign; or by failing as a housekeeper. Thus although the text overtly castigates the killer, John Perry, there is also a parallel, powerful covert message contained which hints that Arminda did not measure up as a wife and so deserved her fate. Arminda Perry's culpability is again suggested in the *Daily Mirror*: the word 'affair' appears under her picture, and her history as a prostitute in the Philippines is recounted.

In the Tanner and Perry cases the woman victim seems to attract most column space but when Pamela Sainsbury was in court for killing her husband, again it was still the woman, this time the perpetrator, who received the full attention of the press. The gender of the actors in *intimate* killings seems to hold more news value than the role played in the crime. In the *Mirror* report both front pages and inside headlines refer to Sainsbury as if a dog, 'Mercy for the killer who bit back', and, 'Whipped and forced to eat out of bowl on the floor'. The report seems to make sense of the act by placing her outside the normal range of woman/human, making her *other*, and stressing her need for psychiatric counselling, the basis of her plea for manslaughter due to diminished responsibility. Sainsbury was so disturbed by her ill-treatment during eight years of marriage that she kept her dead husband's head in the garage for nearly a year, 'to reassure herself he was not suddenly going to come through the door' (*Daily Mirror* 14.12.91)

Linda Calvey is described throughout the papers as a *'platinum blonde, gangster's moll from the East End'*. She is nicknamed the 'Black Widow' (after the female spider which eats the male after mating) and constructed as a vamp in accounts with distinctly *film-noir*[5] overtones. She is described as a 'passionate, ruthless' woman who made 'Cook kneel on the floor and shot him in the head (*The Times* 13.11.91). Little is made of her claim to have been beaten and in fear of her life and (unlike the reportage of the defendants in the other cases) there is hardly any reporting of her own comments.

Intuitive interpretation of such accounts of men and women who kill, elicits a contradictory reading. The violence of the men concerned *is* castigated; there is empathy for women who have been abused; reports also reveal and debate the increasing controversy of apparent judicial gender bias, all of which supports the efforts of feminists to seek justice for women. But alongside these readings others also appear to exist: readings which resurrect old stereotypes about appropriate female behaviour; which situate danger for women outside the home among strangers; place it in a world of fiction and fantasy and perpetuate a concept of male violence as being beyond the control and thereby the responsibility of men.

Although interesting and worrying, such description and interpretation does not begin to address Young's concern that 'despite the fact that our perceptions of criminality and deviance are deeply rooted in the structures of representation, no systematic analysis of the extent and subtlety of representation's influence has been carried out'(1990: 89). Going beyond merely 'providing accounts of topical images of crime'(ibid.) necessarily involves integrating such interpreting with attention to the systematic analysis of the context of its representation, both within and across press accounts.

Method

Systematization of my analysis of representations included the confinement of data collection to a closed six-month period July–December 1991 and matching of samples case-by-case in popular, quality, left- and right-wing daily newspapers. Where possible, articles appeared on the same day. *Intimate* killers themselves were matched with variables reduced as far as possible. The remaining systematization involved close attention to style, syntax, content and narrative.

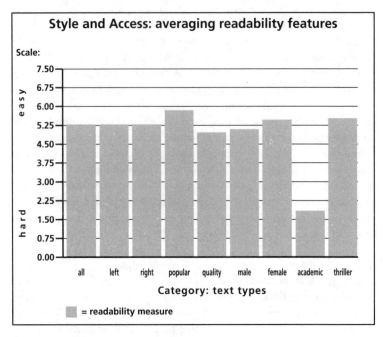

Style and Access: averaging readability features

Scale:

Graph A

There is a common-sense notion that the press offers an immediate, influential and accessible 'window on the world' by virtue of its pervasiveness; but that some 6 million people buy the *Sun*, daily, does not necessarily mean they understand it. Because my analysis concerns textual accounts likely to be well-known in the public domain, I felt any kind of audience research would be too readily confounded. In its place I turned to technology.

By highjacking software intended for style checking in the teaching or practice of writing I found a computerized audience. Text samples are simply word-processed and saved. The software provides a variety of measures – word length; active verbs; sentence length and so forth, all of which contribute to the overall readability of the text. Graph A shows the readability measure for the press texts and equivalent readings for two different texts: a USA Senate report on violent women[7] and the popular, sexually violent novel *American Psycho*.[8] The easy readability of the press accounts suggest no more nor less than that newspapers are effective providers of written information. It is likely that most readers will be able to understand these news reports because in order to score an *easy* rating texts only require 6–9 years of schooling to be comprehensible.[9]

The software style measure is not sophisticated enough to recognize more complex syntactic structures. Verb clauses have been investigated with meaning-significance by other linguistic analyses of the press;[10] such clauses broadly assume three types:

1. relational/associative clauses which categorize, classify and describe;
2. actional/attributional clauses which are transactive in that they include an agent/transitive verb/patient;
3. non-actional/declarative clauses which state a process but not one involving acting on a patient/object.

Verb clauses may have potent ideological roles in text, signifying as they do processes either of relation (which may exist as mood, time, space) or action by an agent on a recipient. For Trew (1979) the actional clause holds the potential to account for an event through the attribution of responsibility. Actional (transactive clauses) offer the syntactic construction for assigning causality. Relation clauses delineate other features which by association may support the interpretation of meaning. Non-transactive clauses offer complete events or undirected activity. Fairclough (1989) argues that selections and use of clause types in text contribute significantly to the ideological role of the text. The transactive or actional clause offers a direct route to identifying a responsible agent; the relational contextualizes an event in broader discourses and the non-transactive forecloses a process. The following graph compares frequency of representation of responsible agency in the press samples by a count of transactive clauses.

All the press samples favour a heavily attributional style more similar to the popular violent novel than the academic research report. The samples of female cases showed a slightly greater tendency to use transitive syntax, than male accounts. At this stage the analysis seemed to hover between the structural and interpretative: held in the structural by the syntagma of lexical forms agent/verb/patient but moving towards the interpretative by assigning the nouns for agency to their categoric paradigm. Arguably this is only possible through cultural knowledge, for example that detective is a label for an agent of

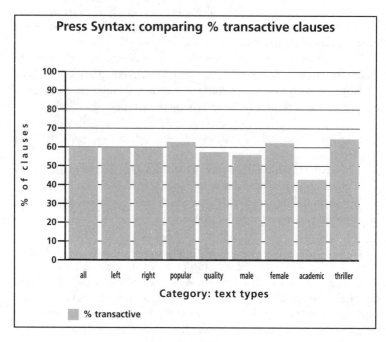

Graph B

the law. For the purposes of the discursive investigation I wanted to make explicit where agent responsibility is assigned in the press discourse of intimate violence. In the narrative structure,[11] this is shown in a clear tendency towards a story which begins with the resolution/sentencing; moves on to the problem/crime; attributes cause/motive; describes struggle/killing; introduces heros/detectives; satisfies/states legal position and validates/supports legal position.

Such labelling brought me to the limit of the contribution of linguistic structures to meaning. The only thing left was to use content analysis to simply count occurrences of lexical types, e.g. legal, victim. Alongside this process I moved away from simple denotative description of category labels, towards exploring connotative evaluation, signification (Barthes 1977). This symbolic level offers up referents in ritual, history and cultural context which prompt a development of meaning through association and comparison. Using a comparative grid, as devised by Chibnall (1977) to assess positive/legitimate and negative/illegitimate British values in

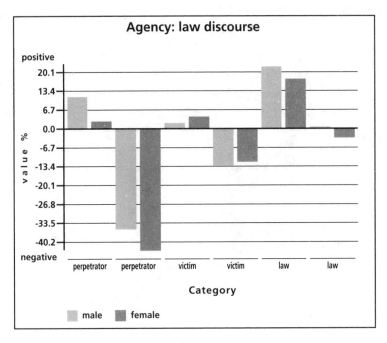

Graph C

crime reports I produced the following models of the incidence of agency, and also a value assignment in terms of the legal discourse of deviant behaviour. Hence 'killer' connotes negative evaluation and relates to criminal agency, whereas 'jury' connotes a positive one and relates to the law as agency.

As might be expected the lexical/syntactic forms connoting/denoting the perpetrator for each case readily attract negative value-judgements. Whether male or female the killers are syntactically blamed for their acts, by holding the agent place most frequently in the actional text and being labelled through denigratory 'names'. Perhaps significant is the way both kinds of victims (the battering man and innocent woman) are also denigrated in the text.

The differences between reports of men and women who kill 'intimate' partners seem fairly minimal. In a world of equal gender relations and factual accounts, where other variables such as time, race, sexuality do not apply, this might be the expected profile of agency. Although in such a world there might be some curiosity about

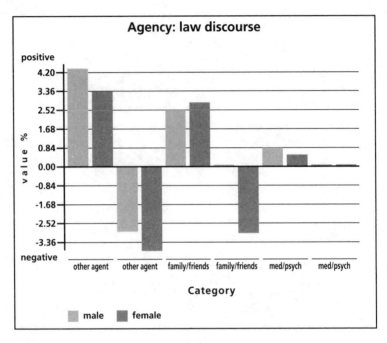

Graph D

the way male killers get some 'positive' press, although female killers get almost none; about the negative labelling of female victims none of whom attacked their killers and the few negative evaluations of the law in cases of women who kill (despite the historicization of all these cases in public debates about injustice to women).

Also interesting is the narrowness of the categories of agency that prevail. In the male cases some 50 per cent of agency is occupied by terms for the male killer; 23 per cent the law and 16 per cent the female victim. In the female cases 47 per cent of agency is the female killer, 22 per cent the law and 18 per cent the male victim. Accounts are therefore contained within tight semantic boundaries of explanation circumscribed by killers, victims and the law. Little reference is made to broader socio-cultural-medical influences, as the second graph shows. In terms of the law these accounts seemed not to support the sense of difference and contradiction elicited from the interpretative readings of accounts of men and women who kill. Cautiously it seems issues of gender are foreclosed in the law discourse in the press. Any reading of gendered differences must be promoted through the other accounting framework common to these texts – the sexual discourse.

If the legal account of gendered killing is similarly castigatory of male and female killers and victims then it is clearly working to uphold the law and resolve a crisis of deviance. However, the press must also address a second area of conflict – gender or specifically marital roles. How might the press having castigated 'intimate' killing as a crime then legitimate male power and promote the feminine norm of passivity? If the discourse of 'intimate' killing in the press is working as a sexual as well as legal account it may circumscribe all gendered agency whether victim or perpetrator in the same terms, i.e. it may evaluate them as men or women as well as in terms of crime.

The final component of my systematic analysis makes explicit any such process in the press. Using similar grids to those developed by Chibnall to map the legal discourse, this stage of analysis evaluates the lexical selections made for male or female perpetrators and victims, in terms of gender norms or values. The value judgements inherent in the grids are subjective, based on my own experience and perception of the preferred 'dominant' models of male and female attributes and roles. In assigning value I referred to other lexes in the immediate syntactic context for explication. For example 'Blonde Pam killed' is adjudged to be negative not only as already evaluated in breaking the law but also through the association of 'blonde' with a specific denigratory female sexual stereotype. 'Husband who murdered his Filipino wife' is judged negative in the legal discourse but positive as a gender label; in contrast 'unemployed man who murdered' would be labelled negative on both counts. The graph which follows shows the occurrences of discourses of explanation and the interpreted value-judgement. Where labels are disguised or deleted the meaning is inferred from the text. The terms man/woman are excluded unless qualified or modified with a value judgement, as in 'strong' man. Proper names provide an interesting exercise because male proper names are always used in full or with the surname only. Women are very frequently referred to by their Christian names, whether victims or killers. This seems significant and I have judged it as devaluing women as child-like and also perhaps hiding their marital status. Assignment for pronouns is treated as neutral and excluded from the profile unless the pronoun is qualified or modified by a verb or adjunct.

Gender Value Grids: Guide to Dominant Model

male positive	male negative	female positive	female negative
heterosexual	homosexual	heterosexual	lesbian
virile	impotent	wife	single woman
working	unemployed	maternal	non-maternal
strong	weak	passive	aggressive
aggressive	passive	dependent	independent
mature	immature	monogamous	polygamous
		natural	artificial
		frail	powerful
		slender	gross
		married mother	single mother

The values cover areas of sexuality, physicality, social role and psychology. The range of available terms for women is much larger, and many more can be inferred but this grid offers an *aide-mémoire* and some account of the evaluation process. I found gendered labels for men less readily accessible with a distinct paucity of male-negative labels. This lack seems to show the extent to which language encodes the view of the world from a masculine position with women the subordinate object requiring labelling as 'other' and 'lesser' than male.

Graph E indicates a much broader range of accounting for women in these accounts than men. Women are denigrated not only as criminal but more in terms of their various gender roles: sexual (wife/lover/mother/attractive); social (housewife/work/leisure); and psychological (caring/stable/intelligence). Although male nouns include some broader discursive references these are often positive references. The majority of negative evaluation of men falls within the legal discourse. In accounts which might be expected to be broadly similar there are firstly more sex-value labels for women than men (57% compared to 43% indicating a greater textual focus on women involved in these crimes); more negative labels (46% compared to 30% indicating a more castigatory evaluation of women perpetrators and victims) and more non-criminal-value labels (48% compared to 28% indicating that women are being evaluated not just for breaking the law but also for going against their gender grain).

The process of quantification is perhaps stretching the structural framework beyond its valid limit. It would, for example, be possible

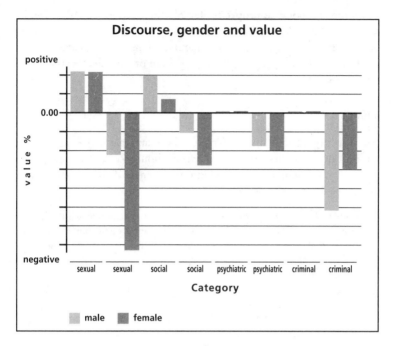

Graph E

to argue with the value assignments I offer gender attributes, according to other experience and perception. Perhaps not always or wholly applicable, I would still insist that my reading of gender norms and values has sufficient cultural capital and currency to support an attempt to map their use systematically. In other words I feel for many instances they would be meaningful in the interpretation of gender discourses at a preferred, top or first level of reading.

Men in these accounts are accounted for as breaking the law rather than as breaking any taboos of masculinity. In contrast, women are depicted as having broken taboos of gender behaviour three times more often than men. Accounts are skewed towards a focus on women participants. The lack of attention to violence as usually masculine is apparent, as is the shifting of any discourse on women into a second-order account of gender roles, especially sexual roles. Thus the press accounts manage to perpetuate the legitimacy of male violence in gendered terms whilst castigating it in legal terms, and castigating female violence in legal terms whilst 'resurrecting old stereotypes about appropriate female behaviour'. In the gender discourse, violence (whether male or female) is associated with deviant femininity; in the law discourse violence is associated with criminality. What is missing is any critique of violence as associated with masculinity.

Summary

Foucault argues that much of male power over women relates to the 'monotonous nights of the Victorian bourgeoisie. Sexuality was carefully confined; it was moved into the home' (1976: 3). That sexual discourse defined sex as:

> That which belongs in common to men and women; that which belongs *par excellence* to men, and hence is lacking in women; but at the same time, as that which constitutes woman's body, ordering it wholly in terms of function of reproduction and keeping it in constant agitation through the effect of that very function.
>
> (Foucault, 1976: 153)

Collier (1994) cites the period 1870–1920 as witnessing the legal reforms and welfarism which underpin the domesticization of sexuality. The family is constructed as the site of legitimate sexual behaviour in monogamous marriage. Women's sexual role is delimited to wife and mother.

The challenges to such definitions brought about by women through the consciousness-raising of feminism, have made of the sexual discourse an arena for the battle of the sexes. Gender conflicts, highlighted by the feminism of the sixties, are still largely unresolved and patriarchy seems currently to be exercising more and more power through social institutions (for example the Pro-Life campaign in the USA, and its recent incursion into the UK; lack of state nursery provision for working mothers in the UK; and the current scapegoating of single mothers) in the effort to restore men's dominance in the Victorian tradition and keep women 'barefoot and pregnant in the kitchen'.

The economic crisis of the last decade underwrites the need for capitalism to reconstruct sexual conditions conducive to its survival. Such reconstructions in policy are also evident in the language of cultural forms. Symbolically, old (even arcane given women's changed social, economic and sexual sensibilities) ideas infuse public discourses; discourses which provide for audiences models of gendered behaviour. Not surprisingly, in the home, in personal and intimate relationships, the pattern of reasserting patriarchy (and concurrently capitalism) seems similar but the means is sometimes more directly an exercise of power through real violence by men on women; an exercise that some women who 'finally decide they won't be bullied any more' are now resisting – sometimes by 'counter-investing the violence . . . endured . . . with arms which may seem disproportional' (Kristeva 1989: 208).

In accounts of 'intimate' killing the dominant sex-violence discourse in the institutions of the law and the media is thus presented with a dilemma. In dominant ideological terms it needs to account for broadly similar crimes, the killing of sexual partners, differently for men and women, in order to promote dominant interests. Also the discourse faces another contradiction; violence in law is illegal, violence as transformed into power through patriarchy and represented in language is essential for dominance.

Given the place of the media and journalism in relation to capital and patriarchy the press discourse is likely to represent the interests of dominance. This paper is drawn from a broader study of:

> who does the speaking, the position and viewpoints from which they speak, the institutions which prompt people to speak about it [violence] and which store and distribute the things that are said . . . to locate, the forms of power, the channels it takes and the discourses it permeates in order to reach the most tenuous and individual modes of behaviour.
> (Foucault 1978 trans.: 11; author's bracketed inclusion)

Analysis of press accounts of 'intimate' killing shows a process of calling to consensus, indicative of conflict within gender paradigm. Such evidence also demonstrates the contribution discourse analysis can make to clarifying social processes.

The message is repeated systematically and is so often the same old story about the havoc wreaked by 'wild and wicked women'; a story that is reworked so effectively that whether the 'real' exercise of violent power is male or female, it is male power that is secured, symbolically, with women urged to conform and comply. But the recycling of such accounts in cultural forms is not entirely containing, or neither this paper, nor the opening comments of Sara Thornton, would be possible. The textual analysis indicates the active exercise of patriarchal power and in that very process reveals the possibility of a different reading and resistance. Such analysis can contribute to the struggle for gender equality by exposing part of the process of oppression and foregrounding the reality of women's experience. If the political goal is to change the world:

> The critical steps are, first, using what we know about our lives as a basis for critique of the dominant culture and, second, creating alternatives.
>
> (Hartsock 1990: 172)

Notes

1 This paper includes only part of the full analysis undertaken and focuses specifically on the usefulness of a structured approach to support analysis of the press discourse. The full analysis is in (1994) 'Accounting for intimate killing: Press, Gender and Discourse' by M. Wykes, Ph.D. thesis, unpublished.

2 (*Applies in two cases.*) Richard Dyer (1993) recognizes a lack of attention in analyses of representation to 'groups with most access to power: men, whites, heterosexuals or the able-bodied' (p. 4). He argues that by focusing on the powerful in 'images work' it becomes possible to make 'normality strange and thus ultimately to decentre it' by exposing the social dominance of certain groups as not natural but won through the exercise of power. Hartsock (1990) argues similarly in her critique of Foucault and calls for 'women to use what they know about their lives as a basis for critique of the dominant culture'.

3 The Mcgrail case was little reported but seemed essential as a pair with Sara Thornton, whose high-profile case was pivotal to my research. Her case was also largely ignored in the tabloids, perhaps, as Julie Bindel of Justice for Women commented, because of the complexity of the legal and feminist debates it inspired.

4 Detailed and systematic discourse research of this kind consumes huge amounts of time and space. It involves multi-level (intertextual, intratextual, stylistic, narrative, metaphoric, mythic, clausal and lexical) mapping and both structural and interpretative analysis. This paper offers only a snapshot of some of the findings of the more structured clausal/lexical work.

5 The influence of the Gothic in these newspaper articles (and the contemporary prevalence of the Gothic in music, film and literature) is fully discussed in M. Wykes and K. Jones (1994) 'Danger, desire and identity: myth, the macabre and the construction of sexual subjects' – paper presented at the BSA conference 'Sexualities in the Social Context' March 1994, University of Central Lancashire.

6 N. Jouve (1986) *The Streetcleaner: The Yorkshire Ripper Case on Trial.* Peter Sutcliffe claimed, during his trial, to have been instructed by voices

from God to cleanse the streets of *bad* (sexual and therefore sinful) women. Feminists criticized judicial comments on the case which seemed to concur with Sutcliffe's view that prostitutes somehow deserved their fate. Sir Michael Havers's view was that, of the victims, 'some were prostitutes, but perhaps the saddest part of this case was that some were not'.

7 The formal report (Ward *et al.* 1969) on violent women was used as a control text to shown how the press offers a particular discursive space different to the factual, academic, complex and inaccessible report.

8 Easton-Ellis's sexual, violent, popular, post-modern novel offered a second control text. Although fictional it provided a textual profile very similar to the average for the press samples.

9 The style checker used for the 'readability' analysis uses scales derived from Flesch 1949, 1979. These relate to sentence length, word length, use of pronouns, use of passives, etc.

10 See especially Trew 1979 (in Hodge *et al.* 1979) in a comparative analysis of the accounts of the 1977 Notting Hill riots in the *Sun* and the *Morning Star*.

11 The full analysis includes a detailed exploration of the way narrative works in these accounts. It draws on film theory, semiotics, Russian formalism and anthropology.

12 Chibnall 1977 developed a grid (below) in order to assess the values of legitimate and illegitimate behaviour he felt were central to the British way of life. He argued that we (as text producers and consumers) cognitively evaluate events according to such a grid of binary opposites.

Legitimate (positive) values	*Illegitimate (negative) values*
legality	illegality
moderation	extremism
co-operation	confrontation
order	chaos
peacefulness	violence
tolerance	intolerance
constructiveness	destructiveness
openness	secrecy
rationality	irrationality
compromise	dogmatism
industriousness	idleness
equality	inequality
responsibility	unfairness
firmness	weakness
freedom of choice	monopoly/uniformity
impartiality	bias
realism	ideology

References

Allen, H. (1987). *Justice Unbalanced* (Milton Keynes, Open University Press).

Barthes, R. (1977). *Image, Music Text* (Fontana).

Carlen, P. (1983). *Women's Imprisonment* (London, Routledge & Kegan Paul).

Carlen, P. (1985). *Criminal Women* (Cambridge, Polity Press).

Carlen, P. (1987). *The Cultural Construction of Sexuality* (London, Tavistock).

Carlen, P. (1988). *Women, Crime and Poverty* (Milton Keynes, Open University)

Carlen, P. and Worrall, A (eds.) (1987). *Gender, Crime and Justice* (Milton Keynes, Open University Press).

Chibnall, B. (1977) *Law and Order News* (London, Tavistock).

Cohen, S. (1972). *Folk Devils and Moral Panics* (London, Paladin).

Cohen, S. and Young, J. (eds.) (1980) *The Manufacture of News. Deviance, Social Problems and the Mass Media* (London, Constable).

Collier, R. (1994). 'Waiting 'til father gets home: Family values and the reconstruction of fatherhood in family law' (pub. forthcoming, *Socio-legal Studies*).

Curran, J. Gurevitch M. and Woollacott, J. (eds.) (1977). *Mass Communication and Society* (London, Open University).

Dyer, R. (1993). *The Matter of Images* (London, Routledge & Kegan Paul).

Easton Ellis, B. (1991). *American Psycho* (London, Picador).

Edwards, S. (1984). *Women on Trial* ((Manchester, Manchester University Press).

Edwards, S. (1989). 'Policing domestic violence' (paper presented BSA conference 1989, Plymouth Eiser).

Fairclough, N. (1989). *Language and Power* (London, Routledge & Kegan Paul).

Fairclough, N. (1992). 'Discourse and text: linguistic and intertextual analysis within discourse analysis', *Discourse and Society* Vol. 3 (2).

Faludi, S. (1991) *Backlash: the undeclared war against women* (London, Chatto and Windus).

Flesch, R. (1949). *The Art of Readable Writing* (New York, Harper Row).

Flesch, R. (1979). *How to Write Plain English* (New York, Harper Row).

Foucault, M. (1978). *The History of Sexuality* (London, Penguin).

Fowler, R. (1991). *Language in the News* (London, Routledge).

Fowler, R., Hodge, B., Kress, G. and Trew T. (1979). *Language and Control* (London, Routledge & Kegan Paul).

Fraser, N. and Nicholson, L. (1990) (eds). *Feminism/Post-modernism* (London, Routledge & Kegan Paul).

Galtung, J. and Ruge, M. (1965). 'Structuring and selecting news' in S. Cohen, and J. Young (eds.) *The Manufacture of News. Deviance, Social Problems and the Mass Media* (1982 edn., Constable, London).

Gardiner, M. (1992). *The Dialogics of Critique* (London, Routledge & Kegan Paul).

GUMG – Glasgow University Media Group (1980). *More Bad News* (London, Routledge & Kegan Paul).

Golding, P. and Middleton, S. (1982). *Images of Welfare: Press and Public Attitudes to Poverty* (Oxford, Blackwell).

Hall, S. (1970). 'A world at one with itself' in S. Cohen and J. Young (1980) (see above).

Hall, S. (ed.) (1980). *The Manufacture of News. Deviance, Social Problems and the Mass Media* (London, Constable).

Hall, S. (1978) in C. Critcher, T. Jefferson and J. Clarke (eds.) *Policing the Crisis. Mugging, the State, Law and Order* (London, Macmillan).

Harland, R. (1987). *Superstructuralism* (London, Routledge & Kegan Paul).

Hartsock, N. 'Social criticism without philosophy: An encounter between feminism and post-modernism' in N. Fraser and L. Nicholson (eds.) (1990) *Feminism/Post-modernism* (London, Routledge and Kegan Paul).

Heidensohn, F. (1985). *Women and Crime* (London, Macmillan).

Hodge, R. and Kress, G. (1988). *Social Semiotics* (London, Polity Press).

Holloway, W. (1989). *Subjectivity and Method in Psychology: Gender, Meaning and Science* (London, Sage).

Husband, C. (1975). *White Media Black Britain* (London, Arrow).

Husband, C. (1984). *Social Identity and Race* (E3542: 5-6, Milton Keynes, Open University).

Jouve, N. (1986). *The Streetcleaner: The Yorkshire Ripper Case on Trial* (London, Marion Boyars).

Kristeva, J. (1988). 'Women's time' in C. Belsey and J. Moore (eds.) (1989) *The Feminist Reader* (London, Macmillan).

Lacan, J. (1976). *The Language of the Self* (Baltimore, Johns Hopkins).

Lees, S. (1989). 'Naggers, whores and libbers: provoking men to violence' (paper presented BSA conference 1989 Plymouth).

Lukes, S. (ed.) (1986). *Power* (Oxford, Blackwell).

Matelart, M. (1986). *Women, Media, Crisis: Femininity and Disorder* (London, Comedia).

Murdock, G. and Golding, P. (1977). 'Capitalism, communication and class relations' in J. Curran, M. Gurevitch and J. Woollacott (eds.) (1977) *Mass Communication and Society*.

Rabinow, P. (ed.) (1984). *The Foucault Reader* (London, Penguin).

Radford, J. and Russell, D. (eds.) (1993). *Femicide: The Politics of Woman Killing* (Milton Keynes, Open University Press).

Smart, C. (1975). *Women, Crime and Criminology* (London, Routledge and Kegan Paul).

Smart, C. (1979). 'The new female criminal: reality or myth', *British Journal of Criminology* (19 Jan. 1979).

Smart, C. (1989). *Feminism and the Power of Law* (London, Routledge and Kegan Paul).

Trew, T. (1979) 'What the papers say: linguistic variation and ideological difference' in R. Fowler, B. Hodge, G. Kress and T. Trew (1979) *Language and Control* (London, Routledge).

Tunstall, J. (1983). *The Media in Britain.* (London, Constable)

Van Dijk, T. (1987). *Communicating Racism: Ethnic Prejudice in Thought and Talk*, (London, Sage).

Van Dijk, T. (1988) *News as Discourse* (Hillsdale NJ, Erlbaum).

Volosinov, V. N. (1929). *Marxism and the Philosophy of Language* (1983, trans. L. Matejka and I. R. Titunik, Seminar Press, USA).

Ward, D., Jackson, M. and Ward, R. (1969). 'Crimes of violence by women' (USA White House staff report in F. Alder and R.J. Simon (eds.) (1979) *The Criminology of Deviant Women*, Houghton Mifflin, New York).

Wykes, M. and Jones, K. (1994). 'Danger, desire and identity: myth, the macabre and the construction of sexual subjects' (paper presented at BSA conference 1994 University of Central Lancashire).

Wykes, M. (1994) 'Accounting for intimate killing: press, gender and discourse' (unpub. Ph.D. thesis).

Young, A. (1988). 'Wild women: the censure of the suffragette movement', *International Journal of the Sociology of Law* 16, 3.

Young, A. (1990). *Femininity in Dissent* (London, Routledge and Kegan Paul).

4

Women's crime and media coverage: Making explanations

BRONWYN NAYLOR

Finding explanations for offending behaviour is central to the task of labelling the behaviour as criminal, of attributing responsibility, of deciding on disposition. There is also a strong common-sense impetus to finding explanations in order to make sense of the behaviour. A number of routine explanations for women's crime can be identified. They arise in discussions of intentionality and the use of various defences; in pleas in mitigation of sentence; and in sentencing decisions and judicial comments on sentence. They can be observed both in criminal trials, and in the reporting of crime in the media. This chapter discusses the author's current research on newspaper reporting of crimes committed by women, and outlines some of the attempts at explanation to be found in media stories about women's violence.

The Violent Woman

Michelle Taylor was the obvious choice as the killer of Alison Shaughnessy. She was an adulterer who indulged in sordid liaisons with her lover, Alison's husband. She was a woman scorned, passed over by her lover when he married Alison. She was young, female and attractive.

The police obviously concluded she had killed her lover's wife, in the face of the most circumstantial and contradictory evidence. The tabloids certainly did, and so ultimately did the jury. But in June 1993 the Court of Appeal quashed the conviction as 'unsafe and unsatisfactory'. The police had wrongly withheld evidence supportive of the defence case, and the press coverage was held to have been so prejudicial as to make the conviction untenable.

My interest is in the search for explanations, and in the ascription of explanations, for violent behaviour by women. Women are, by and large, not expected to be violent. Current gender relations, and the social structures built on those relations, are premised on women's non-violence. When they are violent, these fundamental structures are challenged. Explanations are sought to reduce the contradiction. Explanations may or may not be based in 'reality', but those which are found most 'satisfactory', most consistent with what is seen as a society's 'common sense', are likely to say important things about the position of women in that society. The public explanations within the criminal justice framework take the form of stories compiled by police and lawyers in putting a case together for a trial, stories in the press, and stories in pleas in mitigation of sentence. There may of course be competing stories; those of defence and prosecution counsel, of the judge when sentencing, of rival newspapers.

The Taylor appeal was based on challenging the case as presented at trial, and on the nature of the press coverage. First, the construction of the prosecution case. Police and lawyers identify and select 'facts'; they want to present a coherent, understandable story. Particularly in a case like this, where there was no direct evidence that Michelle Taylor actually killed the victim, the prosecution depended on persuading a jury that the prosecution story was credible, that the circumstantial material added up to proof of guilt, that the projected scenario was predictable.

McConville, Sanders and Leng (1991) and others have shown how the process of preparing a prosecution inevitably involves selection and construction of a case. Ambiguity and uncertainty are uncomfortable conditions. Police and lawyers have both a personal motivation to 'understand' the events, and also a professional need to present a winnable case. Michelle Taylor provided an obvious scenario – the jealous woman. The witness who saw two young women leaving the victim's house at the relevant time may originally have thought one was black, but as he now thought they were both blonde (as were Michelle Taylor and her sister Lisa) his earlier statement could be ignored, even, on the most generous analysis, genuinely regarded as irrelevant.[1]

Second, the press coverage. I will be discussing this in more detail later. You may recall the pictures and headlines in the tabloid press such as 'The "Killer" Mistress who was at Lover's Wedding' and 'Cheat's Kiss'. With the latter headline, the *Sun* published on page 1 a still from a video of the victim's wedding, showing Michelle Taylor kissing the groom (her lover) – a peck on the cheek turned into a passionate kiss by creative editing. This is obviously the stuff that sells papers. It is not suggested that this was a conspiracy against the Taylor sisters themselves. But it provided a 'script', and excluded other scripts, in a way which the Court of Appeal recognized to have been powerfully prejudicial.

The Media Response

Much work has of course been done on the media and their role in the construction and maintenance of dominant institutions and ideologies (for example, Glasgow University Media Group 1976; Hall *et al.* 1978). News stories are addressed to an assumed public and constructed around a taken-for-granted consensus. By selecting and then explaining 'problematic' events, events which contravene the assumed consensual values, the media play a powerful role both in defining what the consensus is, and then in identifying the nature of deviation.

Chibnall observes that news reporting is effective ideologically because it presents explanations as self-evident and unchallengeable.

> . . . the power of newspaper interpretations lies in their ability to make events intelligible at a mundane, 'commonsense' level, to provide a guide for practical activity and to alleviate the need for further investigation and consideration. The self-confident and assertive style in which the interpretations are communicated complements their general claim to represent the opinions of all right-minded people and encourages their ready acceptance as self-evident and 'obvious' . . . This commonsense mode of understanding trades off myths and stereotypes which provide simple, comfortable, ready-made pictures and explanations of things. (Chibnall 1977: 44)

In the first half of 1993, 2.7 million people bought the *Daily Mirror* each day, and 3.5 million bought the *Sun*.[2] These popular tabloid newspapers are written in simple language, requiring minimal reading skill. They are therefore likely to be enormously effective vehicles for the dissemination of written information.

Young (1990) stresses the importance of press analysis on the basis of the ubiquity and consumability of the medium. The discourse of the press, she argues, 'is an important subject for analysis in the inquiry into the construction of definitions of deviance and their representation because of its pervasive, non-specialist and everyday nature. The reading of a newspaper is an accepted part of the daily ritual of millions' (Young 1990: viii). People are, as a general stance, probably sceptical of newspapers, and it is important to know what they make of the stories they read. Nonetheless, as Chibnall notes,

> . . . it is easier for most readers to reject the open, substantive (factual) content of newspaper accounts than the more latent and implicit interpretive scheme in which that content is embedded. These schema are easily absorbed into the common stock of knowledge in a largely subliminal fashion. (1977: 45)

The media give a lot of space to death and violence, as is widely recognized. Williams and Dickinson (1993) found that on average the main national UK papers devoted 64.5 per cent of their crime reporting to stories of personal violence, although official figures suggest that only 6 per cent of crime actually involves personal violence. Violence by *women* seems to be doubly fascinating; criminal women are titillating and at the same time horrifying in ways that violent men generally are not. Around one-third of violent crime stories in newspapers are about women offenders[3] whilst their representation in the criminal statistics is around one in ten. Katz (1987) argues that crime stories instruct as to 'the nature and limits of personal competence and sensibility . . . Reports of armed robberies by children . . . by women, and by the elderly challenge our stereotypes not simply about crime but about the capabilities associated with those age and sex statuses' (1987: 50).

Violence in itself usually incorporates the drama, the human emotion, the shattering of 'normal' expectations that are required for a story to be newsworthy. Violence by women offers not only human drama and emotion but *sexualized* drama and emotion. The expectations breached are not just those of normal human interaction but also gender expectations. The story is more readily personalized than stories about men, and can double as entertainment – as soap opera, as humour, or indeed as soft porn.

There are also, however, differences in the amount of coverage given to different types of stories, just as there are differences in the coverage of other crime stories. Love triangles are very newsworthy, as are 'contract killings'. Stories given prominence speak of current anxieties about women, and about their role and activities in society (see Birch 1993). Such fascination and anxiety are evident not only in the choice of stories in the media, but also in the language in which the stories are told. A journalist commented recently on the reporting of stories about delinquent teenage girls:

> When a boy does terrible things, people always know what he is: he's a thug, a hooligan, a lout. But when a girl does terrible things, she becomes almost literally unspeakable. Pick through the shuddersome tabloid accounts of what Maria Rossi and Tina Molloy, both 17 and from near Aberdare, did to Edna Phillips before and after they strangled her with a dog chain, and see satanic transformations afflict the standard language of moral panic. 'Devil Girls' screams the *Daily Mirror*. 'Evil Beyond Belief' proclaimed the *Daily Mail*, harking directly back to Myra Hindley, the child killer still stalking the nation's nightmares from inside her prison cell. (Hill 1993)

I am proposing that there are a number of 'common-sense' stories used in the press writings about women, particularly violent women, and that these stories are inherently gendered, in important ways. Major stories, or explanations, seem to be:

1. Madonna/whore
2. Sexual passion/love as an 'excuse' for crime
3. Reproduction and madness
4. The figure of evil – the witch – the monster
5. The criminal woman as 'not-woman'
6. The female as devious and manipulative

I will discuss each of these in some detail, drawing for illustration primarily on a review of tabloids (the *Daily Mirror* and the *Sun*) and broadsheets (the *Guardian* and *The Times*) for the period February–April 1993 but also on a number of longer-running cases.

Madonna/whore

This has become a cliché, but it turns on the well-known operation of women's sexuality as a 'master status'. It can be crucial to the presentation of a woman claiming rape; the defence has simply to raise some previous sexual behaviour to throw the victim's *general* credibility into doubt.[4] The woman who has engaged in extramarital sex, or kinky sex, or perhaps is just 'sexy', is capable of any deviance.

Michelle Taylor is a case in point. Although her sexual relationship with the victim's husband was clearly relevant to the story, in that it provided the 'common-sense' motivation for the killing, the specifics were exposed in titillating detail in shocked and sanctimonious tabloidese. There was much coverage of the deceptive and sordid nature of the relationship. They were said to have had sex the night before the wedding, and to have had surreptitious liaisons after work. This was clearly a woman with no morals and no dignity (leaving aside for the moment the light it threw on her partner). She was, by extension, the 'sort of woman' who might well kill someone who stood in her way. She accordingly had no authority at all when trying to present an alternative story. It was a made-for-media story; no ambiguity was acknowledged and the conclusion was foregone.

Another recent story, not strictly of a violent woman but very striking, was of Yasmin Gibson, the 'home alone' mum who left her eleven-year-old daughter (allegedly with a neighbour) while she went on holidays. She was single, a 'bit-part' actress, partying in the south of Spain. Faced with the numerous photos of a tarty blonde in saucy poses, or looking angry and tearful with mascara running down her cheeks, our condemnation is assured. It was a story which could have been reported in more than one way. There was the hardworking single mum whose arrangements had fallen down, or there was the irresponsible tart. The connotations of 'bit-part actress' – sleazy, artful *and* unsuccessful – and the visual images were irresistible for the tabloids. She is at the one time unwomanly, being a bad mother and sexually immodest, and too much a woman, being openly sexual and deceitful. She is 'artificial' (an actress; exposed make-up) where woman should be 'natural'. Her claim to have made arrangements for her daughter (and the school's evidence that she was attending regularly and was tidy and well-fed) were not heard, nor was her honest comment that she found her daughter demanding and difficult at times. These were literally 'irrelevant', raising issues outside the common-sense presentation of the story. Yasmin Gibson's confession also challenged the idyllic and unproblematic concept of mother-hood, with its effortless martyrdom, which is presented as the proper female model. It did not help that her 'offence' was exposed at the same time as little Jamie Bulger was abducted and murdered in Liverpool, when his caring mum turned away for a moment. Some papers initially even linked the two stories in their layouts.

Sexual passion/love as an 'excuse'

I put under this heading stories which turn on women's supposed emotional frailty, and the centrality of love in their lives; their potential for 'love madness'. They may be shown as 'doing it for love' (Millman 1975) or as committing a crime when betrayed in love.

Audrey Lamb was convicted with her Irish lover in connection with IRA bombings in February 1993. She was described as dumpy, sixty, confused. She did it all for love. She was portrayed (using, for example, her own diaries) as desperate for love – a 'proper' desire as a woman, but made incongruous by emphasizing that she was fat and old. She was gullible, 'a pathetic creature who has lost everything' according to her own defence counsel.

> Odd couple from bungalow lovenest are jailed/The Lonely Heart and the Bomber/Audrey, 60, fell for IRA conman, 37.
> A lonely 60-year-old woman took an IRA bomber into her home and her bed . . . because she was desperate for love.
> And yesterday sobbing Audrey Lamb went to jail with evil terrorist James Canning after being labelled a 'pathetic creature who had lost everything'. (*Daily Mirror* 11 February 1993)

Noeleen Hendley had a 'hitman' kill her husband, after she fell in love with someone else. She was said to have been 'lovecrazed' and 'consumed by a terrible passion'. The prosecutor referred to it as a 'fatal attraction'.[5] Her defence counsel argued that his client was scarcely responsible, so infatuated was she. He said she was 'no cold Lady Macbeth-type figure' but had 'found herself being dragged along by what was happening' when her lover suggested they have her husband killed (*Guardian* 4 December 1992). It was obviously important both to avoid the operation of a calculating 'Lady Macbeth' image – a problem when you employ a hitman – and to draw on current mythologies about blind passion, by making reference to popular films. In the end, though, she was convicted of murder with the two men. The result, the shift in her position, is reflected in the *Guardian* which set out in a row recent photos (apparently mug-shots) of the three accused. Noeleen Hendley looks plain, unmade-up and bedraggled; juxtaposed is a blurry wedding photo where she 'presents' in an attractive and feminine way, in her 'other' life. The judge was particularly unimpressed by the deliberate nature of the killing, planned over some weeks. In the tabloids most of the space was again given to the woman. The polarized madonna/

whore image has taken over: in the *Sun* for instance she becomes the 'Evil tattoo temptress' who 'became hooked on sex' with her new lover and had her thigh tattooed to please him (4 December 1992).

Susan Christie was similarly labelled a *Fatal Attraction* killer. She was also an 'Army girl' or 'soldier girl'; some stories opened ambiguously with sentences about 'soldier killing lover's wife'; did we expect to hear of a girl or a boy? Every article mentioned that she 'slit her victim's throat', often 'with a boning knife' and 'from ear to ear'. A girl soldier who slits throats is a stunning image, an outrageous contradiction. She is too womanly, in having become mentally unbalanced owing to her passion for her victim's husband (according to the medical evidence accepted in support of her successful diminished responsibility plea). But she is a 'soldier', and kills like a skilled butcher. Which way will sympathy lie?

The *Sun* did not consider her attractive. It judged her to be plain and naïve, a 'virgin soldier', and asked why 'dashing' Captain McAllister would fall for her, when he has a 'stunning wife' (16 June 1992). This does make her argument about being totally besotted look more credible. The inference is that *she* must have had a lot invested in it; *he* obviously wouldn't have. It is a (type of) story we all apparently know:

> The story of Susan Christie, according to her defence counsel, is one 'as old as history – the inexperienced young girl falling for the dashing young officer'. (*Daily Telegraph* 16 June 1992)

A plea to manslaughter by diminished responsibility was rejected by the prosecutor but accepted by the jury, in contrast to the media story which emphasized her calculating jealousy and the lies she told after the killing.

The 'doing it for love' explanation might have been appropriate for Michelle Taylor but I do not recall seeing it pursued. Perhaps if sex, rather than 'love' is seen as the motivation, it overrides any possible romanticization of the woman's acts. It implies deliberate action rather than behaviour driven by passion. Only stigmatization is permitted.

This explanation was also potentially appropriate for Myra Hindley, who was involved with her (apparently dominating) lover in killing several young children in the early 1960s. Again it did not take hold as an explanation in the media, probably overwhelmed by the unwomanly factor of a woman killing children. When we look at the narrow range of images which have developed around Myra Hindley (essentially, monster/not-woman) it is clear why she has been unable to be considered for parole, many years after men in similar cases have been released.

One case in which at least two different explanations were clearly available was that of Mabel Hyams, aged seventy-nine, who battered her husband (also seventy-nine) to death with a bedpan. Every newspaper report mentioned the bedpan, and their ages.

> One-leg Wife, 79, Beats Sex Cheat Husband to Death with Bedpan.
> One-legged Mabel Hyams battered her husband to death with a plastic bedpan – because of three affairs he'd taunted her with for 50 years.
> Half a century of bitter resentment erupted as powerfully-built 79-year-old Mabel heaved herself from her wheelchair to attack Harold, also 79, in their bedroom. (*Daily Mirror* 27 February 1993)

The easy route was going to be trivialization, turning the participants into freaks. Not only had she used a 'comic' weapon; she killed him after he allegedly persisted in boasting of his sexual conquests – at his age! This is Punch and Judy material. According to the prosecutor, 'Various neighbours described her as domineering and argumentative. By contrast, her husband was described as calm and placid' (*The Times* 27 February 1993). She had reportedly been seen hitting him 'quite ferociously' with her handbag on an earlier day. She claimed however that he had abused her in the past, and that he had hurt her with his affairs. It became a 'tragic case' and she was given a suspended sentence.

There is a category of news story about female violence which fits less easily into this typology but may be noted here. It is not about major crime, but about the so-called 'cat fight' or 'love battle'. The tabloid press delights in stories of women brawling – elegantly, with long red fingernails, preferably. The women will be rivals, and may be celebrities: supermodels, soap-opera stars and others. The dispute will be trivial, a vehicle for indulgent amusement. The *Sun* did a double-page spread in the period I was reviewing on a reported fist fight between the lover and wife of boxing promoter Frank Warren. Tabloid headlines were: 'Two lovely black eyes for Susan' (*Daily Mirror* 30 March 1993); and 'War of Warren Women/ Boxing boss's wife and his ex-mistress in amazing fight at front door' (*Sun* 30 March 1993). The wife was described as a 'former Vogue model' and the lover a 'one-time flower girl' (*Daily Mirror* 31 March 1993).

The comparison with 'real' (masculine) violence, such as duels, renders it a diminutive form of violence. There is a clear subtext that this is deviant behaviour, but, like that of children, almost wholly unthreatening. It is the embodiment of women's alleged emotionality.

Reproduction and madness

This is a variant on the theme of women's mental frailty. The explanations focus on the influence on women's mental state of their biological functions. Such explanations can also permit the denial of responsibility in (some) cases of battered women who kill, and women who kill their children.

This may offer one of the few images which permit sympathetic treatment, in the press and in the courts. It does so by denying the offenders agency in their act, 'rendering them harmless' in Hilary Allen's phrase (Allen 1987). The battered wife who kills *may* receive the benefit, provided she bases her argument on diminished responsibility arising out of the long-drawn-out horrors she has suffered.

> The judge sentencing Sandra Fleming to 3 years' probation after killing her violent husband said, 'It was a terrible thing to do but the doctors say you were suffering from an abnormality of mind when you did it.' (*Guardian* 14 January 1993)

Defence counsel said,

> Her mental state at the time was acutely abnormal as a result of severe and terrifying threats. She has no tendency or record for violence. (*Guardian* 14 January 1993)

Sympathy will be more likely if she can show that she is generally a loving mother (and if possible, wife). This minimizes the contradictions in the representation of the event, explaining the violence as totally out of character. Helena Kennedy (1992) recently provided the following (only slightly ironic) advice:

> . . . whatever drives you to do the old man in, you must be as clean as a whistle yourself, with not a hint of impropriety . . . You have to keep a tidy house, scrub the children, and it helps if you are still proclaiming love whilst holding the bloodstained carving knife. (Kennedy 1992: 218)

Kiranjit Aluwahlia burned her violent husband to death in 1989. She was released from custody in September 1992 after her murder conviction was replaced with a conviction for manslaughter on the grounds of diminished responsibility. The Court of Appeal refused to consider arguments about provocation but seemed as satisfied as the newspapers were with excusing her behaviour as an aberration caused by her awful life. The *Guardian*'s coverage of her successful appeal provided a very striking image. On page 1 the decision was headlined 'Battered wife who killed wins freedom'. Placed centrally was a domestic-style photograph of Kiranjit Aluwalia greeting her husband's uncle after her release, with bowed head and submissive pose, receiving the confirmation of the family.

Battered Woman Syndrome, a behavioural pattern which is claimed to be found in battered women who ultimately kill their abuser, has been proposed as a medical 'way in' to defences otherwise unavailable to women in such cases. It may explain, for instance, why the woman acted after the passing of time, to bring her within self-defence, and therefore to make a full acquittal possible.[6] It has not, as far as I am aware, yet been accepted in an English court, though Australian courts have permitted evidence of BWS to be given (Sheehy *et al.* 1992; O'Donovan 1993). Whilst it constructs an explanation which can be beneficial to some women offenders, by bringing them within formal defences leading to lenient sentencing or acquittal, BWS obviously works within the stereotype of women as 'crazy or helpless or both' (Schneider 1989: 85; Dobash and Dobash 1992).

An image based on women's incipient mental instability does provide the most sympathetic explanation of Beverley Allitt's murders of children in a hospital ward. It is claimed that she suffers from Munchausen by Proxy Syndrome (an almost entirely female disorder), a claim which was made public only after the trial, and therefore had no impact on its result. It may be queried whether this diagnosis is correct. But it does allow her intentionality to be challenged – she couldn't help herself. MBPS also brings with it important images of femininity and mothering. It represents a perversion of the 'good mother', who conscientiously cares for her children, whilst herself inducing their illness in the first place, perhaps (it is argued) to gain approval for her good care, and/or to maintain a position in the powerful and privileged medical world (Schreier and Libow 1993). The MBPS explanation seems to have been covered in most detail in the broadsheets, the tabloids contenting themselves with less complex analyses around the notion of evil. Interestingly however, those papers which did cover it also hinted at the sinister possibility that a lot more children's deaths should be attributed to their mothers than previously believed (for example, the *Guardian* 19 May 1993).

Susan Christie was convicted of manslaughter by diminished responsibility, following evidence of her 'exceptional mental stress' at the time of the killing: emotional stress over her relationship, *and* premenstrual tension. Was this special consideration for a woman who is able to raise a biological-type defence? Angela Neustatter in the *Guardian* thought it totally unwarranted

> The reason Susan Christie was not convicted of murder, we gather, is that she suffered 'overwhelming emotion', had just completed a 24-hour shift and was suffering from premenstrual tension. So did she deserve special pleading on this account? Are these good enough reasons to say that selecting a particularly vicious weapon, feigning friendship to get the victim to a quiet spot and then killing her was not murder but manslaughter? I would say absolutely not. Her actions sound to me like those of a woman of chilling lucidity, whose mind was sound enough for her to carry through an act that would be unthinkable to most of us. (17 June 1992)

The figure of evil – the witch – the monster

The idea of the offender as evil, or a monster, or a witch, seems to be an umbrella 'explanation' for badness which is felt to be otherwise inexplicable. It is found with other attempts at explanation, such as the 'not-woman' but also the 'true woman', Eve, the deceiver, discussed below.

Beverley Allitt is one woman who was castigated in the tabloids in this way: 'Murdered by the Angel of Death' (*Today* 14 May 1993), 'Evil behind her smiles' (*Sun* 14 May 1993). The *Guardian* coverage was also criticized by a reader, for portraying Allitt as a monster. 'Angel of Death' has multiple resonances; woman as the Angel in the Home, as life-giving, but also the biblical Angel of Death. Myra Hindley is another whose awful crimes against children seem to have taken her outside the scope of other, more sympathetic, explanatory devices. Allitt is in fact compared to Hindley. The *Daily Mirror* concluded that 'Britain's first woman serial killer' was 'Deadlier than Myra Hindley'. She is worse, according to the *Mirror*, because she had no man helping her, and her victims had been specifically entrusted to her.

Maria Rossi is another recent example of this process. With

another young woman she killed an elderly woman neighbour, using extreme violence, while drunk and on drugs.

> Just 17, they murdered an old lady for kicks/ Devil Girls/ Drink & drugs pals' sickening orgy of violence . . . (*Daily Mirror* 9 March 1993)

Rossi's mother was, however, blamed for allowing her daughter to behave in this way; she was too disorganized to be able to provide the proper control. The *Sun* trumpeted:

> Evil teenager Maria Rossi sang 'We killed Edna' to the tune of 'The Wizard of Oz' after murdering a half-blind elderly spinster.[7]
>
> Rossi, 17, chanted at the breakfast table – as her mother recovered from a booze session and victim Edna Phillips, 70, lay mutilated in her house next door. (*Sun* 9 March 1993)

Two days later it reported:

> Killer's Mum in Booze Den Fury.
>
> The mum of teenage killer Maria Rossi is *still* holding booze parties for youngsters at her home. (*Sun* 11 March 1993)

In an apparent attempt to bring his client back into the realm of understandable female stories, Rossi's defence counsel endorsed the culpability of the mother and focused on Rossi's sad life history:

> . . . his client had shown remorse and suffered nightmares. She had abused drugs and alcohol since 14 and had miscarried twice. Her mother had had little control over her daughter since the break-up of her marriage when Miss Rossi was 10. (*Guardian* 9 March 1993: 20)

The criminal woman as 'not-woman'

The tabloid coverage of Beverley Allitt combined the broad-brush 'monster' image with one which emphasized her 'masculinity'. She was big, she was butch, she beat up her boyfriend, who became (according to the *Daily Mirror*, 18 May 1993) 'a sex-starved target of her ugly violence'. And for good measure, she is a lesbian.

The syllogism is, real women do not commit crimes, so a woman who does commit a crime is not truly a woman. Lady Macbeth certainly perceived the dissonance between being female and plotting the murder of a king, crying,

> Unsex me here;
> And fill me, from the crown to the toe, top full
> Of direst cruelty!   (*Macbeth*, Act I, sc. v, 38–40)

Authorized explainers fasten on to the woman offender's failure to conform to heterosexual expectations, her defective mothering, her ugliness or unfemininity, even her assertiveness, to confirm that she was masquerading all along. The corollary is that we do not need to feel sympathy for her. She can be dealt with as a male criminal, but with the additional stigma of being a failed woman too.

A striking recent example of this has been the frequent publication of 'before' and 'after' photographs of Beverley Allitt. She is apparently anorexic, and all the papers carried references to her huge loss of weight. The interest in this is consistent with the general focus on feminine appearance in news reporting (and elsewhere). Normally women are praised for losing weight. In this case, however, it seems to be used to suggest that she is chameleon-like, or fraudulent, or sick (e.g. *Daily Mirror* 18 March 1993). It also suggests that the apparently plump and jolly ('buxom') female is now stripped back to reveal her thin – boyish – self. The *Guardian* referred to her as 'gaunt', allowing the more sympathetic possibility that she is gnawed by remose (16 February 1993). She is also referred to, in her new form, as 'tiny' – and so perhaps less threatening.

Deviant women have been portrayed as non-maternal, as the 'anti-mother' (Blum and Fisher 1980). This is an obvious theme in the treatment of Myra Hindley, who after all killed children. Beverley Allitt's crimes against children bring her special opprobrium too. Further, she explicitly betrayed her role as a nurse; this was probably the most shocking aspect of her crimes. Her name was rarely mentioned in the headlines; the word 'nurse' was sufficient (for instance, 'Killer nurse' in the *Guardian* 20 May 1993).[8] Her acts were a rejection of her caring role. But the coverage also reflects anxieties of the sort discussed under the next heading, of the woman as most dangerous when she puts on the soothing appearance of femininity, whilst consciously betraying that image.

Explicit reference is sometimes made to a female standard, of which the offender has generally fallen short. The *Guardian*, for instance, reported of Beverley Allitt (20 February 1993), 'Nurse showed no emotion when told of collapses, court told'.[9] Tears can allay suspicion. But if the weeping widow is ultimately shown to have been the killer, her tears will be held even more powerfully against her. No one likes having been conned, or having their emotions manipulated, but when it has been done by a woman, manipulating our chivalric impulses, it is especially evil. Jean Daddow wept, when her husband was killed on his own doorstep. (Every paper mentioned the location; it was clearly an aggravating factor!) But these were crocodile tears. In reality she was the most Lady Macbeth-like of cold and calculating killers, and had hired the killer for herself. For the *Sun*, she was not a woman – she was not even human:

> Black Widow Married to Kill Hubby for Cash / Gunned down in £300,000 plot. (*Sun* 9 April 1993)

The female as devious and manipulative

This version of the story, on the face of it, runs counter to the previous one. It proposes that women are *inherently* likely to commit crime. And they are peculiarly adept at hiding their crimes. This is the 'true woman', Eve. It is the *femme fatale*, the poisoning wife, the infanticide hiding both fact of pregnancy and the baby's body. It is also the scheming woman masking her evil under the appearance of goodness. Indeed, women may be regarded as playing on the chivalric foolishness of men, who would never suspect a woman, simply by reason of her sex.

This has been a popular source of images of women, both frightening and glamorous. The *films noirs* of the 1940s and 1950s drew on the manipulative and sexually powerful woman, and the hero's attempts to extricate himself from her lures. He may be destroyed in the process, but the direction of the film is usually towards the restoration of patriarchal order by the exposure and destruction of the woman.[10] This has also been a theme in recent films about women, such as *Fatal Attraction*.

Beverley Allitt betrayed the trust of those who thought she was a caring nurse. Particularly painful was the betrayal of a family who made her the godmother of one of the children she injured:

> The Godmother. Killer nurse won mum's trust. (*Daily Mirror* 17 February 1993)

'Godmother' has a number of interesting connotations here. She was literally the child's godmother, a social/religious nomination under which she would be expected to take an interest in the child during its life. But there is also the sense of fairy godmother, and other 'good angels' and, in opposition, the 'Godfather/mother' associated with Mafia activities.[11]

A police officer considered Jean Daddow 'one of the most evil women he had ever known' (*Sun* 9 April 1993). She 'lured' or 'stole' her husband Terry from his first wife (though she was also 'dumpy' and 'mousey' and a 'former hairdresser': *Daily Mirror* 9 April 1993); she had had 'a string of lovers' before she married 'her besotted victim'. She was a temptress *and* a betrayer. Looking like an ordinary woman she was in fact a *sexual* woman. Neighbours saw them as a 'demure suburban couple' but it was not so: they 'had a torrid sex life, keeping a video at the end of their bed to film themselves having sex orgies'. When her husband was shot dead, 'cold-blooded Jean' cried for the cameras and had a loving memorial engraved for him. But detectives 'dug deeper' and 'uncovered a chilling saga of sex, greed and violence'.[12] Although Daddow 'continued to play the heartbroken widow' it was no use; in court 'the mask had been stripped away'.

Discussion

These themes, or explanations, are not mutually exclusive. They compete literally in court, where a 'weak' or 'victimized' image may be presented by the defence to combat a devious or cold-blooded prosecution image. They can also be seen operating in the press coverage itself – though still only chosen from a narrow range of alternatives. Complex explanations are not allowed.

In the Taylor case, the tabloids took a simple line, the evil manipulative woman, based around sexuality. 'The sisters' (Michelle was charged with her sister Lisa) even came to suggest a witches' coven. The quality papers, especially *The Times*, allowed more play with the uncertainties. Reviewing the trial and conviction of Michelle and Lisa Taylor, *The Times* mused:

> Besotted mistress driven by jealousy to kill her lover's wife – or guiltless girl whose heart was broken by her first infatuation? . . . Could the baby-faced Michelle, who gave chocolate teddy bears to her lover John Shaughnessy and said in the witness box she wanted 'just to be cuddled', have become the monster who rained more than 50 knife blows at her rival. (25 July 1992: 3)

The images almost always seem to turn on characteristics of the offender as a woman. Her sexuality, or her femininity are crucial. Women can be censured for being feminine or for *not* being feminine. However, they are more likely to receive sympathetic treatment if they conform to a weak or sick model of femininity, and deny responsibility for their actions by reason of 'love-madness' or biological circumstances.

Ascribing intentionality to a violent woman offender is much more fraught. Legally, of course, if intention can be found the offence will be regarded as more serious and the offender treated more harshly. This is so for male as well as female offenders. But the images which arise where it is concluded that a woman acted intentionally are powerfully stigmatizing – the monster, the non-woman, the betrayer. Stories about violent women are extremely attractive to producers of newspapers. In the tabloids at least, some criminal women can take on something like celebrity status, and have their lives presented in much the same way as those of soap stars and royalty.[13] Only some women though: as Duncan Campbell noted (*Guardian* 4 August 1992) when a violent crime has been committed 'an attractive young white woman remains the likeliest person to attract media coverage'.

Crime news *is* news, as Hall said, because 'its treatment evokes threats to, but also reaffirms, the consensual morality of the society' (1978: 66). Media reports therefore select the most shocking and deviant aspects of the offender and her behaviour. Gender is treated as central when a woman is violent. Deviance from (or at times conformity to) gender roles for women is itself seen as causing the violence, and provides the base from which the story is presented.

Katz (1987) claims that people read crime reports to help them deal with their own life dilemmas. I would argue that reporting women's crime is about not only the morality of personal relations, as perhaps most interpersonal crime is, but is also about negotiating the particular place of women in this society, at this time. We have to look much more closely at what is being said, how it is said, and who is saying it.

Notes

[1]   On the construction of 'relevance' as evidentiary criterion see for example Temkin (1993: 5).
[2]   National newspaper circulation figures as reported in the *Guardian*, 12 July 1993.
[3]   Based on the writer's current research.

4 See for example Temkin (1993); *R* v. *Seaboyer*; *R* v. *Gayme* (1992) 7 CR (4th) 117, in particular the dissenting judgement of L'Heureux-Dube, J.

5 Newspaper crime stories often make reference to popular culture – films or books – to imply a common understanding of the problem (and incidentally to obviate the need for any real analysis of the particular case). The films *Fatal Attraction, Basic Instinct, The Hand that Rocks the Cradle*, and *Home Alone,* for example, are often cited in press reports of crime. A *Fatal Attraction* reference seems to connote any sort of 'triangular' crime of passion.

6 See for example Dobash and Dobash 1992; Gillespie 1989.

7 Many reports referred to Rossi having sung about the killing, a sinister variant on 'proper' women's behaviour (my note).

8 Susan Christie was also widely referred to as 'soldier'. Soldier is perhaps a female contradiction whilst nurse is almost synonymous with femininity (*male* nurses usually have their sex specifically identified). Occupational attribution contributes to the evaluation. For instance, Jean Bradley, a murder victim, was a 'career woman'. She was thus not a wife or mother, and might even be blameworthy for having made this choice. 'Career Woman Murdered' carries a message to us all.

9 I am not ignoring the fact that much newspaper reporting picks up on the way the case is presented in court.

10 See Kaplan 1980.

11 Only a week or so earlier the papers had reported the arrest of an Italian mafia 'Godmother', 'Ruthless Rosetta Cutolo, who has the blood of more than 100 dead gangsters on her hands' (*Daily Mirror* 9 February 1993).

12 It was mentioned, only in passing, that Daddow's husband apparently battered her, and that some of his wealth seemed to come from blackmailing elderly female banking clients. These points were not developed in the reports. The chilling saga was Jean's alone.

13 They may represent a (per)version of the rags-to-riches story which much of the conservative press, at least, likes to offer its readers. A *Guardian* article about Beverley Allitt began 'Bev Allitt was nobody special' (22 May 1993).

References

Allen, Hilary (1987). 'Rendering them harmless: the professional portrayal of women charged with serious violent crimes' in Pat Carlen and Anne Worrall (eds.) *Gender, Crime and Justice* (Milton Keynes, Open University Press).

Birch, Helen (ed.) (1993). *Moving Targets: Women, Murder and Representation* (London, Virago Press).

Blum, Alan and Fisher, Gary (1980). 'Women who kill' in Delos H. Kelly (ed.), *Criminal Behaviour: Readings in Criminology* (New York, St Martin's Press).

Chibnall, Steve (1977). *Law-and-Order News: An Analysis of Crime*

Reporting in the British Press (London, Tavistock).

Dobash, R. Emerson and Dobash, Russell P. (1992). *Women, Violence and Social Change* (London, Routledge).

Gillespie, Cynthia K. (1989). *Justifiable Homicide: Battered Women, Self-Defense, and the Law* (Columbus, Ohio State University Press).

Glasgow University Media Group (1976). *Bad News* (London, Routledge & Kegan Paul).

Hall, Stuart *et al.* (1978). *Policing the Crisis* (London, Macmillan).

Hill, Dave (1993). 'When she was bad she was . . . well what exactly?', *Sunday Times* 21/3/93.

Kaplan, Ann E. (1980). *Women in Film Noir.*

Katz, Jack (1987). 'What makes crime "news"?' *Media, Culture and Society* 9, 47.

Kennedy, Helena (1992). *Eve was Framed: Women and British Justice* (London, Chatto & Windus).

McConville, Mike, Andrew Sanders and Roger Leng (1991). *The Case for the Prosecution: Police Suspects and the Construction of Criminality* (London, Routledge).

Millman, Marcia (1978) '"She did it all for love": a feminist view of the sociology of deviance' in Marcia Millman and R. Moss Kanter (eds.) (1978) *In Another Voice* (New York, Anchor).

O'Donovan, Katherine (1993). 'Law's knowledge: The Judge, The Expert, The Battered Woman, And Her Syndrome', *Journal of Law and Society*, 20, 427.

Schneider, Elizabeth M. (1989). 'Describing and changing: women's self-defense work and the problem of expert testimony on battering', in Sara Lee Johann and Frank Osanka (eds.), *Representing . . . Battered Women Who Kill* (Illinois, Charles C. Thomas Publisher).

Schreier, H. and J. Libow (1993). *Hurting for Love: Munchausen By Proxy Syndrome*

Sheehy, E., Julie Stubbs and Julia Tolmie (1992). 'Defending Battered Women on Trial', *Crim. LJ*, 16, 369.

Temkin, Jennifer (1993). 'Sexual History Evidence – the Ravishment of Section 2', *Crim. LR3*.

Williams, Paul and Julie Dickinson (1993). 'Fear of Crime: Read All About It? The Relationship between Newspaper Crime Reporting and Fear of Crime', *Brit.J.Crim.*, 33, 33.

Young, Alison (1990). *Femininity in Dissent* (London, Routledge).

5

Sex crime news from abroad

KEITH SOOTHILL

The media reporting of sex crime cases began to attract interest in the early to middle 1970s in Britain when the controversy about the crime of rape began to build up. Some of the concerns of the women's movement gained a public stage following some spectacular rape cases and judgements reported in the press. The Home Secretary appointed an advisory group chaired by Justice Rose Heilbron to consider the law of rape in June 1975. A systematic study (Soothill and Jack 1975) to investigate how much the newspaper reporting of rape had changed since the Second World War directly influenced the advisory group's recommendations to place some restrictions on the reporting of rape in the media. The recommendations that the media should be banned from publishing the name of the raped woman and that the courts should be prohibited from enquiring into her previous sexual history except at the discretion of the judge were embodied in the Sexual Offences (Amendment) Act 1976.

The belief was that these restrictions might encourage the newspapers to lessen their interest in reporting rape in a manner which could well deter rape victims from reporting the offence to the police. A study found that sadly the 1976 Act had *not* had the expected impact (Hay, Soothill and Walby 1980). In fact, media interest had substantially increased, not declined. We argued that the circulation battle of the tabloids which developed in the late 1970s used the reporting of sex crime, and particularly rape, as part of a soft-porn package to sell newspapers. It was not chance that many lurid rape reports were set adjacent to the page 3 topless pin-up in the *Sun*.[1]

Sex crime coverage in British newspapers in 1985 and 1992: a comparative study

A project was launched to monitor the reporting of sex crime in the mid-1980s. The study was more ambitious than previous work in three ways – firstly, a much wider sample of newspapers was examined; secondly, all types of sex crime were considered; and thirdly, all stages of the criminal justice process were included. Soothill and Walby (1991) report both continuity and change in media reporting of sex crime. The popular daily papers had further increased their coverage of rape cases, particularly focusing on some quite spectacular cases. A dramatic shift was the sudden decline of the *News of the World*'s interest in reporting court cases involving rape. Unable to compete with the *daily* coverage of the popular dailies, the Sunday newspapers had shifted to providing 'exclusives' lined up at the conclusion of spectacular trials which had excited national interest. Incorporating some valuable data from a Home Office study (Lloyd and Walmsley 1989), Soothill (1991) was able to show how the court and media profiles were diverging and there was an increasing focus on very particular kinds of sex crime in the media.

Recently the question of media reporting has become important not only in sex cases (such as the notorious date rape cases) but also the relevance of media reporting has been identified in the dismissal of the cases of the policemen in the Birmingham Six fiasco as well as in the case of the Taylor sisters where the judges felt that the media focus prevented defendants from getting a fair trial. Certainly media coverage itself has come back into the news! However, the focus on media representations of crime and violence *against women* needs to be maintained.

While the reporting of sex crime continues to attract interest (e.g. Benedict 1992), a major shift in sex crime reporting seems to have been overlooked. In fact, the reporting of sex cases from abroad has been a major development in the 1990s.

Marshall McLuhan's (1962, 1964) vision of the world as a global village through the development of the media and communications network has largely come about and so one should not be surprised with the inclusion of more newspaper reports on sex crime coming from all parts of the world. More importantly, such cases provide the scope for highlighting the very essence which interests newspapers in the area of sex crime reporting. There may not be the same constraints on the selection and delivery of news from abroad, and so for example, despite the ban imposed in Britain by the Sexual Offences (Amendment) Act 1976 on revealing the names of rape victims, Benedict notes that in the case of the alleged rape of a woman in 1991 by William Kennedy Smith, Senator Edward Kennedy's nephew, on the Kennedy estate in Palm Beach, Florida, 'initially, the woman had been named only by *The Sunday Mirror*, an English paper, and Florida's *The Globe*, both sensationalist, supermarket tabloids' (Benedict 1992: 252).[2]

What attracts newspapers to foreign news? Some popular newspapers in Britain can be so cursory in their coverage of foreign news that governments may be overthrown, earthquakes may occur and communities may starve, and few of their readers will be aware of such events. Hence, it is fascinating to ask why certain sex crimes happening abroad feature in British newspapers. What are the types of messages which are being put across with the use of this material from abroad? What are the patterns in the kinds of cases which are actually selected and appear in British newspapers? Are there changes taking place in the coverage of this kind of material? In brief, are the stories potent symbols of what is of widespread concern throughout the world or is the choice of cases from abroad simply guided by the more prurient interests of newspapers?

The method of the study

The dearth of previous studies perhaps brings special responsibilities of rigour. In the two sample years I have taken, 1985 and 1992, the same set of nine British newspapers was considered. The series consisted of two 'quality' national dailies (*The Times* and the *Guardian*), two 'popular' national dailies (*Daily Mirror* and the *Sun*), three 'popular' Sundays (*Sunday Mirror, Sunday People* and the *News of the World*), one 'quality' Sunday (*Observer*) and one evening newspaper (the London) *Evening Standard*.[3] The systematic search of well over 3,000 newspapers in the two years provides scope for measuring both the nature and extent of the use of such material as well as any shifts which seem to be taking place.

In the sample newspapers, all items originating from abroad where there was activity which indicated the commission of a sexual offence were included in the basic data set. Here, however, the focus is on all the material from outside the United Kingdom which related to sex murder (including attempted sex murder) and rape (including reports identifying 'attempted rape'). Cases of 'statutory rape', which is, in British terms, unlawful sexual intercourse with a girl under 16 where consent is not a legal issue, were excluded. In brief, the focus is on coercive sex. Further, the focus is entirely on those occasions where a specific case is mentioned (even if the case occurred some time ago), and so general discussions about rape and sex murder (such as reviewing the amount of such crime) have been excluded from this analysis.[4]

The amount of material from abroad involving sex crime

Questions can be clearly posed. For example, is such material from abroad a source used liberally by British newspapers? From which countries is the material drawn? Do particular newspapers make greater use of this overseas material than others? Is the situation changing? Is there an increasing use of such material? In short, what is the current situation?

While the focus is entirely on sex murder and rape, Table 1 still provides powerful evidence to suggest that sex crime news from abroad is quite extensively used and that, furthermore, there is an increase in the use of such material. The number of items mentioning a 'sex murder' case have more than doubled (51 in 1985 to 113 in 1992), while those focusing on 'rape' have increased almost sixfold (with an increase from 74 items in 1985 to 422 items in 1992).

However, this dramatic rise in rape reports is almost entirely explained by the remarkable interest in the rape trial of the former world-champion boxer, Mike Tyson. In fact, in this sample of British newspapers there was a total of 213 items which mentioned this trial or its aftermath. Curiously, if this trial had not been reported (and no other American case had taken its place) the number of items on rape cases from the United States would have been exactly the same as in 1985. While the proportion of rape items emanating from the Untied States for the two years has actually remained constant at 61 per cent, the Tyson trial must certainly be seen as quite freakish in the amount of coverage and one suspects that, as with 'sex murder', the United States does not have quite the same dominance in terms of the *amount* of coverage in the 1990s, as reports from other countries become more frequent.

Probably a more appropriate measure of change than the raw number of items appearing from abroad is a count of the *different*

Table 1: Sex crimes from abroad reported in British newspapers in 1985 and 1992

		Total no. of items	No. of items from USA	No. of different news stories	No. of stories from USA	No. of countries with reports
Sex murder	1985	51	35	19	8	11
	1992	113	51	31	19	9
Rape/ Attempted Rape	1985	74	45	40	18	14
	1992	422	258	61	20	26
Total	1985	125	80	59	26	22
	1992	535	309	92	39	28

Notes:

1. The newspapers searched in both years were *The Times, Guardian, Daily Mirror, Sun*, (London) *Evening Standard, Observer, News of the World, People* and *Sunday Mirror*.

2. If an item refers to a 'sex murder' *and* a 'rape', the 'sex murder' category takes priority. Hence, as there is no double-counting, it is legitimate to add the figures except for the last column indicating the number of countries with reports, where the totals indicate the number of countries involved in each of the years.

3. An 'item' refers to an entry about a case in one newspaper on a particular day. So, if a case is headlined on the front page and has a four-page report within the newspaper, this counts as one item just as does a one-inch 'filler item'.

news stories in the two years. With this approach, however, there is the opposite problem from using the total number of items, where one extraordinary and quite exceptional case can distort, for by this second measure the total coverage of the Tyson trial counts the same – namely, as one news story[5] – as a one-inch 'filler' item from abroad which appears in only one newspaper. In other words, this measure fails to identify the differential impact of various cases. Nevertheless, it clarifies more appropriately the *number* of sex crime cases from abroad which are actually covered.

By this measure 'sex murder' news stories have increased more rapidly between 1985 and 1992 (from 19 to 31 cases – an increase of 63 per cent) than news stories featuring rape cases (from 40 to 61 cases – an increase of 52 per cent). However, it is the question of the dominance of stories from the United States which is of particular interest, for 'sex murder' and 'rape' cases tell a different story.

While news stories of sex murder cases coming from the United

States have more than doubled (an increase from 8 in 1985 to 19 in 1992), the numbers from all other countries have risen only from 11 in 1985 to 12 in 1992. Interestingly, this contrasts strongly with the fact that the overall proportion of *items* on sex murder emanating from the United States has fallen from 69 per cent in 1985 to 45 per cent in 1992. This apparent paradox is resolved when one simply appreciates that news stories of sex murder from places other than the United States are getting much more extensive coverage recently although the *number* of such cases has not significantly increased. However, it is equally important to note that the United States is now the major source of overseas sex murder cases, for the majority of these cases (61 per cent) come from this source.

For rape, the pattern is almost the reverse. Between 1985 and 1992, there was only a marginal rise in news stories of *different* rape cases from the United States – from 18 to 20 – while the number of rape cases from other places abroad almost doubled in this period from 22 to 41 cases. The particular feature which needs to be stressed is that by 1992 only one-third of the rape cases from abroad had the United States as their original source.

The differences and shifts in the reporting from overseas sources of sex murder and rape cases in British newspapers are instructive. It is argued that the United States remains the major source of *new* interests and is the source of definitions of what is problematic in the world. So when a focus on rape was a major expanding interest in the media in the 1980s, of cases coming from abroad those from the United States clearly dominated. By the 1990s, however, as the concern about rape gathered momentum throughout the world, then rape cases from many other countries began to be included in the coverage of British newspapers and, although the exceptional Tyson rape trial has masked the effect, the total *number* of rape cases from the United States has generally become less dominating. In contrast, the *number* of sex murder cases coming from the United States has increased significantly in the 1990s, while there has actually been a slight decline of sex murder cases reported from other countries. However, if the pattern of rape is repeated, then one would expect more sex murder cases from other countries by the end of the century if the definitions of what is problematic in the world continue to be set by material emerging from the United States. In brief, a powerful message from Table 1 seems to be that concern about rape is being maintained by editors of British newspapers choosing to include material from more countries, while the increasing focus on sex murder in British newspapers is being fuelled by cases coming from the United States.

Different countries?

There were reports of *either* sex murder *or* rape cases from 22 countries in 1985 and 28 countries in 1992. However, these figures mask an important difference as Table 1 shows – reports of sex murders came from 11 countries in 1985 and only nine countries in 1992 (interestingly the countries involved in the two years were almost completely different), while rape cases increased dramatically (from 14 countries in 1985 to 26 countries in 1992). In brief, this further illustrates how by 1992 interest in rape had become a world-wide phenomenon and was being used as media fodder for British newspapers.

While the scale of the increase in the number of items from the United States – owing to the special circumstances of the Tyson trial – is perhaps more tenuous than expected, the importance of the use of material from across the Atlantic, however, cannot be denied. Perhaps the most telling measure is the source of the *different* news stories on sex murder or rape cases coming from abroad, for this measure just regards the Tyson trial as *one* news story. Forty-three per cent (or 65 out of 151) different news stories emanated from the United States with no other country routinely providing this amount of material for British newspapers. There is no location which begins to approach this domination and France (5.3 per cent) only emerges marginally as the next most important source, followed closely by South Africa (4.6 per cent) and Italy and Spain (each 4.0 per cent). Hence, while sex crime from places other than the United States is being reported in British newspapers, it is the *wide dispersion* of countries rather than an increasing amount from any particular country which is the remarkable feature.

Different newspapers?

The question examined here is which British newspapers use this potential source of information and/or titillation. Table 2 shows some quite dramatic shifts which are taking place. The crucial distinction in the table is between the number of *different* news stories (where, of course, the coverage of the Tyson trial or its equivalent counts the same as a one-inch 'filler' item from abroad) and the *total* number of items on either sex murder or rape cases from abroad. In fact, while

Table 2: Coverage of sex murder and rape cases from abroad in nine British newspapers

	Murder Cases				Rape Cases			
	Total No. of items		No. of different cases		Total No. of Items		No. of different cases	
	1985	1992	1985	1992	1985	1992	1985	1992
POPULAR DAILIES								
Daily Mirror	7	24	6	10	8	75	7	16
Sun	11	28	8	20	18	89	15	34
QUALITY DAILIES								
Guardian	8	20	4	11	17	73	11	10
The Times	17	23	8	9	18	78	13	13
LONDON EVENING								
Evening Standard	6	10	2	8	13	53	11	13
POPULAR SUNDAYS								
News of the World	2	4	2	4	-	19	-	8
The People	-	1	-	1	-	13	-	3
Sunday Mirror	-	2	-	2	-	11	-	3
QUALITY SUNDAY								
Observer	-	1	-	1	-	11	-	3

these are two significantly different kinds of measures, the outcomes are very similar.

Among the tabloids there has been a considerable increase in the focus of reports of sex crime from abroad. For sex murder the number of cases covered by the two popular dailies (*Sun* and *Daily Mirror*) has doubled while the coverage (i.e. the number of items) has trebled. For rape the increase has been even more dramatic although the vast increase in the number of items in 1992 has been distorted by the widespread interest in the Tyson case.

Almost as significant has been the shift among the national Sunday newspapers. Sex crimes committed abroad escaped almost unnoticed in 1985. However, all the Sundays were involved to some extent in reporting sex murder or rape cases from abroad in 1992. The increase is particularly noticeable among the tabloid Sundays.[6]

The quality dailies (*The Times* and *Guardian*) produced a rather different pattern. While the coverage of sex murder in *The Times* remained almost identical in the two years, the coverage on this crime in the *Guardian* increased so that by 1992 the two 'quality' national dailies were very similar. With regard to rape cases from abroad, these two newspapers had similar profiles covering a similar number of cases in both years. The massive increase in the number of items in 1992 in both these papers largely reflected the widespread interest generated in the Tyson case.

What kind of material attracts the most attention?

Most attention in analysing sex cases usually falls on the *major* news stories rather than the rest of the material which contributes to the newspaper coverage of sex crime. Indeed, Benedict (1992) in her recent book on how the press covers sex crime in the United States focuses exclusively on four cases – 'The 1978–1979 Greta and John Rideout Marital Rape Case', 'The 1983–1984 New Bedford "Big Dan's" Gang Rape', 'The 1986 Killing of Jennifer Levin' and 'The 1989–1990 Central Park Jogger Case'. Similarly, Soothill and Walby (1991) show how a limited number of sex crime cases get quite enormous publicity.[7]

Taking the two years, 1985 and 1992, the aim here is to consider the press coverage of the *major* sex crimes in British newspapers culled from abroad. This is against a backcloth of emphasizing that 'the norm is for a solitary item from abroad to appear in just one newspaper'[8] but, of course, the cases with the more extensive coverage make the greater impact.

The criteria for inclusion as a major sex case were rigorous but not very demanding.[9] All sex murder or rape cases from abroad which either attracted coverage in more than three newspapers or gained more than three items overall were included. This latter category enabled appropriate news stories where there was a more extended focus in just one or two newspapers to be included. In the event there were no major cases identified in this way, so indicating that if cases were attracting any sustained attention from abroad they were most unlikely to be confined to particular newspapers.

Table 3 shows that in each year there were very few cases indeed which achieved the criteria for inclusion, but there are shifts over time which merit comment. In brief, there is an increase in the number of 'sex murder' cases from abroad which gain more extensive coverage – from three in 1985 to six in 1992. More interestingly, however, the increase comes not from the United States – from which there were two cases in each year – but from reports of cases from a wider range of countries (namely, Kenya, Russia, South Africa and Israel in 1992).

Table 3: Sex crime cases from abroad attracting the most coverage in 1985 and 1992

Type of case	Country	No. of items	No. of news-papers	Cumu-lative total
SEX MURDER CASES				
1985				
Two ex-marines accused of sex killings of around 40 victims.	USA	15	4	29
The 'Night Stalker' accused of 16 murders and 20 rapes.	USA	12	4	53
Two British teenagers killed after a brutal sex attack.	Hong Kong	5	3	63
1992				
Cannibal serial sex killer, 31, confesses to killing 15 young men.	USA	22	7	19
Kenyan game wardens accused of killing British woman, 27, after six-day sex ordeal.	Kenya	16	5	34
A Ukrainian man, 56, accused of 53 serial killings – mostly children and women.	Russia	16	5	48
Two British women, both 30, raped and murdered on beach.	South Africa	13	6	59
Man, 33, executed for rape and murder of his sister-in-law in 1981.	USA	7	6	65
British woman, 20, sexually assaulted and murdered at an Israeli desert settlement.	Israel	5	4	70
RAPE CASES				
1985				
Confession by woman of false evidence that jailed a man for 25 years.	USA	15	4	20
Woman, 26, clamed that she had been abducted as sex slave for seven years and raped.	USA	8	5	31
American football player turned actor, 49, accused of raping woman, 33.	USA	5	3	38
1992				
Former world boxing champion accused of raping woman, 18.	USA	213	9	50
Girl, 14, made pregnant by rapist, banned by law from having an abortion.	Ireland	107	9	76
Aftermath of 1991 trial of nephew of former Presidential candidate and member of Kennedy family	USA	19	7	80

In contrast, rape cases seem to exhibit a different pattern. There were only three cases which qualified in each year. While the monopoly of such cases coming from the United States was broken by a widely reported case originating in the Republic of Ireland, the main interest is in the hugely increased number of items which each of these cases attracted in 1992.

In summary, therefore, there are more 'sex murder' cases from abroad gaining widespread coverage in 1992, while the comparatively few rape cases with widespread coverage in 1992 became very dominant stories indeed with many more items per case than in 1985.

There are many ways of analysing the material on sex crime cases where there has been extensive coverage. Benedict (1992: vi), for example, focused on the press as 'a prominent part of the cycle of injustice that traps victims' arguing that journalists 'tended to perpetuate rather than debunk the myths and misunderstandings that so hurt victims'. Benedict (1992: 42) noted that 'in general, during the 1970s, the focus of the press shifted from the suspects to the victim' and, in turn, by choosing four cases for in-depth analysis where the victim was particularly in focus, she may indeed be helping to develop a new myth that these kinds of sex crime cases are now the current reality in press reporting. Certainly, for example, the lack of a serial sex killer among her cases for analysis and interpretation is fascinating. However, without the more systematic approach of the present study, it is difficult to know whether the omission of such a case was Benedict's choice or that there was quite simply no widespread coverage of such a case in the various years of her interest. Certainly the cases which gain the attention of Benedict are those where women suffer badly at the hands of the press, particularly in the perpetuation of the virgin/vamp dichotomy.

In contrast to Benedict's focus on the victim, Caputi (1987), in a powerful and at times compelling analysis of the apparent rise of serial sex murders, characterizes these crimes as a form of twentieth-century terrorism. In fact, for Caputi it is the sensationalized killers and their atrocities relating to women which she regards as the archetypal actors and acts in what she characterizes as the Age of Sex Crime. Certainly her emphasis on the importance of serial sex killing is something which the Benedict material lacks.

How do the cases from abroad which attract most attention in the British press fit into this kind of classification and competing claims of importance? In fact, for sex murder and rape each seems to have three different kinds of cases which generate interest. The differences in the focus between sex murder and rape cases from abroad are as interesting as their similarities. While the elements which seem to contribute to an interest in a particular case are analytically distinct, they may be at their most powerful when they are combined.

For sex murder the two main elements seem to be 'horror' and 'links with Britain', while exceptionally the focus on an impending death sentence for a sex murder gains attention beyond the usual brief mention. In contrast, for rape, a crucial ingredient for widespread attention seems to be *either* the involvement of the famous *or* an issue involving the female victim. More rarely, the titillation provided by an unusual court case involving rape may be all that is required to capture the imagination of British sub-editors.

I will now consider these elements in relation to the cases briefly identified in Table 3. Of the three sex murder cases in 1985 which met the criteria for inclusion, two directly involved serial killings in the United States. While both of these cases were horrendous in scale, the one that gained the most coverage had the additional element of a link with Britain. This latter case involved two ex-marines, one of whom committed suicide after being arrested while the other, Charles Ng, born in Hong Kong, had been educated for a year at a school in Yorkshire in the north of England. The joint ingredients of 'horror' and 'links with Britain' accentuated the interest in this case. In fact, there was still mention of this case in the 1992 series of newspapers. The reason for the inclusion of the third case was a direct link with Britain. Two British teenagers were killed in Hong Kong after a brutal sex attack. Seven months later the coverage continued with the arrest of five members of a Triad gang.

These three cases (which produced 63 per cent of the coverage of sex murder cases in 1985) highlight the ingredients for coverage of sex murder cases from abroad. The two serial sex murder cases became media fodder because of the scale of the atrocities and the later discovered link of Charles Ng with Britain, albeit tenuous, helped to prolong the coverage. The third case only gained the coverage because of the link with Britain, for two teenagers killed in Hong Kong would not normally be of interest to British readers.

Of the six sex murder cases in 1992 which met the criteria (and which produced 70 per cent of the coverage in that year), again two involved large-scale serial killers but the focus of the coverage had changed in line with the increased interest of the popular press in sex murders from abroad. In covering the so-called cannibal killer, Jeffrey Dahmer, the echoes from the popular film, *Silence of the Lambs*, were very explicitly made (e.g. *Daily Mirror*, 13 January 1992), while the widely reported atrocities of the Russian serial killer, Andrei Chikatilo, were similarly linked with fantasy and he was described as bearing a 'chilling resemblance to Anthony Hopkins' *Silence of the Lambs* fiend, Hannibal the Cannibal' (*Sun*, 16 April 1992). The increasing interest of the popular press together with the clearly stated parallels linking reality and fantasy provide new dimensions to these records of 'horror'. Indeed, the adaptation of real cases to form the bases for films and television series makes it increasingly difficult to disentangle fact from fantasy.

A further three cases involved the rape and murder of British women in foreign lands (Kenya, South Africa and Israel). The Kenyan court case was the outcome of the drive and energy of the murdered woman's father who had overcome attempts to cover up the murder because of the potential damage to the country's tourist trade. Two game wardens were acquitted of the murder. In the second case the popular press made much of the discovery of the bodies of two nude bathers but, while there were perhaps hints of the dangers of 'globe-trotting', the comments were generally measured. In the third of these cases the murder of a 28-year-old woman after a sexual assault appeared to be linked with a fellow worker in a kibbutz. The remaining case from the United States was reported as one of the country's most controversial executions in recent years. After failing a lie-test the accused was executed for the rape and murder of his sister-in-law eleven years earlier in 1981. The main focus was on the protestation of his innocence but in the reports there was certainly no challenge to the reputation of the dead sister-in-law. In fact, a crucial feature of all the reports on the nine cases was that there was no serious challenge to the conduct of the victims (usually women) of these killings. Indeed, in reporting sex murder cases from abroad, the focus is especially on the crime and the criminal rather than on the actions and behaviour of the victims.

This outcome is not unexpected, for with serial killing cases there is rarely a contested trial in which cross-accusations are made and, similarly, with murdered British citizens the media focus is on the shock of the discovery of dead British bodies. As most of the latter kinds of cases take place in areas with a tourist industry, the aim of the authorities will be to minimize the publicity – as the father of the murdered Julie Ward found to his emotional and financial cost. Hence, the sex murder cases from abroad which attract the attention of the media rarely involve the reputation of the dead victim in the ways which are so vividly portrayed by Benedict.[10]

In contrast to the sex murder cases, none of the widely reported rape cases from abroad involved British attackers or British victims. While it would be presumptuous to generalize too freely from these two years, it seems fair to suggest that the rape of British women abroad does not merit sustained interest in the British press. Certainly there are reports of British holidaymakers being raped,[11] but the interest is not maintained and the eventual outcome is never mentioned.

In fact, there are different triggers which produce *widespread* interest in rape cases from abroad. In 1985 the three relevant cases could be identified separately as highlighting an issue about rape, as providing some titillation from the unusual and as focusing on the downfall of the famous. In the case gaining the most coverage the issue emerged with the confession by a woman of having provided false evidence that had jailed a man for twenty-five years. The world-wide coverage of this case of a confessed false accusation of rape seemed to be providing a symbolic message about the dangers of women to men at a time when the women's movement was beginning to make some impact in highlighting to the world the dangers of men to women. A focus on titillation came with the reports of a woman claiming that she had been abducted as a sex slave for seven years and raped repeatedly. The 'bondage slave' was allegedly forced to have oral sex while tied to a torture stretcher and was kept locked in a box under the accused's bed. More straightforwardly, the interest generated by the potential downfall of the famous provides another form of titillation to the readers of the mass media. In 1985 the famous football player turned actor, Jim Brown, was arrested on suspicion of raping a 33-year-old woman. While the case first attracted some widespread interest in the British press, one suspects that he was not quite famous enough for a British audience for the interest to be sustained. Although a judge dismissed the rape charges three months later after the prosecution admitted that there were contradictions in the evidence, none of the sample newspapers reported this outcome.[12] These three rape cases in 1985 only attracted 28 per cent of the total coverage while, in contrast, the three relevant cases in 1992 attracted 80 per cent. So what were the ingredients which helped to develop this overwhelming interest in these three cases?

In 1992 there was a much greater focus on the famous who were well known enough for the interest to be sustained. The preliminaries, the trial and the aftermath of the case against Mike Tyson, the former world boxing champion, gained quite incredible coverage. The second case of a focus on the famous was less clear-cut. William Kennedy Smith was famous by association as part of the Kennedy clan. Although Smith had been acquitted at the end of the previous year, the case continued to be 'milked' so that there were reports in 1992, for example, of the rape trial packaged as a £10.99 video (*Guardian*, 10 January 1992) and other similar peripheral mentions which ensured that interest in the case was maintained. Benedict (1992: 251) suggests that 'all in all, rape as a societal problem has lost interest for the public and the press, and the press is reverting to its pre-1970 focus on sex crimes as individual, bizarre, or sensational case histories – witness the furore over the celebrity rape case against William Kennedy Smith'. Certainly, the reporting of the Tyson trial strongly endorses this view of developments in the 1990s. However, the exception to this rule reminds that wider issues can still be addressed.

The third rape case from abroad which attracted a vast amount of coverage – matched only by the Tyson trial – concerned a girl aged fourteen who had been raped by a friend's father and made pregnant in the Republic of Ireland but denied by law the opportunity of having an abortion. Clearly this fell neatly into the 'virgin' category in Benedict's classification but the case set in motion the exploration of wider societal issues. More recently, it has been suggested that 'the fuss that ensued made her an emblem of Ireland's troubles with sex' (*Guardian*, 5 July 1993). Perhaps Britain's troubles with Ireland are also relevant for the case provided an opportunity to highlight some fundamental cultural and structural differences.

Conclusion

This study highlights the importance of considering the reporting in British newspapers of sex crime from abroad. It provides the opportunity to consider what sub-editors regard as sufficiently important to bring to the attention of British readers without the constraints imposed by British legislation. The scale of importing sensational news from abroad is increasing and the recent interest among the tabloid press presents new dimensions. In particular, the links between reality and fantasy are being developed and will increasingly confuse the audience in terms of what is actually happening in the world.

The differences in the coverage of sex murder and rape need to be recognized. In the case of sex murder it is argued that some of these reports from abroad are helping to fuel a global fear of serial killing. The reports of British women being killed after a sexual assault seem to have much more of a domestic interest although they are also highlighting the dangers for women abroad and so implicitly focusing on the social control of women. However, in reports of sex murder, there is no significant evidence of the reputation or the behaviour of the victims being inappropriately challenged. This contrasts strongly with many of the rape cases. Indeed, the often titillating coverage of rape from abroad reminds again of the concerns for the victim which the women's movement has so strongly fought for.

Benedict (1992: 251) detects that 'rape as a societal problem has lost interest for the public and the press' and goes on to suggest that 'the press is reverting to its pre-1970 focus on sex crimes as individual, bizarre, or sensational case histories.' This study supports this assertion as appropriate for the United States, but elsewhere this may not necessarily be true. Certainly the case of the fourteen-year-old Irish girl raped by a friend's father illustrates quite powerfully how in some contexts the wider societal issues can still be drawn out into the debate. Hence, while the United States certainly remains secure in setting the agenda of what should be regarded as problematic in the world, the process is certainly dynamic as reports from more countries begin to attract the interest of British editors. The situation is changing but, whatever else might happen, one can confidently predict that sex crime news from abroad will continue to increase in British newspapers and we need to understand its impact.

Acknowledgements

This study was financially supported by the Nuffield Foundation under the Small Grants Scheme in the Social Sciences. An earlier version of this article was presented as a paper at the British Criminology Conference, Cardiff, 28–31 July 1993.

Notes

1 After some controversy this practice seems to have been discontinued from the early 1980s. Sexual harassment cases heard in industrial tribunals now seem to fill this role on occasions.

2 Benedict (1992: 252) also notes that 'the woman's attorney said later that the victim's "low point" came when she was publicly identified.' This comment is interesting in so far as the anonymity provision in British law has been particularly strongly criticized by American commentators (e.g. Geis 1978).

3 The author has considered the reporting of sex crime, particularly rape, in a series of British newspapers in ten-year (1951, 1961, 1971) and more latterly, seven-year (1978, 1985, 1992) intervals. The newspapers considered since 1951 have been *The Times, Daily Mirror, News of the World, Sunday People,* and (the London) *Evening Standard. The Sun* has been included since 1971. Since 1985, the *Guardian, Observer* and the *Sunday Mirror* have been added to the series. The most obvious gap in the current series is in the middle range of newspapers (e.g. *Daily Mail, Daily Express* and *Today)* which appeal to a more staid middle-class Conservative readership. In 1985 a wider selection of newspapers, including the *Daily Mail* and the *Mail on Sunday* as well as some local evenings and weeklies, was studied (Soothill and Walby 1991).

4 Probably the most contentious omissions from this article are the reports of mass rape and sexual assault by Serbian forces. While the EC investigation into the allegations concluded that 'around 20,000 women had suffered sexual assault at the hands of Serbian forces and gave credence to the claim that rape was being used as a systematic weapon in the campaign of ethnic cleansing' (Grant 1993: 10), the reports in the sample period involved general discussions about the phenomenon rather than a focus on specific cases. Grant (1993: 10–11) discusses how the media quickly lost interest in the issue of sexual violation in Bosnia.

5 It would, of course, be possible to regard the various developments in the Tyson saga as different news stories, but the aim here is to group the reports which derive from a particular case.

6 As the Sundays appear once a week and the (London) *Evening Standard* only appears on five evenings compared with six times a week for the daily newspapers, the raw figures need to be weighted for a strict comparison. Weighting the scores indicates more strikingly the increasing significance of the popular Sundays and more especially the importance which both the Murdoch newspapers, the *Sun* and the *News of the World*, have recently attached to including sex crime from abroad in their news pages.

7 So, for example, Soothill and Walby (1991: 58) note in the press reporting of rape trials how in 1985 'three cases (out of 114) had one-third of the total number of pages devoted to rape cases, while nine cases had over half.'

8 Of the 151 different sex murder and rape cases identified in 1985 and 1992, 100 (or 66 per cent) were solitary items appearing in only one of the nine newspapers. Of the 50 sex murder cases, 29 (or 58 per cent) were solitary items, while of the 101 rape cases, 71 (or 70 per cent) were solitary items. Of course, there is the possibility that some entries were missed and, if there had been an even larger number of newspapers surveyed, this percentage would have probably fallen although again there may have been a further series of solitary items uncovered.

9 While termed 'major sex cases', it is important to stress that cases from abroad which get extensive coverage may get it for reasons of titillation rather than of importance.

10 Murder victims are not, of course, necessarily sacrosanct. Benedict's analysis of the press coverage of the murder of Jennifer Levin portrayed as the 'voracious vamp' exemplifies this point. Furthermore, with serial killing there are, of course, distinctions made between victims, for a concern with the search for the Yorkshire Ripper was that the matter was not taken seriously until a 'respectable' woman became a victim of Peter Sutcliffe. However, the burden of that latter concern must be laid largely at the door of law enforcement agencies rather than the press.

11 So, for example, there is a report of a 21-year-old woman claiming she had been raped by at least eight men at her hotel in San Antonia, Ibiza, with the headline, '30 Ibiza Brits Say: We had Sex with Rape Girl' (*Daily Mirror*, 10 July 1992) but the coverage is not sustained. However, as this headline portrays, the victim's account in such circumstances can be seriously undermined.

12 In fact, this outcome was noted by the author in a report in the *Coventry Evening Telegraph* (21 June 1985).

References

Benedict, H. (1992). *Virgin or Vamp: How the Press Covers Sex Crimes* (New York, Oxford University Press).

Caputi, J. (1987). *The Age of Sex Crime*. (London, The Women's Press).

Geis, G. (1978). 'The case of rape: legal restrictions on media coverage of deviance in England and America', in C. Winick (ed.) *Deviance and Mass Media* (Sage).

Grant, L. (1993). 'Anyone here been raped and speak English?', *Guardian*, 2 August.

Hay, A., Soothill, K. and Walby, S. (1980). 'Seducing the public by rape reports', *New Society*, 53 (924), 214-15.

Lloyd, C. and Walmsley, R. (1989). *Changes in Rape Offences and Sentencing*. Home Office Research Study no. 105 (London, HMSO).

McLuhan, M. (1962). *The Gutenberg Galaxy: The Making of Typographical Man*. (Toronto, University of Toronto Press).

McLuhan, M. (1964). *Understanding Media: The Extensions of Man*. (New York, McGraw-Hill).

Soothill, K. (1991). 'The changing face of rape', *British Journal of Criminology*, 31, 4, 383-92.

Soothill, K. and Jack, A. (1975). 'How rape is reported', *New Society*, 32 (663), 702-74.

Soothill, K. and Walby, S. (1991). *Sex Crime in the News* (London, Routledge).

6

Conceptualizing violence by women[1]

MARGARET SHAW

> The images that cross the borders in magazines, movies, or videos are . . .
> more dangerous than any secret weapon, because they make one desire
> that 'otherness' badly enough to risk one's life by trying to escape.
> (Drakulic 1993)

> The photograph came to establish and delimit the terrain of the *other*, to
> define both the *generalized look* – the typology – and the *contingent
> instance* of deviance and social pathology. (Sekula 1989: 345)[2]

The explosion of public concern with violence involving women in
the past ten or more years has had a powerful impact on many
sections of society. But as with many social movements not all of that
impact has been beneficial to all women. The focus on women as
victims of violence was and remains an essential one. Among women
from many social groups there are clearly very high levels of
experience of violence in terms of physical, sexual and emotional
abuse. In the context of the criminal justice system, however, this
focus has had some important consequences for women, not all of
them beneficial.

Much of the current discourse about the position of women in
conflict with the law centres around their low social and economic
status in society, the extent of social controls over their behaviour,
and, particularly in Canada, their position as victims of violence
(*Creating Choices* 1990; Coté 1991). This status has tended to replace
one social label with another – the unfit mother or the fallen woman
. . . becomes the helpless victim with low self-esteem. This has
become a universal label and as such it oversimplifies the explanation
of women's situation and behaviour (Naffine 1986). At the level of the
courts it has become 'incorporated', particularly in terms of the

Battered Woman Syndrome, into legal and medical discourse, in a way which, as Comack (1993a) argues, is not always in the best interests of women. There is still a tendency to pathologize violence by women (Allen 1987). It has also led to counter-claims that women are just as violent in domestic situations as men, claims which Dobash and Dobash (1992) vigorously demolish.

For feminists, for professionals who work with women who have been victimized, for criminologists, perhaps for all women, however, it is difficult to talk about women as perpetrators of violence, *except* in terms of their own reactions to victimization: the battered women who hit back. And almost all attention has been on the issue of women who kill. This ranges from statistical accounts of women who kill (Silverman and Kennedy 1993); historical and descriptive accounts (Jones 1980; Carrigan 1991); feminist analyses of the impact of the Battered Wife Syndrome (Comack 1993a; Noonan 1993); journalistic 'moral tales' of women accused of murder (Priest 1992) to, more recently, accounts which try to contextualize representations of such women (Walford 1987; Birch 1993). Finally, almost all that attention has been focused on the early stages of the criminal justice process, discovery, arrest, speculation, investigation, trial, verdict, and perhaps appeal. There, however, most interest and discourse stops. The focus is upon the drama and the stage. What happens next? How much attention does the justice system subsequently pay to the issues facing those women? How far do the discourses of the correctional system, the prison, the classification system, the parole board ignore, or incorporate or really contemplate the implications for women? And how many other women use violence apart from those who kill an abusive partner, and outside a domestic situation? How can we contextualize and understand their behaviour?

One of the problems has been the understandable difficulties which feminists have had in thinking about women as violent, although some have tried (Carlen 1988; Heidensohn 1992). Another is that women who kill have become the focus of attention in the media and in Hollywood films, with all the implications for locating their actions which this implies (Birch 1993). There is a lack of information about the range of violent offences by women, but partial and sensational information about certain offences. Certainly there are those who are willing to talk about violent women. It is a familiar journalistic device to portray the unusual, the lives of extraordinary women, or more recently the 'soaring' rates of crime by women.

In Montreal, for example, a female bank robber, Machine-gun Molly/Monique la Mitraille, achieved the status of a notorious fantasy figure in the 1960s courtesy of a journalist for the *Montreal Star*. She was killed by the police in 1967 after a robbery, and suspected of involvement in twenty others. Numerous articles, a TV documentary and even a musical *Monica la Mitraille* followed. She was portrayed as a tough woman who wore men's clothes and carried a machine gun. Similar intense interest was shown in the 'discovery' of 'the first female serial killer' Aileen Warnous in the United States in 1991 (Skrapec 1993). And in 1992 Lisa Priest, a young *Toronto Star* journalist, published *Women Who Killed*, the 'stories of Canadian Female Murderers', inappropriately classified as 'True Crime' by the publishers.

Yet such accounts are of little help in explaining why there were some 13,000 women charged with violent offences in Canada in 1991 (Canadian Centre for Justice Statistics 1992) or accounting for the fact that 58 per cent of the population of women under federal sentence in Canada in 1989 – that is a sentence of two years or more – had been sentenced for a violent offence. Nor are they helpful in dealing with evidence of a long-term upward trend in violent offences among women (and men) in Canada and the sensationalism attached to its reporting.[3]

Thus there are a number of interrelated issues to be considered in confronting women as perpetrators of violence. These include:

a) representations by the media of women who use violence and the focus on the early stages of the criminal justice process;

b) the problem of oversimplification, of reducing explanations of women's offending to a single one; of assuming that all women are victims (or alternatively all tough and masculine non-women);

c) the tendency to conceptualize violent behaviour in masculine and simplistic terms and to see women's violence from the perspective of violent acts by men;

d) the related problem of what is meant by the use of the word 'violent' in the context of the criminal justice system and society in general;

e) the problem of the links between being victimized and using violence; and

f) – this is one of the primary reasons *why* we should confront violence by women – the implications of this labelling for the criminal justice system, the problem of what we should do with or for women designated as violent.

This paper examines some of these issues in the light of current Canadian knowledge of violent behaviour, including the findings of a survey of women serving federal sentences in 1989 (Shaw *et al.* 1991).[4]

How many women are violent?

Certainly, compared with men, women commit very few offences, and violence by women forms an even smaller proportion of all acts of violence committed. Around 110,000 men were charged with offences against the person in Canada in 1991,[5] compared with 12,915 women – or 10 per cent of all violent offences.

The number of women who have been charged with violent offences has, however, increased in the past twenty years, from 8 per cent of all women charged with offences in 1970, to 12 per cent in 1991 (Johnson and Rodgers 1993). This represents a greater increase in violent offences than among men.

Among those people serving federal sentences of two years or more, women represent only 2 per cent of the total population. This amounts to around 300 women compared with 12,000 federally sentenced men. At the time of the 1989 survey of women serving federal sentences, however, 69 per cent of those in prison were there for an offence against the person – 42 per cent for murder or manslaughter, 27 per cent for robbery or assault (see Table 1).[6]

Table 1: Current offences of federally sentenced women: 1989 survey

Offence	No.	%
Murder	44	
Attempted murder	3	42
Manslaughter	38	
Robbery	24	
Assaults	21	27
Theft, fraud	30	
Drug offences	24	31
Others	9	
Population Total	203	100

Among provincially sentenced women the proportion serving sentences for violence will be considerably lower, since, by definition, women convicted of crimes perceived to be serious receive sentences of over two years. Figures for six provinces indicate that 10 per cent of women admitted to provincial custody in 1989–90 had committed violent offences (Canadian Centre for Justice Statistics 1990). Recent figures for the province of Ontario suggest that 19 per cent of women in both institutions *and* under community supervision have been convicted or charged with offences involving violence.[7] In Quebec, Savard and Biron (1986) reported that 34 per cent of the women in the provincial prison in Montreal were serving sentences for offences against the person, although this included federally sentenced women.[8]

How do we explain these figures and these women? Are they all Machine-gun Mollies or have they all been victims of violence at some stage of their lives?

The problem of oversimplification

The oversimplification of explanations, as Naffine (1986) has pointed out, is particularly common in relation to explanations of crime and gender. Traditional explanations for women's offending stressed a biological determinism which explained women's behaviour in terms of child-like impulses and sexual drives, or more recently, menstrual cycles (Kendall 1991). Shoplifting, theft and fraud, infanticide or murder could all be 'explained' in these terms as irrational behaviour. Even as late as 1969, designs for the replacement of the main women's prison in London (Holloway) with a psychiatric prison for women were justified on the grounds that women are not 'bad' but 'mad' (see for example Dobash, Dobash and Gutteridge 1986).

But there has also been a dualism which characterized women as angels or whores, and enabled correctional administrators to divide women into child-like creatures capable of reform, and recidivists and older women 'too far sunk in criminality to respond to reformative influences' (Rafter 1982). Comparing the discipline problems of male and female convicts in England in 1978, a prison matron described the latter as 'desperately wicked, deceitful, crafty, malicious, lewd and void of common feeling . . . in the penal classes of the male prisons there is not one man to match the worst inmates of our female prisons' (quoted in McConville 1981).

Since the 1970s, the development of feminist approaches to women's offending has profoundly challenged the assumptions on which such explanations are based. The control and power exercised by society over women, in the home, school and work-place have been shown to be persistent and pervasive (Bertrand 1969; Heidensohn 1986). The 'discovery' of domestic abuse and violence against women in society as a whole has had a major impact upon our understanding of this 'control' over women. Women are seen to be victims of their circumstances, lacking independence and status, subject to control at the hands of their partners and a patriarchal society. And we now know that many of the women who end up in the criminal justice system have experienced considerable abuse, both physical and sexual, in the course of their lives. Yet our current, and justifiable, concern with levels of violence against women runs the risk of oversimplifying the explanation of women's crime and violence by portraying women as 'helpless' victims whose offending derives from that experience.[9]

The lack of basic information about women who commit violent offences is a particular problem in Canada although it has been noted elsewhere. Sally Simpson, for example, suggests that women who commit violence are not seen to exist in the USA: 'The simplistic assertion that males are violent and women are not contains a grain of truth, but it misses the complexity and texture of women's lives' (Simpson 1991: 129). In Canada there are no national court statistics or in-depth studies which would allow us to look at the issue of violence by women in any detailed way. There exists only a handful of studies which have attempted to approach the issue. Savard and Biron (1986) interviewed nineteen women convicted of serious violence outside their family. Girouard (1988) interviewed thirteen women to investigate the importance of their role in robbery offences. There are two very different biographical accounts of twenty-two women charged with homicide (Walford 1987; Priest 1992).

In the absence of any in-depth accounts we are left in many cases relying on general truisms about 'most women'. In one of the most often quoted texts about women's contribution to crime in Canada, for example, Holly Johnson writes of women's violence as follows:

> The small body of research in this area suggests that violence by women for the most part consists of acts of rebellion or retaliation against abusive or exploitative domestic situations. (1987:30)

One of the sources of this comment is the earlier, and again much referenced, study of violence by women published in 1974 by

Rosenblatt and Greenland. In this article, which explores the backgrounds and circumstances of cases of homicide and wounding, women's violence is seen to be very different from that of men. They argued that it is characterized as primarily altruistic, in that many of the women killed a child to save them from pain or suffering, that women's violence rarely involved the use of alcohol, and was almost exclusively domestic or family-related. By contrast, men's victims were not always relatives but strangers too, and their acts were often under the influence of alcohol or drugs.

Much of Greenland's admirable work on violence and dangerousness has been particularly concerned with domestic violence and childhood abuse. It is worth underlining here, nevertheless, that this particular study was based on a sample of twenty-two women psychiatric patients retained under a Warrant of the Lieutenant Governor for murder, attempted murder or wounding, and just four federally sentenced women at the federal penitentiary in Kingston (P4W) (as well as 69 and 96 men). This highly selected sample bears very little relationship to the current population of women serving federal sentences in Canada for such offences. A number of selective factors concerning the representation of those women by the legal and medical professions will have separated out those women from those sentenced to serve a prison term.[10]

Thus one of the problems has been the almost exclusive focus on women offenders in relation to domestic violence in recent years, which by definition excludes other kinds of events and situations. By focusing only on domestic violence, we are unable to begin to understand the complexity of violent behaviour and its generation among women.

If we examine the federal population surveyed in 1989, for example, we find among those eighty-five women convicted of murder or manslaughter a variety of circumstance (Shaw 1992a):

— there are those women who represent the battered women we recognize, who had killed a spouse or common-law husband, for example, after twenty years of physical abuse, and
— those who killed an acquaintance after sexual advances (19 cases);
— those who killed someone in a very complex situation, after several days of drinking or drug use, and who often remember nothing of the event itself and

— women who committed a *crime passionnel*, killing a lover or a lover's wife or husband, or to get back their child (31 cases);

— women who killed clients or acquaintances, such as 'Johns' or drug dealers, for money or drugs (12 cases);

— women who were convicted for murder in the course of a robbery (although none of them had actually done so themselves) (4 cases);

— women who killed a child, their own or someone else's, by accident, because of depression, for vengeance . . . (11 cases).

Mostly, these women did not plan the act, it happened – it was a combination of circumstances, of situation, it involved a life crisis, depression, alcohol and drugs misuse, physical or sexual abuse – in almost all cases it was a very *complex situation* and chain of events.

So brief an outline of the 'circumstances' of these events cannot take into account all of the factors which led to those acts. The purpose here is to demonstrate that not all such events can be defined as 'domestic' and that even among those which are, they are not necessarily directly related to an abusive relationship. Apart from these women convicted of murder or manslaughter, there were those fifty-five women convicted for assaults and robbery. Is the behaviour of all these women to be understood and classified in terms of their status as victims?

What *is clear* is that many of the federally sentenced women do not *present* themselves as victims – without personality, resolution or self-esteem. There are a number of women with considerable strength, intelligence, many regrets for what had happened, but a lot of determination, humour and anger.[11]

Images of violent women

Our image of violence is based on that of male violence – macho, tough, aggressive; we have no ways of conceptualizing violence by women except in terms of its 'unnaturalness'. Lisa Priest's account of the eleven women 'who had killed', much of which she gathered from interviews with those involved in the trials as well as court transcripts, displays the familiar intense interest in the details of the act itself. She focuses on the drama, the details of the events leading up to the act, the details of the scene of the crime, the amount of blood and tissue.

She describes her interest in these terms: 'it is the human equation I find riveting' (Priest 1992:13).

While she provides graphic accounts of women who killed abusive partners, there is also a tendency to dichotomize, to separate out the 'genuine killers', the 'dark characters who disturb and fascinate' from the rest. This she does by relying on the strangeness of the dress or behaviour of those women to help to account for their acts. Their failure to act, dress, behave 'normally' is emphasized, and they are represented as unnatural. A 55-year-old woman who worked for Northern Telecom is described as follows:

> A . . . it seemed, had a craving for diversified sex in the form of clandestine affairs . . . although a strong, somewhat dowdy woman, [she] oozed and smouldered sex. (Priest 1992:249)

Elsewhere she was described by the Crown as 'a cold-hearted blue-eyed killer' who did not cry when it was thought appropriate (p. 261). Another woman is described as being 'extremely manipulative . . . university-educated, articulate and ruthless' and as having very sinister-looking eyes, 'eyes so dark they are almost black'. She too is found to be not above clandestine sex and not fazed by being caught in a 'compromising position'. A third is described as 'a woman of privilege . . . best known for her tasteless wardrobe' and a 'grotesque appearance':

> Her rouge was a strong red and heavily applied in streaks. . . Her lips were painted unevenly with a creamy red geranium lipstick. She was a short, stocky woman with the gait of an old, fat dog. It was hard to believe that she came from a family of . . . notables. (Priest 1992: 163)[12]

Other accounts also testify to this apparent need for women defendants to appear 'normal'. Myra Hindley, convicted in 1967 for her involvement in the murder of children in England, was thought to be too smartly dressed in court to be a repentant accomplice, too expressionless. Her own account of her appearance in court was that because of the intense scrutiny, she cultivated an expressionless face, interpreted by others as evidence of her callousness. A police photograph which always accompanies newspaper articles about her shows a brooding face with hooded eyes staring 'blankly from beneath a heavy fringe' the epitome of 'feminine evil' (Birch 1993).[13] As Helen Birch argues:

Her attempts to represent *herself*, to locate an explanation for her actions somewhere between the polarities of victimization and evil, are doomed to failure. (Birch 1993: 59)

The mythology of Myra Hindley reveals above all that we do not have a language to represent female killing, and that a case like this disrupts the very terms which hold gender in place. (Ibid. 61)

A similar point is made by Bonny Walford (1987) in her sensitive account of the lives of eleven women convicted of murder or manslaughter, including herself. She warns that many women awaiting trial for murder will be given tranquillizers to calm them, and risk appearing unemotional or cold-hearted. This separation of the 'true killers' from the 'victims' is comparable to the dichotomy noted by Lorraine Radford (1993) who argues that 'legal and popular discourses separate "true" women victims of domestic violence from the not really battered, undeserving viragos' (p. 195).

What is violent offending?

What is meant by the use of the word 'violent' in the context of the criminal justice system and society in general? Like many other concepts, violence has layers of meaning and covers a vast range of behavioural events and legal definitions apart from murder or manslaughter. These range from 'planned aggressive attacks', to threats and scuffles on the street – between a prostitute and the arresting police officer as he tries to search her for possession of drugs, for example.

Among the federally sentenced population, there were those convicted for robbery involving the handing over of notes, threatening bank tellers with the use of a gun (which did not exist); and others who drove a get-away car but did not enter the building. And among the women charged with assault, there was one with fifteen previous convictions ('a recidivist too far sunk. . .'?) only three of which had involved a charge of violence. These had included hitting victims on the head and snatching their bags in two cases, and grabbing money from a supermarket cashier in another.[14] None of this is to discount the experience of the victims of those events themselves, but it does demonstrate the range of those actions we call violent.

Of the few studies of violence by women other than killing, most have used conventional empirical methods or theoretical approaches to 'measure' the acts themselves, and to see how they 'measure-up' to violent acts by men. Girouard (1987) in his study of women convicted for robbery uses conventional measures of offence seriousness developed on the basis of the male offender population to assess the extent of their actual involvement in the offence. His purpose is to test the extent to which women's role in such acts is secondary as traditionally argued (e.g., sitting in the get-away car, holding the door, acting as decoy), or demonstrates the emergence of the more active violent woman promised in the 'women's liberation' thesis. Campbell (1986), concerned at the lack of anything other than anecdotal accounts of female violence or studies of extreme cases such as homicide, compared self-reports about fighting among groups of adolescents and young women.

As Savard and Biron have shown (1986), violence was a rare event in the lives of the nineteen women they interviewed. Even among those with considerable offending histories, the use of violence was rare, as it was among the women in the federal survey. As they also point out, the great majority of those 13,000 women charged each year in Canada with offences against the person will have been charged with assaults, often of a very minor kind, and with very little physical harm ensuing. Among women in Ontario, the *majority* of those charged with assault received a sentence of probation, not incarceration, suggesting that the behaviour was not seen to be very serious (Shaw 1994). Some of these studies go a little way towards understanding the involvement of women in violent offences. What are missing are more detailed studies which examine in greater depth and in terms of their own experiences the contexts and lives of women convicted of violence.

The links between being victimized and using violence

We were told by the women in the federal survey, both those convicted of violent offences and non-violent offences, that 68 per cent of them had been physically abused at some stage in their lives, and 53 per cent of them sexually abused. Among the Aboriginal women as many as 90 per cent said they had been physically abused and 61 per cent sexually abused (Shaw 1991). We do not know how far that 'knowledge' reflects what actually happened – they may not be prepared to talk about it, they may not recognize that they were abused. Some said that they had 'got over' what occurred, others that they felt they needed a great deal of help.

It is, nevertheless, very difficult to say how far this experience is *directly related* to the use of violence, when there are in their lives many other experiences – 75 per cent had an involvement with substance abuse, 66 per cent had no work skills or regular legitimate employment, almost half had severe disruption in their early lives. The Aboriginal women in particular have a history as victims of racism, violence in the home and on the street, dependence on drugs and alcohol from a very young age, being sent to institutions or white foster homes with sometimes as many as forty-seven different placements before the age of fifteen or sixteen. For some women, although not all, their contact with society has been one of violence and punishment almost all their lives.

Bonny Walford (1987) in her account of women 'lifers' at P4W, certainly details the abuse some of these women experienced, but she also stresses other aspects of their lives including alcohol and drugs, bad companions and bad luck.

What should be done with women convicted of violent offences?

The problem remains of what we should do with or for women designated as violent – and in a climate which sees violent crime as a contemporary crisis.[15] As Bonny Walford has argued, 'the media has misrepresented us so much that even outside professionals have misconceptions about us' (1987: 97). Are they a 'risk' to themselves or others; should we label them as troublesome; what are the implications of their status for the criminal justice system?

Here I am concerned less with the processes by which women came to be labelled as 'violent' than with what that signifies to society and to a correctional system given the responsibility of 'managing' offenders. While the conditions under which women serving federal sentences in Canada will be considerably different with the closure of the Prison for Women and the implementation of the recommendations of the Task Force report *Creating Choices*, the issue of understanding women's violence remains.[16]

The 'violent' label attached to many Aboriginal women, and to others in the federal population has led over the years to a syndrome of consequences, based on the traditional masculine model of corrections. This model stresses security, discipline, punishment and control. A conviction for a violent offence attaches meanings to those women. They are labelled, segregated, controlled. They are likely to be categorized as risks because they have resisted the controls placed on them. Six of the Aboriginal women have committed suicide since the beginning of 1989; a number of other women have slashed themselves. The case of Marlene Moore is another very clear example of the problems of attaching male categories of violence to women. She was the first (and so far only) woman to be retained in prison under the Dangerous Offender legislation introduced in Canada in 1977. She had spent much of her life in training school or prison, had a history of slashing herself and died in prison probably from suicide.[17] Complex as it was, in no way did her history of offending approximate to that of the kind of violent offender from whom the legislation was intended to protect the public.

What the women themselves argue is that they need not control, but understanding and support. By punishing and controlling minor misdemeanours in the prison setting, we create a situation where the response is more likely to be violent. This is particularly likely to be the case for someone whose primary experience in relation to others has been of the use of violence to deal with difficult situations.

Somehow, we must begin to understand how to respond to women who use violence, avoiding both the control–punishment reflex, and the person/individual-blaming approach. And we have to try to understand, as Simpson has argued (1991), 'the complexity and texture of different women's lives', and to avoid seeing them all as victims devoid of any capacity to make rational choices. To do so is an injustice to the women themselves, and risks replacing the masculine control system by a more benign but still controlling net which sees them all as victims. As Pat Carlen has put it:

> however meagre women's contribution to the sum total of crime, the relatively small numbers of female criminals have over the years embraced the whole spectrum of criminal ingenuity and socially injurious behaviour. And they have not always been women in poverty and without power. (Carlen 1988: 19)

Notes

1   Part of the work on which this paper is based was conducted under contract for the Secretariat of the Ministry of the Solicitor General of Canada, and I am grateful to them for their support. The views expressed in the paper are my own and do not necessarily reflect those of the Solicitor General.

[2] Allan Sekula (1989: 345) on the development of photography as a means of classifying and catching offenders. I am grateful to Cheryl Simon for alerting me to this paper, as well as Helen Birch's book.

[3] See for example the headline in the Montreal paper the *Gazette*, 'Crime rate among women skyrocketing: StatsCan', 15 December 1990, in response to the publication of a Juristat on women and crime (1990).

[4] The survey was conducted in conjunction with the Task Force on Federally Sentenced Female Offenders whose report *Creating Choices* was published in 1990.

[5] Criminal statistics include under the category of crimes of violence, or offences against the person, homicide, attempted murder, assaults including sexual assaults, abduction and robbery.

[6] The 1989 survey was based on all those 203 women actually in prison at the time of the study, whether in Prison For Women, the women's penitentiary at Kingston, Ontario, or in provincial prisons under Exchange of Service agreements. It excluded women out on day parole or temporarily absent.

[7] M. Shaw (1994) *Ontario Women in Conflict with the Law*, Ministry of Solicitor General and Correctional Services; and Ministry of Correctional Services (Ontario), *Annual Report*, May 1992.

[8] Most federally sentenced women from Quebec stay in the province under an Exchange of Service Agreement.

[9] See also Shaw (1992b) for a discussion of some of these problems.

[10] See Hilary Allen (1987) for a discussion of some of these issues.

[11] Elizabeth Comack (1993b) emphasizes that the women she interviewed in Portage provincial prison, Manitoba, were active survivors rather than victims.

[12] I have a recent photograph of her. She looks healthy, vital and splendid.

[13] Her own explanation is that the photograph was taken after four sleepless nights, and in expectation of the kind of interrogation she had seen in films (Birch 1993: 53).

[14] Girouard (1985) in a small study of thirteen women convicted for robbery argues that their offences were as serious and violent as those of men. However, he uses traditional categories of seriousness based on the male population, and relies only on case records.

[15] See, for example, the *Globe and Mail* 21.1.93, 'Crime and punishment – it's a topic inching to the top of the political agenda as violence raises public anxiety on both sides of the Canada–USA border, and even across the Atlantic.'

[16] The penitentiary is to be replaced by four regional facilities for women and a Healing Lodge for Aboriginal women, to be focused on providing programmes for the special needs of women in a supportive environment. See *Creating Choices* (1990) and Shaw (1993).

[17] See Kershaw and Lasovitch (1991) for an account of Marlene Moore's life and death. The Dangerous Offender legislation was introduced to respond

to public fears about the release of violent offenders, and has been used primarily to retain violent sex offenders. Around 90–100 men have been retained under the legislation.

References

Allen, H. (1987). *Justice Unbalanced: Gender, Psychiatry and Judicial Decisions* (Milton Keynes, Open University Press).

Bertrand, M. A. (1969). 'Self-image and delinquency: a contribution to the study of female criminality and women's image', *Acta Criminologica: Etudes sur la conduite antisociale* 2 (January), 71–144.

Birch, H. (ed.) (1993). *Moving Targets: Women, Murder and Representation* (London, Virago).

Campbell, A. (1986). 'Self-report of fighting by females', *British Journal of Criminology*, 26(1) 2846.

Canadian Centre for Justice Statistics (1990). *Women and Crime*. Juristat Service Bulletin, Vol. 12 No. 20, December. Ottawa.

Carlen, P. (1988). *Women, Crime and Poverty* (Milton Keynes: Open University Press).

Carrigan, D. O. (1991). *Crime and Punishment in Canada: A History* (Toronto, McClelland and Stewart).

Comack, E. (1993a). 'Feminist engagement with the law: the legal recognition of the Battered Woman Syndrome', in the *CRIAW Papers*, Canadian Research Institute for the Advancement of Women, Ottawa.

Comack, E. (1993b). *Women Offenders' Experiences with Physical and Sexual Abuse: a preliminary report* (University of Manitoba, Criminology Research Centre).

Creating Choices (1990). Report of the Task Force on Federally Sentenced Women (Ottawa, Correctional Service Canada).

Coté, A. (1991). *La rage au coeur: Rapport de recherche sur le traitement judiciaire de l'homicide conjugal au Québec* (Regroupement des femmes de la Côte-Nord, C.P. 2486 Baie-Comeau G5C 2T2).

Dobash, R. P., Dobash, R. E. and Gutteridge, S. (1986). *The Imprisonment of Women* (Oxford: Basil Blackwell).

Dobash, R. E. and Dobash, R. P. (1992). *Women, Violence and Social Change* (London, Routledge).

Drakulic, S. (1993). *How We Survived Communism and Even Laughed* (New York, Harper Collins).

Girouard, D. (1988). 'Les femmes incarcérées pour vol qualifié, au Québec, en 1985: importance de leur rôle', *Canadian Journal of Criminology*, 30(2), 121–34.

Heidensohn, F. (1985). *Women and Crime: The Life of the Female Offender* (New York, New York University Press).

Heidensohn, F. (1992). 'Sociological perspectives on violence by women' (unpublished paper given at University of Montreal, February 1992).

Johnson, H. (1987). 'Getting the facts straight: A statistical overview', in E. Adelberg and C. Currie, *Too Few to Count: Canadian Women in Conflict with the Law* (Vancouver, Press Gang Publishers).

Johnson, H. and Rodgers, K. (1993). 'Getting the facts straight: A statistical overview', in E. Adelberg and C. Currie, *In Conflict with the Law: Women and the Canadian Justice System* (Vancouver, Press Gang Publishers).

Jones, A. (1980). *Women Who Kill* (New York, Holt, Rinehart & Winston).

Kendall, K. (1991). 'The politics of premenstrual syndrome: implications for feminist justice', *The Journal of Human Justice,* 2(2), 77–98.

Kershaw, A. and Lasovitch, (1991). *Rock-a-Bye-Baby: A Death Behind Bars* (Toronto, McClelland and Stewart).

McConville, S. (1981). *A History of English Penal Administration*, Vol. 1, 1750–1877 (London, Routledge & Kegan Paul).

Naffine, N. (1986). 'Women and crime', in D. Chappell and P. Wilson (eds.), *The Australian Criminal Justice System* (Sydney, Butterworths).

Noonan, S. (1993). 'Strategies for survival: moving beyond the Battered Women Syndrome', in E. Adelberg and C. Currie, *In Conflict with the Law: Women and the Canadian Justice System* (Vancouver, Press Gang Publishers).

Priest, L. (1992). *Women Who Killed* (Toronto, McClelland and Stewart).

Radford, L. (1993). 'Pleading for time: justice for battered women', in H. Birch (ed.), *Moving Targets: Women, Murder and Representation* (London, Virago).

Rafter, N. H. (1982). 'Hard times: custodial prisons for women and the example of the New York Prison for women at Auburn 1893–1933', in N. H. Rafter and E. A. Stanko, *Judge, Lawyer, Victim, Thief* (Boston, North-Eastern University Press).

Rosenblatt, E. and Greenland, C. (1974). 'Female crimes of violence', *Canadian Journal of Criminology and Corrections,* 16(2), 173–80.

Savard, C. and Langelier-Birion, L. (1986). *Female Perpetrators of Serious Offences* (User Report No. 1986–16: Ottawa, Ministry of the Solicitor General).

Sekula, A. (1989). 'The body and the archive', in R. Bolton (ed.), *The Contest of Meaning: Critical Histories of Photography* (Cambridge, Mass., MIT Press).

Skrapec, C. (1993). 'The female serial killer', in H. Birch (ed.), *Moving Targets: Women, Murder and Representation* (London, Virago).

Shaw, M. with Rodgers, K., Blanchette, J., Hattem, T., Thomas, L. S., and Tamarack, L. (1991). *Survey of Federally Sentenced Women: Report to the Task Force on Federally Sentenced Women on the Prison Survey* (User Report 1991–4: Ottawa, Ministry of the Solicitor General).

Shaw, M. with Rodgers, K., Blanchette, J., Hattem, T., Thomas, L. S., and Tamarack, L. (1992a). Paying the Price: Federally Sentenced Women in Context (User Report 1992–13: Ottawa, Ministry of the Solicitor General).

Shaw, M. (1992b). 'Issues of power and control: women in prison and their defenders', *British Journal of Criminology,* 32(4), 438–52.

Shaw, M. (1993). 'Reforming Federal Women's Imprisonment', in E. Adelberg and C. Currie, *In Conflict with the Law: Women and the Canadian Justice System* (Vancouver, Press Gang Publishers).

Shaw, M. (1994). *Ontario Women in Conflict with the Law: A Survey of Women in Institutions and Under Community Supervision in Ontario* (Toronto, Ministry of Solicitor General and Correctional Services).

Silverman, R. and Kennedy, L. (1993) *Deadly Deeds: Murder in Canada* (Scarborough, Nelson Canada).

Simpson, S. (1991). 'Caste, class, and violent crime: explaining differences in female offending', *Criminology,* 29(1), 115–35.

Walford, B. (1987). *Lifers: the stories of eleven women serving life sentences for murder* (Montréal, Eden Press).

7

In the name of love:
Women and initiation to illicit drugs[1]

LISA MAHER

One of the most persistent observations found in the literature on illicit drug use is that men are responsible for the initiation of women (e.g. Freeland and Campbell 1973; Waldorf 1973; Eldred and Washington 1976; File 1976; Rosenbaum 1981a; Hser, Anglin and McGlothlin 1987; Parker *et al.* 1988; Blom and van den Berg 1989; Moore 1991). In the early twentieth century, the ultimate menace of both cocaine and heroin was seen as their role in the seduction of young white women by Chinese and black men (Kohn 1992). Concurrent themes of decadent sexuality and racial degeneration emerged on both sides of the Atlantic (Musto 1973; Kohn 1992). As a British newspaper account of the capture of drug 'king-pin' Edgar Manning reported under the headline 'Evil Negro Caught', 'This negro was money mad, and he made it at the sacrifice of the souls of white women and white girls' (*News of the World*, 2 July 1923, cited in Kohn 1992: 158).

The aetiology of drug use by women has traditionally been examined in the context of prostitution where a familiar trope has been the innocent young woman as hapless victim, lured into prostitution by the 'evil doper' (Lemert 1951: 254–5). As noted by Bingham Dai in 1937, that 'the pimp in his attempt to entice a girl to his service not seldom "dopes" her and makes her an addict so that she will have to depend on him for her drug and thereby she becomes his woman is a matter of common knowledge' (Dai 1937: 136).

Such accounts perpetuate stereotypical images of women as weak and submissive; as incapable of exercising agency and unable to make any kind of choice in relation to drug use. As Campbell has pointed out in relation to criminological research on gangs, there has been 'until recently, a consistent tendency to view the girls as being led into crime through their sexual relationships with "bad" boys' (Campbell 1990: 56). This is due to the premiss that women define their worth almost exclusively in the domestic sphere and a belief in women's inability to form same-sex friendships (Campbell 1990: 56). These same assumptions underpin most research in relation to women and illicit drugs. Unlike criminology, where, for the most part, representations of women lawbreakers have vacillated between the volitional and inherently evil 'female criminal' and the silent, passive accomplice of male deviance, drug research has historically portrayed women as 'doing it all for love' (Millman 1975). Myths about women's 'natural' passivity and dependence condition the production of knowledge concerning the motivations for, and modes of, women's drug use.

Following the literature, this paper focuses on race/ethnic differences and differences between smokeable cocaine and heroin and cocaine hydrochloride (hereafter cocaine HCl) initiates in order to examine the social and cultural processes involved in becoming a woman drug user. This research suggests that although the complex situational and motivational dynamics that characterize female initiation are profoundly gendered, initiation cannot be reduced to the omnipotence of male others. Rather, women's experiences of initiation were mediated by many factors including the influence of same-sex peers, previous drug use experience, availability and cost of the drug, patterns of consumption and the reciprocal relationship with popular cultural images.

Initiation as a social process

Drug careers are not dissimilar to conventional careers in so far as they usually develop in stages (Becker 1963; Preble and Casey 1969; Waldorf 1973; Agar 1977). Neophytes are generally taught the 'cultural recipes' of drug use by trusted and experienced users, including the quantities to use, manners, customs, norms and rituals surrounding use, perceptions of the effects or 'high' and sanctions for inappropriate behaviours (Becker 1963; Zinberg 1984; Hamid 1990; Grund 1993). Most of these studies describe initiation as a 'ritualized' affair confined to familiar and relatively stable social milieus. Hamid (1990) has described this process of learning and teaching as a period of 'incubation' whereby the skills and rules of using new substances are developed and diffused among drug users.

Ironically, while this literature emphasizes the fundamentally social process of becoming a drug user, it simultaneously neglects what is often one of the most crucial structuring axes of social interaction – sex/gender.[2] As Pearson (1987) has noted in relation to heroin use: 'The role of friendship in helping to spread the heroin habit cannot be over-emphasized' (Pearson 1987: 11).

For the most part, the gendered composition of these friendship networks has been ignored. 'Friends' are generic. They are simply people – ungendered and unraced. Introduction to heroin via friendship networks is only one of many accounts provided by the women in this sample. The privileged significance afforded [male] peers in the initiation process has served to mask the extent of variation between sexes and across ethnic and racial groups and to overshadow the role of family and kin networks in facilitating initiation to drug use (but see Rubin and Comitas 1976; Moore 1991).

By contrast, where women have been the focus of detailed research, explanations have tended to be constructed almost exclusively in terms of family, kin and domestic variables (e.g. Gerstein, Judd and Rovner 1979). Here it is assumed, rather than documented, that men and women enact drug use within separate spheres. By viewing men in the context of peer groups/public life and women in terms of domestic settings or the private, drug research not only occludes women's roles as public citizens and men's roles within families but evades questions concerning the possible overlap between these spheres.

Women and initiation

Little is known about the contexts of women's initiation to cocaine. Greenleaf (1987) reports the results of a recent survey of callers to a cocaine hotline which claimed that 87 per cent of women were introduced to cocaine by men and that 65 per cent of women continued to receive cocaine as 'gifts' (Greenleaf 1987: 5). This is echoed by Greenleaf's own conclusion that 'most women are introduced [to cocaine] by men, whether it is on a date or via a platonic friendship' (1987: 101).

Although there is a paucity of contemporary empirical research on women and cocaine, several empirical studies have examined women's initiation to heroin. O'Donnell (1969) reported that while marriage to male addicts was related to subsequent initiation and addiction for previously non-addicted female partners, non-addicted men married to women addicts did not generally become addicts. Freeland and Campbell (1973) found that both men and women are typically introduced to drugs by men (see also Waldorf 1973). In research based on a sample of thirty women current or former treatment clients of a programme specializing in methadone maintenance, Gerstein, Judd and Rovner (1979) found that the presence of 'intimate' (primarily siblings or spouses) or 'casual' (peer group) others at first use differentiated subsequent patterns of use into high and low heroin consumption respectively. Asserting the primacy of kin group relations for women, these authors conclude that both the problem and the solution lie in family liaisons (Gerstein *et al.* 1979: 21).

Based on a sample of 180 matched pairs of institutionalized men and women, Rosenbaum (1981a) found that 'women addicts, for the most part, are introduced to heroin use by one man – a boyfriend or spouse' (1981a: 864). However, in later qualitative research with a sample of 100 women who were primarily active users, Rosenbaum suggests that women introduced to heroin by boyfriends or husbands tended to be older than women who initiated heroin use in other contexts. For the most part, these women were introduced to heroin use prior to the impact of the 'Women's Liberation Movement' and without involvement in the hippie scene or criminal activity (1981c: 31). Rosenbaum also found that initiation in this context held important consequences for subsequent patterns of use: 'After having been introduced to heroin by a man, the woman tends to immerse herself in his world and become an addict in far less time than it takes most men. She then builds up a more costly and sizeable habit than her male counterpart' (Rosenbaum 1981a: 875).

Assuming that women's initiation to heroin takes the form of 'immersion in the world of her man', some researchers have sought to examine the extent to which this may differ across class, racial and ethnic groups. Recent research suggests that a significant proportion of Mexican-American or Chicana women were introduced to drugs by their boyfriends or spouses (Anglin, Hser and McGlothlin 1987; Hser, Anglin and McGlothlin 1987; see also Long 1990). Using a sample of eighty Chicana ex-gang heroin users, Moore (1990) found that initiation to heroin was most likely to occur in social settings, with 46 per cent of the women first using heroin in a party situation, 38 per cent with a boyfriend or husband, 11 per cent with a relative and 5 per cent first using alone. Moore also notes that 17 per cent of these women concealed their first-timer status from the person who injected them and that comparatively few women reported being 'urged' to use heroin for the first time. However, in a separate study of two Chicano gangs in East Los Angeles and how they changed over time ($n = 106$ men and 52 women), Moore's research tends to confirm the conventional wisdom, suggesting that,

> Women [tecatas] are more likely to grow up in a household with an addicted brother or father. Women were also much more likely to have their heroin use bracketed by a mate: they tended to start heroin use with a boyfriend or husband, and, even though each liaison might be short-lived, the street world almost dictates that a tecata's next boyfriend will also be a heroin user. To some extent, then, *women's heroin use is enacted within a familial context*. It might be seen as a twisted version of the usual Mexican emphasis on family roles for women. (Moore 1991: 109, emphasis added.)

Miller's (1986) sample of Milwaukee 'street women' includes ten women for whom substance abuse provided a route to deviant street networks. Somewhat surprisingly given that only three of these women were Hispanic, Miller argues that,

> Hispanic women seem more likely to be introduced to hard drug use within their own extended households. The difference between Hispanic women and white women seems to be a matter of availability and the strength of competing norms governing use. Not only are the norms against use, especially among peers, weaker for Hispanic women, but the values that foster use are deeply embedded in the culture with which the young woman is likely to be surrounded. (Miller 1986: 113)

Miller suggests that, among Hispanics, extended households combine with an absence of cultural norms against use and the presence of pro-use cultural values to facilitate the initiation of women into drug use and deviant street networks (1986: 113). This contrasts sharply with previous research findings on the relationship of Hispanic cultures to drug use or its avoidance. For example, Fitzpatrick (199), in an ethnographic study of Puerto Rican communities in New York during the 1970s, found that, 'The most significant variable that emerged in the cases of the non-addicts was the extended family. . . It was this controlling and protecting network that was significantly related to the absence of addiction' (Fitzpatrick 1990: 104).

Upon initial examination these findings appear to be consistent with those of Moore's (1990) study of Chicana female heroin users who were ex-gang members (*n* = 80). Moore found that, in general, Chicanos in Los Angeles communities where heroin use is endemic did not ostracize their heroin users. However, many of the families of women heroin addicts – particularly the more conventional families – did in fact reject their addicted daughters, suggesting the operation of a sexual double standard. However, focusing on the differences between women from poor but conventional homes and women from 'cholo families', Moore suggests that women from more conventional families are more likely to experience problematic heroin use and street life. By contrast, women from families with a history of heroin use appear to have benefited from familial norms and limits governing use – even though few of these women actually initiated use within the family setting.

This research suggests that measures of family conventionality may be more important than either race/ethnicity *per se* or household composition in determining the degree to which women heroin users are rejected by their families and communities. Such findings represent a welcome departure from the great bulk of literature which seeks to characterize particular ethnic/racial groups and their family structures as pathological, dysfunctional and responsible for perpetuating successive drug epidemics in the United States. Indeed, as Moore suggests, the intergenerational transmission of established norms and values regarding drug use may serve to regulate consumption, resulting in, if not benign use, at least less problematic lifestyle correlates (see also Rubin and Comitas, 1976).

> Women from cholo families, with illegal incomes during childhood, are quite different. Few went overboard with heroin in this fashion. Ironically they sounded less deviant and more under social controls. Such families gave women something of a head start in the street life. Along with the gang, they provide a basic grounding in street roles. Women avoid the tragic discontinuity with other roles, and they are used to a greater degree of control over life circumstances. For one thing, if one's family is dealing, then heroin is less surrounded by chaos, and the women users may be less dependent on male partners. (Moore 1990: 141)

Nonetheless, the image of the woman drug user as dependent and passive is pervasive and finds considerable support in the literature. Although not representative of their major work, even articles by outstanding researchers such as Rosenbaum (1981a) and Moore (1991) manifest traces of what Naffine (1985) has called 'masculinity/femininity theory' or M/F theory. In the criminological context, M/F theory asserts that socialized masculinity and femininity account for the gender differential in offending. Although the linkage with M/F theory is mostly implicit in drug research, sometimes it is made explicit: 'Their [women's] subsequent usage is indicative of traditional role differentiation. The physical use of the drug is one of dependence, as is the situation in which women "turn on" – in the company of others, often sharing the actual injection device' (Rosenbaum 1981a: 864). Rosenbaum has sought to illustrate the extent to which traditional gender socialization operates to render women 'doubly dependent' in the drug world. However as Naffine has pointed out in relation to crime, 'although the feminists clearly take issue with the assumptions underlying Parsons' account of gender roles, in particular the implication that they are positively functional, they display tendencies to caricature and stereotype women in precisely the same way as the early "masculinity" theorists' (1985: 370–1). Whether implicit or explicit, the adoption of M/F theory in the drug field has overdetermined both research and theoretical conceptualization in relation to women's initiation to illicit drug use and subsequent patterns of consumption.

However, even within this literature there are important exceptions – at least for certain groups of women. For example, in the same article Rosenbaum (1981a) observed that 'black women tended not to lose control and sit back and let their spouses take care of them when they became addicted' (1981a: 868).[3] Pettiway (1987) also found that black women drug users had a reduced likelihood of committing illegal acts with other members of their domestic and criminal networks (Pettiway 1987). A promising direction for future research is suggested by Moore's previously noted study of women from 'cholo' families. As she concludes,

> The 'street person' addict stands in sharp contrast to these women from cholo families. Though the latter form only slightly more than ten percent of our sample, they are a significant social type in this subpopulation of Chicana gang-member addicts. In many ways they resemble male gang-member addicts in that their heroin use and scoring occur within fairly stable social networks. They do not seem to fit the gender deviance model. (Moore 1990: 142).

Sample and research methods

During 1990-92, I conducted ethnographic fieldwork in three Brooklyn (New York) neighbourhoods with women drug users. The only criteria for initial involvement in the study were to be *a.* women and *b.* crack smokers. Subjects were recruited through chain referral or 'snowball' sampling procedures (Biernacki and Waldorf 1981) and tape-recorded interviews were conducted with more than 200 women across the three study sites. Interviews were unstructured and lasted anywhere between half an hour and three hours. Each woman was paid $10 or equivalent per interview. The final data base for the study consisted of more than five thousand pages of transcribed interview narrative, several hundred pages of typed fieldnotes, a field diary and photographs, as well as personal letters, poems and drawings provided by individual women. Forty-five women in the principal study site formed a core group of 'key informants'. These women were all street-level drug users in one of the poorest neighbourhoods in New York City. Most were racial/ethnic minorities. Nearly all were homeless. Many were mothers and a large number were HIV positive. These women were both the perpetrators and victims of violence and all engaged in law-breaking – principally street-level sex work – as a means of supporting their drug consumption. The data presented here consists of repeated interviews and multiple field observations with these forty-five women over the three-year period. In addition, a small number of interviews and observations were undertaken in the primary research neighbourhood with female kin and male partners of women drug users.

Analysis

The women in this sample formed two groups: poly-drug users (intravenous drug users who also smoked crack cocaine) and those women who only smoked crack at the time of first interview. These groups also reflect substance of initiation, with all the women in the first category having initiated use with heroin or cocaine HCl and women in the second group initiating with cocaine freebase or crack cocaine. Freebase or alkaloidal cocaine is a derivative of adulterated cocaine HCl powder. Users inhale the fumes or 'smoke' it. Conversion to freebase also means the substance is no longer water-soluble and cannot be injected.

The mean age of women at first use was 18.85 years, with heroin and cocaine HCl initiates significantly younger (mean age 17.5) than cocaine freebase and crack initiates (mean age 20.2). Although street drug use often takes place within the context of social networks which are racially and ethnically heterogeneous, all of the women reported initiating drug use within the context of their own racial/ethnic group.

Race/ethnic differences in initiation

Table 1 presents women's accounts of persons present at their introductory experience. The majority of women, 25 or 26 per cent of the sample, initiated use within the context of a male–female dyad. However only seventeen of these women, or 38 per cent, were introduced by a boyfriend or husband. Of the remaining twenty women, two initiated use in the context of a mixed-sex group or social setting and eighteen women or 40 per cent initiated with other women. Of these eighteen women, fifteen initiated with one or more girlfriends, two with their sisters and one with her mother.

For Latina women, initiations in male–female dyads were the modal category with 70 per cent (*n* = 14/20) experiencing initial use with a male. For ten of these women (50 per cent), initiation occurred with a boyfriend or husband. A similar pattern appears for European Americans with six out of a total of nine women, or 66 per cent, initiating use with males. Five of these women (55 per cent) initiated use with either boyfriends or husbands.

While these data suggest that males continue to play a significant role in the initiation of both Latinas and European American women, as the women's accounts demonstrate, the relations involved took multiple forms and often decisions to initiate use (even within the context of a male–female dyad) were inscribed with multiple meanings. Although there were some women, like Yolanda, who initiated use with a neophyte male, this was atypical and most women initiated subsequent to a boyfriend or husband's use (see also Rosenbaum 1981a; 1981b). For Yolanda, a 38-year-old Latina, introduction to heroin occurred within the context of a very traditional relationship, where as she states, her husband was 'like her father'.

> My first apartment. . . That's where it all started. All the drugs, that's where the first time, you know, the drug scene started. We, you know, he had a job. He used to work for the Navy Yard. I had the kids. But you

Table 1: Race/ethnic differences in initiation

	Latina		Afro-American		Euro-American	
	No.	%	No.	%	No.	%
Boyfriend/husband	10	50	2	12	5	56
Girlfriend	3	15	11	69	1	11
Brother	2	10	0	0	1	11
Father	1	5	1	6	0	0
Mixed-sex group	1	5	1	6	0	0
Male associate	1	5	0	0	1	11
Male cousin	0	0	1	6	0	0
Sister	1	5	0	0	1	11
Mother	1	5	0	0	0	0
Total	20	100	16	99	9	100

know someone always comes along and says, 'Oh, you know, you want to make some money?'. . .you[re] young. It sounds good, but we didn't know that drugs was a habit forming thing. All we knew was that it could make you some money. So he had a good job, and I didn't know nothing about being a housewife, but I use to keep the house. . . He was like my father – a father figure. He was a strong, strong person and I, to him, I was like a doll, a china doll. He use to dress me, I had real long hair, so to him I was the most gorgeous little thing he seen, and I was a virgin. . . So, when we had the two kids, things were fine until the drug thing started. When he fell into jail, see, when the drug wasn't there that's when we realize that it was . . .habit forming.

Similarly, Debbie, a 31-year-old European American woman initiated (heroin) use within the context of a relationship with a man she very much loved and admired.

When I was about nineteen I got into dope, and by the time I was twenty-two, I have a daughter. . . I met her father when I was fourteen and fell very much in love with him. It was probably the one thing in life I loved. . . Well, I started doing dope with my daughter's father. He was brilliant. . . He had the first loft I had ever seen on the lower east side. He had a hundred and eighty IQ. He was a guru type person, he was absolutely brilliant.

Blanca, a 24-year-old Latina, also initiated her (crack) use within the context of a relationship with a live-in boyfriend. Not only was her boyfriend an experienced user, but he exerted considerable pressure on Blanca by, among other things, blowing the smoke into her mouth.

I started using crack. We was livin'. . .in a little two family house. My boyfriend was doing it, and he would sometimes blow the smoke in my mouth; but it never did nothing to me so I wouldn't pay no mind to it. . . I would fight about it but it would go in through one ear and go out through the other – they really don't care when they're on that. . . I was pregnant at this time. I didn't know what it really felt like. . . And I tried it, yeah. But I thought that maybe I, just by trying it, by the fun, you know, just to find out what it is like, so I can say 'Yeah, I know what it's like', I wouldn't do nothing. They kept telling me 'Naw, you do it once, you're going to do it twice' and I was like 'No, I won't'; and yes, I did.

Most women however, were not pressured by their husbands or boyfriends to initiate drug use.[4] More often, initiation in this context was, as Rosenbaum also found, the product of a woman's desire to understand or share what her partner was experiencing. Only two of the women in my study fitted Rosenbaum's category of women for whom initiation resulted from the ready availability of heroin due to the partner's dealing activities and none of the women reported initiating heroin use because they wanted a share of what drained the household resources (Rosenbaum 1981c: 31). Perhaps most Latina and European American women's experiences are best captured by what Moore has described as women partners of male addicts who 'seemed to just slide into use, partly out of curiosity and partly out of boredom' (Moore 1990: 138). As the following quote from Candy, a 41-year-old European American woman indicates, these women epitomize the 'if you can't beat 'em, join 'em' approach: 'He was always doing it [heroin]. There was never time for me. There was no sex, there was no nothing.' Similarly, Jo-Beth, a 23-year-old European American, recalled that although initially she thought she could help her addict boyfriend, her curiosity about the attraction heroin held for him eventually got the better of her. And while he did not pressure her, she claims that her boyfriend was 'very happy' when she became an 'addict':

I started doing heroin with my ex-boyfriend. . . I just happened to get involved with him through friends, and he was addicted to heroin. . . Like two years before I met him. He was shooting it. . . I guess I tried to help him and I couldn't, so I accepted the fact that he did that and then I got curious about it and I tried it. . . He's like an evil person. He, he was very happy when I became a heroin addict.

For a small minority of women, although initiating drug use was done 'behind their boyfriend's backs', the relationship was clearly integral to the decision to begin using. Most of these women viewed their decision to initiate as a way to ameliorate the growing distance that their partner's use was causing – as a way of maintaining a relationship that was important to them. As Bee, a 31-year-old Latina put it,

> To be honest I was about 16, 17 years old. My boyfriend introduced me to marijuana. . . then I started with drugs, I mean with glue. Then after glue I started with valiums. I was 19. I kept on getting high with a little bit of pot, a little bit of glue and the valiums. I was feeling out of sight. I felt like I could do whatever I wanted. I was free. . . I was happy but I had problems with my boyfriend because he was trying to leave me. After he got my virginity he wanted to leave me. But the only way I figured I could hold on to him is if I got high with him, and I don't be boring with him he still probably stay with me. . . I said I'm going to try it, fuck it. If Miguel does it I'm going to do it too.

In contrast to both Latinas and European Americans, African American women evinced a distinctive pattern of initiation in female dyads or triads. Among the sixteen African American women, only five initiations occurred in mixed-sex dyads and only two of these were with boyfriends or husbands. A majority of eleven women, or 69 per cent of African American women, initiated use with one or more girlfriends. Below, Sissy, a 34-year-old African American woman, recounts her first experience of heroin use with a teenage girlfriend.

> I was like about fourteen. I had a girlfriend – she died of AIDS a few years back. . . I was helping her get the party together in the basement, and she was sniffing – this something out of a little white bag. So I was so gullible – I wanted some, right? But she says 'No, no. Don't mess with it.' The phone rang and like an idiot, she put down the bag, and like an idiot, I picked up the bag, and before I knew it I snorted it all up. She pitched a bitch, and she gave me money, you know, to go out and cop. I knew the guy that was selling it, Vincent, lived right around the corner – cop a bag. . .

The experiences of Jonelle and Princess, both 32-year-old African American women, are somewhat unique in that both women were sexworkers prior to their initiation to heroin use. However, their stories illustrate that, within this context at least, women can be put under considerable pressure to initiate drug use, not only by men, but by female peers. Jonelle was introduced to heroin at age sixteen by her co-workers on a Chicago prostitution stroll. As she told me:

> When I started I was messin' wid syrup, cough syrup. I used to get high jus' on Sundays. I was sixteen. . . Den all the other pros-tutes I used ta be with, they used to be like 'C'mon les' go get high' [on heroin]. . . I dn' wanna go even when I went. I wanna keep them from saying 'you a faggot', whatever.

Similarly, Princess was introduced to heroin by her girlfriends whilst working a prostitution stroll in lower Manhattan.

> . . .my friends used to. . .snort dope. I would never do it. . . 'cos it was a bad feeling, jus' y'know getting nauseous and all that. . . till one day I bought a bag on my own. And then it started from there. . . [So it wasn't like men, it was women you first started getting high with?] No, it was women. . . Workin' women.

Keisha, a 26-year-old African American, was also introduced to smokeable cocaine (in the form of coke cigarettes) by a girlfriend. As she recalled,

> Dey were called coolies. Coke cigarettes. I decided to come back up here [New York] to live. Thas when I got on welfare. I learned it from a friend o' mine. . . we used to sit aroun' and' I used ta see her jus' take coke. . . An' thas how I learned.

These apparent 'women-centred' initiations are discussed in detail below where they are located firmly within the immediate context of the crack culture. However, it is important to note the existence of a number of cultural and historical factors which may render African American women more likely than other women to initiate drug use with female companions. The impact of institutionalized racism in the United States has given African American women a long history both as economic providers and purchasers. The significance, strength and durability of bonds between female kin and women-centred domestic networks has also been well documented. In addition, while African American women in this study were no less likely than their Latina counterparts to have grown up in low-income urban settings, their families of origin were more likely to evince fairly stable residence patterns in impoverished neighbourhoods characterized by the long-standing presence of a strong informal economy and at least some exposure to drug sales and use. Such findings clearly underscore the need for future research along the lines of that undertaken by Moore (1990) and referred to above.

Differences between smokeable cocaine initiates and heroin/cocaine HCl initiates

Research on the developmental cycles of drug epidemics suggests that a stable and protracted incubation period and the presence of an experienced user culture are necessary pre-conditions for the safest or 'most benign' introduction of a substance to a population (Hamid 1989, 1992, forthcoming; see also Becker 1963; Zinberg 1984). During the 1980s a rapid succession of cocaine products were introduced into economically and socially destabilized inner-city neighbourhoods in the United States before appropriate rules and norms for their use could be properly developed and institutionalized. As Hamid has argued, concentrated in neighbourhoods which, in the decades preceding the advent of crack, suffered a massive exodus of human and economic capital, 'the activities of drug [cocaine] users and distributors accelerated or facilitated these transformations and expressed them at the ideological level' (Hamid 1990: 68).

Subsequent research has confirmed the groundbreaking work of Hamid (1989, 1990, 1992, forthcoming). Fagan and Chin (1991) found that the learning processes during crack initiation, unlike that for other drugs, involved techniques for maximizing the high rather than safe use and appropriate behaviours, suggesting that informal controls were either neutralized or defeated. Most respondents in their study of male and female drug users ($n = 559$), including crack smokers, were introduced to their primary drug by friends (86.2 per cent) or a spouse or family member (21.5 per cent).[5]

Cheung, Erickson and Landau (1991) in a sample of seventy-eight Canadian crack smokers, found that men played a more active role in introducing neophytes to the drug than women (1991: 124). Some three-quarters of respondents were initiated to crack by males and almost 20 per cent were introduced by women, although only a quarter of the sample were women. Only 10.3 per cent were introduced by a spouse, common-law husband or 'intimate friend'. However it is unclear how many of these were women. These researchers found that, unlike cocaine HCl and marijuana users (Erickson and Murray 1989), only 30 per cent of respondents reported heavy peer use (Cheung, Erickson and Landau, 1991).

As noted previously, the few studies that have been done on initiation to crack or smokeable forms of cocaine tend to either ignore women or, where women are included in samples, they remain marginal to the analysis. Williams (1992) has suggested that most of the women in his 'crackhouse' study were initiated to crack use by boyfriends who were dealers and had access to large quantities of the drug. However, in the present sample there was only one smokeable cocaine initiate whose boyfriend was a dealer – Christina, a 28-year-old Latina – and her story was atypical. As she told me,

> Then I found another guy, I wasn't into drugs yet. I found this other guy . . . a drug dealer. . . He use to take care of me and my son. He use to give us everything. I was a happy, normal woman. I use to work as a dental assistant. I was a dental assistant. . . making $9 a hour, and he has a spot [for dealing drugs] that use to make 22G's a day, or every two days. . . boy he use to make good money. We had it made. We had white rugs, we had a beautiful apartment. My son had everything and me too. But, all of a sudden, he started smoking weed with crack inside. And that's when everything started, so you know one day he told me, 'Try it this one night.' There was a party at the house. You know, everybody left. And he told me, 'Look, try it. Try it. Smoke a weed.' I said 'Naw, man, I can't take the smell of it.' A headache – he kept on and on until I tried it. I tried it and the next day I tried a little more, the third day I smoked a whole joint, and the fourth day I was smoking blunts, and then he came to see I was into this shit. . . The spot went down, and down, and down the drain. I lost my job . . . and I just left. I left everything behind.

In order to examine whether there were any differences in patterns of initiation between women who initiated heroin or cocaine HCl use prior to their use of crack and women who initiated with smokeable forms of cocaine (including crack), the data were analysed by group. Group 1 consists of thirty-one women (69 per cent of the sample), all of whom were intravenous heroin and/or cocaine users prior to initiating crack use. Twenty-two of these women initiated use by sniffing heroin, five by snorting cocaine, three skin-popped heroin and one skin-popped cocaine. Group 2 consists of fourteen women (31 per cent of the sample) who used crack exclusively. Crack was the first experience of smokeable cocaine for a majority of nine women. Of these nine women, five began smoking crack in the stem and four started out smoking wullas – marijuana cigarettes sprinkled with crack. Four women were introduced to smokeable forms of cocaine through freebasing and one woman smoked coke cigarettes prior to commencing crack use.

Table 2 illustrates the differences between these two groups. Firstly, it must be noted that there are no European Americans among the

Table 2: Differences between smokeable cocaine initiates and
heroin/cocaine HCl initiates

| | Group 1 | | Group 2 | |
	No.	%	No.	%
Boyfriend/husband	16	52	1	7
Girlfriend	7	23	8	57
Brother	1	3	2	14
Father	1	3	1	7
Mixed-sex group	2	6	0	0
Male associate	1	3	1	7
Male cousin	0	0	1	7
Sister	2	6	0	0
Mother	1	3	0	0
Total	31	99	14	99

Note Group 1: women who had initiated heroin, cocaine HCl and smokeable
cocaine prior to crack use. Group 2: women who used crack exclusively.

smokeable cocaine initiates. The European American women in this
study all initiated intravenous heroin and cocaine HCl use prior to
their use of crack. The figures suggest that heroin and cocaine HCl
initiates were more likely than smokeable cocaine initiates to
experience first use in the context of a male and in particular with a
boyfriend or husband. Of Group 1, sixteen women (52 per cent) were
introduced by a boyfriend or husband and an overall total of twenty
women (65 per cent) were introduced by a male.

For Group 2, initiation appears more likely to occur in the context
of other women. Out of fourteen women, eight (57 per cent) initiated
use with girlfriends and only one woman was introduced to
smokeable cocaine by a boyfriend or husband. Six of the eight women
who initiated use with girlfriends were African American while five of
the seven Latinas started in mixed-sex dyads.

Previous research has found that, despite its widespread availability,
crack is not likely to attract drug neophytes (Fagan and Chin 1991;
Johnson 1991). The present study confirms this, with thirty-six
women, or 80 per cent of the sample, having initiated either heroin,
cocaine HCl or freebase cocaine use prior to commencing crack use.
The remaining women had all used alcohol and smoked marijuana
prior to initiating crack use. There has also been considerable
speculation as to whether crack acts as a 'gateway' drug by facilitating

the progression of former neophytes to other drugs. This sample provides little evidence for such claims with only two women out of the fourteen smokeable cocaine initiates 'progressing' to heroin use during the course of the study. What the experiences of the women in this sample overwhelmingly indicate is that crack, rather than acting as a gateway, is readily incorporated into an existing repertoire of poly-drug consumption by experienced users (Johnson, 1991).

The available literature also suggests that there will be substantial differences between heroin and cocaine HCl initiates and smokeable cocaine initiates in terms of motivations and reasons for initiating use. In response to probes as to their reasons for initiating use, women implicated a range of factors including: curiosity, peer influence, relationships, avoidance of needles, depression, financial or emotional pressure and the 'high'. Smokeable cocaine initiates were more likely to report curiosity, peer influence, the 'high' or 'rush' and the drug's perceived 'sociability' than either heroin or cocaine HCl initiates. Heroin and cocaine HCl initiates tended to focus on intimates, relationships, external pressures and emotional problems.

Although few women talked specifically about age, emotional status or a lack of material resources as contributing to their decision to initiate heroin or cocaine HCl use, it is clear that these elements were contributing factors in many cases in the sense that they rendered women vulnerable. Slim, a 29-year-old African American woman who was twelve years old when she used heroin for the first time, provides a good example of what I call the 'vulnerability' thesis.

> [So, tell me the first time you tried dope, the very first time, you remember that?] I sick as damn dog. [Where were you?] Screwin'. [Laughs uproariously] [So you were with a man.] He said it wasn' gonna hurt but I was a virgin too. [You did it all at once.] Thas right. [Laughing] And he lied on both counts – it did hurt and I got sick as a dog. Mmm hmm. Then I got pregnant. [What off the first time? Oh man, you caught 'em all at once.] I was twelve.

Similarly, Rosa, a 31-year-old Latina, illustrates how young women who are runaways may be particularly vulnerable to illicit drug use.

> I was just sixteen. . . Well my father. . . was punching me a lot. And one day I just left the house and didn't come back to the house. . . I was, lost in New York City, you know, catch the train. I was sleeping, you know, start living on the train, I be riding on the train. . . I end up going to the Bronx.

Yeah, so that's where I end and started being a junkie, and stayed with the people, you know the junkie people.

Aiesha, a 24-year-old African American woman, ran away from her home in the Midwest at age eleven with a man fifteen years her senior.

[How long you been using drugs now?] Since I was about 12. . . I started off with heroin. . . I was sniffin' at first, and then I squeezed. . . My man hit me the first time.

Although Jenny, a 25-year-old European American, had experimented with other drugs in the context of her relationship with a violent and abusive husband, it was not until after they split up that she began to use heroin, cocaine HCl and crack. Evicted from her apartment in Queens because she could no longer afford to pay the rent, Jenny and her two children were made homeless and wandered the streets before eventually being relocated to a single-room occupancy (SRO) hotel in mid-town Manhattan. Her story clearly illustrates the way in which social and economic factors converge with situational factors such as the availability of drugs and the proximity of experienced [usually male] users.

After I split up with him I couldn't pay the rent, and he wouldn't give me no money unless I let him stay with me. So I had to take him to court. But in the meantime, I still couldn't pay my rent. So I went down to Welfare, and Welfare wouldn't pay that amount. So they got me in the welfare hotel . . . And it was like pimps, crack, dope, you know, drug hotel – pimp hotel . . . I never knew anything about this stuff you know 'cause I came from Queens, in a quiet area. . . He conned me into staying with him, and I did you know. I was vulnerable, hungry, you know. I lost my welfare, and they were kicking me out of the hotel; and he had a room in the same hotel. . . It wasn't like welfare benefits. He just paid to keep that room and I was staying there because I had no other place to stay, and then he turned me out to the streets. I was sniffing dope, coke and smoking a lot of crack. . . and that's how I became like really hooked because I had a habit and I didn't know.

For one woman, even though the actual initiation took place with a girlfriend, her decision to use drugs was characterized by emotional vulnerability in the wake of losing her children and a recently failed relationship. As Carmen, a 31-year-old Latina, told me,

I broke up with my boyfriend, and because I found out he was shooting up, and I wanted to see what he was so in love with so I tried it myself. . . I met this girl Maria and we went up in her house, and she got me off. . . She didn't know that I was new to it. . . I got very sick. But I loved it. Yeah, 'cause I did too much. You know I liked it at first, but then I started gettin' nauseous. . . I just kept doin' it – yeah because, uh, I was hurting inside – and I didn't want to do nothin' but get high because I didn't have my kids, and I didn't have the man that I was in love with, and I was just like falling apart.

Lady B. is a 32-year-old European American heroin initiate. The product of an affluent upper-middle-class Jewish upbringing, Lady B. got into heroin and later cocaine freebase in California, where for a time she was 'living large'. Her initiation to heroin, however, was prompted by a combination of factors, including the break-up of a long-standing relationship, the loss of her apartment and depression.

It was at the end of me and this guy for three years, when he sliced up my clothes 'cause I wouldn't marry him . . . That's when I started using, but I didn't start on my own. This girl that was supposedly my best friend – started me. We were in her apartment. She lived in the Hills. She was my supposedly best friend. She was getting high on dope – she was shooting it. You know, whatever – she's the one that introduced me to like um, [famous person]. But I introduced her to [famous person]. So I wasn't doing anything like that yet, but I was dealing drugs in quantity, and ah, you know, as I said, I lost my job, and then this incident happened with the guy I was living with, and so it's – everything was happening at once. Of course I – I ended up losing my apartment 'cause this guy moved all my things out, anyway I was getting depressed and one day I said, 'Okay, I'll try it.'

There were relatively few differences between the groups in relation to the setting for first use with the great majority of initiations occurring in private indoor settings. Significantly, while crack initiates were not more likely to initiate in a public space they were more likely to experience a rapid 'progress[ion] to the streets' and accordingly, to consumption in public places. Drug-using subcultures have historically displayed strong norms against the public consumption of drugs, especially intravenous consumption, and in particular, when the consumer is a woman.[6] Crack is widely perceived as responsible for the breakdown or erosion of these norms. As Jonelle, an African American heroin initiate told me,

I jus' started bein' aroun' – seein' people do dat like since I came to New York. I mean, they're so open down here. Where I'm from you don' see –

you don' walk pass an' see people smokin' outside or stickin' needles and stuff in their arms. . . I saw somebody in tha' res'room across the street smokin' crack. It's like. . . one time a guy was givin' samples. . . an' you hadda tell 'em you shoot dope to get a sample, so I was sick I said 'Well I do it, I do it, I shoot dope.' So he said 'Well, do it, ya gotta do it now.' I said 'I'm not gonna do it right here'. . . Later on that night when I started sayin' yeah, he say 'Ya know what, I respec' you fa dat. An' I'm sorry about, y'know.' He say, 'I guess I used to women, if dey messin' wid it, y'know dey gotta shoot it right dere on da corner.'

Heroin and cocaine HCl initiates also appeared more likely to have been *given* their first taste of the drug rather than smokeable cocaine initiates. A minority of women in both groups recalled either exchanging or alluding to the possibility of sexual services in return for their introductory experience. As Linda, a 31-year-old European American heroin and cocaine HCl initiate recounted,

I was about fifteen. My sister got me started on it, 'cause we were hanging out on Delancy, right? Yeah, Delancy Street in Manhattan. And, she wanted to get high, so she got me high first, right?. . . So, she started me off. We were hanging out with these two guys, two big dealers, and they wanted to go out with me, 'cause I was young. So, I went out with them, 'cause my sister wanted to get some more stuff. . . I was curious. I wish I was never curious, but. . . they had something on them.

Or as Connie, a 25-year-old Latina told me,

Well I went to a club. . . I went in and older people than me was sniffing, and – this older man came up to me and offered me a blow, and I said 'I don't use it.' He said 'Try it. It will make you feel good.' I said 'Well, let me try it.' And I sniffed it. I kept on sniffing, and sniffing, and sniffing that night, till the next day. [Tell me about this guy though, how come he was giving it to you?] He liked me, right. [Yeah, he wanted sex or something?] Well, I wasn't going to give him sex. [But that's what he – that's what he, had in his mind though, right?] Right. There were a whole bunch of them offering me. . . And I'm not gonna lie, sometimes I use to go with big guys with a lot of coke to hotels. We use to have fun parties.

Kizzy was one of four smokeable cocaine initiates who purchased crack on the occasion of first use, although ostensibly she was purchasing the drug for her male cousin.

Oh well, here come D. [cousin], the destroyer wi' 'is crack an' reefer. 'Oh you wann smoke a wulla?' I say, 'Wulla, what the fuck is a wulla?' He said 'It's crack an' reefer.' I say, 'What?' An' I smoked it an' I said, 'Oh I don' like this, take this shit back, gimme the reefer joint and I smoke dat.' At that time I din know what de effects was o' what ta look for. So I'm spendin my money and he happy 'cos he's hooked, you know, he's like a fiend.

Although evidence was not collected on a systematic basis, this study suggests that heroin and cocaine HCl initiates were just as likely as smokeable cocaine initiates to report insignificant time lags between first and second episodes of use. As Peggy, a 34-year-old European American cocaine HCl and heroin initiate told me,

And, I loved that. I loved that feeling! It was like nobody could touch me, you know. So, the next day, I did a bag, and the next day. . . I just kept doing it. [But then, you were dependent on him to cop it for you?] At first, but I'm very independent person. So, within three or four days. . . I'd be down there myself doing my own thing.

Or, as Rachel, a 35-year-old European American heroin initiate, put it,

You know, so finally one day he gave me. . . He said 'Fuck it', and he went and got it. I used the whole bag, and I said, 'I don't feel this. I want more.' He said 'Well, wait.' 'Hold up. No, I don't feel it. I want more', and about three minutes later the trip came. My belly slipped, and, uh, it was the only drug that I could say that I fell in love, you know. The warmth, you know. I like that trip. I loved it. I threw up all over the place. It was the most wonderful feeling I felt in my whole life. I loved it. From that day on I never stopped doing dope. I mean there have been times that I have stopped, I might have been in jail or whatever.

However, the time between first and subsequent episodes of use does not provide an accurate measure of 'dependency' because, as heroin initiates often commented, obtaining a 'habit' was hard work. As Debbie recalled,

It took me about three years to become strung out, I mean three years of doing it every day. I worked hard at becoming strung out. I wanted to become strung out. People aren't born dope fiends, they are made into that. It is not as easy to become strung out as people might have you believe.

Similarly, although none of the smokeable cocaine initiates recounted the arduous process described by Debbie and other heroin users, this study produced little evidence that crack induced the 'instant addiction' for which it has become notorious.

The literature also suggests that different classes of initiate will display differences in terms of the perceived positive and negative aspects of drug use.[7] Initially, most heroin initiates reported negative effects in terms of being sick on the occasion of first use but persisted in order to secure more pleasurable effects over time. Many of these women reported that they loved the feeling of being 'cut off' and removed from the problems and pressures of life. Others spoke of the glowing feeling or warmth. Dee Dee, a 29-year-old African American woman who had previously snorted cocaine, simply like the 'down head'.

> [Tell me about the first time you tried heroin.] I was giving my father some cocaine and he said that he would give me something to try. And we exchanged and it turned out that he gave me heroin to snort. And he told me that when you get that nasty taste in your throat, thas when you feel it. And thas when I started feelin high, and I liked that better. I did it with the cocaine but the heroin still overpowered the coke and I could really feel it. I liked it. Thas when I discovered I liked the down head better than the up head.

For most, but not all heroin and cocaine HCl initiates, initiation was a protracted process because they commenced use as sniffers and often took considerable periods of time before 'progressing' to either skin-popping or mainlining the drug. As sniffers, most women were aware of the symbolic potency attached to shooting up or 'getting off'. Although economic considerations also weighed heavily, a major shift in perception usually accompanied the decision to move from sniffing to injecting. Interestingly, none of the smokeable cocaine initiates mentioned the fact that it did not require intravenous administration as a positive feature, although it is likely that this factor played a part in some women's initial decisions to use. Given that all but one of these women were cigarette smokers and all had previously smoked marijuana, smoking cocaine clearly did not necessitate the major psychological or symbolic shift that often precedes the intravenous administration of drugs. As Boy told me, she was frightened by needles.

> I'm scared of dat. [What are you scared about?] I don' know, the consequences. I don' know, it just doesn't seem right to me. I be scared of needles, period.

Most smokeable cocaine initiates claimed that initially crack had many positive attributes. Among these were its cheap unit cost, widespread availability and the rapid, intense high. However, a minority of women reported not really feeling anything when they first started using crack – exemplifying the literature on the 'learned effects' of drug use (Becker 1963; Zinberg 1984). As Yolanda recalled,

> But when I first started smoking crack – I didn't know – I didn't feel nothing. Nothing at all. I use' to say 'You know this is a very stupid hit.' The thing was the guy. . . didn't teach me how to smoke.

The bulk of smokeable cocaine initiates also reported that – at least initially – the drug stimulated or 'motivated' them and enhanced their sociability. However, smokeable cocaine initiates were more likely than either heroin or cocaine HCl initiates to mention and elaborate on the rapid onset and intense nature of negative consequences in relation to their drug use. Most of the smokeable cocaine initiates recounted in considerable detail the ways in which crack had led them to do things which they found degrading and were ashamed of, including sexwork. As Boy recalled,

> It [crack] progressed more women out on the street. You see things you never seen before. . . Changin' clothes inna street. Y'know shit dat females would never do, dey do now. Y'know, dat you would never see before. In dis day an' time you see now.

In particular, the perception that crack use leads people to steal from their families was a recurrent theme among the freebase and crack initiates. None of the heroin or cocaine HCl initiates mentioned this. The following account from Keisha illustrates its strength.

> I said, what is dis all about. Everybody say it's so good. But den dey say, when de girls get ta smokin' crack dey start stealin' stuff from dere parent. Uh uh. I will never steal. I could never steal from no one. . . The firs' time, I took a fall. Guy said pull real slowly (demonstrates a slow pull), like takin' in an inhale of a breath. An' 'e say exhale it out. An' ma head started spinnin'. It was like – Whoa, was goin' on? An' he said, 'Issa min' game now. Don' go home an' go steal from no one.'

Boy's account illustrates the guilt and complex emotions that inhere when collective folklore becomes individual reality.

Dis morning I was in my mother's house and I had to leave because I was on the verge of stealing something and I know when I get to dat point I walk out. . . I have been through where you suck dicks and shit and it's not me. I have been where you steal from your mother, my sister, I have even got down to stealing my fuckin' baby's milk a while back. . . But can you change it? Can you come back home? Hey Boy you did dis for a fuckin' cap, a three minute high and it's gone. What da fuck you gonna do now? You can't go home now so I'm going to stay here out on the street.

However, both smokeable cocaine and heroin and cocaine HCl initiates agreed that, in the long run, using drugs had had a negative effect on their lives and relationships and estranged them from their families. As Boy said,

It destroyed ma life. It messed wi' ma kids. Ma family, it caused me problems with dat. If I wasn' smokin' I would have dem [kids]. Y'know, in dat way. An' far as my family, y'know, if I wasn' smokin' we would be closer.

Esmeralda, a 28-year-old Latina heroin initiate, had six children, five of whom were in foster care. During the course of the study Esmeralda entered a detoxification facility, stopped using drugs and became a regular at Narcotics Anonymous meetings. She found an apartment, regained custody of her children and gave birth to a seventh child. As she told me after she stopped getting high,

It [drugs] damages a lot of areas in your life in general. First of all it's your home, your family, people in general, your friends, your education, your health, your self-respect and your self-esteem. Those are everything you lose on the illicit drug.

There were few differences between the groups with respect to the women's perceptions of the effects of their drug use on their relationships with their children. As Esmeralda recalled,

When I was getting high I had control over my kids and the reason I say that is because they had fear. . . To me the drugs was the most important thing in my life. Without it I could not function. . . There were times like I stayed home, my house was like what you call a shooting gallery OK, so you get high. I didn't care if people were smoking in front of my kids.

However, smokeable cocaine initiates were more likely to feel that they were being judged and punished in their roles as mothers, and not without good reason (Maher 1990, 1992). As Blanca, a 24-year-old Latina who had five children and was also pregnant during fieldwork, told me,

> I lost a lot. I lost my apartment; I lost my kids. I know people weren't respecting us like they use to, you know, everything was 'Well, you're crackheads. You're crackheads. You're this, you're that. Look, you lost your kids', and 'Oh look, she don't have her kids with her. Why? She's using crack.'

Smokeable cocaine initiates also spoke at length about the negative effects on their physical well-being and in particular, rapid and sustained weight loss and a perceived decrease in their physical attractiveness.[8] Smokeable cocaine initiates also reported a quicker progression to the streets than heroin and cocaine HCl initiates. As Keisha saw it,

> Dere's a lotta girls out dere dat trick for smokin' crack, but dey don' take no care. Dey not healthy. Dey don' eat no food. Dey not takin' care dey hair. Dey not takin' care deyself. Dey pickin'. Dey layin' out in de street.

None of the women reported experiencing drug-induced feelings of violence or aggression although a minority of smokeable cocaine initiates reported violence by boyfriends or husbands whilst under the influence of crack. Most of the women also had experiences with violent dates, some of whom were also crack users (see Maher and Curtis 1992). As Kizzy, a 24-year-old African American smokeable cocaine initiate, told me,

> He [boyfriend] started buggin' out. . . He actually put me through da glass window. He god mad 'cos he wanted a hit.

Smokeable cocaine and cocaine HCl initiates were also more likely to have experienced paranoid feelings than heroin initiates. However, a powerful common sense among the women was that crack affected different people differently, and as a consequence, was a highly unpredictable drug. As Yolanda explained,

> Some can't speak, some act [like] they're paranoid. Some people think they got – they got things on their clothes. You know, and I said 'What is it? Is it their mind? Is there some kind of small thing in their heads?' That's what they should experiment, to find out why is it that everybody gets a different reaction – of it.

As a group, the women were more likely to attribute negative effects or consequences to their crack use than to either heroin, cocaine HCl or cocaine freebase. As Debbie put it,

> The crack is the ultimate evil in terms of drugs. Crack took me down faster in two years than dope did in ten. Crack is by far the ultimate evil.

While women who were heroin, cocaine HCl or cocaine freebase initiates had experienced ill effects in terms of deterioration of physical health, family life and economic position prior to crack use, they clearly felt that these effects were exacerbated once they began to use crack, confirming the limited power and partial nature of pharmacological explanations. That many of the women had considerable experience with cocaine HCl use prior to initiating crack use confirms that drug effects are mediated by, among other things, modes of ingestion (Waldorf *et al.* 1991) and patterns of consumption (Hamid, forthcoming).

Compared to just over one-fifth of heroin and cocaine HCl initiates, more than half the women who initiated use with smokeable cocaine did so in the company of other women. These women-centred initiations were the dominant mode of introduction to smokeable cocaine for the women in this sample. Initiation in the context of other women may reflect an adaptive strategy in the face of the purported and much publicized sex/crack nexus and its consequences for women. In contrast to both media and scientific reports of rampant female 'hypersexuality' in the context of crack use, none of the women reported that crack acted as a sexual stimulant or enhancement. Below, Boy articulates both her own feelings and the broader resistance of women crack users to this nexus.

> He'd be – ya wanna make love? Get the fuck away from me. I don' wanna make love . . . you can get five hundred people and five hundred people can smoke . . . And every five hundred people will have a differen' reaction. One will start pick onna floor, one of 'em migh' ac' violent. One might start talkin' a lot, one might feel sexy. It reacts on everybody differen'.

I went on to ask Boy specifically about media claims that crack stimulates women's sexual appetites.

> It's a crocka shit. . . They're not doin' it fa da feeling and then half the time they not doing it because dey want to. All while dey humpin' an' pumpin' their man, they're thinkin' about – Man I wish I could hurry up an' jerk da

fuck off or somethin', 'cos I wanna go get ma fuckin' shit – thas the main line. . . You enjoy makin' da money, you enjoy smokin' da crack, but you do not enjoy standin' out there makin' fifty dates – fuckin' to get it, but das the only way you know how. . . Dey enjoy da money and da high, dey don' enjoy doin' it, y'know, but iss somethin' they have ta do. If dey want dat hit ya have to gimme a blow job.

Users' perceptions of effects are mediated by social, economic, cultural and political variables. These effects both structure, and are structured by, cultural representations. It is clear that smokeable cocaine initiates are both aware of, and influenced by, media accounts and broader cultural imagery as well as by their own experiences of male behaviour within such contexts – which may to a large extent be a product of these same cultural representations. In the absence of a stable incubation period and an experienced user culture (Hamid 1990, 1992), the perceived effects of crack may be as much structured by broader cultural discourse in relation to crack as by the users themselves – which is to say that if men are repeatedly told that (at the minimum) the pharmacology of crack sexually arouses women (and increases male potency) then they will act accordingly.

Keisha, who recalled her initiation to smokeable cocaine with a girlfriend (above), went on to initiate crack use with a male associate. Here she explains why she prefers to smoke crack in the company of women:

See when I started smokin' I never smoked by myself. I always started wid a guy firs'. Den I notice, guys get choosy. So I sat down an' started smokin' wid females. Dey buy dey own, I buy my own an' we jus' siddown an' party. [It's different, smoking with women to smoking with men?] Yeah. 'Cos men get horny behind it. . . See men have imagination of sex. Sex dis, sex dat. When dey see a female. . . – Oh boy, I'm ready ta go screw somebody now. Oh no, not I.

Keisha's comments were reflected in many women's accounts, suggesting a relationship between women's perceptions of men as undesirable smoking partners and the fact that initiation with girlfriends was the dominant category for smokeable cocaine initiates. Many women spoke to me during the course of the study about how, given a choice, they preferred to smoke crack with other women. Most of the women were of the opinion that if they had control of, or access to, either quantities of the drug or large amounts of money, they would choose to exclude men from crack smoking sessions. As they saw it, this would allow them to avoid unwelcome sexual advances, remove the threat of violence implicit in many male–female encounters, and permit them to concentrate on 'smoking lovely'.

This apparent shift to women-centred initiations has been facilitated by the ease with which crack has been incorporated into established patterns of marijuana consumption by these women via the wulla joint. Additionally, both the widespread availability and low unit cost of crack may operate, at least in the early phases of use, to render males somewhat redundant – at least in so far as they have traditionally been perceived as the suppliers of illicit drugs to women. It is ironic that one of the many contradictions of the commodity culture which produced crack cocaine has been a decentring of men in their role as suppliers of illicit drugs and the elevation of women as consumers or purchasers in their own right.

Discussion

To a large extent, I began this component of the research guided by the literature. In particular, I expected to find that the majority of women were introduced to drugs by boyfriends and husbands. I further anticipated that many of these women would experience initiation in the context of either seduction or manipulation by a male partner. The women soon caused me to question my assumptions. The process of becoming a drug user cannot be reduced to a singular essence. The women in this sample were introduced to drugs in the company of boyfriends, husbands, girlfriends, cousins, brothers, sisters, mothers and fathers. Additionally, they were initiated in the context of male associates and mixed-sex groups. Contrary to the dominant stereotypes of boyfriends, husbands and pimps, relationships with male others in connection with the initiation of drug use take multiple forms and require multiple explanations.

This research suggests that initiation in the context of male others, particularly boyfriends and husbands, does not necessarily mean that women are either duped or merely passive accomplices. Certainly none of the women in this study viewed themselves as lambs led to the slaughter. I was, however, struck by the vulnerability of a small subgroup of those women who did initiate use with boyfriends or husbands. For these women, several dimensions or strands of vulnerability were present at the time of initiation. These 'vulnerabilities', in terms of a lack of material and emotional resources, including cases of homelessness and adolescent runaways, were clearly gendered.

Equally important, initiation in the context of other women does not suggest that women drug users, and crack users in particular, have broken free of the patriarchal yoke and are somehow more 'liberated'. Pressures to initiate drug use – both subtle and not so subtle – are placed on women by other women. Moreover, the consequences of their drug use are no less real and just as painful as those experienced by women who initiated in other contexts. Thus the process of becoming a drug user, while gendered in a number of specific dimensions, cannot be captured by an over-arching logic. Human relations take many forms and the contexts in which they occur are diverse. What is needed are empirical studies of women drug users that attempt to capture the complex interplay between sex/gender and culturally and historically specific contexts in producing decisions to initiate drug use.

Conclusion

It is certainly easier to say 'she did it all for love' – especially as feminists concerned to minimize the harms perpetrated against women in the areas of crime and justice. The notion that 'dependency is an integral part of women's daily lives – use of substances is only the outward sign of it' (Merfert-Diete and Soltai 1984 in Oppenheimer 1989: 186) views drug use as yet another instance of the relentless and universal subordination of women. However, white feminists in particular need to think about the extent to which this paradigm frames the lives of black and Hispanic women as emanating from the phallocentricity of 'other' cultures rather than as emerging out of the culture of racism.

Moreover, it is a paradigm which denies women agency. Women, like men, choose to use drugs. Not one of the women in this study was forced to stick a needle in her arm or coerced into taking a blast off a crack stem. However, the choices which they and women like them have made are choices which are sorely in need of contextualization. While it is stating the obvious to note that the process of initiating drug use will be different for women because women's lives are different to men's lives, one of the dangers is in slipping into explaining gender differences without reference to the specific and local forms of social life which give them their meaning.

We need to be wary of reducing women's lives to sociological and anthropological clichés about (dysfunctional) extended families and (deviant) domestic networks or ignoring the specifics of women's lives by invoking the public/private dichotomy. As Brittan and Maynard have argued, 'family forms differ in organization. . . it cannot be assumed that women's involvement in them is everywhere the same' (1984: 120). We also need to begin to examine the role of women's peers and friendship groupings. These are things that are done almost without question for men. At the same time, we should continue to explore the specific and local forms of women's domestic networks, taking care not to privilege these at the expense of other explanatory frameworks.

My examination of the literature, combined with the actual research process and the experiences of the women presented here, suggests that the dominant paradigm – encapsulated by the notion of initiation 'in the name of love' – simply does not capture the range and complexity of women's experiences. This research suggests that the dynamics of gender are not revealed in terms of either the sex of the person one initiates use with or traditional theories of gender socialization, but rather the complex process and negotiations involved in becoming – both defining oneself and being defined by others as – a drug user. The complexity of this process is mediated by factors such as peer influence, previous drug use experience, availability and cost of the drug, patterns of consumption and the symbiotic relationship between individuals and broader cultural forms and discourses that produces particular (gendered and raced) social subjectives.

In spite of the 'fact' that women in this sample overwhelmingly initiated smokeable cocaine use in the company of women, it remains necessary to explicate this finding in terms of the gendered and sexed consequences of continued crack use. While women's significance as consumers has to some extent been recognized within the highly commodified crack culture, they continue to bear the brunt of social stigma and economic marginalization attributed to drug users (Maher and Curtis 1992). While some women may have control over the initial decision to use and relative autonomy as to the purchase of the product and the setting for consumption, these initial features may be illusory. For once women are immersed in consumption, their options are circumscribed by the structure of the drug economy – hardly an equal opportunity employer – and the role of non-market statuses in creating and sustaining segmented labour markets in the informal sector (Maher, forthcoming).

Women, like men, initiate drug use in a variety of settings and circumstances with diverse motivations and rationales that cannot be captured by a singular theory. Empirical research into the relationships between gender and other variables in establishing the conditions of women's illicit drug use illustrates the need to develop concepts that, in explaining why women's drug use takes the particular forms it does, also deny a necessary and unitary existence to women's experiences. Despite the fact that there is no essential female drug user, conventional understandings of women's reasons for initiating use are underpinned by stereotypical images of women. The woman drug user – at home, on the street, in the treatment centre, and in the literature – remains overdetermined by her identity as a sexual partner.

Notes

[1] This paper was originally presented at the British Criminology Meeting, Cardiff, July 1993. I would like to thank the women whose lives form the grist for this particular ethnographic mill; Richard Curtis and Ansley Hamid for my own (male-sponsored) initiation into drug research; and Kathleen Daly and David Dixon for critical comments on an earlier draft. In Memory of Cherrie, 12 December 1992.

[2] Not only is drug research dominated by studies of male users but for the most part it assumes that drug use behaviours are gender-neutral. For the most part, this literature fails to recognize that addicts, junkies, dopefiends, crackheads, pipers hos and bitches are both sexed and gendered.

[3] Rosenbaum attributes this to black women's historical role as economic providers in matrifocal households (1981a: 868). However it could also reflect the disproportionate impact of the criminal justice system on African American males – i.e. they simply may not be around to 'take care' of their (*sic*) women.

[4] As Rosenbaum (1981c) has noted, 'It is very often the case, therefore, that the woman coaxes the man to *let* her use some of the heroin, rather than the popularly depicted scenario where a man coerces a resisting woman to use heroin' (1981c: 31).

[5] The conflation of spouse and family member may serve to mask the gendered dimensions of initiation.

[6] Although, once established, I hung out with women while they were smoking crack on numerous occasions, it was not until very late in the

fieldwork phase that women permitted me to observe them while they were shooting up. This was because, in their words, they did not want to 'disrespect' me.

[7] The range of positive responses to drug of initiation included: the ability to 'block out' problems, the feeling of being cut off or removed, warmth or glow, down head, up head, cheap cost, rapid high, intense high, easy to use, availability and quick high. Negative perceptions included: compulsion or cravings to use, inability to stop, short duration of the high, expensive cost, initial sickness, fear of HIV infection, paranoia, anxiety, stealing, degrading behaviour or things to be 'ashamed' of, problems with family, loss of sexual desire, loss of appetite and weight, picking and consequent scarring of the face and body, nausea, heart palpitations and a burning sensation in the lungs.

[8] A particularly gendered phenomenon which struck me was the considerable time women crack smokers spent poking and picking at their faces, often resulting in terrible scarring. Although women were reluctant to discuss this practice, they could often be observed on 'Crack Row' peering intently into bits of mirrors, digging at their faces with pieces of broken glass, stem scrapers or any other sharp object they could get their hands on.

References

Agar, M. (1977). 'Into that whole ritual thing: ritualistic drug use among urban American heroin addicts', in B. du Toit (ed.) *Drugs, Rituals, and Altered States of Consciousness* (Rotterdam, A. A. Balkema).

Anglin, M. D., Hser, Y. and McGlothlin, W. H. (1987). 'Sex differences in addict careers: becoming addicted', *American Journal of Drug and Alcohol Abuse*, 13, 253–80.

Auld, J., Dorn, N. and South, S. (1986). 'Irregular work, irregular pleasures: heroin in the 1980s', in R. Matthews and J. Young (eds.) *Confronting Crime* (London, Sage).

Becker, H. (1963). *Outsiders: Studies in the Sociology of Deviance* (New York, Free Press).

Biernacki, P. and Waldorf, D. (1981). 'Snowball sampling, problems and techniques of chain referral sampling', *Sociological Methods and Research*, 10(2), 141–63.

Blom, M. and van den Berg, T. (1989). 'A typology of the life and work styles of "heroin prostitutes": from a male career model to a feminized career model', in M. Cain (ed.) *Growing up Good: Policing the Behaviour of Girls in Europe* (Newbury Park, CA, Sage).

Brittan, A. and Maynard, M. (1984). *Sexism, Racism and Oppression* (Oxford, Basil Blackwell).

Campbell, A. (1990). 'The invisibility of the female delinquent peer group', *Women and Criminal Justice*, 2(1), 141–62.

Cheung, Y. W., Erickson, P. G. and Landau, T. C. (1991). 'Experience of crack use: findings from a community-based sample in Toronto', *The Journal of Drug Issues*, 21(1), 121–40.

Curtis, R. (1993). Personal communication.

Dai, B. (1937). *Opium Addiction in Chicago* (Montclair, NJ, Patterson Smith).

Eldred, C. A. and Washington, M. M. (1976). 'Interpersonal relationships in heroin use by men and women and their role in treatment outcome', *International Journal of the Addictions*, 11, 117–30.

Erickson, P. G. and Murray, G. F. (1989). 'The undeterred cocaine user: intention to quit and its relationship to perceived legal and health threats', *Contemporary Drug Problems*, 16(2), 141–56.

Fagan, J. and Chin, K. (1991). 'Social processes of initiation into crack', *Journal of Drug Issues*, 21(2), 313–43.

File, K. N. (1976). 'Sex role and street roles', *International Journal of the Addictions*, 11(2), 263–8.

Fitzpatrick, J. P. (1990). 'Drugs and Puerto Ricans in New York City', in R. Glick and J. Moore (eds.) *Drugs in Hispanic Communities* (New Brunswick, NJ, Rutgers University Press), pp. 103–26.

Fitzpatrick, J. P. and Martin, J. M. (1978). 'Puerto Rican addicts and non-addicts: a comparison', unpublished report, Institute for Social Research, Fordham University, Bronx, New York.

Freeland, J. B. and Campbell, R. S. (1973). 'The social context of first marijuana use', *International Journal of the Addictions*, 8(2), 317–24.

Gerstein, D. R., Judd, L. L. and Rovner, S. A. (1979). 'Career dynamics of female heroin addicts', *American Journal of Drug and Alcohol Abuse*, 6(1), 1–23.

Goldstein, P. J. (1979). *Prostitution and Drugs* (Lexington, MA, D.C. Heath).

Goldstein, P. J., Ouellet, L. J. and Fendrich, M. (1992). 'From bag brides to skeezers: a historical perspective on sex-for-drugs behavior', *Journal of Psychoactive Drugs*, 24(4), 349–61.

Greenleaf, V. (1987). *Women and Cocaine: Personal Stories of Addiction and Recovery* (Los Angeles, Lowell House).

Grund, J.-P. C. (1993). *Drug Use as a Social Ritual: Functionality, Symbolism and Determinants of Self-Regulation* (Rotterdam, Erasmus University, Instituut voor Verslavingsonderzoek (IVO) Series 4).

Hamid, A. (1989). 'Incubation times and subsequent use', paper presented at the annual meeting of the American Ethnological Society, Santa Fé, New Mexico, May.

Hamid, A. (1990). 'The political economy of crack-related violence', *Contemporary Drug Problems*, 17(1), 31–78.

Hamid, A. (1992). 'The developmental cycle of a drug epidemic: the cocaine smoking epidemic of 1981–1991', *Journal of Psychoactive Drugs*, 24(4), 337–48.

Hamid, A. (forthcoming). *The Political Economy of Drugs* (New York, Guilford Press).

Hser, Y., Anglin, M. D. and McGlothlin, W. H. (1987). 'Sex differences in Addict Careers, 1. Initiation of use', *American Journal of Drug and Alcohol Abuse*, 13, 33–57.

Inciardi, J. A., Pottieger, A. E., Forney, M. A., Chitwood, D. D. and McBride, C. D. (1990). 'Prostitution, IV drug use, and sex-for-crack exchanges among serious delinquents: Risks for HIV infection', *Criminology*, 29(2), 221–35.

Inciardi, J. A. Lockwood, D. and Pottieger, A. E. (1993). *Women and Crack Cocaine* (New York, Macmillan).

Johnson, B. (1991). 'The crack era in New York City', *Addiction and Recovery*, May/June, 24–27.

Kohn, M. (1992). *Dope Girls: The Birth of the British Drug Underground* (London, Lawrence and Wishart).

Lemert, E. M. (1951). *Social Pathology* (New York, McGraw-Hill).

Long, J. (1990). 'Drug use patterns in two Los Angeles barrio gangs', in R. Glick and J. Moore (eds.) *Drugs in Hispanic Communities* (New Brunswick, NJ, Rutgers University Press).

Maher, L. (1990). 'Criminalizing pregnancy: the downside of a kinder gentler nation', *Social Justice*, 17(3), 111–35.

Maher, L. (1992). 'Punishment and welfare: crack cocaine and the regulation of mothering', *Women and Criminal Justice*, 3(2), 35–70. Also published in C. Feinman (ed.) (1992), *The Criminalization of a Woman's Body* (New York, Haworth Press).

Maher, L. (1994). 'Dope girls: gender, race and class in the drug economy', Ph.D. dissertation, Rutgers University, Newark, New Jersey.

Maher, L. and Curtis, R. (1992). 'Women on the edge of crime: crack cocaine and the changing contexts of street-level sex work in New York City', *Crime, Law and Social Change*, 18(3), 221–58.

Merfert Diete, C. and Soltan, R. (eds.). *Die Alltägliche Verstickung in Abhängigkeit* (Hamburg, Rowohlt).

Miller, E. (1986). *Street Woman* (Philadelphia, Temple University Press).

Millman, M. (1975). 'She did it all for love: a feminist view of the sociology of deviance', in M. Millman and R. Moss Kanter (eds.), *Another Voice: Feminist Perspectives on Social Life and Social Science* (New York, Anchor Books).

Moore, J. W. (1990). 'Mexican American women addicts: the influence of family background', in R. Glick and J. Moore (eds.), *Drugs in Hispanic Communities* (New Brunswick, NJ, Rutgers University Press).

Moore, J. W. (1991). *Going Down to the Barrio: Homeboys and Homegirls in Change* (Philadelphia, Temple University Press).

Musto, D. F. (1973). *The American Disease: Origins of Narcotic Control* (New Haven, Yale University Press).

Naffine, N. (1985). 'The masculinity–femininity hypothesis: a consideration of gender-based personality theories of female crime', *British Journal of Criminology*, 25(4), 365–81.

O'Donnell, J. A. (1969). *Narcotic Addicts in Kentucky* (Washington, DC, US Government Printing Office).

Oppenheimer, E. (1980). 'Young female drug misusers: towards an appropriate policy', in M. Cain (ed.), *Growing up Good: Policing the Behaviour of Girls in Europe* (Newbury Park, CA, Sage).

Parker, H., Bakx, K., and Newcombe, R. (1988). *Living with Heroin* (Milton Keynes, Open University Press).

Pearson, G. (1987). *The New Heroin Users* (Oxford, Basil Blackwell).

Pettiway, L. E. (1987). 'Participation in crime partnerships by female drug users: the effects of domestic arrangements, drug use, and criminal involvement', *Criminology*, 25(3), 741–66.

Preble, E. and Casey, J. (1969). 'Taking care of business: the heroin user's life on the street', *International Journal of the Addictions*, 4, 1–24.

Puyo, A. M. (1979). 'Family headship and drug addiction among male Puerto Rican youths: an investigation of quality of family life, Ph.D. dissertation, Fordham University, New York.

Ratner, M. S. (ed.) (1993). *Crack Pipe as Pimp: An Ethnographic Investigation of Sex-for-Crack Exchanges* (New York, Lexington Books).

Rock, P. (1977). 'Review Symposium on Women, Crime and Criminology', *British Journal of Criminology*, 17, 392.

Rosenbaum, M. (1981a). 'Sex roles among deviants: the woman addict', *International Journal of the Addictions*, 16(5), 859–77.

Rosenbaum, M. (1981b). 'When drugs come into the picture, love flies out the window: love relationships among women addicts', *International Journal of the Addictions*, 16(7), 1197–206.

Rosenbaum, M. (1981c). *Women on Heroin* (New Brunswick, NJ, Rutgers University Press).

Rubin, V. and Comitas, L. (1976). *Ganja in Jamaica* (New York, Anchor Press).

Smart, C. (1977). 'Reply to Paul Rock', *British Journal of Criminology*, 17, 397.

Vigi, D. (1988). *Barrio Gangs* (Austin, TX, University of Texas Press).

Waldorf, D., Reinarman, C. and Murphy, S. (1991). *Cocaine Changes: The Experience of Using and Quitting* (Philadelphia, PA, Temple University Press).

Waldorf, D. (1973). *Careers in Dope* (Englewood Cliffs, NJ, Prentice Hall).

Williams, T. (1992). *Crackhouse: Notes From the End of the Line* (New York, Addison-Wesley).

Zinberg, N. E. (1984). *Drug, Set and Setting: The Basis for Controlled Intoxicant Use* (New Haven, Yale University Press).

8

Child-killing by parents:
Social, legal and gender issues

ANIA WILCZYNSKI

Child abuse first became labelled as a major social problem in England in the late 1960s. Since that time, there has been an increasing awareness of violence towards children in all its forms, including physical, emotional, sexual and ritual (or 'organized') abuse. The most extreme form of violence towards children is that which results in the child's death. Filicide – or child-killing by parents or parent-substitutes such as stepfathers – has received a great deal of media and public attention in the 1980s and 1990s, largely due to a number of widely publicized inquiries into child deaths such as those of Jasmine Beckford, Tyra Henry, Kimberley Carlile and Doreen Aston. However, there has still been relatively little systematic research carried out on the subject in England and Wales. The literature is also predominantly psychiatric in orientation, rather than examining the role of social and gender issues.

This paper describes some of the major findings of a research study on filicide carried out in England and Wales in the mid-1980s (Wilczynski 1993). Sixty-five files from the Director of Public Prosecutions (DPP) in London were examined from 1983 and 1984. The findings reported below are drawn from the sample of forty-eight cases from 1984 (28 female and 20 male). This included all cases in 1984 in which the police felt there was a prima-facie case of homicide by a parent or parent-substitute in England and Wales. The year 1984 was the most recent for which a centralized national sample could be obtained, since in 1985 the Crown Prosecution Service was created, and after it commenced operation in 1986 all homicides were prosecuted at a regional level.

Three aspects of filicide are focused upon: the motivations for the crime, the common background features of the cases, and the criminal justice response to offenders. Particular emphasis is placed on the similarities and differences between men and women. All case names used are pseudonyms.

The motivation for filicide

Various attempts have been made to classify filicide, using a variety of criteria such as the offenders' psychopathology (Royal Medico-Psychological Association 1970, cited in Scott 1973), the 'source of the impulse to kill' (Scott 1973), a 'cluster of common features' (Wallace 1986) and various social and psychiatric stress factors such as mental illness and social isolation (Simpson 1992). The present study used a classification based on the offender's motive for the killing. This was a modified and expanded version of the motivational classifications used in some previous studies (Resnick 1969; Baker 1991).

Filicides were classified into eleven categories of motive: 'retaliating' killings; jealousy of, or rejection by, the victim; the unwanted child; discipline; altruistic; psychosis in the parent; Munchausen Syndrome by Proxy; self-defence; killings secondary to sexual or organized abuse on the victim or another person; no intent to kill or injure; and cases where the motive is unknown. The classification took account both of the sample cases, and other types of cases reported in the literature not represented in the sample. Emphasis was placed on the suspects' explanations for their behaviour immediately after the offence and in police interview. Since filicide cases often involve more than one motivation (Simpson 1992), cases were classified according to both their 'primary' (major or predominant) and 'secondary' (apparently less significant) motives. In cases which appeared to involve two major motivations, 'psychosis' was always classified as a primary motivation, and 'discipline' was always classified as a secondary motivation (since it was the more immediate and transitory reason for the killing).

It should be noted, however, that whilst a 'motive' in cases of filicide can often be identified, most of the killings in the sample, as in other studies, were not instrumental or premeditated – they were usually sudden and impulsive. Thus care must be taken not to 'over-determine' motives.

In *retaliating killings*, anger towards another person – typically the person's partner – is displaced on to the child (d'Orban 1979). Men were more likely than women to commit these killings. A common hallmark of these cases was a history of severe marital conflict, often involving physical violence by one or both partners.

The male 'retaliating' filicides were often characterized by possessiveness, sexual jealousy and the exertion of power within the marital relationship. For example Mohammed, a man of Pakistani origin, had an arranged marriage to an English woman. Initially his career in his brother's business prospered. Mohammed then started abusing alcohol and heroin, gambling and frequently assaulting his wife. His wife left him, taking the two children of the marriage. She went to live with Mohammed's brother and his wife and children, and refused Mohammed's attempts at reconciliation. Mohammed's brother had also advised business associates to deny Mohammed credit, which he needed to re-start his section of the business. One night Mohammed threw a can of petrol and a match into his brother's home, and in the ensuing fire his daughter died. The other occupants of the home escaped with no or minor injuries. Mohammed said he had set the fire because he was 'fed up' with his wife and brother and was under 'mental pressure'.

Conversely, the female 'retaliating' cases were rather different. In these the female perpetrator tended to be motivated by resentment at her *lack* of power. For example one woman was angry at always being told what to do by her husband, whilst another resented her second husband's constant emotional abuse and harsh physical discipline of her mentally retarded teenage son.

Jealousy of, or rejection by, the victim (Baker 1991) was an exclusively male category, apart from one case in which both the man and the woman had abused and killed the child. The reasons for the perpetrators' resentment included: suspicion or knowledge that they were not the child's biological parents; resentment of the attention the child received from the mother; or 'rejecting' behaviour by the child due to illness or prior abuse.

Unwanted child (Resnick 1969; d'Orban 1979) filicides usually involve female perpetrators. These cases were classified according to the age of the victim (neonates or older) and also the stage at which the child became unwanted. Most of the unwanted victims were *children unplanned and unwanted from the time of conception.* These cases usually involve *neonaticide,* the killing of new-born babies within twenty-four hours of birth (Resnick 1969), usually by somewhat passive and immature young single women who deny and conceal their unplanned pregnancies. Less commonly, the victims are *older than one day*, such as one boy whose teenage mother was pressured by her parents to keep him rather than let him be adopted as she had wanted. The one victim who was *wanted by the parent at conception but not after the birth* was unwanted because of her characteristics after birth. The baby girl was completely rejected by her father because she had Down's Syndrome.

Discipline killings occur as a result of attempts to discipline a child for behaviour regarded as annoying or disobedient (Baker 1991; Greenland 1987). Although both men and women killed during the course of discipline, it was more common amongst the male offenders. For example Alan shook his three-year-old son and banged his head against a wall in a fit of temper. The child, who was frequently disobedient, had fallen down the stairs. As is typically said by parents who kill during the course of discipline, Alan said that he hadn't meant to harm the child seriously.

In *altruistic* filicide, the parent (usually the mother) perceives the killing as being in the child's best interests (Resnick 1969; Steele 1978). '*Primary*' *altruistic killings* are what have been termed 'mercy-killings', in which there is a real degree of suffering in the victim (for example mental or physical handicap or disease) and an absence of secondary gain for the parent (Scott 1973). There was one of these cases in the sample. The much more common '*secondary*' *altruistic killings* involve no real degree of suffering in the child. In these cases the parent, virtually always the mother, is suffering from depression. These women expressed acute feelings of failure to measure up to society's standards of 'good' mothers or wives. For instance, one woman regarded herself as a bad mother and wife, worried that the child was abnormal in some way, and felt that she did everything but it was never enough.

Psychotic parents include those diagnosed as psychotic at the time of the killing (Resnick 1969). There were both men and women in this category, but more women than men. In some cases the killing was committed directly under the influence of delusions, such as a schizophrenic man who repeatedly stabbed his daughter because he believed she was possessed by the devil. In other cases the killing was in some way altruistic: either the parent delusionally believed the child was suffering in some way (such as one mother who believed her children had venereal disease and had therefore stopped growing), or their psychotic illness led them to want to commit suicide and the child was killed secondarily to this primary suicidal urge.

In *Munchausen Syndrome by Proxy* (MSBP), the parent fakes or induces illnesses in a child, and presents them – often repeatedly – for medical assessment and care (Rosenberg 1987). Smothering to induce seizures or fits is the most common method (Rosenberg 1987). Some children die from the abuse. There was one case in the sample in which there may have been Munchausen abuse by the mother, although none of the professionals involved in the case mentioned the possibility. Maria had had four cot deaths. In each case Maria had been alone with the child at the time of death, and two of the children had only recently been discharged from hospital when they died. However, Maria denied any involvement in any of the deaths, and the pathological evidence could not prove otherwise. Maria was not prosecuted owing to lack of evidence.

The following three categories were not represented amongst the sample cases.

Some filicides are *secondary to sexual or ritual (or organized) abuse*, either on the child or another person (see Wallace 1986). There were no sample cases of this type, and there were no suspected cases of sexual assault. However, sexual abuse is particularly difficult to detect, and at the time of the sample cases (1984) there was not the current level of professional awareness of this type of abuse. Where filicides involving sexual abuse do occur, the child may be killed inadvertently during the course of the sexual assault, or else deliberately killed in order to prevent disclosure of the abuse. For example in a recent case a 14-year-old girl told a teacher and social services that her stepfather had been sexually abusing her. Her stepfather was then charged, but subsequently electrocuted his step-daughter, after forcing her to write a 'suicide' note in which she asked to be forgiven for her 'untrue' allegations (Joseph Nelson-Wilson, reported in the *Guardian*, 19 February 1992).

Self-defence is rarely a motive for filicide, which is not surprising given children's physical inferiority and lack of power. Baker (1991) describes one instance only, which it is perhaps questionable to classify as truly self-defence. In this case a solid and aggressive 16-year-old boy threatened his mother when she told him she was marrying her boyfriend. He then started to threaten the boyfriend and allegedly started to become violent. The boyfriend then shot the boy (Baker 1991).

In some filicides there is *no intent to kill or injure* the child at all. This excludes cases in which there was *any* intention to harm the child (for example cases typically classified as 'battering' in some prior classifications, where there is at least an intent to injure, if not to kill). This category includes many cases where children die from neglect. These deaths are usually due to ignorance of the food and health requirements of the baby, compounded by the stresses of social disadvantage and personal inadequacies (Wallace 1986).

The final category is cases in which the *motive is not known* or suspected. There was one case of this type in the sample.

Overall, the most common categories of filicide motivation were retaliating, discipline, the unwanted child (both neonaticides and older children), secondary altruism, psychosis and jealousy. This was true both of primary motivations alone and when analysed together with the secondary motivations. It is also clear that men and women tend to kill their children for very different reasons. Men's motives tend to be associated with retaliation, discipline, or jealousy of or rejection by the victim. Women tend to kill because they are psychotic, or the child is unwanted (typically a neonate killed by a passive and immature young woman), or for altruistic reasons. This sex difference reflects an extreme version of traditional gender roles, in which men are socialized to be aggressive, dominant and sexually possessive, and women are taught to internalize stress and anger, and be passive, nurturing and self-sacrificing. Although the use of select samples and differences in classification in previous studies makes direct comparison difficult, the literature reports comparable results on both these findings (Wallace 1986; Resnick 1969; Daly and Wilson 1988).

Common background features in filicide cases

Prior research indicates that there are numerous common background 'risk' factors in cases of filicide (Wallace 1986; d'Orban 1979; Goetting 1990). The incidence in the sample of a total of ninety-two demographic, social, psychiatric, victim, and situational character-istics was examined. It was found that filicidal parents tend to be characterized by the following three features.

Firstly, they have multiple problems of various kinds (d'Orban 1979; Fein 1979) 'imposed on them by their oppressed worlds of racism, sexism, poverty, mental illness, and general social disorganisa-tion' (Goetting 1988: 345). Put simply, misery, isolation and instability are strongly correlated with filicide. Numerous social stresses are a very prominent feature of filicidal parents' histories, such as financial and housing problems, youthful parenthood, marital conflict, lack of preparation for parenthood and children who are difficult to care for. Filicide offenders are also a psychiatrically vulnerable group, and many have, for example, suffered depressive symptoms, received prior psychiatric treatment, used either legal or illegal substances, and (at least after the offence) been diagnosed as suffering from psychiatric disorder. A second common feature of filicidal parents is that they usually have a lack of compensatory personal and social resources with which to cope with their problems (Goetting 1988; Korbin 1986). For instance, they are often extremely socially isolated. Finally, filicidal parents tend to perceive their situations as essentially negative (Korbin 1987). Thus as Wallace (1986: 133–4) notes, filicide is the product of a 'complex interweave' of individual, psychiatric, social and cultural factors, rather than any one of these factors alone; often it is the clustering of the various factors together which proves fatal.

The three common features of filicidal parents identified above applied equally to male and female offenders. In fact, overall male and female filicide cases were found to possess many of the same common background features. Nonetheless, a number of important sex differences emerged also. Those differences reaching the level of statistical significance are concentrated on below. Levels of significance are designated as follows: <.05 (*), <.01 (**), and <.001 (***).

Men tend to have somewhat higher levels of 'social' problems – for instance related to the victim's behaviour, and material difficulties such as finance and accommodation. Women are more likely to be middle class,* not in paid employment,* to have the sole or primary care of the child,*** and to have either no or an unsupportive partner.** Thus problems related to the female gender role seem to be particularly important in filicide by women. Women also tend to have higher levels of 'psychiatric' stress factors than men. However, given that this difference is relatively modest and that men also have high levels of such stress factors, it is perhaps surprising that women are so dramatically more likely to be diagnosed as suffering from some form of psychiatric disorder** at the time of the filicide. This coincides with the very different legal treatment of filicidal men and women discussed further below.

Other major sex differences are also apparent. Whilst men more commonly kill by manual assault or shaking,*** women are more likely to use methods from which a clear intent to kill or cause grievous bodily harm could be inferred,* such as asphyxiation. Women are also more likely than men to kill children aged under one.* General patterns of family violence are much more characteristic of male filicide perpetrators than of female. Men are both more likely to be violent to the child before the filicide,* and to have violent relationships with their partners** (and to be the perpetrators of that violence). They are also more likely to have prior convictions,*** illustrating their tendency to demonstrate more general social deviancy than filicidal women. Generally, filicidal men conform more to the typical profile of the non-fatal child abuser than do filicidal women – for example in having chaotic family relationships and multiple social problems.

The criminal justice response to parents who kill their children

Turning to the legal treatment of filicidal parents, it is clear that men and women who kill their children are perceived and treated in very different ways by the criminal justice system. This is in accordance with the view that 'men are bad and normal, women are mad and abnormal'. Generally men are treated in accordance with the 'legal/ punishment' model of child abuse, and women in accordance with the 'welfare/treatment' model (see Tilley 1989; Newberger and Bourne 1978).

This difference is apparent at all stages of the criminal justice process. Women are less likely than men to be prosecuted, or convicted of murder, and more likely to be granted bail and to receive psychiatric treatment before trial. Most female filicide offenders use 'psychiatric' pleas such as infanticide and diminished responsibility, and receive psychiatric or non-custodial supervisory sentences such as probation orders. Their killings tend to be seen as aberrant 'tragedies' for which they are not responsible. On the other hand, men tend to utilize 'normal' pleas such as involuntary manslaughter (a lack of intent to kill or seriously injure) to reduce the charge to manslaughter. They usually receive prison sentences, even in the relatively few cases where a 'psychiatric' plea is used. Their killings tend to be seen as less surprising, and more in need of punishment and deterrence.

Two examples – one female and one male – illustrate this. On the one hand Janet's case illustrates the readiness with which filicidal women can be 'psychiatrized' (see Allen 1987), and the liberal definition of mental disorder used to satisfy the Infanticide Act 1938. The Act only applies to a woman who kills her child aged under one when the balance of her mind was disturbed as a result of childbirth or lactation. The legislation is premised on the belief that women kill their children because of disturbed hormones after childbirth.

Janet battered her two-month-old child's head against a wardrobe during the course of discipline, and had abused the child previously. She had come from the Philippines to marry an Englishman, after they met through a dating agency. She had the sole care of the baby (who cried constantly) and suffered from lack of sleep, extreme social isolation, and racist comments by neighbours. Her husband was unsupportive in both a practical and emotional sense. Janet also experienced continual vaginal bleeding after the birth. Acquaintances, relatives and her husband described her as appearing unhappy, tired and depressed.

Janet's GP refused to make a statement, but implied that he did not think Janet was suffering from (clinical) depression. The DPP lawyer noted that 'There is no evidence that the defendant was depressed following the birth of the child' (by which he presumably meant suffering a depressive disorder) '*other than the very nature of her actions*' (my emphasis). This illustrates the contradiction perceived between Janet's 'normal' character and her violent actions. The DPP lawyer noted that there was no evidence to justify reducing the murder charge to infanticide, although he believed the defence was obtaining medical reports. He then somewhat startlingly went on to state that:

> It seems likely that a plea will be offered to. . . [infanticide], and if so I am of the view that such a plea would be acceptable.

Both the defence and prosecution obtained lengthy psychiatric reports. These reports concluded that Janet was *not* suffering from any mental disorder. She had a reserved, passive personality, was subjected to very severe stressful factors and suffering from mild depression, and experienced amnesia after the killing. Both reports concluded that Janet satisfied the Infanticide Act 1938 on the basis of these factors and because the effects of childbirth (including her tiredness and continued vaginal bleeding) were 'likely to have crucially disabled her from withstanding all the stresses to which she was subjected'. On the basis of these reports, Janet's plea was accepted and she was sentenced to a three-year probation order with a condition of psychiatric treatment.

Janet's case illustrates how a plea of infanticide can be accepted even when the causes of a woman's mental distress are at least as much social as hormonal. Further, the case shows how a filicidal woman can use a psychiatric plea and receive a psychiatric disposal, even though she is not actually suffering from any mental disorder.

On the other hand, Mark's case illustrates how the 'potentially pathological' (Allen 1987: 83) behaviour and mental state of male filicide offenders can be neutralized, and the case ultimately dealt with on a non-psychiatric basis. Mark shook his ten-week-old baby son, punched him hard in the face twice and once in the stomach, and threw him into his cot. He was alone with the child for a few minutes, and became angry about the child's crying because he did not know what was wrong with him and felt the child was rejecting him. He said he was tired, not having slept for two and a half days, and had 'snapped'. He said he had not meant to kill his son.

Mark had a chaotic life characterized by numerous stresses. The child he ultimately killed cried constantly due to colic and appeared to become apprehensive around Mark. Mark had been severely beaten as a child, and was seen by a child psychiatrist at a young age. According to his wife, relatives, various professionals and Mark himself, he had an extremely bad temper which resulted in numerous outbursts of violence. Mark frequently physically and emotionally abused his own wife and two children, and had also assaulted his father-in-law, neighbour and pet dog. There were numerous social problems including severe marital conflict, extreme social isolation, poor accommodation, debt and alcohol abuse. In police interview Mark said that he had been 'crying out for help' for months but 'no one wanted to know'. He had received tranquillizers from his GP because of his suicidal impulses and bad temper; his wife described him as very depressed and aggressive.

The police charged Mark with murder. However the investigating police officer said that he felt Mark was mentally disturbed, immature, lived in a world of fantasy, was totally intolerant and destroyed everything he could not have in fits of 'extreme illogical temper'. He described Mark's violent outbursts as a 'cry for help', and felt a plea of diminished responsibility was clearly made out. The DPP lawyer, however, was rather sceptical about this view and felt

> . . . he is a wicked boy but not off balance. However, the case might well go the way of a diminished responsibility matter. . .

A more senior DPP lawyer who examined the case also expressed the view that the case was 'likely to end as a diminished responsibility manslaughter'.

The case then swung back to being seen more within the framework of normality. A psychiatric report prepared said only that Mark was of relatively low intelligence, immature and not suffering from any mental illness. The report was typical of those on male offenders. As Allen (1987) found also in her examination of the construction of psychiatric reports, the reports on men tended to be short and impersonal, with the offender's mental life 'referred to only negatively, as an absence of anything worthy to report' (Allen 1987: 36).

At trial the prosecution accepted that the violence was not premeditated and there would be problems proving specific intent. The prosecution therefore accepted a plea to manslaughter on the basis of lack of intent because Mark was 'immature and with a violent temper he cannot control'. In mitigation defence counsel argued that Mark regarded the children's screaming as a 'rejection of the love he was trying to show them' and that each violent incident was a 'reaction to external pressures'. Mark received a four-year prison sentence. Thus whilst Mark had originally been perceived as an 'internal' and mentally disturbed being, by the end of the case he had been reconstructed as someone who was 'bad', 'normal' and 'external'.

The marked sex disparity in criminal justice treatment found in the sample cases was also apparent in an analysis of 474 of the 493 cases in the 1983–89 Criminal Statistics for England and Wales in which a parent (including substitute) had killed their child. This analysis was obtained by the author and another from the Home Office Statistical Branch (Wilczynski and Morris 1993). Although conducted on a much larger sample, a very similar pattern emerged. Mothers were less likely than fathers to be convicted of murder and to be sentenced to prison, and were more likely to be given psychiatric and probation disposals.

Other studies have found similar results concerning the differing disposals of male and female filicide offenders in England (Marks and Jumar 1993; Greenland 1987), Australia (Baker 1991; Lansdowne 1987), Canada (Greenland 1987), America (Showers and Apolo 1986), and Denmark (Harder 1967). There is, however, some evidence to suggest that filicidal women in America are more likely to receive prison sentences (often of some length) than for example in England (Maeir-Katkin 1992; Jones 1986).

Whilst men and women are clearly treated very differently by the criminal justice system, the interpretation of this difference is by no means clear. An examination of the sample cases indicated that there are certainly some differences in the circumstances in which men and women kill their children, which could be used to justify women's more lenient treatment. This could be on traditional tariff criteria – for example women are less likely to have prior convictions or to have abused the child on a previous occasion. Their typical categories of motivation are also those which tend to be regarded as less morally reprehensible than those in which men predominate. Alternatively, women's more lenient treatment could be justified on the grounds of women's social role and responsibilities, since women still retain primary responsibility for child-rearing with little support. Nonetheless, it would still appear that the differences which do exist between male and female filicide are exaggerated by the criminal justice system, and that such dramatically different treatment cannot be justified. It is also apparent that more informal means of social control can have a greater impact on the legal processing of women than men – for example to justify the imposition of a non-custodial sentence. These informal means of control were found to include psychiatry, social work, the family, being perceived as a 'good parent', and self-punishment through remorse.

To conclude, filicide is often viewed as an aberrant and inexplicable act committed by someone who is either evil or mentally deranged. Nonetheless, whilst it is a relatively rare act, it is important to place it in its social context and to see that there are strong connections between filicide and both non-fatal abuse and so-called 'normal' parenting. The very different legal responses to filicidal men and women also represent in more extreme form the way in which gender can impact on the legal processing of offenders. And whilst the enforcement of traditional sex stereotypes can be very oppressive to women, it would also appear that they can at times benefit from them. When a woman kills her own child, she offends not only against the criminal law, but against the sanctity of stereotypical femininity: it is therefore assumed that she must have been 'mad'.

References

Allen, H. (1987). *Justice Unbalanced: Gender, Psychiatry and Judicial Decisions* (Milton Keynes, Open University Press).

Baker, J. M. (1991). '"You can't let your children cry": filicide in Victoria 1978–1988' (MA thesis, University of Melbourne, Australia).

Daly, M. and Wilson, M. (1988). *Homicide* (New York, Aldine De Gruyter).

d'Orban, P. T. (1979). 'Women who kill their children', *British Journal of Psychiatry*, 134, 560–71.

Fein, L. G. (1979). 'Can child fatalities, end product of child abuse, be prevented?', *Children and Youth Services Review*, 1, 31–53.

Goetting, A. (1988). 'When parents kill their young children: Detroit 1982-1986', *Journal of Family Violence*, 3(4), 339–46.

Goetting, A. (1990). 'Child victims of homicide: a portrait of their killers and the circumstances of their deaths', *Violence and Victims*, 5(4) 287–96.

Greenland, C. (1987). *Preventing CAN Deaths* (London, Tavistock Publications Ltd.).

Harder, T. (1967). 'The psychopathology of infanticide', *Acta Psychiatrica Scandinavica*, 43(196), 196–245.

Jones, A. (1986). 'Mothers who kill', *Newsday* (October), 12–31.

Korbin, J. E. (1986). 'Childhood histories of women imprisoned for fatal child maltreatment', *Child Abuse and Neglect*, 10, 331–8.

Korbin, J. E. (1987). 'Incarcerated mothers' perceptions and interpretations of their fatally maltreated children', *Child Abuse and Neglect* 11, 397–407.

Lansdowne, R. G. (1987). 'Child killing and the offence of infanticide: the development of the offence and its operation in New South Wales 1976-1980' (Master of Law Thesis, University of New South Wales, Sydney, Australia).

Maier-Katkin, D. (1992). 'Infanticide, law and penal policy in England and America' (unpublished paper).

Marks, M. and Kumar, R. C. (1993). 'Infanticide in England and Wales', *Medicine, Science and the Law*.

Newberger, E. H. and Bourne, R. (1978). 'The medicalization and legalization of child abuse', in J. M. Eekelaar and S. N. Katz (eds.), *Family Violence: an International and Interdisciplinary Study* (Toronto, Butterworths).

Resnick, P. J. (1996). 'Child murder by parents: a psychiatric review of filicide', *American Journal of Psychiatry*, 126, 73–82.

Rosenberg, D. A. (1987). 'Web of deceit: a literature review of Munchausen Syndrome by Proxy', *Child Abuse and Neglect*, 11, 547–63.

Royal Medico-Psychological Association Seminar (1970). 'Royal Medico-Psychological Association Seminar', *Forensic Psychiatry Section*.

Scott, P. D. (1973). 'Parents who kill their children', *Medicine, Science and the Law*, 13(2), 120–5.

Showers, J. and Apolo, J. (1986). 'Criminal disposition of persons involved in 72 cases of fatal child abuse', *Medicine, Science and the Law*, 26(3), 243–7.

Simpson, A. I. F. (1992). 'Maternal filicide: an approach to classification and understanding', *Progress in Forensic Psychiatry* (Conference Proceedings), Auckland, New Zealand.

Steele, B. F. (1978). 'Psychology of infanticide resulting from maltreatment', in M. Kohl (ed.), *Infanticide and the Value of Life* (New York, Prometheus Books).

Tilley, N. (1989). 'The abuser – punishment or treatment', in W. S. Rogers, D. Hevey and E. Ash (eds.), *Child Abuse and Neglect* (London, Batsford).

Wallace, A. (1986). *Homicide* (Sydney, NSW Bureau of Crime Statistics and Research).

Wilczynski, A. and Morris, A. (1993). 'Parents who kill their children', *Criminal Law Review*, 31–6.

Wilczynski, A. (1993). 'A socio-legal study of parents who kill their children' (Criminology Ph.D. thesis, Institute of Criminology, University of Cambridge).

9

Men's own stories, lives and violence: Research as practice

RICHARD THURSTON AND JOHN BEYNON

This chapter presents some preliminary results of a study (supported by the Leverhulme Trust) of masculinity and violence. The project's focus has been on making links between the cultural construction of masculine identities, the cultural context of men's everyday lives, and men's use of violence. A key question underpins the research: what compels some men, in demeanour, attitudes and style, to use physical and/or symbolic violence? This 'show of violence' is viewed as learned male behaviour, both a product and an expression (or 'performance') of socialization, genderization, and acculturation into narrow and persisting values of 'being a man', and into a society underpinned by asymmetrical power relations. The project aims to explore qualitatively how male violence is neither inevitable nor accidental, but at the heart of how some men as individuals and in cultural groups define their masculine identities. This is not viewed in either a pathological or psychological light, or even in the tradition of sociological studies of delinquent behaviour (although some of these are pertinent to the research). Rather, at the starting-point are the recent debates in 'reading masculinities' and the cultural production, anchored in time and place, of male subjectivities and aggressive identities; to which 'being hard', and its performance, 'showing hard', are often central.

The project does not view violence exclusively from within a gender perspective, but rather seeks to explore the intersection of a number of social, cultural, and personal factors with men's lives, identities and behaviour. Keeping firmly in mind the cultural ecology of post-industrial south Wales, where the study was conducted, the intention of the project has been to unpick the link between displayed and lived definitions of masculinity and male violence by reference to the reproduction of gendered lives and identities in a number of interrelated 'life-spheres', such as: domestic, street, leisure, education, media, penal, etc. Clearly, these 'life-spheres' are not readily separated. Indeed, they transcend both the public and private, local and global. As such, they facilitate purchase upon male violence as simultaneously a personal act and a vehicle for cultural expression, group identity and the regeneration of men's personal and social power. The research is qualitative and ethnographic, focusing particularly on life-history interviews on a one-to-one basis over a number of weeks with thirty male offenders – both in prison and on probation orders; and through undertaking in-depth semi-structured interviews and participant observation. The intention here is to comment on some of the key concerns of the project; particularly issues relating to the cultural politics of identity, and life-history work with men as both a research and practice method. This will provide a context for some initial analyses from one of the life stories.

Cultural studies and the politics of identity

In trying to make sense of the connections between violence and masculinities, in a way that accounts for both cultural determination and individual agency, the project draws on a number of academic insights that are often constituted under the umbrella of cultural studies.

As an interdisciplinary subject, cultural studies draws on a range of theoretical and methodological discourses and approaches, and from the outset has offered a number of critiques of social science through its concern with the politics of knowledge, cultural transformation, practice, cultural politics and power (Johnson 1985). In this respect it shares strong common links with women's studies both epistemologically and politically (Franklin 1991). Indeed, a central theme has been the study of gendered power relations in terms both of social institutions and cultural practices; and symbolic meanings and the formation of identities. Of particular interest here is the acknowledgement of the fragmented nature of subjectivity and the difficulty of maintaining stable, unified identities; along with a conception of the 'cultural' as the site and the product of collective human praxis where subjects do not passively 'inherit' transferred internal structures (as in some versions of Marxism). Simply put, cultural studies has been interested in the ways identities are constructed through an interaction between self and others within particular contexts and for particular reasons and motivations, whether conscious or unconscious.

The primary interest for the perspective of our study is to gain a better understanding of the following: the process through which some men construct their sense of masculinity through violence in certain contexts; how this is used to produce and sustain certain identities; and, how this view of masculinity might provide a useful, practical, and personally political challenge to men's violence. Furthermore, an integration of theory and method with practice might provide some valuable and desirable outcomes from the research. Indeed, this paper forms part of an on-going attempt to explore the possibilities of critical life-history work with men for both theory, politics and practice.

The life-history approach

Our research is firmly based in the life-history method, extended to include practical and pragmatic issues. The life-history method – integrated within broadly sociological or cultural perspectives – has a long and illustrious past with the social sciences as a means of collecting highly revealing insights into lived experience. Acts often assumed as individual and idiosyncratic can be unpicked as culturally shaped in a nexus of area, time, place, sexuality, race, gender, class, disability, and age.

George Mayhew used the life-history method novelistically in mid-Victorian London to document the life-styles and attitudes of rich and poor, but it was at the University of Chicago in the 1920s and 30s that the life history came to be employed in a more focused and principled manner to 'map' the cultural ecology of the city and its range of human environments, from 'hobomania' to the suburban middle class. It was particularly insightful on the 'criminal class', especially when used in harness with ethnographic observation and strategies for 'social treatment'. *The Jack Roller* (Shaw 1930), the story of a petty thief and hustler, stands as one of the most celebrated products of the genre, with its assertion that its subject's (Stanley's) criminal behaviour was a rational response to adverse circumstances. Shaw uses the 'boy's own story' to depict the cultural net of 'streetwiseness' which provided many young working-class men in the city, from an early age, with a cultural clothing of values, attitudes, and events, responses and repercussions. The life history has subsequently been allied to a range of sociological theories and research (Plummer 1983).

Whilst many of these perspectives are pertinent to the present project, this paper will focus on work currently emerging from cultural studies; the emphasis being on 'reading identities' as 'texts in context'. One of the values of applying this approach in this instance, is that it enables an in-depth understanding of the cross-overs between the individuals' experiences (represented and reconstructed in the life-story text) and the cultural and historical contexts that frame the subjects' life and the construction of their identity.[1] Our interest in this project has been to develop the life history as a way into understanding the cultural construction of masculine identities and how they impact upon a variety of forms of male violence within specific cultural and institutional contexts. Moreover, from the outset the main concerns of the project have not been pursued as a narrowly academic enterprise. Rather, we have set out to apply recent approaches to understanding both men and violence so as to articulate a range of policy, practice-related, and pragmatic outcomes relevant to a range of initiatives being developed by professional and voluntary bodies.[2] Subsequently, the aim has been to explore the value and desirability of developing the life history simultaneously as a method for data collection, and as a form of intervention in order to challenge men's use of violence in a variety of contexts.[3]

Collecting and 'reading' life-story accounts as cultural codings of male identities

A brief description of the life-history technique developed in this project is as follows. One-to-one interviews were set up with men, in prison and on probation, likely to have had experience of perpetrating violence. The interview process was open, semi-structured, and necessarily flexible. Interviewees' participation was voluntary, and confidential. Typically, the first interview involved talking about early memories, with subsequent meetings centring on themes and key events arising through progressive focusing. Significant issues, themes, memories, relationships, and events were returned to in subsequent interviews. A certain degree of encouragement to explore taken-for-granted 'truths', attitudes, and interviewees' interpretations of experiences formed the focus of more in-depth meetings nearer the conclusion of the process. The life-history interviews were also accompanied by in-depth observation of the various contexts in which the interviews took place, and informal interviews with staff in both prison and probation services.

Men's life-story accounts are representations. As such, they are a way into exploring men's attitudes, feelings and identities, particularly here in relation to gender, along with class, race, age, sexuality and disability. All these factors intersect in the cultural construction of masculinities. It is because of this that life stories can offer to the cultural reader or decoder the opportunity to examine how certain masculine identities – sets of attitudes, values and beliefs – underpin (some) men's violence in specific situations. They give clues as to how certain narrow definitions of 'what it means to be a man' or 'manly' are learned, discovered, expressed, and sustained (or reproduced) through violent acts and interactions (either intimated, symbolic, or physical). Identity in this sense is not an already accomplished given. As Stuart Hall argues, 'We should think, instead, of identity as a "production", which is never complete, always in process, and always constituted within, not outside representation' (1990: 222). As such, the practice of representing one's self through the production of a life story always implicates the position of the speaker – the position of enunciation. When we speak of life experiences we do so from a cultural position that is always specific in place, time and history. This context bears greatly on the form, content and telling of the life story – through language, discourse, narrative, and interpersonal relations. These communicative practices are dialogic, in the sense that they are particular incidences of an interaction between many factors: private and public, local and global, micro and macro.

In this sense the project's respondents are not seen as passive recipients of gendered (or any other) ideologies or childhood experiences that socialization theories would suggest (Brittan 1989); or as individuals separate and free from social structures and cultural contexts. Rather, the cultural construction of identities is viewed as an active, on-going process, and as a complex interaction between social structure, institutional context, lived experience, and sense-making or subjective processes.

As in film or literary genres, the narrative form of the life story is neither given nor neutral. Rather, it is in fact active in conveying or producing meaning. In our experience of doing life-story work with men it is apparent that the attempt, sometimes quite active and conscious in choice, is to construct a coherent sense of self from childhood through to adulthood through narrative continuity or linearity. Within these narratives continuous frames of reference and meaning are drawn upon (e.g., 'I've always been . . . a man, heterosexual', etc.). The representation of 'self' in the life-story interviews involves tensions and contradictions which are created in the process of exploring taken-for-granted pasts in relation to a fixed sense of present identities and identifications. These contradictions and tensions are most clearly communicated in relation to key events or direction markers – expressed as significant by the life-story-teller. They are indicators of transitional moments in the interviewee's life, often remembered in relation to changing circumstances, and sometimes accompanied by a change in attitudes or beliefs.

What this process reveals in the interviews, and what cultural and feminist theories have been arguing for some time, is that the process involved in the production of identities is never simple, never unitary, and never cohesive. As Beechey and Donald (1985) note:

> . . . the idea that the person or the self is a culturally and historically malleable category is probably one of the most scandalous axioms of the social sciences. It offends not only common sense, but also our sense of who and what we are. It calls into question the very integrity and cohesiveness of ourselves as conscious, rational, self-directed beings. (1985: ix–x)

For men, who are centrally located *vis-à-vis* the locale of cultural power and knowledge, this critique is more risky (Rutherford 1990). Some men, quite simply, have more to lose (and arguably something to gain) by questioning the myths that are both circulated within culture and internalized, and that underpin and are integral to the sustaining of asymmetrical power relations between men and women. Simply put, the argument is that when this sense of self is questioned or disputed, the response may be through various forms of behaviour broadly defined as violent. Jonathon Rutherford (1990: 10) argues that, 'it is the threat of the dissolution of self that ignites the irrational hatred and hostility as the centre struggles to assert and secure its boundaries, that construct self from not-self.'

For white heterosexual masculinities, fear of difference prompts strong defences and well-policed borders against the potential threat of challenges and transformations that a recognition of differences provokes. Thus, the resultant hegemonic struggle to maintain the cultural, racial, sexual, and gendered dichotomies of Self and Other – relationships of polarity – makes and reproduces social formations of domination and inequality.

Of course, we all do 'identity work' through telling stories and constructing narratives about experiences in our everyday lives. Indeed, as Arthur Brittan notes, 'every social situation [. . .] is an occasion for identity work' (1989: 36). We tell (or rather reconstruct) stories in social interactions not only to other people – our friends, our family, our colleagues – but also to ourselves. And in this way story-telling functions as a way not only of communicating but also of constructing a sense of who we are in specific locations of place, time, and cultural context. The stories men tell about being violent, and the language and manner and context in which such stories are told, can provide insights into the gendered nature of some men's violence.

Most of the time the gendered attribution of identity – a 'production ' (Hall 1990) or 'accomplishment' (Brittan 1989) – is taken for granted as natural and inevitable. This is predictable given the choices that men make about who they talk to and in what contexts. However, there are, in all our lives, moments when we become aware of the tentativeness of our cultural identities. For the men interviewed, a potential point of self-reflection had been opened up for them on starting a period in prison or on probation. The process of doing life-story work offered another opportunity and context for this to take place.

One of the men interviewed ('Nigel') was serving a probation order for domestic violence against his second wife. He was white, aged thirty-two, and had lived all his life in south Wales. At the time of the interviews he was unemployed. The life-history process clearly encouraged Nigel to reflect on his past experiences in relation to his present situation, negotiating various definitions of what it means to be a man through reconstructing his (auto)biography. The following extracts and analyses, closely following Nigel's own story, attempt to highlight the main themes emerging for further analysis and as possible starting-points for transformative/re-educational intervention.

'Fighting to survive': Nigel's life story

'The polio has given me my character, because as a child everything was a fight': reconstructions of childhood identity

At an early age Nigel contracted polio. This is the first issue that he noted in the interviews. He goes on to describe in much detail both the emotional and cultural effects of dealing with it. And, it is Nigel's experience of contracting polio which forms a central and recurring theme in his reconstruction of his life story, simultaneously affecting the on-going construction of his self-identity:

> The polio has given me my character, because as a child everything was a fight.

Of all the effects on producing his 'fighting character' Nigel notes the physical and bodily ones first and foremost:

> You see, well, my leg, I limp. It's better than it used to be. The difference between my left leg and my right used to be three inches or more.

Subsequently, learning how to walk was not easy for Nigel. One might consider the paradigm (choices) of adjectives possible to describe the ways in which such a disability is coped with: through patience, calmness, perseverance, etc. Nigel, however, uses fighting as an analogy to explain firstly how he learned to walk, and then to justify his 'fighting character':

> Because I had to fight to walk. Now, I'd kill myself if ever I couldn't walk. . .

While Nigel's experience of schooling was understandably disrupted by his frequent hospital visits, his memories of school are mediated through his polio and fighting identity:

> All the time I was at school people used to call me names, and I think it made me aggressive. I can remember one day at high school, I must have been in about the second year. I made a conscious decision to punch the first person to call me 'hop' or 'puny'. Well, this boy did, and I punched him and everybody else who called me names that day (. . .) I was pretty disruptive at school.

> The kids were cruel, and the teachers didn't care. I had a fight with a teacher once and got pushed down the stairs. I was always fighting, mainly verbal, so I never really bothered with school.

There are a number of issues that come from a 'decoding' of these life events and that relate to Nigel's construction of a masculine self. Clearly, he believes that fighting when he was at school was a way he could prevent others calling him names, which were damaging to his sense of self. His awareness of physical inadequacy is not a purely individual phenomenon however. It is related to his perception of other boys and the way they treated him.

As an adult he looks back at how he felt about his body which did not match up to the ideal of masculine physicality. The way in which Nigel responded to these feelings of 'puniness' and inadequacy, and subsequently, anger, are clearly seen in his attempts to prove his masculinity through fighting. The following vignette (mini-episode) works as a metaphor for this process: from feeling inadequate, cutting-off from the pain of that, and projecting it on to what he constructs in his story as the source of that anger:

> I can remember running home once to take the leg iron off, because I wanted to fight with this boy. I took the leg iron off, and I was holding it in my hand, so that I could hit him with it. A teacher turned up though and stopped me. Afterwards, I was so angry that I went upstairs to my room, and I started crying.

In this instance, Nigel ends up having to express the intensity of his emotions through crying. That he does this in private is significant, as is the fact that he recalled this incident as indicative of his childhood experiences.

'I was outside the system and I learnt to survive': Biker culture and a new location of self

Nigel explains how he got involved in the biker culture, and the pleasure he got from this in relation to the difficulties he experienced at both school and at home. If he felt let down by his body and excluded from, and hostile to, the institutions of home and school, he found a new locale for (constructing) his male identity in the 'biker gang':

> I got into motorbikes. Because I couldn't, well, I rebelled. My father hated the biker image. No long hair, no earrings, the biker image, being a Hell's Angel for a day. It's all to do with rebellion [. . .] Because of my leg, well, anyway, it gave me some freedom [. . .] I got streetwise, got my education that way. I was interested in all sorts of other groups at that time, hippies

and punk. But, with the bikers I was outside the system and I learnt to survive. I was always fighting to survive!

So, why didn't Nigel identify with the hippies and punks? What was it that appealed to Nigel at this particular moment in his life (he was thirteen when he first got involved); and which sustained his interest well into adult life?

Here, Nigel notes many factors which together formed his identification with the bikers. Firstly, there is the image: rebelliousness, aggression, operating on the peripheries of acceptable society. There was also the feeling of belonging after rejection:

> . . . they just accepted me for what I am, and that was a poke in the eye for my dad.

The bikers' culture was homologous to (fitted alongside) Nigel's self-identity at the time. It was at this time he started perceiving himself as autonomous; he was becoming 'his own person'. Central to joining the bikers, then, was that they provided a space where he could relocate his sense of self apart from family and school. Furthermore, the sense of escape and freedom was intensified by riding motorbikes in a group of other men:

> . . .it's the rush, adrenalin, high, whatever you want to call it. I enjoy riding, and to flout the law is part of it. I could ride all day, anywhere [. . .] There's so much freedom on a bike. More camaraderie too.

> It's cosy when you're in a crowd. I got a lot of status and street cred from it. And, I never felt intimated by the bikers. They were my brothers, it's all like that. There is a lot of fellowship with the bikers and I felt like I had to join a group, a gang.

It is no coincidence that Nigel refers to the gang as a 'fellowship', and his companions as 'brothers'. In doing so the implication is that women were absent, or at least, not worthy of inclusion or mention. This is not to suggest either that women were not part of the biker culture or indeed that they were not central in the on-going construction of Nigel's masculinity.

'We were called the DLFPC': locating a masculine identity in relation to women

Creating and sustaining an aggressive masculine identity for Nigel is closely tied to being heterosexual. His memories of the biker culture illustrate this:

> The image is macho, that's what attracts women. In school a bike was always an attraction. The girls put on a show, like.

The values associated with this self-perceived attraction for women underpin Nigel's approach to sexual relationships at this time in his life:

> I'd chase anybody. I've done the knight in shining armour bit [. . .] To tell the truth, I've always enjoyed the thrill of the chase as much as the reward for winning! [. . .] After, like, I would always tell my mates about it.

Confirming and locating his sexuality in relation to his 'mates' is a necessary part of 'social-bonding'. Attitudes to women in the biker culture contributed greatly to Nigel's heterosexual identity as a man. However, on reflection, there are some important tensions in his account. His acceptance and internalization of these values and attitudes towards women and sex is not best represented as a simple, straightforward process. Rather, the changing locations of self intersect at various points in his life in his constant reconstruction of his sexuality. Whilst illustrating his sexual exploitations of women within a male 'gang', the following mini-narrative also highlights some of the contradictions of such a subject position in the present as Nigel retrospects:

> I'm sorry for the way I treated women [. . .] There was a group of about four or five of us. We were known as the DLFPC. Well, that was because we were known as the 'dirty little fuck a pig club'. We tried to pull the ugliest woman in the place. I never went to bed with an ugly woman, but I've woken up with a few! [. . .] This all sounds really macho. There have probably been some broken hearts along the way.

> I'm glad I grew up before now, Aids and all that [. . .] They'd say though that a girl doing the same would be a tramp, but a guy would be a stud. That's what society says. I don't agree with that, but in principle that's how it is. I don't think that a woman should be demeaned if that's how she is, but a guy is boosted by it.

The motivation behind Nigel's desire for membership in the subculture of the bikers seems to be intimately linked to proving his masculinity in terms of aggression, rebellion, heterosexuality, and flouting the law (of his father as well as the police). This process of identification, and subsequent relocation of the main site of identity-formation has been described here in relation to the term 'homology'. Paul Willis (1978) first applied the term to describe the symbolic fit between the values and life-styles of a group, its members' subjective experience and the cultural forms (music, clothing, film, etc.) they use to express or reinforce its/their focal concerns. Dick Hebdidge (1978) explains: 'each part is organically related to other parts and it is through the fit between them that the subcultural member makes sense of the world.' Nigel perceives and represents his activities as a biker as the most positive and integrated (homologous) experience of his life. But the process and experiences of personally and culturally aligning himself to this particular group, as Nigel did (and attempts to do still), are ambiguous and contradictory; and have also had their negative side.

It could be suggested that such tensions are 'written into' Nigel's life story through his attempt to place a static self-definition of his identity within a shifting cultural context of changing attitudes of acceptability *vis-à-vis* sexuality and masculinity (his reference to Aids points to this). Ultimately, Nigel's life is homologous in some contexts and activities and not in others. Some of the ambiguity here comes from Nigel actively seeking the reassurance of belonging to the 'male club' because of his precarious purchase on 'being male'. Subsequently, he learns to conform to the accepted codes and conventions of hetero-sexual masculinity through his experiences in his family, and at school, and with the bikers' culture. In all these contexts the ambiguous relationship with his sense of self as a man exists within a social network of male power. The cultural and institutional locales for this constitute together, and in relation to the wider cultural dimension, an important force for regulating women and powerless masculinities.

> I've hit men, see, when I've been sober. I'd rather talk or walk away, but you know once there's been a push and a shove I become possessed, it's like I've lost my temper. It doesn't frighten me if there's no other option. I try to avoid losing my temper. I don't know if one punch is enough. You've got to do as much damage as possible once I lose control.

Nigel's constant reference to his experiences with this subculture, then, illustrates his continued desire to find a place for the reconstruction of a masculine sense of self as he gets older. In the process of doing this he attempts to keep hold of a sense of power and control and autonomy. It could be argued that this is intimately related to his violence – particularly to both his wives – who were on the peripheries of the bikers' subculture:

> Well, you get the blokes first, and then normally the girlfriends and wives follow [. . .] that's what attracted my wife. She used to be on the fringe of it all, but she's pulled away.

In terms of gender Nigel finds he has access to a powerful subject position; one that he is reluctant to give up:

> I still want to be wild for a while sometimes, I still miss the partying.

The location of his sense of self-identity in the present is mainly in relation to his own family with his second wife. To get there he had to first 'break off' from his parents and relocate his identity within the bikers' culture of fighting for escape, and misogyny, and subsequently to relocate his identity again back to the 'familial'. This process is not resolved for Nigel. The desire to return to his 'biker identity', and concomitant life-style, is a reminder of the tensions that exist in Nigel's life in the present as a father, husband and adult man; and in the past as a son. Therefore, it seems apposite to examine in more depth his family experiences as represented throughout his life story, which mainly focused on his father.

'We always had a physical relationship. I used to get hit!': (dis)locating a sense of self-identity

There are two levels of interpreting Nigel's life-story material relating to his father. On one level, there are the ways in which his father's relationship to Nigel affected him during his childhood. Whilst on another, interrelated level, there is the changing manner in which he has negotiated his sense of masculine identity in relation to his father. The former approach engages more with the gendered aspects of family life and social relations; the latter, with the on-going, active construction of masculinity in relation to these familial relations in a broader context. I would argue that, through reference to his father's effect on family life, Nigel moves through his life, constantly having to amend his cultural identity in relation to 'what his father stood for', first as a boy, then as a young man, and now in his present position as an adult, father, and husband.

In this way he positions or locates his self-identity *vis-à-vis* the family largely in relation to his father; this is in spite of his father's marked absence:

Well, my dad, he was always at work when we were kids. Never around when I needed him.

Nigel's father was working to establish his own retail business. And Nigel sees this as 'the' explanation for his father not spending a great deal of time together with him and the family. It was only in relation to Christmas that Nigel had anything positive to remember about his father:

As a kid, all the troubles were always put aside at Christmas. We'd go shopping with my father, and he'd spend like it was going out of fashion. If we said we liked something, we got it. We always had plenty of presents. That was the once in a year I gave my father a hug and a kiss.

Not only was there a general lack of presence on the part of his father, there was little emotional closeness either. This, in Nigel's own descriptions, had a profound effect on his own sense of self and attitudes towards emotions and relationships:

My dad never cried. I think that men don't have emotions. They bottle them up. I bottle everything up and then release it all, mainly verbally.

The significance of this for Nigel requires 'unpacking'. Drawing on the popular myth that men don't have emotions, Nigel makes sense of the impact of his father on his own emotional attitudes. A central, and very closely related theme, is Nigel's experiences of domestic violence as a child; and how he has responded to these in his adult life.

Nigel grew up in an environment where his father's violence was a way of life:

There was a lot of fighting, but mainly when we'd gone to bed. I can remember going to sleep crying because I could hear the arguing downstairs. Sometimes, it was so bad that I used to go downstairs and shout at my old man [. . .] I used to think of how I could get rid of the bastard. He was always the aggressor in our family, always where the aggression came from.

And, in the process of making sense of his father's violence towards himself, Nigel attempts to excuse it both through humour and deflection of blame:

We always had a physical relationship. I used to get hit! But it wasn't always my father's fault.

Perhaps it is in this process of transferring blame, and thus legitimating to some degree his father's violence, that it becomes easier for Nigel to justify his own violence in his adult relationships with women. Furthermore, Nigel felt it necessary to note the connections and tensions that existed between himself and his father:

> We were a lot alike after I was eleven, when I became my own person. He used to see himself through me. He put his head on my shoulders if you know what I mean. On reflection I can see that he's got no control over me, though he'd still like to think that he has.

Nigel's experience of family life, and his relationship with his father, prompted him to move out. He reconstructs this transitional period as one of rebellion. In the life-story interviews he attempts to relocate his sense of identity, and the site of this – as a 'biker' – was an active and meaningful choice; not least because of his father's reaction.[4]

'Our love is like a cake and each time I hit her it's like a piece of the cake being taken away': masculinity, alcohol and domestic violence
Whilst Nigel dismisses his violence against his first wife ('that relationship doesn't matter'), it is his violence towards his present wife that most concerns him. This does not mean that his first marriage is not significant. By constructing his previous marriage as insignificant he denies the impact of his violence on his first wife and the effects he has had as an absent father to his children from that marriage, along with a concomitant denial of his feelings towards these people. In both cases he plays down the significance of, and thereby cuts off or separates, that time from his present predicament. By doing this he (actively) fails to make any links that might bear significance on his relationship now. He also separates off previous relationships with women as unimportant; not 'serious'. For Nigel, these relationships are part of being a young man. They are significant, however, because they give an insight to the values Nigel associates with women. They may provide some clues as to the difficulties he has now in making a commitment (to a non-violent relationship) especially when 'commitment' is represented in his narrative as one of the causes of his violence and his desire to escape – 'to be wild again'.

'My problem is drink-related'

On a number of occasions Nigel makes a connection between his domestic violence and his drinking: 'For me, alcohol increases my aggression.' This is central to Nigel's conceptualization of his violence towards his wife. By making this connection he is drawing on the popular and widespread public belief that alcohol is a moral and behavioural incapacitator or disinhibitor. This is not to argue that alcohol does not produce chemical changes in the body that impair sensor–motor performance. What is at stake is Nigel's social construction of the role of alcohol. This is an example of 'the self-interested use of a motive' (Scully 1990).

By saying that he is always drunk when being violent to his wife, he casts doubt on his ability to control himself ('I'm not in control'); or to remember events as they actually happened ('I didn't know what I'd done'; 'I'm not aware of what I'm doing'). Scully (1990: 124) argues convincingly that this is in the interest of men who abuse their partners. MacAndrew and Edgerton (1969: discussed in Scully 1990: 122) argue that the relationship of alcohol to disinhibition is culturally learned and varies according to situation:

> Over the course of socialization, people learn about drunkenness and what their society 'knows' about drunkenness; and, accepting and acting upon the understandings thus imparted to them, they become the living confirmation of their society's teachings.

For Nigel, the specific location and social acceptability of his drinking is, then, significant:

> Part of my drinking is the social side, going to the pub with your mates. It's socially acceptable. The thing is not to take a problem home with me, that's when the trouble starts [. . .] It was easier to run away, go to the pub.

Nigel's use of violence when drunk is not a biological given. Rather, the emotional consequences of his drinking are culturally regulated through the expectation that violence can result from drinking. Because it is culturally approved that disinhibition is caused by drunkenness, men can exempt themselves from the ordinary behavioural limits that are associated with sobriety. Nigel seems to have internalized the social belief that he is not really himself when drunk. Through this social construction, he enables himself to interpret the changes brought about via alcohol to result in violence which is perceived as not representative of his 'true' self.

A further expectation of Nigel's is that to be drunk and take his troubles from the pub to his home can lead to his violence. As noted elsewhere in his life history, Nigel feels 'at home' with his mates and the pub is often the context for this social acceptance. There is a tension here with another type of security offered by home/family life. Nigel seems to reproduce this tension through separating the public (house) from the private (home). This is a subtle distinction, but through it Nigel attempts to construct a distance between his violence against his wife and the violence he uses against other men. This is closely related to Nigel's attempts to sustain a particular purchase on his sense of maleness. This is mediated – or rather constructed – through the social regulation of masculinity. Whilst it is unacceptable to hit women, it is acceptable to hit men. Indeed, Nigel claims to hit his wife only when he is drunk; but, to hit other men when he is sober is quite 'normal' and 'acceptable'. Clearly, Nigel conceptualizes his domestic violence and violence towards other men differently. It is as though he has been able to compartmentalize the two at a 'safe' distance from each other. However, by doing this he reproduces a central contradiction. This contradiction, embedded in the meanings and lived experience of violence, clearly underpins, and is used to support through justification and excuse, his continued identification with violence and aggression.

The contradiction and its ramifications are central to under-standing Nigel's present identity-work as he acknowledges his violence towards his wife. However, by viewing his masculinity as 'neutral' he is blind to the types of links that may be possible and desirable in order to enable him to change. Nigel focuses on his drinking and his father's violence as the root causes of his own violence:

> I can see that I'm doing the same as my father did. I was conditioned into it.

The centrality of violence and aggression in his on-going reconstruction of self is not decoded any further than this by Nigel. To do so would mean acknowledging the potential of having to give up the power he enforces over others, including his partner and children.

Summary/preliminary conclusions

Nigel reconstructs numerous childhood, teenage, and adult experiences through the telling of his life story. He starts with alienation and ridicule at school; lack of love from – but also identification with – his father; and competition in the family (from his two sisters, one of whom had epilepsy). In this way Nigel tells of a childhood in which he was constantly battling to find acceptance as a young man.

This might be 'read' also as a search for more 'livable' and secure location for the uncertainty/tentativeness of his masculine self-identity. Clearly, this new location is the biker culture wherein he is accepted (without 'stigma'). Moreover, he (over-)compensates for his self-perceived 'puniness' through a cultural clothing of leather, fast bikes, flouting the law, fighting, heterosexuality. How 'secure' this proved is a central and recurring contradiction for Nigel as he negotiates being an adult and a father and a husband within the parameters of his and others' expectations and what it is to them to be masculine.

The focus here has been on the contradictions of Nigel's masculine identity within a range of cultural contexts or locations: from family, to school, into the bikers' subculture, and back to the family. Across these sites, and through the shifting purchase on his sense of self-identity as a man, Nigel himself centralizes aggression, fighting, sex, and violence. These are appropriated in different ways at different moments and with different cultural meanings, but, nevertheless, run through his life story.

He sees his father's violence against his mother, for example, in largely negative and revengeful terms: 'I used to think how I could get rid of the bastard.' Significantly, he minimalizes that blame in relation to his father's aggression towards himself: 'I used to get hit but it wasn't always my father's fault.' For Nigel this is different from his and others' fighting at school: 'The only way I got accepted was through fighting.' And different again to his more positive(?) or celebratory association of the bikers' subculture with aggression: 'fighting the system' and 'doing as much damage as possible'.

The criteria Nigel uses to differentiate between the meanings and uses of violence in different contexts seem to be ambiguous and fluctuating across his life history. At times he legitimizes and justifies it; at others he believes it to be wrong and damaging. This is not to say that there is no common link. And one way of starting to make sense of this is to 'decode' the gendered meanings Nigel uses to relate his violence to his self-identity.

Possibilities for challenging research, men, violence and masculinities

It has been argued that a cultural understanding of the complex construction and regeneration of male identities may be a useful and productive way into understanding and responding to male violence. This has been demonstrated in relation to arguments about the constitution of 'normal' and 'legitimate' masculine identities situated in specific cultural and institutional contexts. Whilst these analyses are at an early stage of development, it is possible to make some useful observations linking some men, with some versions of masculine subjectivities, with some forms of violence.

It has also been noted that the process of research has encouraged us to consider the value of critical life-story work as a possible basis to pragmatic intervention – as a form of reflexive identity-work. In her research of the practices and experiences of black women in secure psychiatric hospitals, Sally Westwood (1992: 197) has suggested that life-history work might provide a focus for challenging and transformative research. She argues that such 'research methods and skills can be appropriated for counter-hegemonic work' (Westwood 1992: 197). Whilst it must be acknowledged that 'counter-hegemonic work' with men who are violent may need to be markedly different, a focus on critical life-story work might be usefully explored in relation to interventions with some violent men. From the research to date, it is emerging that this might best be done at critical incidents, or 'transition points'. The narratives that the respondents have produced in the interviews illustrate that their sense of self has undergone, or is in the process of undergoing, a potential transformation as a result of their prison or probation order.

Other evidence from the research, however, suggests that there are many barriers to such potential transformation, particularly in the context of prison culture, where the institutional and procedural relations of power are often modelled on the same sets of values underpinning narrowly aggressive ways of feeling, being and communicating.

One of the main issues, then, emerging from the project has been about recognizing the transformative possibilities of applications of the research that engage in a critical, challenging and cultural understanding of men, violence and masculinities. These ideas for change or intervention are centred around the life-history method as a technique for encouraging men to reassess their histories, attitudes and cultural and subjective positions of power. Moreover, the effectiveness of such re-educational strategies for change relies heavily on the institutional contexts in which they are implemented.

Afterword

A new project has now emerged, necessarily focusing on how a cultural critique of masculinities and violence, drawing on theories of cultural identities and social power, can effectively engage men in a process of change that results in the reduction of their violence. The site for this project is the Mid Glamorgan Probation Service, where pilot programmes for male perpetrators of violence, and sexual violence, are currently being developed. This work incorporates policy-led, and theoretically informed, evaluative research assessing the effectiveness and politics of such intervention.

Acknowledgements

We would like to acknowledge our thanks to the following agencies for their involvement and interest: Gwent Probation Service, HMP Cardiff, Mid Glamorgan Probation Service, and South Glamorgan Probation Service.

Notes

[1] A recent example of how this might work in relation to understanding the cultural construction of masculinity is David Jackson's *Unmasking Masculinity: A Critical Autobiography* (1990). For a critical and useful – although brief – discussion of the possibilities of 'life-story' research on masculinities see also David Morgan's *Discovering Masculinity* (1992).

[2] For example, in south Wales a number of agencies have taken an interest in the project in relation to their own development of work in this area, for example: Mid Glamorgan Probation Service, Gwent Probation Service, the Prison Service, Women's Aid, Victim Support, and Mid Glamorgan Domestic Violence Forum.

[3] Part of the process or 'praxis' of doing this is to rehearse a range of theoretically, politically and personally related arguments, in order to integrate the research work and subsequent insights in practical contexts.

This paper is part of this on-going process; so, comments and feedback are welcome.

4   A key debate in recent theorizations of the gendered self, which might throw some light on this, is the psycho-social framework of object relations theory. This provides some analytical strategies which can encompass an analysis of Nigel's life story, (and within this the dislocated and fragmentary aspects of his identity-work in relation to family relations), in relation to his sometimes violent, sometimes contradictory relationships with women, children, and other men. Of course, the position of his mother in Nigel's life story is of much relevance here; and we note the absence of relevant discussion around this.

References

Beechey, V. and Donald, J. (eds.). *Subjectivity and Social Relations* (Milton Keynes, Open University Press).

Brittan, Arthur (1989). *Masculinity and Power* (Oxford, Blackwell).

Connell, R. W. (1987). *Gender and Power* (Cambridge, Polity Press).

Franklin, Sarah *et al.* (eds.) (1991). *Off Centre: Feminism and Cultural Studies* (London, Lawrence and Wishart).

Griffin, Christine (1992). 'The researcher talks back', in Shaffer and Stebbins (eds.) *Experiencing Fieldwork: An Inside View of Qualitative Research* (Newbury Park, CA, Sage).

Hall, Stuart (1990). 'Cultural identity and diaspora', in Jonathon Rutherford (ed.) *Identity: Community, Culture, Difference* (London, Lawrence and Wishart).

Hebdidge, Dick (1978). *Subculture: the Meaning of Style* (London, Methuen).

Jackson, David (1990). *Unmasking Masculinity: A Critical Autobiography* (London, Unwin Hyman).

Johnson, Richard (1985). 'The story so far: and further transformations?', in Punter *Introduction to Contemporary Cultural Studies* (Harlow, Longman).

Morgan, David (1992). *Discovering Masculinity* (London, Unwin Hyman).

Plummer, Ken (1983). *Documents of Life* (London, Unwin Hyman).

Rutherford, Jonathon (1990). 'A place called home: identity and the cultural politics of difference', in Rutherford (ed.) *Identity: Community, Culture, Difference* (London, Lawrence and Wishart).

Scully, Diana (1990). *Understanding Sexual Violence* (London, Harper Collins).

Shaw, Clifford (1930). *The Jack-Roller: A Delinquent Boy's Own Story* (Chicago, University of Chicago Press).

Westwood, Sally (1992). 'Power/knowledge: the politics of transformative research', in *Studies in the Education of Adults*, 24 (2), October.

Willis, Paul (1978). *Profane Culture* (London, Routledge).

10

'A father's "normal" love'?: Masculinities, criminology and the family

RICHARD COLLIER

Men? Who needs them? Far from single mothers being the objects of shame or pity they once were, more and more women are opting to have babies independent of traditional reproduction and family structure. And age seems no barrier. But is this a revolution out of control? (*Guardian*, 18 February 1993)

During July 1993 a high-profile and apparently orchestrated political row took place following comments made by the Cabinet Minister John Redwood.[1] He had suggested that some single women were deliberately becoming pregnant, with no intention of marrying, in the knowledge that they would then be supported by the state. Moreover, he declared, lone mothers should not receive state benefit until the 'errant father' had been found and forced to return to the family. He was not simply suggesting that fathers should make a financial contribution to the upkeep of their child. This was already the task of the Child Support Agency and government policy under the Child Support Act 1991. He was also requiring that fathers return to the household so that they might offer 'the normal love and support that fathers have offered down the ages'.

This article is about that 'normal love and support'. It seeks to explore the ways in which a range of issues around lone motherhood, the family and the criminality of male youth are at present being constructed as an 'attack', not simply on fatherhood, but on men and the 'traditional reproduction and family structure' generally. It is concerned with how, in the 1990s, deeply problematic ideas of masculine 'crisis'[2] and 'renewal'[3] are currently serving to deflect attention from important changes taking place in the social production of discourses of masculinities.[4] Far from single mothers no longer being the 'objects of shame and pity they once were' a range of issues around questions of morality, economics and criminality continue to attach to the 'social problem' of lone motherhood. They tend not to attach to the problematic nature of fatherhood.

One result of this has been to deflect attention from the ways in which the construction of an idea of masculine 'crisis' has itself been an important element in the restructuring of the welfare state and a 'wider project of patriarchal reconstruction' (Smart 1989). . . . a 'backlash against long term changes in gender relations and against feminism' (Mann and Roseneil 1994: 5). Or, as the *Guardian* asks about those reproductive technologies which have recently, and controversially, facilitated 'motherhood without men',[5] 'Men? Who Needs Them?' The time is propitious to ask such questions. For, a year on from John Redwood's comments and the debates of the summer of 1993, just what we as a society understand 'responsible' fathering to involve has moved to the centre of the political stage in Britain in relation to both the family and, in particular, to crime.

A context: masculinity, criminology and the family

What has all this to do with criminology? Criminology is, at present, at something of a critical juncture with regard to what is being increasingly called the issue of the 'masculinity of crime'. On one level contested understandings of paternal masculinity have been central to recent developments around crime and criminal justice. The Home Secretary, Michael Howard, has vigorously sought to 'defend' the father from those who would wish to 'sack' him from the family (Morgan 1986).[6] By highlighting a purported connection between absent fatherhood and criminality, a correlation between 'dangerous' male youth and single motherhood has been constructed as central to the retributivist 'law and order' agenda which has emerged in the wake of the now discredited 1991 Criminal Justice Act reforms. Politicians,[7] the media[8] and academics from diverse political persuasions (Dennis and Erdos 1992; Halsey 1992; Murray 1990) have each, in the aftermath of the murder of James Bulger, drawn on the language of a new urban 'underclass'[9] in seeking to valorize fatherhood and the 'traditional' family. Meanwhile the numbers of single mothers, and the consequent 'breakdown' of the family, are blamed on such diverse influences as the Church, 'politically correct' ideas[10] and a feminist movement which '. . . has given encouragement to the concept that it is all right to have a child and bring the child up on your own.'[11] The scapegoating of single mothers as 'undeserving' poor which followed John Redwood's remarks in 1993 did, of course, conveniently place on the political agenda the possibility of further cuts in welfare benefits (Mann and Roseneil 1994).

Such debates on the family and juvenile delinquency have a long history. It had been commonplace for the early Victorians of the mid-nineteenth century to relate juvenile delinquency to a breakdown in parental control and the family (Pearson 1994: 1162). My concern here is on a rather different level, however. Whether criminology is to make sense of recent events depends in part on how the 'masculinity problematic'[12] – the range of changes taking place around masculinity at present – is to be conceived. To do this we need to comprehend both the terminal masculinism which has historically been at the heart of criminology's own project *and* locate historically the emergence of specific discourses of masculinities. To begin to make sense of the present it is instructive to look to the past. What follows, therefore, is a discussion of the history of fatherhood in law. It is an attempt to address present concerns through exploring what has been a substantial failing of criminology's past – its inability to 'take masculinity seriously'.

Criminology: 'taking masculinity seriously?'

The discipline of criminology illustrates this problem of 'taking masculinity seriously' (Stanko and Hobdell 1993). It is, perhaps, the classic masculine discourse, pervaded by an ideology of masculinism[13] in terms of its methods and epistemological assumptions (Gelsthorpe and Morris 1990). Criminology has traditionally concerned itself with men and crime (Allen 1988). Yet in so doing it has failed to recognize the social and contingent nature of the masculinity/crime relation and the fact that it has been men, and not humankind, who have constituted the object of study (Cain 1990; Smart 1990; Brown 1986). Criminology may not have necessarily *excluded* women from its discourse – women are present – but women and women's subjectivities have been rendered systematically marginal to the discipline (Smart 1976). Criminology has failed, in other words, to address the gendering of its object of study (Scraton 1990) – and the crucial fact that most crimes remain unimaginable without the presence of men.

It is interesting therefore, but not surprising, that recent advocates of a critical 'sociology of masculinity'[14] should have used examples from criminology to highlight the gender-blindness of sociology in a more general way. Thus 'juvenile delinquency', street-corner gangs, understandings of legitimate 'goals' and 'means' – indeed, of the myriad causes of educational underachievement, deviancy and criminality amongst groups of males (the 'very stuff' of criminology) can all be seen as the exemplar of a gendered discourse. In speaking of 'men', criminology has remained largely blind to the social production of men *as men*, to the communality and differentiation within male experiences. Criminology has, in short, failed to ask what it may be about men,

> . . . not as working-class, not as migrants, not as underprivileged individuals but *as men* that induces them to commit crime? Here it is no longer women who are judged by the norms of masculinity and found to be 'the problem'. Now it is men and not humanity who are openly acknowledged as the objects and subjects of investigation. (Grosz 1987: 6, quoted by Allen 1988.)

Feminist perspectives have redrawn (or perhaps irretrievably undermined?) the masculinist and positivist foundations of this model of criminology (Heidensohn 1994; Smart 1990). Yet in the almost twenty years that have passed since the publication of Carol Smart's influential *Women, Crime and Criminology* (1976) it is only now, in the 1990s, that criminology is beginning to 'take seriously' masculinity as a social construct. Criminology has, albeit reluctantly, been forced by feminism to face up to the partial and evasive nature of its past accounts of crime. Feminism has clearly transformed our understandings of 'malestream' criminology. The multifarious ways in which criminology has, in the past, been gender-biased has been well documented elsewhere (e.g. Gelsthorpe and Morris 1990; Smart 1976). However what I am interested in here are the *ways in which* masculinity is now, as a result of feminist interventions, presently being addressed within criminology.

There has occurred a subtle, but significant, shift. At national criminological conferences, at day schools on criminal justice, at workshops on the family and crime, whenever 'new directions' in criminological research are being discussed (where do we go from here? what new areas are there?) one thing repeats itself again and again – the need to 'tackle' the masculinity of crime and criminology, to take this subject 'seriously'. The 1993 Conference on Masculinity and Crime held at Brunel University is perhaps the most tangible manifestation, in Britain at least, of the recognition of the problem of men and masculinity within criminology. At the 1993 British Criminology Conference, however, what one colleague described as 'the "m" word' – masculinity – appeared in many guises.

This development in criminology cannot, however, be seen in isolation from the construction of a 'masculinity problematic' in society in a much more general sense. Without reference, that is, to the range of cultural and economic developments which have combined to render the social consequences of hitherto dominant models of masculinity[15] increasingly problematic; and any discipline concerned with a social phenomenon such as crime cannot, of course, remain impervious to such developments. The impact of feminism, the increasing proportion of women in the workplace, wider shifts in employment patterns resulting from economic restructuring, mass unemployment and shifts from industrial-based to service economies (as well as an increasing cultural valorization of leisure time) have all thrown into question the traditional ideas of masculine subjectivity based on the centrality of work and male sexual prerogative. Nowhere, perhaps, have the results of these tensions been more evident than in the domain of family law and around changing perceptions of fatherhood and men's role in the family.

Family law: constructing the 'crisis' of masculinity

The 'problems' of single motherhood and the 'flight of fathers' from the home referred to above have involved a range of issues central to both criminology and family law. The construction of 'father-absence' as problematic *per se* is, in a sense, at the *interface* of criminology and family law. What we are dealing with is a nexus of more general concerns about family maintenance, legitimacy, access to children, public spending, delinquency and crime. If the story of criminology is one of 'dangerous' or 'wild' masculinities (and in particular of urban male youth) the representations of masculinity to be found in family law are replete with constructions of 'the good father'; that is, of masculinities which have been judicially assigned a positive value usually, though not exclusively, in the context of assessing the desirability of the presence of a certain kind of fatherhood in the family. Yet what has been unspoken in the recent debates is what we actually understand by this father-presence – the 'good father' as it were – in the first place.

This failure to engage with the sociality of paternal masculinities has a particular significance in the arena of family law. It is here that a perceived diminution of men's legal rights in relation to women, children and property has been singled out for critique by those who would argue that the law has now swung too far in favour of its 'spoilt darling'. Given a gloss of legitimacy by the powerful (if empirically questionable) ideology of the 'new fatherhood' (Lewis and O'Brien 1987; Lewis 1986) the politics of family law and fatherhood have thus become enmeshed within debates around contemporary masculinity and ideas of masculine 'crisis'. Recent men's liberationist texts have simply brought to these debates a particularly bitter and vituperative anti-feminist twist (e.g., Lyndon 1992; Thomas 1993; Farrell 1993; see further Faludi 1992; Roberts 1992). As developments around the Child Support Agency show only too clearly, contemporary matrimonial politics, notably around post-separation child care and maintenance, continue to cut to the heart of tensions and contradictions within men's responses to feminism. Any critical discussion of paternal masculinity, informed by what I have identified as the crucial awareness that discourses of masculinity are themselves historically and culturally specific, remains sorely lacking in recent debates.

Fatherhood, families and 'dangerous' masculinities

The question remains to be asked therefore. Just who is this 'normal father' – this man whose 'love and support' so binds together the family? When did he emerge? Where is he now? The rights and obligations which married men have historically had over 'their' children can be socially, economically and politically located in the context of broader changes in family structure which resulted from the transformations of the agricultural and industrial revolutions of the eighteenth and nineteenth centuries. By the time of the late nineteenth century the law had already begun, albeit slowly, to move away from the common law 'empire of the father' position declared by Blackstone (*Commentaries on the Law of England*, Vol. 1: 453, quoted in McKee and O'Brien 1982: 27). A succession of legal reforms had gradually brought increased legal rights to the mother. However as the apotheosis of nineteenth-century 'absolute father right', the 1883 case of *Agar-Ellis* v. *Lascelles* (1883) 24 Ch.D 317 illustrates the nature of the married father's rights at the time.[16]

Father right was a natural and 'sacred' right based on the reciprocity of obligation and paternal prerogative (*per* Brett MR 327–8: 337. See also *In Re* Curtis 28 LJ 458.) Paternal authority is naturalized; it needs no explanation, justification or further deliberation – it is impervious to questioning.

The paternal masculinity invoked in *Agar-Ellis* (broadly, one of the Victorian paterfamilias) only related to the lives of fathers socialized into the '. . . civilized self-control . . . rigidity of character structure' which marked the middle-class Victorian Man (Cominos 1963; quoted in Richards 1987: 27). Class, geographic (e.g., rural/urban), religious and ethnic differences all divested the legal authority of the father (as well as beliefs about sexuality) in different ways. Cases such as *Agar-Ellis* which came to court at the time involved wealthy families, and divorce was heavily restricted and permeated by a sexual double-standard. What this means is that the passionate homilies of judges to the symbolic good of 'the family' must be seen as prescriptive rather than descriptive. They were addressing a particular *kind* of paternal masculinity. It also means that any contemporary recourse to ideas of 'the normal love . . . that fathers have offered down the ages' must be treated with caution. Emotional and physical distance has marked fatherhood more than the ideal of affection in the modern sense.

Crucially, with regard to recent debates around the new urban 'underclass', the idea of 'modern' fatherhood – the father of the egalitarian, 'symmetrical' family – has been constituted through reference to social and economically specific ideas of 'respectable' masculinity and sexual propriety. The 'man of law' (Naffine 1990), we must remember, was established in legal discourse around the same time as urbanization, industrialization and capital accumulation were transforming pre-industrial conceptions of civil society and, crucially, of ideals of parenthood itself. The impact of industrialization and urbanization had brought with it an undermining of the traditional social controls which had regulated sexuality in the pre-industrial world. The 'sexual waywardness' perceived to be endemic amongst the dangerous classes was in fact a consequence of a more general proliferation of pre-, extra- and intra-marital sexual styles which accompanied industrialization. The sexual transgressions of the lower orders were to be, however, rapidly seen from the viewpoint of a sex- and class-based notion of sexual propriety (Finer and McGregor 1974: para 59).

These changes brought about no less than a reconstitution of familial, household and gender relations at the same time as male power within the 'public' domain of work, the market and industrial capital was being entrenched through the incorporation of 'public' masculinities (Hearn 1992). It is the history of these 'competing masculinities', in both North America and Britain, which is now beginning to be mapped by historians (e.g. Rotundo 1993: Davidoff and Hall 1987) and sociologists of masculinity (Hearn 1992). Central to this history, it is clear, has been the idea of the reconstruction or *modernization* of fatherhood.

The 'modern' father is very different from the paterfamilias of *Agar-Ellis* and the 'wild' and unrespectable masculinities of the urban mob. The efforts which have gone historically into legitimating and promulgating this ideal of a responsible and 'respectable' familial masculinity '. . . through the printed word and via prestigious and proliferating educational institutions' (Mangan and Walvin 1987: 1) should not be underestimated (Rotundo 1987; Vance 1985). At its heart is the ideology of separate spheres, the rational imperatives of industrialization, industrial production and the standardization of labour and products. It is, above all, a model of the father as provider which remains with us today (Naffine 1990: 105). Domesticating masculinity, moving from the dangerous masculinities of dangerous classes (immoral, promiscuous, drunk, violent and so forth) involved also ridding masculinity of that which was the perceived essence of maleness at the time – the 'natural' force of male sexuality and its potentially destructive expression. It is no wonder, therefore, that this process involved a de-sexualizing of the father as he is transformed into the sex-less, safe and recognizable 'dad' of today. The temperance movement (Hey 1984), campaigns around 'moral purity' (Walkowitz 1980) and more generally the prescriptive moral order and gender ideology of the urban Victorians all sought to discipline both men and women to the strictures of the hearth and home and to the tempo of the industrial order.

The 'respectable' masculinity of the man of law was set against something else; the irresponsible and sexually licentious 'dangerous classes' who haunted the Victorian imagination and whose pre-industrial pursuits informed the policing and demarcation of urban areas into areas 'safe' for both capital development and 'respectable' domestic space (Cohen 1981; Storch 1981). From 'darkest Africa to darkest England' (Showalter 1992: 5), and trading on eugenic fears of race degeneration, chroniclers of the nineteenth century had begun to depict a netherworld of a chronically poor class who were yet to be civilized into the gender norms of the new familial order (e.g., Booth 1976; see Stedman-Jones 1976; Keating 1976). This process, however, was to be and remains partial: as criminologists we come up against our familiar friend (or enemy?) time and again – the 'unreconstructed' (a telling phrase) 'dangerous' masculinities of a 'wild' and 'disorderly' male youth.

Though the ideal of respectable familial masculinity,

> . . . made important inroads . . . in middle-class schools, churches and homes . . . it is open to serious doubt whether [it] managed to take root and grow at the lower end of the social scale, where it encountered the antipathy of the poor, ill-educated and aggressive urban youths who remained the perennial but hostile target of proponents of this middle-class ideal. (Mangan and Walvin 1987: 5)

It is these 'poor, ill-educated and aggressive urban youths' who continue to be cast as the 'other' of a respectable familial masculinity. These are the 'sacrificial men' (Naffine 1990) of the law, the economically and culturally marginalized 'subordinated' masculinities (Connell 1987) of an apparently 'undomesticated' group of men who do not understand, or who reject, the responsibilities of their 'betters'. The 'young, poor and uneducated' males (Naffine 1990: 124) who, we must remember, remain the primary object of criminological discourse and the criminal justice system (Box 1981).

It should not surprise us that competing accounts of these dangerous and destructive masculinities should have surfaced so powerfully in both recent debates around the 'new underclass' (Dennis and Erdos 1992) as well as feminist interventions concerned with gendering the youth/crime debate (e.g. Campbell 1993). Given the power of élite males to construct a moral discourse of their own gender, the marginalization of working-class cultures and these masculinities has a long and revealing history in legal discourse. In relation to recent constructions of lone motherhood as a social problem, however, the hypocrisy which has marked readings of this hierarchy of masculinities is offensive and misleading. This has been particularly clear in relation to the recent controversy surrounding the Child Support Act 1991 and the Child Support Agency (CSA) where, I have argued above, the idea of a masculine 'crisis' has been most forcefully articulated within a political economy of fatherhood. The example of the CSA shows just how this division of masculinities can be reproduced in a contemporary setting.

Errant fathers, family men and dangerous masculinities
There has been a systematic failure in recent debates around child support to address the fact that generations of men have been considered effectively redundant by the women with whom they have children either because they cannot or will not pay maintenance. Rather, when paternal masculinity is considered it has been through reference to the familiar myths and images of fathering: in particular, that of the 'irresponsible' feckless (lower-class) father and, in contrast, the 'normal love' offered by responsible and respectable married men (such as John Redwood and his Conservative Cabinet colleagues). A number of commentators have noted the class-based nature of the campaign against the Child Support Act 1991 in which ideas of competing masculinities have been central. James Pirrie of the Solicitor's Family Law Association captures well this aspect of the protest:

> Looking back, the most astounding thing about this fiasco is how middle-class left and right-wingers created the mythical bogeyman of the absent father who wandered around council estates, siring children without a care in the world. (*Independent on Sunday* 1 July 1993)

For many fathers, encountering the CSA has been their first experience of the welfare benefit system. As with the Campaign for Justice on Divorce in the late 1970s and early 1980s (Alcock 1984) the government has appeared once again to have listened to the complaints of middle-class men in a way it fails to do with other groups in society (notably, single mothers). Yet the deceit and gender-blindness with which the debate about single mothers and child support as a whole has been constructed is indicative of much more than simply the contemporary purchase of the underclass thesis (Mann and Roseneil 1994). What it also reveals is how it has been within one particular section of society – read underclass – that the 'problem' of the 'flight of fathers' has been primarily constructed. Such an image is deliberately misleading.

The continued political concern with single mothers who have never married obscures the fact that around two-thirds of lone mothers are divorced, separated or widowed. That is, made up of women who have tried the nuclear ideal but have found, for whatever reason, that it does not always work. Moreover, the dominant construction of single mothers and absent fathers promotes a belief that the 'problem' is really a question of the individual irresponsibility of a single group of men and women – and, crucially, not a problem of cultures of masculinity which pervade socio-economic groupings. It is thus the *invisibility of fatherhood*, secured through reference to a catch-all, benign but illusive, 'family man', which has functioned to make the scapegoating of single mothers possible. What are these errant fathers like? Well, they are not like us. 'We' are 'family men' – or we might potentially take up the subject position of family man (the heterosexual narrative of courtship, coupledom and breakdown is quite clear).

The failure to engage emotionally and economically with women and children cannot be confined to a particular class of men. It is not just the 'irresponsible' behaviour of a 'bunch of jobless teenagers' but is one end of a continuum of what is considered to be 'acceptable' masculine behaviour; and therein lies the problem:

> It is not only unemployed men from inner city dumps who feel that it is perfectly OK to procreate and move on. All kinds of men think children basically belong to women, that their part in the process ends as soon as they put their trousers back on . . . we can't even have a debate if no one is going to ask the most obvious and fundamental question: how do you get men to change? (Suzanne Moore, *Guardian* 16 July 1993)

How, that is, do you put 'changing men' on the political agenda – the very question, I have argued, that criminology is now attempting to do? These are issues about the diversity of masculinities which criminology must now face. In the context of an anti-feminist 'backlash' and a resurgent retributivism it is insufficient to fall back on naturalized ideas of masculinity, on notions of 'functional' male roles and masculine 'deviance'. The past of criminology is bedevilled by such ideas. Dominant notions of masculinity are themselves more likely to be inherently crimogenic – part of 'being a man' is, in a sense, to walk the line between danger/deviance and conformity (a dynamic positivist criminology has systematically failed to explore). It is through disturbing the perceptual grid which renders male heterosexuality invisible that it becomes possible to '. . . recognise the extent of the complex, mutually reinforcing nature of men's power, as a class, and the diversity of men and men's power' (Hearn 1992: 96). Meanwhile, in relation to the stigmatizing of single mothers, it should not surprise us that the corporeality of women continues to be assigned sexualized meanings which reflect the class-subjectivities of those who are in a position to so label women. For every 'good father', a 'loyal wife'; for every 'errant father', a 'scrounging' lone mother.

The gendering of the underclass debate as a whole is as insidious and misleading as it is crude. The historical emergence of these ideas of 'underclass' masculinity must be seen in relation to a discourse of 'respectable' masculinity. The 'errant' fathers, aggressive youths and dangerous masculinities (the very stuff of traditional criminological discourse)

> . . . have more in common with the men who represent the nation, the rowdy louts in the Palace of Westminster, whose manners are modelled on an upper-class cult of conflict. The lads on the terraces behave more like MPs on the benches than school dinner ladies and secretaries, and the women who have to put up with them. (Campbell 1993: 313)

It would be misleading at this point simply to '. . . enlist sympathy for the working-class family as subject to surveillance by experts', however (O'Donovan 1993: 22). The politics of gender cuts across traditional party-politics and what we are in fact dealing with here are discourses of 'respectable' and 'irresponsible/dangerous' masculinities which are, in fact, two sides of the same coin. It is a *male* culture – contested ideas of masculinity – and not simply a *class* culture which is at issue here. If we confine our analysis of masculinity and power to either the private or public spheres then we misunderstand the nature of an apparently seamless web of masculine authority which encompasses the familial and institutional terrains of interpersonal relationships, employment, the state and the 'public spaces' of leisure and the street. That is, we write out of the analysis the fundamental insights of feminist criminologies. It is misleading, Beatrix Campbell has argued, to interpret the 'flight of fathers' either as a purge orchestrated by mothers or through reference to a 'heyday of respectability as the proper regime of family life' (which is, in effect, John Redwood's stance) where that 'respectability' was expressed through the economic power of the father (Campbell 1993; cf. Dennis and Erdos 1992). That 'respectability' was premised in the first place on a legally structured male authority derived from the man/work relation and if '. . . authority is defined as legitimate power, then we can say that the main axis of the power structure of gender is the general connection of authority with masculinity' (Connell 1987: 109).

Authority is a key in relation to the purported 'crisis' of masculinity in family law. In the case of current controversies surrounding child support the reduction of emotional relationships to a financial equation by the CSA, however objectionable in theory, does tell us much about how law has historically constructed the family man. The problem for those contesting the CSA assessments, for example, with their perceived reduction of men to 'cheque signing machines without rights' (Roger Whitcombe, *Guardian* 24 January 1994), is that in law 'being' a father frequently does appear to come down to an economic link with children; to 'being' a remote and authoritarian figure, empowered and identified above all through publicly related activities. In the present context what these classes of males can also be seen to share, alongside an irresponsibility which has in the past been legally endorsed (Smart 1987), is a *lack* of any involvement in child care. There is a growing consensus that fathers should be financially responsible for their children. What there does not appear to be, however, is any understanding of how cultures of masculinity which are inimical to men's involvement with child care have themselves been reproduced through law (notably through reference to the public/private divide) and how they continue to inform our understandings of the morality, economics and politics of single parenthood.

The diminution of fathers' formal legal 'rights' since the time of *Agar-Ellis* has not meant that paternal masculinity no longer embodies claims to power and authority in the family. Rather, the power embodied in paternal masculinity has itself been modernized, or reconstituted, in ways compatible with the new familial order. Specifically, a gendered structuring of domestic labour was entrenched in law as the family sphere continued to be legally structured as the location for the exercise of power, authority and dominance by men (O'Donovan 1985; Smart 1984, 1989; Atkins and Hoggett 1984; Okin 1989). In the reconstruction of fatherhood which has taken place throughout the twentieth century, men's involvement in child care has been brought into the public domain, however (Hearn 1992). No longer can fathers assert, as per *Agar-Ellis* (above) 'this child is mine'. Paternal masculinity continues to seek legitimation through reference to a naturalized idea of fatherhood in which a 'lack' or absence from child care is legitimated. Only now it does so through recourse to the ideology of father-absence.

Is it 'in the best interests of the child' that the father is present? Do 'families need fathers'? The establishment of this child-centred imperative in   determining post-separation arrangements (e.g. Guardianship of Minors Act 1925 s 1: Children Act 1989 s 1) has necessitated no less than constructing father-presence as desirable *per se* in the family (notwithstanding the evidence of men's violences in the home). The 'desirable' paternal presence of the detached father exists first and foremost as an *economic resource* which presumes the physical absence of fathers from the family domain (because they are or should be 'at work': Richards 1987: 32).[17] The ideal of the companionate marriage presumed an increased joint activity on the part of both husband and wife. Yet in reality it appears tasks remain segregated on gender lines with the father a detached and often absent figure (Lewis 1986). But should this surprise us, when it continues to be through a primary reference to work and capacity for paid employment that masculine subjectivity is constructed in family law? Tackling such issues involves embracing a political agenda and policies which would appear anathema to the present government.

(Re)constructing the 'family man'

A Cabinet Minister declares his wish to return to 'the normal love and support' of the father; academics bemoan the 'breakdown' in the family and the lack of male role models. The result – urban disorder, poverty, widespread and growing criminality – is plain for all to see. Newspaper editorials, television and radio programmes and numerous articles question the 'crisis' of masculinity, the 'fashionable' belittling of men and the emergence of a new 'disposable sex' (Farrell 1993). Who can disagree with the 'common sense' of those who argue for a return to 'traditional' values and, of course, the 'traditional' family? And who can argue that criminology has not palpably 'failed' to explain rising crime? That criminology has not itself 'failed' *per se*, unable to transcend its positivist originating paradigm (see, for example, Smart 1990)?

These are arguments which, in the present political climate, have considerable force and appeal and which, importantly, criminologists concerned about recent trends in criminal justice policy must face. The 'back to basics' débâcle might have undermined the plausibility of the wider moral agenda espoused by significant sections of the Conservative Party and the media. Certainly, Cabinet divisions on the correlation between lone parenthood, family breakdown and criminality testify to a more complex scenario than any thesis of a homogeneous 'backlash' would suggest.[18] Nonetheless, in constructing the new 'law and order' agenda of the 1990s – and in legitimating the rejection of reforms which, however partial, marked a progressive approach to crime – the gender politics of fatherhood, family and the underclass debate have been central. The masculinity of crime is, I have argued, central to such a politics.

There have been two elements to the transformation of fatherhood from the times of the 'pre-modern' paterfamilias to the 'modern' father of the purportedly 'symmetrical' and egalitarian family. First, it has been necessary to construct father presence as desirable and father absence as problematic. It has been primarily through reference to their presumed utility as appropriate male 'role models' (utilizing a crude, and intellectually flawed variant of sex role theory) that the law has sought to attach fathers to families. It is also through the language of the male 'role model' that 'underclass' theorists, be they 'ethical socialists' or New Right apologists, have similarly sought to defend a masculinity which is, in so many other ways, now consigned to history.

Secondly, it has been necessary to render fatherhood 'safe'; or, more accurately, to make a distinction between the law's construction of familial paternal masculinities and the other 'dangerous' masculinities we have seen above. Through resorting to the idea of the 'family man' it has been possible to contrast the benign masculinities of matrimonial law with their antithesis – the 'wild' and 'dangerous' masculinities of criminology. The cost of this bifurcation of masculinity, however, has been to divert attention from the problematic nature of masculinity *per se* and, in particular, from the socially destructive nature of masculinities *inside* the family. This has been achieved through assigning to the extra-familial domain values which did not accord with this image of the modern and safe father. It is this idea that the errant father discourse taps into. Thus masculinities outside the familial heterosexual matrix are sexualized; for example, the 'promiscuous' homosexual, the 'irresponsible' unmarried father who evades his responsibilities, the sexually suspect male who fails to marry after 'sowing his wild oats' – a range of ideas involving notions of promiscuity, bodily hygiene and notions of male sexuality as threat to children. Who is it that John Redwood, Michael Howard, Peter Lilley *et al.* wish to return to the home? Those violent men whom the law already fails adequately to protect so many women from?

The reassertion of fatherhood rests, in other words, on a particular *ideal* of fatherhood and family life in which the 'responsible' and 'respectable' 'family man' remains a key player. Yet for all the law's endeavours to construct the 'family man' as a priori 'safe' and desirable, the dangerous and the familial share much more than is commonly acknowledged. At times that which is dangerous (e.g. men's violence and certain transgressive sexual behaviour) filters through (or 'leaks into') the familial domain. In a different context certain values which are traditionally culturally considered to be 'masculine' (e.g. competitiveness, a certain machismo, aggression) may be either celebrated or reviled depending on contingencies of class, timing and locale. Criminologists are familiar with such ideas of 'subterranean values', 'strain' and 'stigma'. What criminology has failed to do is to face what these ideas might tell us about masculinity as a social and contingent construct; how these ideas are themselves *masculinized*. I have argued that criminology needs, as a result of feminist challenges, now to reassess the assumptions it has made about masculinity. This must be part of truly 'taking masculinity seriously'.

Concluding remarks

I have sought to outline how a critical approach to the social construction of discourses of masculinity and 'fatherhood' can help us to understand such issues. The 'family man' in law, as an ideal of (hetero) familial masculinity, remains a dominant motif in law. It has been constituted across a multiplicity of discourses and practices, not towards any one overarching purpose, but as an effect of power which has served to reconstruct fatherhood whilst maintaining economic and social arrangements that benefit all men as men. The shift between absolute father-right and the emergence of the modern family took place alongside the growth of a range of regulatory strategies and techniques of surveillance and normalization more attuned to the disciplinary mechanisms of the modern order. However, these regulatory agencies have also been concerned with reproducing masculinity in ways compatible with maintaining male dominance within the family of the new order.

Imagining the family man as 'dangerous' remains profoundly

difficult so long as he appears to be, a priori, the antithesis of that danger. Challenging the law's foreclosure of alternative subject positions involves fragmenting the purported unity of this hetero-sexual identity and revealing its sociality. Meanwhile consideration of single mothers continues to revolve around issues of the public purse. The role of law in legitimating the positions of élite males in hierarchically organized social institutions has historically facilitated the intergenerational transfer of power between men. It should not be surprising that those to whom power is bequeathed should ascribe to individualistic accounts of de-gendered human agency, merit and social status by way of justification of existing social structures (and, of course, judicial espousal of these values is not hard to find). The 'errant father', the 'scrounging' single mother tap into just such an individualistic discourse. Recent events testify to the scale of politicians' wilful (blissful?) ignorance of the realities of many working-class lives.

Ultimately (re)emergence in public debate around father-absence of an 'unrespectable' working class should be seen in the context of the withdrawal of capital from the industrial areas. The underclass theorists' moral panic about fathers has been ignited, Campbell has suggested, not by their flight and failure – that after all was nothing new – '. . . but by their redundancy . . . To reveal the redundancy of the fathers is the crime of the mothers' (Campbell 1993: 313–14). Given the dominant legal construction of paternal masculinity the nature of the father's 'normal love' is open to question. Meanwhile criminology, as well as politicians' asides, appears to continue to construct the crimes of men through reference to naturalistic accounts of masculinity and a negation of gender configurations and social practices which fall outside the frames of a hegemonic familial heterosexuality. Without 'the family' and an appropriate heterosexual male role model these men will revert to their 'wild' nature; just as, ironically, many affluent men are also embracing the mytho-poeic and seeking to reclaim their 'wild' natures in a rather different context (Harding 1992). It may be on the inner-city streets or back to the woods – but perhaps we have not come so far from those ideas of 'dangerous classes' which so shaped the gender anxieties of the last *fin de siècle*.

The reconstituted paternal masculinity I have outlined – the masculinity of the 'modern' father in law – remains bound up within discourses which continue to construct fatherhood as involving specific claims to power and authority within the family and which involve separating out this 'safe' paternal masculinity from other 'dangerous', extra-familial masculinities. This division *between* classes of masculinities must be seen, I have argued, as an important technique in the construction of social and legal changes which might facilitate motherhood without men as threats to masculinity, the family and ultimately to social order itself. These divisions between masculinities, and the mechanisms by which they are reproduced, are an important part of a patriarchal reconstruction (Smart 1989) in which legal reforms which might have sought to help women continue to be undermined for 'attacking' men. Meanwhile, for increasing numbers of young men and boys, moves towards increasing carceration will mean that even more 'subordinated' (Connell 1987) or 'sacrificial' (Naffine 1990) masculinities will be consigned to a life on the margins. Meanwhile élite, educated men continue to set the parameters of the debate, cut benefits to the young in the name of 'public spending', restrict already limited sex-education programmes and, at the end of the day, return home to their 'loyal' wives and children who might provide them with the 'normal love and support' to which they are accustomed.

Notes

[1] The immediate history of recent debates about 'family values' can be traced back to Margaret Thatcher's speech to the National Children's Home in 1990. Plans for what were to become the Child Support Agency were then put forward with explicit reference to the social problems perceived to follow from absent fatherhood. At the 1992 Conservative Party conference the Secretary of State for Social Security, Peter Lilley, had, in a parody of *The Mikado*, spoken of 'young ladies who get pregnant just to jump the housing list and dads who won't support the ladies they have . . . kissed.' Following John Redwood's comments in July 1993 it emerged that Peter Lilley had known in advance what Redwood was going to say. Further statements from ministers appear to suggest that both Lilley and the Prime Minister were happy for a high-profile debate about single parents at a time of public spending cuts. By the time of the 1993 Conservative Party conference, held during the autumn, the debate over family values had intensified. Subsumed under an ill-defined and ultimately misguided notion of 'back to basics', a range of social ills – the criminality of male youth, family breakdown and urban disorder – were all now being laid at the door of the single-parent family and linked to the detrimental consequences of this father absence.

[2] Recent pro-feminist and men's liberationist accounts of masculinity have

differed in their analysis of the causes and consequences of the nature of the changes taking place around masculinity. What there has tended to be agreement on, however, is that these changes now constitute something of a *crisis* in masculinity (e.g., Brittan 1989: 25–36; Hearn 1987: 16–31; Connell 1987: 183–6). Crucially, this crisis is seen as having a specifically *legal* dimension.

3 The idea of masculine 'renewal' is most marked in the North American 'mytho-poeic' tradition: note, in particular, the influential work of Robert Bly (1990).

4 In order to assign any particular significance to the idea of historically specific representations of masculinity it is necessary to address the social relations within which these representations are reproduced at any given historical moment (Middleton 1992: 142). Outside such an institutional context the idea of a 'discourse of masculinity' has no self-evident meaning. Thus, '. . . to speak legitimately of a discourse of masculinity it would be necessary to show that a particular set of usages was located structurally within a clearly defined institution with its own methods, objects and practices. Otherwise the reference to discourses of masculinity is simply a reference to repeated patterns of linguistic usage, which may be significant, but cannot be theorized . . . Masculinity is produced within some discourses in the stricter theoretical sense, but most examples of "masculine" utterance are not discourses' (Middleton 1992: 142). Law provides just such a set of usages for discourses of masculinity which can be located structurally. Law also provides clearly defined institutions with their own (doctrinal exegetical) method, objects and practices. Discourses of masculinity, in other words, have had an established and entrenched link with the histories of power and knowledge both in and of law.

5 Particularly clear in the UK in relation to the practice of artificially inseminating 'virgin mothers'. The objection of the 'pro-family' Right appeared to be that the practice involved motherhood without men (or, specifically, without intercourse: e.g., see the *Guardian*, 12 March 1991: *Daily Mail*, 12 March 1991).

6 At a fringe meeting at the 1993 Conservative Party conference Michael Howard stated '. . . children born in these circumstances learn to get their own way. With few adult male role models around they are all too likely to . . . emulate the most aggressive and most rebellious boys in the neighbourhood'. This is one of a number of misconceptions which have pervaded the public debate about the single parent in 1993 (e.g., 'Separation: Fiction and the Facts', P. Ghazi and L. Gerard, *Observer* 11 July 1993; 'Single Mothers: How many are there? What do they cost the state? Are the children likelier to go astray?' R. Waterhouse *Independent on Sunday* 14 November 1993). Of such single mothers who have never married, half are older than twenty-five. Whilst it is true that the number of never-married lone mothers has risen sharply (representing, in 1993, 6.4% of all families compared with 1.2% in 1971) changes in family

structures have meant that around 20 per cent of all households are made up of single parents of which 1.4 per cent are headed by men.

7 Note in particular the pronouncements of Peter Lilley, John Redwood and Michael Portillo. Redwood followed his criticisms of lone parents by declaring that the '. . . natural state should be the two-adult family caring for their children. The norm should be the purchase of a home of one's own with the entitlement to live peacefully, rent-free in retirement. The common aspiration should be a good second pension on top of the state retirement pension so that the luxuries and extras in retirement are affordable', *Guardian* 3 July 1993.

8 A view promulgated world-wide notably by Rupert Murdoch's News International Group newspapers. In Britain *The Sunday Times* has given considerable space to the views of Charles Murray (1990, cited in Mann and Roseneil 1994: 16).

9 See further Katz 1993; Mann 1992; Macnicol 1987.

10 As Jolly and Sandland (1994: 32) note, the rubbishing of the purportedly 'politically correct' in recent debates around family law reform has in fact provided an 'ideological photo-opportunity' for the present government. A clear 'anti-pc' and pro-'common sense' ideology has proved a powerful weapon for those seeking to defend the 'traditional' nuclear family and male sexual prerogative. These ideas have recently come together in Britain perhaps most clearly around the issues of women's sexual harassment of men and some highly publicized 'politically correct' comments on heterosexism in education (e.g. see 'Theatre of the Absurd', *The Sunday Times* 23 January 1994).

11 Tom Sackville, *Guardian* 6 July 1993.

12 This idea is explored further in Collier (1994: forthcoming).

13 Brittan (1989) provides a useful definition of the ideology of masculinism: 'Those people who speak of masculinity as an essence, as an inborn characteristic, are confusing masculinity with masculinism, the masculine ideology. Masculinism is the ideology that justifies and naturalises male domination. As such, it is the ideology of patriarchy. Masculinism takes it for granted that there is a fundamental difference between men and women, it assumes that heterosexuality is normal, it accepts without question the sexual division of labour, and it sanctions the political and dominant role of men in the public and private spheres' (Brittan 1989: 4).

14 The literature on masculinity is now voluminous and has expanded vastly since the overview of Carrigan *et al.* (1985). On distinctions within this scholarship see further Middleton (1992). It is possible that the growth of masculinity studies has been prompted in part by a disillusionment with traditional critical theory (and in particular Marxism) whereby, for postmodernist nihilist and post-Marxist alike: 'The experience of being left out, on the sidelines, was the new and threatening reality for many a young male radical, no longer feeling as certain as he had in the 1960s of his own participation in the making of history' (Segal 1990: 280). On the

problematic nature of the 'men's studies' genre generally, see further Canaan and Griffin (1990); Moore (1991).

15 In particular with reference to the role of father as economic provider. The 'nuclear family' to which this breadwinner masculinity is central was very much a phenomenon of the post-war years. The social conditions which supported it have now gone; however, a central problem – still seldom addressed – is the continued desirability of full-time lifelong employment supported by women's unpaid work at home. British men, interestingly, continue to work the longest hours in the European Community (Leach and Hewitt 1993).

16 The modernization of paternal masculinity which follows has also involved treating the unmarried father increasingly *as if* he were married. However, there remain important differences between the legal positions of the married and unmarried father. Legal constructions of unmarried paternal masculinities are explored further in Smart 1987; Collier 1995.

17 The idea that paid employment has a central place in the maintenance of masculine identity and status not surprisingly recurs in a succession of cases in family law, in marked contrast to legal constructions of the correspondence between maternity, child care and women's familial role. Indeed, ideas of the 'natural' abilities of fathers and mothers continue to be pervasive in family law: see, for example, *B* v. *B* 1985 FLR 462: *B* v. *B* 1985 FLR 166: *May* v. *May* 1986 1 FLR.

18 Note the recent divisions within the government on 'family values' and 'lone parents': 'Lilley Lone Parent Row Revived', *Guardian* 21 June 1994.

References

Alcock, P. (1984). 'Remuneration or remarriage? The Matrimonial and Family Proceedings Act 1984', *Journal of Law and Society*, 11, 3: 357.

Allen, J. (1988). 'The masculinity of criminality and criminology: interrogating some impasses', in M. Findlay and R. Hogg (eds.) *Understanding Crime and Criminal Justice* (Sydney, Law Book Company).

Anderson, D. and Dawson, G. (eds.) (1986). *Family Portraits* (London, Social Affairs Unit).

Anderson, D. and Dawson, G. (1986). 'Popular but unrepresented: the curious case of the normal family', in D. Anderson and P. Dawson (eds.), *Family Portraits* (London, Social Affairs Unit).

Atkins, S. and Hoggett, B. (1984). *Women in Law* (Oxford, Blackwell).

Barker-Benfield, B. (1972). 'The spermatic economy: a nineteenth century view of sexuality', *Feminist Studies*, 6, 45–74.

Bly, R. (1991). *Iron John* (London, Element Books).

Booth, W. (1976). 'In darkest England and the way out', in P. Keating (ed.) *Into Unknown England 1877–1913* (London, Fontana).

Box, S. (1981). *Deviance, Reality and Society* (London, Holt Rinehart and Wilson).

Brittan, A. (1989). *Masculinity and Power* (Oxford, Blackwell).

Bromley, P. and Lowe, N. (1987). *Family Law* (7th edn., London, Butterworth).

Brown, B. (1986). 'Women and crime: the dark figures of criminology', *Economy and Society*, 15, 355.

Brown, C. (1981). 'Mothers, fathers and children: from private to public patriarchy', in L. Sargent (ed.) *Women and Revolution: The Unhappy Marriage of Marxism and Feminism* (London, Pluto).

Butler, J. (1990). *Gender Trouble: Feminism and the Subversion of Identity* (London, Routledge).

Cain, M. (1990). 'Realist philosophies and standpoint epistemologies or feminist criminology as a successor science', in L. Gelsthorpe and A. Morris *Feminist Perspectives in Criminology* (Milton Keynes, Open University Press).

Campbell, B. (1993). *Goliath: Britain's Dangerous Places* (London, Methuen).

Canaan, J. E. and Griffin, C. (1990). 'The New Men's Studies: Part of the problem or part of the solution?', in J. Hearn and D. Morgan (eds.), *Men, Masculinities and Social Theory* (London, Unwin Hyman).

Carrigan, T., Connell, R. and Lee, J. (1985). 'Towards a new sociology of masculinity', *Theory and Society*, 14, 551–604.

Cohen, P. (1981). 'Policing the working class city' in M. Fitzgerald *et al.* (eds.), *Crime and Society: Readings in History and Theory* (Milton Keynes, Open University Press).

Collier, R. (1995). *Masculinity, Law and the Family* (London, Routledge).

Cominos, P. (1963). 'Late-Victorian sexual respectability and the social system', *International Review of Social History* 81, 18–48, 216–50.

Connell, R. (1987). *Gender and Power* (Cambridge, Polity Press).

Davidoff, L. and Hall, C. (1987). *Family Fortunes* (London, Hutchinson).

Dennis, N. and Erdos, G. (1992). *Families without Fatherhood* (London, Institute of Economic Affairs).

Donzelot, J. (1980). *The Policing of Families* (London, Hutchinson).

Dorris, M. (1990). *The Broken Cord: A Father's Story* (London, Warner/Futura).

Faludi, S. (1992). *Backlash: The Undeclared War Against Women* (London, Chatto and Windus).

Farrell, W. (1993). *The Myth of Male Power: Why Men are the Disposable Sex* (New York, Simon and Schuster).

Finer, M. and McGregor, O. R. (1974). 'The history of the obligation to maintain', Appendix 5 to the *Report of the Committee on One-Parent Families*, Cmnd. 5629 (London, HMSO).

French, S. (1992). *Fathers and Sons* (London, Faber),.

Gelsthorpe, L. and Morris, A. (1990). *Feminist Perspectives in Criminology* (Milton Keynes, Open University Press).

Halsey, A. H. (1992). Foreword in N. Dennis and G. Erdos *Families Without Fatherhood* (London, IEA Health and Welfare Unit, Choice in Welfare No. 12).

Harding, C. (1992). *Wingspan: Inside the Men's Movement* (New York, St Martin's Press).

Hearn, J. (1992). *Men in the Public Eye* (London, Routledge).

Hearn, J. (1987). *The Gender of Oppression* (Brighton, Wheatsheaf).

Heidensohn, F. (1994). 'Gender and crime' in M. Maguire, R. Morgan and R. Reiner (eds.), *The Oxford Handbook of Criminology* (Oxford, Clarendon Press).

Hey, V. (1984). *Patriarchy and Pub Culture* (London, Tavistock).

Hoch, P. (1979). *White Hero, Black Beast* (London, Pluto).

Hoyland, D. (1992) (ed.). *Fathers and Sons* (London, Serpent's Tree).

Jolly, S. and Sandland, R. (1994). 'Political correctness and the adoption White Paper', *Family Law*, January, 30–2.

Katz, M. B. (ed.) (1993). *The 'Underclass' Debate: Views from History* (Princeton, Princeton University Press).

Keating, P. (ed.) (1976). *Into Unknown England 1866-1913* (London, Fontana).

Leach, P. and Hewitt, P. (1993). *Social Justice, Children and Families* (London, Institute for Public Policy Research).

Lee, J. (1991). *At My Father's Wedding* (London, Piatkus).

Lewis, C. (1986). *Becoming a Father* (Milton Keynes, Open University Press).

Lewis, C. and O'Brien, M. (1987). *Reassessing Fatherhood: New Observations on Fathers and the Modern Family* (London, Sage).

Lowe, N. (1982). 'Fathers and the law', in L. McKee and M. O'Brien (eds.), *The Father Figure* (London, Tavistock).

Lyndon, N. (1992). *No More Sex War* (London, Sinclair Stevenson).

Macnicol, J. (1987). 'In pursuit of the underclass', *Journal of Social Policy*, 16, 3, 293–318.

Mangan, J. and Walvin, J. (eds.) (1987). *Manliness and Morality: Middle-Class Masculinity in Britain and America 1800–1940* (Manchester, Manchester University Press).

Mann, K. (1992). *The Making of an English 'Underclass'? The Social Division of Welfare and Labour* (Milton Keynes, Open University Press).

Mann, K. and Roseneil, S. (1994). 'Some Mothers Do 'Ave 'Em': Backlash and the Gender Politics of the Underclass Debate', paper presented to the Good Enough Mothering Conference, University of Leeds, May 1994.

McKee, L. and O'Brien, M. (eds.) (1982). *The Father Figure* (London, Tavistock).

Middleton, P. (1992). *The Inward Gaze: Masculinity and Subjectivity in Modern Culture* (London, Routledge).

Moore, S. (1991). 'Trivial pursuits of stags at bay', *Observer*, 9 January.

Morgan, D. (1992). *Discovering Men* (London, Routledge).

Morgan, P. (1986). 'Feminist attempts to sack father: a case of unfair dismissal?', in D. Anderson and G. Dawson (eds.), *Family Portraits* (London, Social Affairs Unit).

Murray, C. (1990). *The Emerging British Underclass* (London: IEA Health and Welfare Unit).

Naffine, N. (1990). *Law and the Sexes: Explorations in Feminist Juris-prudence* (London, Routledge).

O'Donovan, K. (1993). *Family Law Matters* (London, Pluto).

O'Donovan, K. (1985). *Sexual Divisions in Law* (London, Weidenfeld and Nicolson).

Okin, S. M. (1989). *Justice, Gender and the Family* (London, Basic, Harper Collins).

Pearson, G. (1994). 'Youth, crime and society', in M. Maguire, R. Morgan and R. Reiner (eds.), *The Oxford Handbook of Criminology* (Oxford, Clarendon Press).

Pinchbeck, I. and Hewitt, M. (1969). *Children in English Society: Vol. 1. From Tudor Times Till the Eighteenth Century* (London, Routledge and Kegan Paul).

Richards, M. (1987). 'Fatherhood, marriage and sexuality: some speculations on the English middle-class family', in C. Lewis and M. O'Brien (eds.), *Reassessing Fatherhood: New Observations on Fathers and the Modern Family* (London, Sage).

Roberts, Y. (1992). *Mad About Women* (London, Virago).

Rotundo, E. A. (1993). *American Manhood* (New York, Basic Books).

Rotundo, E. A. (1987). 'Learning about manhood: gender ideals and the middle-class family in nineteenth century America', in J. Mangan and J. Walvin (eds.), *Manliness and Morality: Middle-Class Masculinity in Britain and America 1800–1940* (Manchester, Manchester University Press).

Rutherford, J. (1992). *Men's Silences* (London, Routledge).

Scraton, P. (1990). 'Scientific knowledge or masculine discourses? Challenging patriarchy in criminology', in L. Gelsthorpe and A. Morris, *Feminist Perspectives in Criminology* (Milton Keynes, Open University Press).

Segal, L. (1990). *Slow Motion: Changing Masculinities, Changing Men* (London, Virago).

Showalter, E. (1992). *Sexual Anarchy* (London, Bloomsbury).

Smart, C. (1976). *Women, Crime and Criminology* (London, Routledge & Kegan Paul).

Smart, C. (1984). *The Ties That Bind* (London, Routledge & Kegan Paul).

Smart, C. (1987). 'There is of course a distinction dictated by nature: law and the problem of paternity', in M. Stanworth (ed.), *Reproductive Technologies* (Cambridge, Polity Press).

Smart, C. (1989). *Feminism and the Power of Law* (London, Routledge).

Smart, C. (1990). 'Feminist approaches to criminology: or, postmodern woman meets atavistic man', in L. Gelsthorpe and A. Morris, *Feminist Perspectives in Criminology* (Milton Keynes, Open University Press).

Smart, C. and Sevenhuijsen (1989). *Child Custody and the Politics of Gender* (Routledge, London).

Springhall, J. (1987). 'Building character in the British boy: the attempt to extend Christian manliness to working class adolescents 1880–1914', in

J. Mangan and J. Walvin (eds.), *Manliness and Morality: Middle-Class Masculinity in Britain and America 1800–1940* (Manchester, Manchester University Press).

Stanko, E. and Hobdell, K. (1993). 'Assault on men; masculinity and male victimization', *British Journal of Criminology* 33, 3, 400.

Stedman-Jones, G. (1976). *Outcast London: A Study in the Relationship between Classes in Victorian Society* (Harmondsworth, Penguin).

Storch, R. (1981). 'The plague of the blue locusts: police reform and popular resistance in Northern England 1840–57', in M. Fitzgerald *et al.*, *Crime and Society: Readings in History and Theory* (Milton Keynes, Open University Press).

Thomas, D. (1993). *Not Guilty: In Defence of the Modern Man* (London, Weidenfeld and Nicolson).

Tolson, A. (1977). *The Limits of Masculinity* (London, Tavistock).

Vance, N. (1985). *The Sinews of the Spirit: The Ideal of Christian Manliness in Victorian Literature and Religious Thought* (Cambridge, Cambridge University Press).

Walkowitz, J. R. (1980). *Prostitution and Victorian Society: Women, Class and the State* (Cambridge, Cambridge University Press).

11

Target women: Women's victimization and white-collar crime

HAZEL CROALL

This chapter is an exploration of some of the ways in which women are victimized by forms of white-collar and corporate crime. It will begin by locating the investigation in the context of studies of both women's victimization and white-collar crime. It will then look at some examples of how women as workers, consumers or investors are at risk from a variety of practices endangering their health, safety and well-being, or which amount to fraud and deception. Finally, some implications for further analysis will be outlined.

A broad definition of white-collar crime as 'the abuse of a legitimate occupational role which is regulated by law' (Croall 1992), will be followed. This frees the concept from the inclusion of the class and status of offenders, which, while by no means irrelevant, arguably diverts attention from the nature of offences themselves (Shapiro 1990; Croall 1992). It thus enables a fuller analysis of the abuse of trust and occupational power involved in white-collar offences which is particularly relevant to discussions of victimization. It also incorporates both 'occupational' and 'corporate' crime (Croall 1992). This chapter will also include practices which are not, strictly speaking, crimes, but which lie in the grey area between criminality and legality. This can readily be justified on the grounds that the borderline between criminal and legal is not only very difficult to determine, but is itself worthy of analysis. Many practices reveal the moral ambiguity of white-collar crime (Aubert 1977), and call into question the social and legal construction of crime (Croall 1992; Wells 1988). Thus many white-collar or corporate offences are not widely defined as 'crime' and victims do not define themselves as 'victims'.

Victimology, whether of the conventional or radical variety, has been criticized for neglecting both the victimization of women, and victimization by corporate crime (Walklate 1989; 1992). Thus Walklate argues that conventional victimology, 'explicitly excludes the private as a domain of personal victimization, alongside a failure to conceptualize corporate crime as a source of much victimization' (Walklate 1992: 106). Realist criminology claims to overcome many of these problems by including both sexual harassment (Jones *et al.* 1986) and aspects of corporate crime (Pearce and Tombs 1992) in victim surveys. Nonetheless the realist association of 'crime' with 'what the community takes seriously' may underplay the significance of domestic violence which many do not define as a problem (Walklate 1992). Much the same could be said of corporate and white-collar crime – often said to be dealt with leniently on the grounds that it is not seen as a 'criminal' problem (see, for example, Croall 1992).

In addition, both realist and conventional analyses of victimization tend to focus on *interpersonal* relationships between victims and offenders – neglecting the significance of offences which involve diffuse and indirect victimization. Thus Pearce and Tombs (1992: 71) ask: 'Would a realist analysis of the violence and harassment suffered by women at work include a discussion of corporate violence and the particular forms it takes against women?' This is not, they add, to argue that it cannot do so – victim surveys can adapt conceptual categories and Lea (1992) argues that classifications of victim–offender relationships should include the indirect and organizational victimization of both individuals and groups. But even refined victimization surveys are limited, as they inevitably exclude offences where victims are unaware of their victimization (Walklate 1989; Croall 1992). Thus Ruggiero (1992) draws attention to the 'invisible victims' of pollution, unemployment, inadequate services, exploitation and dangerous goods. Realists, he argues, 'neglect those dimensions of victimization which involve ordinary people in their relationships with corporations, central and local authorities' (Ruggiero 1992: 138).

Many studies of the 'hidden' victimization of women in the 'private' or domestic sphere have highlighted the way in which assault and sexual abuse of women by intimates, spouses and husbands has not been defined as 'criminal' (Dobash and Dobash 1979, 1992; Hanmer *et al.* 1989; Radford and Stanko 1992). Much of this work focuses on the 'problem of men' and sexual violence, making only passing reference to the victimization of women at work, or to 'corporate violence' and fraud. While Stanko (1990) talks about dangers from 'intimates, friends and co-workers', with the exception of sexual harassment at work much analysis has focused on husbands and lovers rather than on supervisors, managers or service providers.

Like domestic violence, white-collar crime often takes place in 'private', is not seen as a 'public order' problem, and is often invisible (Clarke 1990; Croall 1992). Studies of victimization have been limited by the diffuse effect of many offences which means that victims may suffer only a small loss or be unaware of any damage (Croall 1992; Levi 1992). The victimization of women has been largely unexplored (Weeks and Gerber 1992), and victimization tends to be discussed in terms of non-gendered categories such as 'business workers', 'consumers', citizens' or the 'public'. Nonetheless, white-collar crime may have an unequal impact, with some groups being particularly vulnerable due to their structural location (Croall 1992).

What follows is an exploration of the impact of white-collar crime on women, both as the specific targets of some kinds of offences, and as major victims of others where they are not the direct target. It is not intended to argue that women, or indeed any group of women suffer *exclusively* or *more* than any other group. For example, while 'consumers' as a group may be victimized by a variety of offences, female consumers are victimized by products and services specifically marketed at women. Other consumer offences have a severe impact on women by virtue of their role as mothers or 'housewives'. While all workers are endangered by employers' neglect of protective legislation, the structural position of female employees may make them particularly vulnerable. The following examples will look at the victimization of women workers and consumers, and will cover offences relating to health and safety along with fraud and deception.

The victimization of women workers

The victimization of workers by corporate crime has been analysed in terms of both health and safety and wages legislation (Box 1983; 1987; Pearce and Tombs 1990; Tombs 1990). Many so-called 'accidents' at work result from the neglect of safety regulations and many occupationally induced diseases are similarly avoidable. Women workers, by virtue of occupational segregation, low pay and part-time status, may be particularly vulnerable to the offences of employers – whether corporations or small businesses. In addition, many women workers face sexual harassment and abuse in the workplace. Few of these offences however lead to prosecutions, and reductions in the strengths of enforcement agencies have increased the ability of employers to neglect regulations. Indeed the minimal protection offered to low-paid workers by wages councils has recently been removed – thereby 'decriminalizing' the payment of wages below minimum levels.

The hazards of women's work

Many kinds of 'women's work' involve health hazards – whether in 'high-tech' or 'low-tech' industries. In the garment industry, for example, sweatshop conditions persist. An investigation in 1983 into the textile industry, prompted by the death of five women workers in a clothing factory fire, found many dangerous workplaces, some not even registered with the Health and Safety Executive (*Guardian* 28 February 1985). Only two prosecutions followed. Some clothing factories were also found to be paying workers below the minimum wage. So-called 'high-tech' industries also involve hazards to women, as is the case in the silicon-chip manufacturing industry, currently under investigation by the Health and Safety Executive. In the United States, studies of this industry have shown that women workers face a higher risk of miscarriage, along with respiratory ailments, dermatitis and alopecia. Unions argue that anti-union attitudes within the industry, along with the low union membership of women process workers, have contributed to the erosion of health and safety standards, as implementation of regulations is more difficult in non-union workplaces (*Guardian* 22 June 1993).

Women workers in the food industry risk contracting complaints as a result of working with high concentrations of food additives (Miller 1985). Women working in soft drinks and crisp factories may suffer from dermatitis, and asthma and bronchitis have been associated with the additive tartrazine. Respiratory problems have been connected to exposure to sulphur dioxide, a preservative and bleach used in many foods, including jam, fruit juice and beer. Miller (1985) estimates that more than forty approved food additives can provoke allergic or intolerant reactions amongst food workers. These dangers are not widely recognized, largely because safety requirements are geared towards consumers, who are exposed to lower concentrations.

Women workers, argues Miller, are especially vulnerable, as food processing and manufacturing industries employ a higher percentage of women than any other industry – and 'women's work' is concentrated in the less skilled jobs such as production and packing. As these jobs also have a high turnover, illnesses are less likely to be associated with work, being dismissed as 'women's problems'.

Women's pay

Women workers form a large section of those deprived of legal minimum wages. Box (1987) estimated that in 1984 employees were cheated of around £2.5 million by an increasing number of companies underpaying staff. Approximately one-third of companies were estimated to be paying below the legal minimum wage in 1993 (*Independent on Sunday* 16 May 1993). Despite this, few are prosecuted, and the size of the Wages Inspectorate shrank from 177 in 1979 to 54 in 1993. In Scotland a mere seven inspectors can inspect only 7.5 per cent of establishments, involving 222,000 workers. While around a third of the establishments are found to be underpaying, only two were prosecuted in 1991 (*Scotsman* 30 October 1992). According to Chris Pond, director of the Low Pay Unit, the abolition of the Wages Councils in October 1993 means that Britain is becoming a 'low-tech, sweatshop economy' (*Independent on Sunday* 16 May 1993). It will also, according to the Equal Opportunities Commission, increase the exploitation of women. Presently women are also underpaid in the many sectors not covered by Wages Councils – the Scottish Low Pay Unit cites as some of its worst examples cleaners and care assistants in nursing homes working for as little as £1.65 per hour, often with no overtime rate. The lowest white-collar rates are found amongst administrative assistants working full-time for professionals (*Scotsman* 30 October 1992).

Sexual abuse and harassment at work

Less often listed as a white-collar crime is the widespread sexual abuse and harassment of women at work, which often involves the abuse of an occupational role. Box (1983), discussing exploitative rape, points out that men may abuse their organizational power over women to overcome resistance. Giddens (1989: 182) also points out that, 'sexual harassment in the workplace may be defined as the use of occupational authority or power to try to enforce sexual demands. This may take blatant forms, as when it is suggested to a female employee that she consent to a sexual encounter or be dismissed.' The extent of sexual abuse in the workplace is difficult to estimate. The Islington Crime Survey found that 13.5 per cent of reported sexual assaults took place at work (Jones *et al.* 1986), although they do not indicate how many of these were by clients or colleagues. In the police service, a Home Office study recently reported that 6 per cent of respondents had suffered serious sexual assaults at the hands of male colleagues. Extrapolated nationally this would mean that 800 officers had been the victim of rape or attempted rape (*Guardian* 11 February 1993). High levels of sexual harassment have also been found – in a previous study 48 per cent of women officers interviewed reported that they had been touched, stroked or pinched by fellow officers. While the occupational culture of the police has been noted for its 'machismo' attitudes (Reiner 1985), other occupations may have similarly high rates of sexual abuse.

Complaints about sexual harassment at work have recently been said by ACAS to be 'soaring' (*Guardian* 27 April 1993), although it is often dismissed by men as 'horseplay' (Grint 1991) or treated humorously, as in the film *Nine to Five*. High levels of sexual harassment by colleagues have been found by the European Commission (*The Times* 14 December 1987), and by individual unions such as NALGO – one study indeed found reports of harassment amongst trade-union officials (Grint 1991). A survey by the Labour Research Department of 157 workplaces found that nearly half the complaints involved an immediate supervisor or member of management – and one in ten women reported physical abuse (*The Times* 22 December 1987). Sexual harassment is of course not a 'crime'; however, it has been suggested to the European Commission that employers should have a legal duty to provide a workplace free of sexual harassment (*The Times* 14 December 1987).

Women consumers as victims

Consumers are a major group victimized by corporate or business crime (Croall 1987; 1992), mainly covered by the Trade Descriptions, Weights and Measures, Consumer Protection and Food Acts. Despite a plethora of regulations, these acts contain loopholes and ambiguities, and many unsafe or deceptive practices are inadequately regulated. It is for example often difficult to define precisely when a 'description' is 'misleading' under the Trade Descriptions Act, and many deceptive selling strategies, such as the use of deceptive packaging, lie in the grey area between legality and illegality. Analyses of consumer crime also reveal the narrow line between acceptable selling strategies and fraud, and many deceptive practices are morally unacceptable, whether or not they are criminal.

Women's health and safety is threatened by products marketed for female consumers like cosmetics and slimming products. As reproducers, women are particularly susceptible to the dangers of contraceptives and they are major consumers of drugs. The growing cosmetic surgery industry, much of it in the less well-regulated private sector, has also been the subject of recent investigation. Women consumers are also routinely deceived. Advertisements appealing to the 'cereal packet' (Abercrombie *et al.* 1988) image of the family may make housewives the target of a host of frauds and rip-offs involving packaging, advertising, false descriptions and bargain offers. Gendered assumptions about women's ignorance of financial or technical matters may also make them the targets of unscrupulous sales strategies. This section will look firstly at issues of women's safety before going on to discuss sales and investment frauds.

The safety of female consumers
Many have argued that the multimillion-pound slimming industry is insufficiently regulated. Products causing concern include slimming aids, 'diets', plastic pants to increase fluid loss and skin patches purporting to speed up metabolic rate. Gallstones, constipation, heart stress, infertility, depression and mood swings have all been related to 'dieting' (*Independent* 8 April 1993), and herbal teas sold as slimming aids have recently been associated with potentially fatal liver failure (*The Times* 11 September 1992). In the USA the Food and Drugs Administration have found that 'cholesterol free' products contain highly saturated fats, and some 'sugar free' foods contain ingredients unsafe for allergy sufferers (Simon and Eitzen 1993). Regulations for slimming products, however, are less stringent than those for 'drugs', as they are not subject to the same testing protocols (*Sunday Telegraph* 9 August 1992). This is also the case with alternative medicines, some of which can make conditions worse. A top cancer specialist has estimated for example that as many as 36,000 breast cancer sufferers place themselves at risk by using alternative 'cures' in preference to medical treatment (*Today* 9 May 1989).

The drug industry is itself high on the list of 'criminogenic' industries – with intense competition producing a variety of offences including inadequate or falsely reported testing procedures, deceptive advertising and the suppression of damaging information (Braithwaite 1984). Women are often adversely affected by the activities of these legal 'drug pushers' (Walklate 1989). For example, women suffering from anxiety were widely prescribed the tranquillizers Valium and Librium – despite the fact that these led to addiction and accidental or intentional overdoses.

Contraceptives have been the source of many scandals. The case of the Dalkon Shield intra-uterine device well illustrates the way in which women's safety can be endangered by market forces. At least seventeen women in the United States and unknown numbers in the Third World died and others suffered infertility as a result of using the shield (Perry and Dawson 1985). During intense competition in the 1960s to find a cheap and effective contraceptive, the inventor of the Dalkon Shield falsified test data and made exaggerated claims about its effectiveness. The shield was however taken over by a major drug company and aggressively marketed despite growing doubts by production supervisors, quality controllers and doctors. Many users suffered septic abortions and infertility, but as regulations on devices were less stringent than those on drugs, regulatory authorities were slow to react. No criminal prosecutions were ever brought, although the shield was 'dumped' on at least forty Third World countries where it was sold at a huge discount (Braithwaite 1984).

Women were also sufferers of the Thalidomide tragedy. Like the Dalkon Shield, this never led to a successful prosecution, but caused nearly 8,000 birth deformities world-wide (Braithwaite 1984; Clarke 1990). Reports of nerve damage to women and the growing evidence of deformities were initially suppressed. After its withdrawal in Europe, like the Dalkon Shield it continued to be sold in the Third World. Women's suffering was compounded by the fact that many fathers left mothers to suffer alone (Braithwaite 1984).

Even more dangers are posed by the lucrative market in cosmetic surgery, as indicated by recent revelations about silicone breast implants. Rashes, allergies and arthritis have been found to occur when these leak, releasing silicone into the body. In America, a Federal Court found that Dow Corning had acted with 'fraud, malice and oppression' in failing to disclose information about the product's hazards (*Guardian* 10 October 1993). Implants have now been banned in America, where there is now a growing trade in 'explantations' –

which cost more than the original surgery (*The Times* 15 June 1993). In Britain, however, plastic surgeons, who have dismissed women's claims as 'anecdotal evidence' (*Daily Telegraph* 29 June 1993), have been accused by one solicitor of minimizing the danger to protect the breast-enlargement market, where operations cost about £3,000 (*Sunday Times* 20 June 1993). Women undergoing the operation must now register with the Health Department. An alternative product, the saline implant, now undergoing tests, has been suspected of being more prone to leaking and deflation, and of fostering fungal colonies and micro-organisms (*Guardian* 10 June 1993).

Pregnant women, along with the elderly, may be particularly vulnerable to listeriosis – a form of which, 'materno-fetal listeriosis', can lead to abortion, stillbirth, or brain damage in babies born with the disease. The incidence of this disease, linked to cook-chill foods, rose between 1969 and 1988. While reported incidents have fallen since the publicity in 1989, the real rate may be three times higher than official figures, as many miscarriages are not attributed to the disease (Lacey 1992). While these concerns should, he argues, have caused a major rethink by the food industry, this has not happened.

Danger: men at work

No review of the hazards faced by women consumers would be complete without recognizing the threat of sexual abuse, let alone harassment, faced by female customers and clients of service providers. Often publicly dealt with in the media as 'scandals', these have a wider significance. One recent scandal involved a women client being drugged and raped by the manager of a dating agency – who had in the past been investigated for fondling a girl at a job interview. Also a fraudster, this man had, according to one report (*Daily Mail* 13 February 1993), made his career from 'exploiting the lonely and vulnerable'. A point arising from this case is the ease with which anyone can set up a dating agency – giving them access to personal details about women.

Professional employees also abuse the trust placed in them by women. Doctor–patient scandals are much loved by the media – a recent example being a Harley Street doctor convicted of sexually assaulting four women (*Independent* 1 December 1992). Having falsely presented himself as a gynaecologist and psychosexual therapist he had set up a charity for female victims of AIDS. He thereby created, according to the Detective Inspector in charge of the case, 'the perfect environment in which to commit these offences . . .the charity gave him the opportunity to exploit every vulnerable woman who walked in through the door'. This case highlights the particular vulnerability of female patients, although clients of other professional groups may be similarly at risk. As with other kinds of sexual abuse, this often remains unreported or dealt with by the 'private' justice of professional bodies.

Consumer frauds

Women can be 'ripped off' in a variety of ways by products aimed at female consumers. Jewellery, for example, features strongly amongst prosecutions and investigations under the Trade Descriptions Act, involving the 'passing off' of cheap trinkets as 'brand name' goods, and counterfeiting (Croall 1987). Jewellery stores also feature prominently in investigations of blatantly false 'bargain offer' claims and dubious sales promotions (*Sunday Times* 15 December 1991; Croall 1987). Similar problems occur with perfumes, fashion goods and clothes. Trading Standards Officers recently broke up a forgery ring which involved up to one million pounds worth of designer clothes (*Daily Telegraph* 18 June 1992), and so called 'Gucchi' trainers and 'Naf Naf' T-shirts were widely sold in the North-East (*Northern Echo* 29 November 1991). Many of these apparent 'bargains' are aimed at the poorest consumers, with Cleveland County Council's Consumer Protection Committee having recently issued a warning about 'cowboy' salesmen and 'suitcase sellers' peddling shoddy, inferior, damaged and counterfeit goods at Christmas (*Northern Echo* 7 December 1992). Other bogus bargain offers involve everyday food and household products in both small stores and large supermarkets (Croall 1987, 1989).

The slimming industry not only endangers women's health but also makes exaggerated claims about its products. The spokesperson for a recently formed anti-dieting campaign claims that 95 per cent of diets do not work – if dieting was a product, she argues, most dieters would demand their money back (*Independent* 8 April 1993). The Consumer Association's magazine *Which?* has called for more prosecutions and tougher penalties for the producers of slimming pills, which, they conclude, are a waste of money and possibly dangerous (*Today* 2 February 1989). Other slimming products are marketed with misleading descriptions – Boots was recently prosecuted on the grounds that a 'diet' chocolate bar contained nearly as many calories as other chocolate bars (*Guardian* 11 December 1992). The Consumers' Association has argued that many phrases such as 'low in fat', 'light in calories', 'unsweetened' or 'sugar free' should be banned, as they have no real meaning in the absence of agreed standards of fat or calorific content (*The Times* 12 November 1991). Similar problems occur with so-called 'green' products (*Today* 6 October 1991), and with 'cruelty free' or 'against animal testing' labels on cosmetic products (*Northern Echo* 19 May 1992).

Cosmetic products are also the source of much complaint on the grounds of exaggerated claims. Anti-wrinkle creams, for example, were recently investigated by the *Guardian* (7 January 1992). If these work at all, they may damage skin tissues, but most cannot repair age-related skin damage. Those that appear to have some effect do so by moisturizing, and the effect is short-lived. Advertising is blamed for the large sale of these products – the author of the report argues that 'while the media continues to portray men of all ages alongside young, smooth skinned women as a vision of success, women will go on investing in pots of worthless goop'. The packaging of cosmetics can also be deceptive. Many cosmetic manufacturers use 'double-skinned' containers – giving the impression that the package contains more than it does. This can amount to a 'misleading' description, but prosecutions are rare and costly (Croall 1987; *Daily Telegraph* 2 August 1990). Perfumes are also sold in misleading packages, and have been associated with deceptive price indications. Trading Standards Officers in Cleveland found that major stores regularly conceal the price of perfumes – leading one officer to comment that 'when it comes to expensive perfumes there seems to be a deliberate attempt by some retailers to hide prices from customers' (*Northern Echo* 1 January 1993).

The scent of crime?

The complex relationship between legal and illegal marketing strategies can be seen in the recent controversy over perfume sales. Following a campaign by Superdrug, the Monopolies and Mergers Commission have been asked to investigate whether the 'selective distribution systems' of leading perfume houses amount to rigging the market to keep prices high (*Financial Times* 21 November 1992; *Daily Telegraph* 1 October 1992). Consumer groups have complained that British perfume prices are artificially high, with normal profit margins being estimated at 60 per cent. Superdrug was refused supplies by leading perfume houses, but having obtained supplies on the 'grey market', undercut major retailers. A bottle of Chanel No. 5 Eau de Toilette, for example, was sold for £10 less than in Harrods. Leading perfume houses and retailers justify these practices on the grounds that their product is different, and that high prices are essential to the 'illusion of exclusiveness'. They must therefore be sold in a setting consistent 'with the aura of luxury cultivated by their lavish advertising and marketing campaigns' (*Financial Times* 21 November 1992). An executive from Parfums Givenchy stated that 'we sell a luxury product that relies on the dream it creates' (*Daily Telegraph* 1 October 1992), and a spokesman for Harrods argued that 'when you are selling perfume, you are dealing in romance and you cannot equate buying expensive perfume with buying a bottle of aspirin' (*Sunday Telegraph* 23 August 1992).

Sales frauds

It could also be argued that women are particularly vulnerable to many other sales and service frauds on the grounds that they are assumed to be 'ignorant' of financial or technical matters. Car sales and services are, for example, a notoriously 'fiddle-prone' or 'criminogenic' sector (Mars 1982; Leonard and Weber 1977; Croall 1989, 1992), where women's assumed ignorance may make them more likely to be overcharged or told they need repairs when they don't. While many men may be equally ignorant they may be assumed to be more knowledgeable. An American study by Tracy and Fox (1989) found that cars purporting to be uninsured presented to auto body repair shops by women were given higher estimates than those presented by men.

Women at home may be the targets of the questionable sales techniques of door-to-door salespersons, cowboy builders and plumbers and many other 'hawkers' at the door. These 'shady operators', many of them businesses, are an often-ignored but significant part of white-collar crime (Croall 1989; Sutton and Wild 1985). Indeed, an aspect of women's 'fear' of crime may be a reluctance to open the door to doorstep sellers. Some indication of the greater impact on women of this kind of crime is provided in a case study by Vaughan and Carlo (1975) of the activities of a bogus appliance repairman. Eighty-three per cent of his victims were female, and around one half of these were housewives – both blue- and white-collar. In more than half the cases, the victims were alone when the repairman called – and indeed felt that the outcome would have been different had they not been alone.

Women investors – 'little old ladies' and 'charmers'

The assumed gullibility of women, particularly 'little old ladies', is a popular image associated with financial fraud. This may well derive from the historical vulnerability of widows and elderly ladies (Robb 1992). In an era when women had little control over their own property and were expected to be provided for by men, widows and spinsters, reliant on small inheritances, became the targets of many bogus brokers and financiers. According to Herbert Spencer, victims included, 'widows who have never in their lives acted for themselves in any affair of moment. . .[and]. . .maiden ladies, alike nervous and innocent of all business knowledge' (quoted in Robb 1992: 126).

These kinds of attitudes may well affect sellers of financial products. In a study of victims of an American pyramid-selling scheme, Ganzini *et al.* (1990) found that 48 per cent (of 77) victims were female, and the average age was fifty-three. Citing other studies, they argue that, in comparison with violent crime, victims of white-collar crime tend to be 'older, more affluent, and relatively more likely to be female'. This was however a relatively small study. Nonetheless the elderly may be particularly vulnerable. The majority of the 15,000 investors who lost their savings in the Barlow Clowes affair were elderly, having been attracted by investment in seemingly solid Government gilts. Much of Barlow Clowes's advertising was aimed at elderly investors, and one of Peter Clowes's schemes was to set up a chain of gilts shops – to serve, in his words, the 'thousands of little old ladies holding the wrong gilts' (Lever 1992: 70). Farmers' widows and 'Wimbledon housewives' were among the many 'names' at Lloyd's to suffer most severely from the large losses sustained amid allegations of fraud, which most adversely affected 'outsiders' rather than 'insiders' (Gunn 1992). As with consumer frauds, women investors may be more likely to be targeted because of their *assumed* ignorance of financial affairs.

Little old ladies are not of course the only targets of fraudsters – a popular media image of fraud involves the seduction and defrauding of women by 'charmers'. While many of these cases involve confidence-tricksters rather than white-collar offenders, some fraudsters abuse their position as brokers or financial advisers to cheat investors. A recent example of this kind of case is the conviction of a 'small fat balding financial consultant. . .who could charm the birds from the trees'. This 'charmer' swindled six women out of a total of £500,000. Typically, perhaps, this was attributed to his obsession with his girlfriend. The judge commented that 'having been introduced to six women, none of whom had experience in financial matters, as a broker and financial adviser, you deceived them and took their money' (*Today* 18 October 1989). While Levi and Pithouse (1992) do not look specifically at gender in their study of fraud victims, they point out not only that private citizens may be more likely to be defrauded by family and friends than by strangers, but that being a victim of fraud can be likened to a mild form of rape.

Implications

The above, albeit selective, examples illustrate how women in their various roles as workers, consumers, housewives, mothers or investors are victimized by white-collar crime, from the corporate 'violence' of multimillion-pound enterprises to the activities of small businesses or professionals. These examples are not exhaustive, and many more could be added. Women's sexuality is exploited in marketing campaigns and advertisements; and pornography and the exploitation of women in the legitimate and illegitimate sex industries are further examples of business or 'enterprise' crime (Kelly and Radford 1987). Corporate crime is also increasingly global (Pearce and Woodiwiss 1993), and women in underdeveloped countries may be victimized by exploitation in poorly regulated manufacturing plants or by the dumping of unsafe contraceptives and drugs in the Third World countries. They may also be guinea-pigs for testing drugs or contraceptives. Women in low-income groups in Chile and Puerto Rico were the subjects of early clinical trials of oral contraceptives (Braithwaite 1984), and Depo-Provera, banned in the USA, was used in US-sponsored population-control programmes (Simon and Eitzen 1993).

It could be objected that many of these examples involve practices not legally defined as crime. Many do fall within the ambit of the criminal law, even if they are rarely detected and prosecuted and not widely regarded as criminal. Others involve practices which reveal loopholes and limitations in existing regulations and have been the subject of campaigns for 'criminalization'. Analyses of white-collar crime necessarily raise questions about the legal and social constructions of crime, and the failure to regard these practices as crime in itself indicates the ideological nature of these constructions (see, for example, Croall 1992). Critical criminologists and feminists have challenged the definition of 'criminal', with some arguing that racism, sexism and other forms of exploitation should be defined as criminal (Kelly and Radford 1987). To others the failure to treat such practices as crime, along with the failure to resource enforcement agencies fully, indicates the pervasiveness of the 'hegemony of corporate capital' (Pearce and Tombs 1990).

The exploration of how white-collar crime targets women has implications for analyses of both white-collar crime and victimization of women. Much work on the latter, by revealing the considerable victimization of women in the 'private' sphere, has sought to challenge these conventional definitions of crime. The examples above show that sexual abuse occurs in other relatively 'private' spheres. As Stanko (1990: 175) points out, 'because many of women's social, educational and economic situations take place primarily within a framework of heterosexuality, they are at risk of violence merely because they are in some form of a relationship with a man'. In addition, women's safety is threatened not only by sexual abuse but by corporate or organizational 'violence', arising from the marketing of products and services for women where profits, sales, or efficiency and budgets are given a higher priority than women's health and safety.

Women are also subjected to fraud and deception, both directly and indirectly, by a host of deceptive and fraudulent marketing and selling strategies. Marketing and advertising campaigns play on idealized images of women's sexuality, motherhood or domestic roles to sell a variety of products. Not only are many of these products ineffective and over-priced, but they involve, like the sale of perfume, selling a 'dream'. Charles Revlon is reputed to have said 'we don't sell lipstick, we sell hope' (cited in Ramsay 1989: 375). While it lies beyond the scope of this paper to analyse advertising and its impact fully, a major issue is the extent to which advertising creates consumer wants and needs (see for example, Cranston 1984: Ramsay 1989). As Simon and Eitzen (1993) comment 'in a fundamental way, all advertising is deceptive because it is designed to manipulate'. The spokeswoman for the anti-diet group referred to above argues that the powerful diet food industry has artificially created a 'problem', resulting in the vast majority of women feeling a need to diet – experiencing feelings of 'failure' if they don't succeed (*Independent* 8 April 1993). Like rape victims and victims of fraud, women victims of consumer offences tend to be blamed for their own victimization, given the primacy of *caveat emptor* (Levi and Pithouse 1992). Despite the many calls for stricter regulations and more prosecutions, the current de-regulatory climate places the onus of consumer or worker protection on the individual – most clearly seen in the 'decriminalization' of wages legislation.

Exploring the victimization of women is also important for analyses of the impact of white-collar crime. It suggests the addition of sexual abuse and harassment to the long list of offences where employees, managers or service providers abuse occupational power, in this case combining patriarchal control with organizational power. Other examples also highlight the abuse of occupational roles and the power, for example, of the seller over the buyer or the professional over the lay client. As Hagan (1988) points out, an important dimension of white-collar offending is the differential power that derives from the offender's 'structural location in the social organization of work'. Groups are rendered specially vulnerable by their structural location and powerlessness. It must be recognized, however, that gender inequalities overlap with class, age and racial inequalities. Thus while women in all classes are the victims of products and services marketed for women, lower-class women are structurally more vulnerable – especially in the workplace and the market-place, where low-income consumers become the target of the bogus 'bargain' offer or counterfeiter. They are also less likely to have the resources to seek recompense, unlike the largely middle-class victims of cosmetic surgery, or of the Barlow-Clowes and Lloyd's scandals, who are able to mount campaigns for compensation.

Further work on the structural basis of victimization would undoubtedly reveal other vulnerable groups. Children, for example, are highly susceptible to aggressive marketing of products which, like junk food or video games, may have long-term health implications; and they can be injured or killed by dangerous toys. Parents, of course, are also victims as the often unwilling purchasers of such products. Children also suffer from the sexual abuse and violence of 'caring' professions, the subject of much recent publicity. The elderly may also suffer from such abuse and may be particularly vulnerable to financial frauds, whether by having their pension funds plundered or being sold dubious investment products. Race may also be a factor – not only in relation to workplace offences but also many consumer products. Thus issues of gender, race, class and age are interrelated – which must be recognized in any full analysis of the victim–offender relationships involved in white-collar crime.

References

Abercrombie, N. *et al.* (1988). *Contemporary British Society* (Cambridge, Polity Press).

Aubert, V. (1977). 'White collar crime and social structure', in G. Geis and R. G. Maier (eds.), *White Collar Crime: Offences in Business, Politics and the Professions – Classic and Contemporary Views* (revised edn., New York, Free Press, Collier and Macmillan).

Box, S. (1983). *Power, Crime and Mystification* (London, Tavistock).

Box, S. (1987). *Recession, Crime and Punishment* (London, Macmillan).

Braithwaite, J. (1984). *Corporate Crime in the Pharmaceutical Industry* (London, Routledge and Kegan Paul).

Clarke, M. (1990). *Business Crime: Its Nature and Control* (Cambridge, Polity Press).

Cranston, R. (1984). *Consumers and the Law*, 2nd edn. (London, Weidenfeld and Nicholson).

Croall, H. (1987). 'Crimes against the consumer: an analysis of the nature, extent, regulation and sanctioning of trading offences' (Unpublished Ph.D. thesis, University of London).

Croall, H. (1989). 'Who is the white collar criminal?' *British Journal of Criminology*, 29 No.2, 157–64.

Croall, H. (1992). *White Collar Crime* (Milton Keynes, Open University Press).

Dobash, R. E. and Dobash, R. P. (1979) *Violence Against Wives* (New York, Free Press).

Dobash, R. E. and Dobash, R. P. (1992). *Women, Violence and Social Change* (London, Routledge).

Ganzini, L., McFarland, B. and Bloom, J. (1990). 'Victims of fraud: comparing victims of white collar and violent crime', *Bulletin of the American Academy of Psychiatry and the Law*, 18 No.1, 55–63.

Giddens, A. (1989). *Sociology* (Cambridge, Polity Press).

Grint, K. (1991). *The Sociology of Work* (Cambridge, Polity Press).

Gunn, C. (1992). *Nightmare on Lime Street: Whatever happened to Lloyd's of London?* (London, Smith Gryphon).

Hagan, J. (1988). *Structural Criminology* (Oxford, Polity Press).

Hanmer, J., Radford, J. and Stanko, E. (eds.) (1989). *Women, Policing and Male Violence: International Perspectives* (London, Routledge).

Jones, T., McLean, B. and Young, J. (1986). *The Islington Crime Survey* (Aldershot, Gower).

Kelly, J. and Radford, J. (1987). 'The problem of men: feminist perspectives on sexual violence', in P. Scraton (ed.), *Law, Order and the Authoritarian State* (Milton Keynes, Open University Press).

Lacey, R. (1992). *Unfit for Human Consumption* (London, Grafton).

Lea, J. (1992). 'The analysis of crime', in J. Young and R. Matthews (eds.), *Rethinking Criminology: the Realist Debate* (London, Sage).

Leonard, W. N. and Weber, M. G. (1977). 'Auto-makers and dealers: a study of criminogenic market forces', in G. Geis and R. G. Maier (eds.), *White Collar Crime: Offences in Business, Politics and the Professions – Classic and Contemporary Views*, revised edn. (New York, Free Press, Collier and Macmillan).

Lever, L. (1992). *The Barlow Clowes Affair* (London, Macmillan).

Levi, M. and Pithouse, A. (1992). 'The victims of fraud' in D. Downs (ed.), *Unravelling Criminal Justice* (London, Macmillan).

Mars, G. (1982). *Cheats at Work, an Anthropology of Workplace Crime* (London, George Allen and Unwin).

Miller, M. (1985). *Danger! Additives at Work* (London, London Food Commission).

Pearce, F. and Tombs, S. (1990). 'Ideology, hegemony and empiricism: compliance theories and regulation', *British Journal of Criminology*, 30 No. 4, 423–43.

Pearce, F. and Tombs, S. (1992). 'Realism and corporate crime' in R. Matthews and J. Young (eds.), *Issues in Realist Criminology* (London, Sage).

Pearce, F. and Woodiwiss, M. (eds.) (1993). *Global Crime Connections* (London, Macmillan).

Perry, S. and Dawson, J. (1985). *Nightmare: Women and the Dalkon Shield* (New York, Macmillan).

Radford, J. and Stanko, E. (1992). 'Violence against women and children: the contradictions of crime control under patriarchy', in K. Stenson (ed.), *The Politics of Crime Control*.

Ramsay, I. (1989). *Consumer Protection: Text and Materials* (London, Weidenfeld and Nicolson).

Reiner, R. (1985). *The Politics of the Police* (Brighton, Wheatsheaf Books).

Robb, G. (1992). *White Collar Crime in Modern England* (Cambridge, Cambridge University Press).

Ruggiero, V. (1992). 'Realist criminology: a critique', in R. Matthews and J. Young (eds.), *Issues in Realist Criminology* (London, Sage).

Shapiro, S. (1990). 'Collaring the crime, not the criminal: re-considering the concept of white collar crime', *American Sociological Review*, 44 (June), 346–65.

Simon, D. and Eitzen, D. (1993). *Elite Deviance*, 4th edn., (Allyn and Bacon).

Stanko, E. (1990). 'When precaution is normal: a feminist critique of crime prevention', in L. Gelsthorpe and A. Morris (eds.), *Feminist Perspectives in Criminology* (Milton Keynes, Open University Press).

Sutton, A. and Wild, R. (1985). 'Small business: white collar villains or victims?' *International Journal of the Sociology of Law*, 13, 247–59.

Tombs, S. (1990). 'Industrial injuries in British manufacturing industry', *Sociological Review*, 323–43.

Tracy, P. and Fox, J. (1989). 'A field experiment on insurance fraud in auto body repair', *Criminology*, Vol.27, No. 3, 589–603.

Vaughan, D. and Carlo, G. (1975). 'The appliance repairman: a study of victim-responsiveness and fraud', *Journal of Research in Crime and Delinquency*, 12, 153–61.

Walklate, S. (1989). *Victimology: The Victim and the Criminal Justice Process* (London, Unwin Hyman).

Walklate, S. (1992). 'Appreciating the victim: conventional, realist or critical victimology?', in R. Matthews and J. Young (eds.), *Issues in Realist Criminology* (London, Sage).

Weeks, S. and Gerber, J. (1992). 'The invisible woman: gender, victimization and white collar crime', *Criminal Justice Matters,* No.7, Spring, 14.

Wells, C. (1988). 'The decline and rise of English murder: corporate crime and individual responsibility', *Criminal Law Review*, 789–801.

12

Women-talk and men-talk: Defining and resisting victim status

JULIE M. OWEN

This chapter will consider some of the difficulties faced by anyone attempting to design and carry out a piece of feminist research and some of the choices made, in a discussion of work currently in the process of completion, and explore the motivations for conducting this research. It will consider the influences that theoretical and methodological orientations can have on shaping the approach to and the design of research. The process of developing initial research aims and assumptions will be highlighted by focusing on one particular choice made in my current research: the inclusion of male research participants in a feminist study of violence. I will explore the ideological, personal, practical, and analytical difficulties of including men, as victims, within this frame of reference, and also the rewards and the insights this inclusion has provided. The discussion will conclude with an informal consideration of the findings beginning to emerge from the research.

The research questions the relationship/s between gender and violence in people's lives. In what ways are one's experiences of violence determined by one's social position as woman or man, and how do the experiences of, or attitudes towards violence shape the 'doing' of gender in everyday life? Semi-structured, in-depth interviews were conducted with thirty people: thirteen women and seventeen men. Discussion centred around experiences of violence and threatening/anxiety-provoking behaviour, predominantly as a victim, in childhood and adulthood. The effects of these experiences and of anxieties about potential victimization were considered.

Where I use the term 'violence' to cover a wide range of behaviours ,cluding sexual harassment, bullying, indecent exposure, threats, hysical violence, child physical and sexual abuse, and rape, I do so self-consciously, but aware of the limitations and dangers involved. As a feminist I recognize the need to acknowledge all of these behaviours as rooted in structural inequalities of power, and to do so by using the term 'violence'. Labelling these various experiences as violence, however, does not have to involve labelling them as the same or equivalent, and should not involve denying the very real differences in severity and effect across such a range.

The use of the term 'victim' also needs some elaboration. It is in no way meant to imply any kind of static, universal, or unalterable state. What it does imply is an event/series of events in which one is a victim for which someone else has responsibility. I feel it is essential to retain this sense of responsibility on the part of the perpetrator. This research is based on the premiss that victimization involves a process of becoming, resisting, and surviving, and is not a fixed identity.

The research participants were contacted primarily through occupations and leisure activities where the experience of violence is often considered either part of the job or part of the culture, for example welfare and criminal justice agencies, football clubs, public houses. A number of participants were contacted as a result of snowballing arising from initial contacts. The ages of the participants ranged from twenty-one to thirty-nine, with the majority clustered around the late twenties/early thirties age group.

A major concern, as a feminist researcher, was not only to use this commitment to feminist politics, theory, and ethics in the construction and carrying out of the research, but also to be very self-conscious of this commitment throughout the research process, and to acknowledge (and analyse) this position (and its implications) within the accounts.

The research arose from my political and academic interest in gender inequality and, more specifically, in violence against women. The shape of the project was largely defined by: the influences of a political commitment to feminism; what I saw as the peculiar demands of the topic; a background in sociology; the siting of the research within the academic setting of a social science department; and an orientation towards participating in and producing feminist social science.

Theoretical orientations and conceptual developments

The theoretical starting-point of the study was the feminist perception that women are in a structurally unequal position in society, simply because they are women, (this is not to deny that there are significant differences between women). Violence against women is thus viewed as a manifestation of this inequality and a maintenance strategy in enforcing unequal power relations between women and men. Violence in this sense is a mechanism of social control. Another important concern within this project is the idea that theory and praxis remain inextricably linked for a feminist researcher.

Much valuable research has been done explicating these links and examining the operations of power relations between women and men, at individual and societal levels. Whilst accepting the ideas above as basic premises, this research was designed with the aim of broadening analytic consideration of them. The aim was to explore these operations as dispersed, dynamic, and contextual; to incorporate an understanding or at least an acknowledgement of difference; and to shift the traditional focus from men as perpetrators to enable a continued problematizing of masculinity using a consideration of men as victims.

The project is concerned with the operations of power across different levels and in particular their anchoring in the 'micro-practices' of social life. Thus it focuses on the experience of violence and the effects this may have on the everyday negotiations of one's gendered social position. Recognizing everyday social practice as infused with politics also places added emphasis on the need for reflexivity in recognizing research practice as political too.

By considering the experience of men as victims of violence, my work departs from most of that done in exploring violence against women and male domination. There are a number of reasons for believing that this inclusion may prove insightful, some of which I will consider at a later stage.

Methodological concerns

One of the most important additions of interpretivist and feminist developments in sociological research has been to insist upon the positioning of the researcher within the research process as an active social agent, affecting and affected at all stages of the research act. This reformulation of the 'research act' as a dynamic social process rather than an objectively controlled experimental event, has clearly shaped my ideas around research practice.

I began my research with a number of preconceptions about the appropriate methods of study for a project focusing on such sensitive and complex issues as victimization. I considered it would be more revealing to use qualitative methods of data construction. It must be acknowledged that much valuable work has been done in this area using quantitative methods, particularly in establishing the issue as a widespread social problem. Kelly, Regan and Burton (1992) have suggested that sensitively applied quantitative methods may prove more revealing, and certainly less traumatic for participants when dealing with experiences of child sexual abuse. In seeking to explore the processes and dynamics of violence and victimization, including the defining of situations and events, I felt, however, that qualitative methods would be the most appropriate and productive.

I see my research as located within a tradition of critique of positivistic notions of science and an awareness of the limitations that such a view of the world and of knowledge production can place on the study of the social. In interpretivist social science this critique has largely focused around the claim that quantitative methods are inappropriate tools for the exploration of the social world. Such methods – for example, large-scale surveys, structured questionnaires – are often in danger of eliciting only superficial or stereotypical views. They may lack the depth or flexibility to allow exploration of complex and/or sensitive issues. Hammersley and Atkinson (1983: 2), consider such methods are 'incapable of capturing the meaning of everyday human activity'. Whilst in the field of violence against women, research using large-scale survey methods has been invaluable in highlighting the enormity of the problem, it remains the case that much violence is still invisible to the survey, and if what is sought is an understanding of process, then these methods can indeed be inadequate.

Underlying this critique of quantitative methods is a different conception of valid knowledge. What interpretivist research aims to understand or explore, is the everyday world of the research participants. It considers the ways in which people experience their lives and through these experiences interpret and construct the world around them: how people attribute meanings and significance in their world. Jones (1985: 56) typifies this research aim as 'a concern to understand the world of the research participants as they construct it'. As a result of this concern, qualitative research can offer, 'a theory of social action grounded on the experiences – the world view – of those likely to be affected by a policy decision or thought to be part of the problem' (Walker 1985: 19).

The use of in-depth, semi-structured interviews was decided upon, with the idea that, 'open-ended interview research explores people's views of reality and allows the researcher to generate theory' (Reinhartz 1992: 18). Therefore, it was hoped that the open-ended nature of the majority of the questions would enable the participants to express themselves freely and in as much (or as little) detail as they chose. The loose structure enabled the inclusion of topics the researcher wished to explore without excluding the possibility that these were not the only or the most important ones as far as the participants were concerned, and facilitated (without predetermining) the preliminary analyses.

In considering the new demands placed upon a researcher aware of and sympathetic to interpretivist conceptions of social life and social science, it must be remembered that this need not necessarily result in the prescription of certain methods of research. Although most immediately associated with questions of methodology, what is central is the critique of the epistemological assumptions made by positivistic science. Interpretivist social science questions objectivity:

> Doing field research is therefore not merely the use of a set of uniform techniques but depends on a complex interaction between the research problem, the researcher and those who are researched. (Burgess 1984: 6)

In problematizing objectivity, it also questions what are seen as valid data, and what constitutes the production of credible social science. These decisions and questions of epistemology and methodology are what inform much feminist social science and the debates surrounding it.

Feminist methods? Feminist research

The traditional mainstream of social science has been recognized and refigured as 'malestream' by those on its margins,

> what feminist thought and practice have done is both to empower women and to problematize yet again what we mean by knowledge, reason, objectivity and validity in divided societies. (Ramazonoglu 1992: 209)

What most feminist researchers agree on is that problematizing objectivity (or even rejecting it as an unachievable goal), need not involve producing less rigorous or unscholarly work:

> good feminist research, rather than rejecting academic and scientific rationality, is proposing that we critically re-examine socially constructed notions of just what it is that constitutes scholarship and rationality. (Roberts 1990: xv)

Feminist research need not involve a rejection of 'method', but a redefinition or rather a more conscious awareness of what this method does (and should) involve. As Gelsthorpe (1992: 214) notes, 'a rejection of the notion of "objectivity" and a focus on *experience in method* does not mean a rejection of the need to be critical, rigorous and accurate.' A recognition of one's subjective social positioning and an analytical concern with gender can only lead to more rigorous scholarship.

Critiques of shallow and inappropriately applied quantitative methods, then, are not necessarily critiques of quantitative methods *per se*, but of the epistemological assumptions behind them. What feminism critiques is the assumption of the white, male scientific voice as objective, neutral and universal. The

> permeation of sociology by sexist background assumptions is less a product of the adoption or failure to adopt a particular methodology and much more a product of the social relations of sociological production. (Morgan 1990: 107)

What does constitute feminist research is a much contested matter. It could be seen as a different approach to research, and a concern with a certain type of research practice as opposed to the adoption of a set of prescriptive methods. As Fonow and Cook (1991: 8) note, many feminist researchers consider, 'that carefully designed research grounded in feminist theory and ethics is more useful to understanding women's experiences than an allegiance to any one particular method as more "feminist" than another'.

The relationship between feminist theory and practice, then, is very important in defining work as feminist. As Reinhartz (1992: 249) notes, 'feminist social research utilizes feminist theory in part because other theoretical traditions ignore or downplay the interaction of gender and power.' Thus feminist theory was influential in defining my choice of topic, the experiences of victims of violence. It also affected my approach to theoretical explanations of the issues, a concern with structural power constraints as well as the continual and fluid negotiations of power on an everyday level. Importantly, it lent emphasis to the need for reflexivity within the research process itself.

If the definition of research as feminist lies at an ontological level, as Stanley and Wise (1991a: also 1991b) suggest, or at least an epistemological level, then in practice what does this mean for the process of feminist research? As discussed above, it does not necessarily appear to dictate the use of particular methods. It does involve the researcher in criticism of a dominant tradition which has ignored, marginalized, trivialized, and/or misrepresented topics of enquiry and the people (or women) involved, (Jayaratne and Stewart 1991; Acker, Esseveld and Barry 1991); 'this "normal" way of creating "truths" must not be allowed to persist and dominate research' (Herbert 1989: 175).

Another truism about feminist research is that it is research for, by and on women. The claim that it should be 'for' women is by far the least controversial of the three, although there is debate as to how or to what extent it can and should be, or even whether there is a category 'women' it can be *for*. Reinhartz (1992: 177) argues for a wide definition, '(t)o the extent that feminism is change-oriented by definition, all feminist research has action components'.

Self-consciousness and reflexivity

The question of 'interest' or 'bias' is one often raised in relation to feminist research. Laws (1990) notes how the views of those with power often become seen as unquestioned universals, whereas those arguing from (and acknowledging their position within) oppressed social positions are often accused of partiality. Studying the personal, whether issues/situations/people/experiences, is always controversial, leading to accusations of partiality or bias. It can be particularly hard to avoid, as a feminist, addressing any questions concerning gender. Of course it is because of the researcher's feminism and the fact that she is a woman that she is discussing these questions at all.

Particularly in feminist research it is the personal experiences of the researcher (as a woman) that influence the definition of the research question and the way in which it is approached. Recognizing this is not confessing to bias but exploring the 'researcher's standpoint' (Reinhartz 1992: 259). The choice to study experiences of violence/threatening situations has obviously been influenced by both my personal and my academic development. These concerns will clearly be at issue not just through the choosing of a topic, but throughout the research project. I aim to remain reflexive about this and aware that my concerns and experiences are not necessarily those of all women. In fact, 'hearing other people's stories also provides the researcher with an alternative case that *prevents* her from generalizing exclusively from her own experience' (Reinhartz 1992: 34).

It has therefore become seen as increasingly important to locate the researcher clearly both within the research and within the wider social structure: 'the theoretical reconstruction must be able to account for the investigator as well as for those who are investigated' (Acker, Esseveld and Barry 1991: 145). It is not only the product of knowledge or the process of knowledge production that is opened to scrutiny, but the role of the researcher within this process (Aldridge 1993):

> each sociologist should analytically account for their intellectual products by investigating the material grounds of their own labour processes, recognising that knowledge is situational and contextual and differs systematically in relation to the social location of its producers. (Stanley 1993: 48)

Linked to this and to wider concerns of reflexivity must be an acknowledgement of the potentials for distortion within any research act. The final written presentation of the research, however it may try to do justice to the recounted experiences of participants, must acknowledge that they are being structured and interpreted by the researcher.

> The act of looking at interviews summarizing another's life, and placing it, within a context is an act of objectification
> . . . How do we explain the lives of others without violating their reality? (Acker, Barry and Esseveld 1991: 142)

Problems in adequately reproducing the accounts of participants and combining them with the accounts of researchers must be noted. In explaining or theorizing from participants' accounts, researchers must be aware of what they are doing to the language and explanations of the participants.

'Description' involves selection and interpretation and is therefore more properly to be seen as gloss or theorisation – there is no such thing as untheorised experience for experience is always mediated by these kinds of structuring processes. (Stanley and Morgan 1993: 3)

The motivations and initial framing of the research topic clearly locate this work within a tradition of feminist scholarship. The critique of positivistic and traditionally malestream approaches to research, position this work within the interpretivist and feminist challenge to accepted notions of what constitutes valid and credible social research and knowledge production. The acknowledgement of the researcher as a socially situated agent within the research process is of obvious importance to such an approach.

Researching the unknown? Questions of identity and difference

Let us return to the assumption often made about feminist research, that it will not only be for, but also by and on women (Stacey 1988). In assuming that the research participants will be women, and the researcher a (usually white middle-class) woman, it is often taken for granted that the researcher will be in a more powerful social position than the research participant. This excludes work done on those with higher class status or institutional power, or a more generally privileged position in the social structure, for example, white men.

Other researchers (e.g. Finch 1984) have noted how much easier it is as a female researcher to interview women. This was a potential problem for me, questioning my ability as a female (and feminist) researcher to interview, identify with or even understand male research participants: 'A feminist interviewing women is by definition both "inside" the culture and participating in that which she is observing' (Mies 1991: 57). There are however, ethical problems concerning the use of a perceived shared identity to facilitate research (Finch 1984; Stacey 1988), particularly when considering that it can only be a partial identity at best (Mies 1991).

'Women' can no longer be used unthinkingly as a simple descriptive category disconnected from experiences of ethnicity, age, sexual orientation, dis/ability, or class largely placed on the agenda by black and lesbian feminists critiquing in turn the exclusions of white middle-class feminism; claims of identification and thus a privileged understanding of research participants because of their gender are no longer a straightforward issue (King 1990; Ramazanoglu 1989; Simmonds 1990; Smith 1989). However, if gender is seen as fundamental in defining social experience, and especially experiences of violence, then at least this partial identity might be claimed by female researchers. As Finch (1984: 76) points out, 'both parties share a subordinate structural position by virtue of their gender'.

Self-disclosure and non-disclosure in the interviewing relationship

Feminist attempts to reconstruct the research relationship as a more egalitarian enterprise have often involved the practice of self-disclosure within the research process. Self-disclosure depends to a large extent on recognizing and fostering some sense of shared identity. Many consider it vital (Oakley 1990) that, in challenging hierarchical research relationships and acknowledging the active nature of the researcher in creating data, the researcher should be open to disclosing information and personal experiences. In this way it is hoped that the essentially exploitative nature of the research might be minimized. Self-disclosure is not a simple issue, however, nor a simple solution to the problem of power negotiations within research relationships. Thompson (1990) discusses how self-disclosure can be used by the researcher to alleviate her own pain: Bombyk, Bricker-Jenkins and Wedenoja (in Reinhartz 1992) consider how it can restrict the participants' own disclosures made within the interview setting. It is especially important to note that, regarding the research in its entirety, from conception to production, the researcher will have a measure of control that the research participants will not (and indeed may not want to) have.

The disclosure of personal experience is becoming increasingly at issue in the presentation of the research product itself. Acknowledging experiences related to research concerns can lead to a feeling of personal as well as academic vulnerability. Therefore in acknowledging my personal experiences of violence I do not attribute any detail of these to myself within research accounts. I have chosen to be interviewed myself, but this was with more regard to understanding the interviewing experience from a different angle. Cotterill and Letherby (1993) emphasize that the need to acknowledge one's autobiography outweighs the difficulties involved:

> their [research participants'] lives are filtered through us and filtered stories of our lives are present (whether we admit it or not) in our written accounts. Surely it is better to acknowledge this and explore it analytically

rather than subscribe to false notions of objectivity or to collapse and confuse our respondents' experiences with our own. (Cotterill and Letherby 1993: 74)

This concern with self-disclosure is also a particular issue, as a woman, when considering interviewing men. As already noted, it is often assumed that feminist research will be research solely focusing on women. The studying of men inevitably creates a new set of issues to concern the female researcher.

Turning the focus on to men and masculinity

Increasingly, feminist researchers are including men and sometimes focusing on men in study. Why? In part this is a (not new, but alternatively conceptualized) recognition of the fact that women's lives, socially and personally, are entangled with men's.

> Women do not inhabit a single-sexed universe; the real world involves not only 'actual men', but also the ideologically founded but materially practised discourses by which some men, individually and collectively, actively construct the category 'woman/women' and also and thereby construct the category 'man/men' as well. (Stanley and Wise 1991a: 44).

It is also of importance to recognize that male power affects women's lives even when individual men are not present:

> The production of the various roles and meanings involved in 'doing' masculinity affect me and all women both in their production and their employment, as these seem to centre on power differentials between men and men and men and women. (Layland 1991: 128)

In necessarily attempting to rectify the invisibility and marginalization of women's experiences, little feminist research has considered male experience. A focus on male experience, as specific and not universal, can usefully avoid the danger of keeping women and women's experiences as marginal and, paradoxically, by making masculinity a focus of research, displace men from the centre: 'Thus taking gender into account is "taking men into account" and not treating them – by ignoring the question of gender – as the normal subjects of research' (Morgan 1990: 98).

More specifically, research on victims of violence has not often considered the male experience (notable exceptions being Stanko 1990; Stanko and Hobdell 1993; and recent work on hate crimes and

ethnoviolence, Herek and Berrill 1992). One reason for the involvement of male victims in this study was the consideration that the
relationship between masculinity/experiences of being a man and
violence could be explored equally well through a focus on men as
victims as through the more familiar focus on men as perpetrators.

Issues in interviewing men

One of the main expectations of a feminist piece of research is that
the researcher will aim to make the research process more egalitarian,
that there will be less of a hierarchical research relationship. This is
based on the assumption that the researcher is necessarily in a more
powerful social position than the participant. This poses particular
problems when interviewing men. Laws (1990) notes this problem in
her project involving men's conceptions of menstruation; she
comments on her desire to retain more control over the research
process and (so to a certain extent) over the research participants. It is
interesting to note here that my choice to interview male *victims* as
opposed to *perpetrators* of violence may have been prompted by a
desire to maintain a certain sense of control, and possibly to enable a
sense of identity/sympathy with and valuing of the research
participants that is the goal of much feminist research practice.

One common way of developing a more equal research relationship
is through self-disclosure, answering questions asked by participants
even when involving personal information and sometimes
volunteering information oneself (Oakley 1990). Reinhartz (1992)
notes that this can be a particular problem,

> when feminists engage in research on men, upper-class people, and
> institutions with considerable power [and as a result] they are likely to
> demand less and self-disclose less because self-disclosure diminishes one's
> power. (Reinhartz 1992: 42)

Of course, sympathy with the views or life experiences of any
participant is not assured by sharing of gender (Yeandle in Reinhartz
1992), nor is self-disclosure an unmitigated good thing. Bombyck,
Bricker-Jenkins and Wedenoja (in Reinhartz 1992) note that such
disclosure can at times constrain participants and lead to them
stereotyping the interviewer and what she wants to hear. Thompson
(1990) also considers how such *supportive* interrupting can be a way
for the researcher to escape the pain of what she is hearing. It is

important for the researcher to be constantly aware that her own experiences are not universally generalizable to all women. It remains the case, however, that there is likely to be a certain resonance for the female researcher in female participants' accounts, that is lacking in those of male participants.

It is certainly the case that my disclosures within the interview setting were far less personal (therefore potentially less supportive) and less frequent when I was talking with male research participants than they were with female research participants. I was generally less comfortable with the idea of 'becoming vulnerable' or 'losing power' by revealing personal experiences of violence to male participants.

It was also often the case that my personal experiences simply did not appear so relevant to the experiences of male participants as they did to some of the female participants' experiences. Thus, for me as a woman, there was a resonance between my experiences and women's accounts of negotiating their safety daily, of 'laughing off' being flashed once it became clear that 'nothing really happened', despite being 'really scared at the time'. To use my own experiences as a comparison to enable a woman to recognize that her responses to a violent partner were not necessarily mad or stupid or unnatural is an effective strategy. Self-disclosing in this way can lead to more inclusive, accurate accounts, and most importantly lead to the interview being less traumatic and more productive for the woman involved.

This strategy did not appear to be so readily available for me when talking with, for example, male victims of schoolyard bullying. Of course this could mean that the accounts men revealed were 'cleaner' (not driven by any disclosures of mine) and that I would find it easier to avoid generalizing too simply from my own experiences. However, a concern to avoid this kind of temptation must be continuing in any research project. The main aim of self-disclosure in this has been to lessen the feeling of exposure for the research participants, and to extract painful information in a way that is easier for the participant and not just the researcher. One strategy I did develop to ease men's telling of experiences in the way self-disclosure can be used, was to refer to the experiences of other men I know or have interviewed. This proved productive in this way, and also in facilitating further discussion of the issues involved.

This relative lack of self-disclosure with the male research participants is perhaps also indicative of the gendered dynamics of the interview relationships as a whole. The interviews with the men were more formal than those conducted with the women. There was no physical contact with male participants beyond the occasional introductory handshake. With the female participants I felt freer to offer a hug or hand-squeeze now and then. This was not necessarily because of the potential sexual implications involved in physical contact with male heterosexual participants. I felt more confident of my ability to judge when physical contact would be acceptable to or desired by the women.

My greater self-consciousness with male research participants could be viewed positively in terms of my performance as a social researcher. However, I consider it may have resulted in the interview experience being less supportive for the men, and therefore can only be viewed negatively in terms of my performance as a *feminist* researcher.

There were a number of purely practical issues raised by interviewing men. Discussions with other researchers made me aware of the need to consider my own negotiations of safety in terms of conducting the interviews with male participants. As a result I ensured that someone was always aware of how long I expected to be gone and had a contact number for me. Within the interviews themselves, I never felt threatened or indeed felt any anxieties over my safety, no doubt owing to my relatively 'safe' and powerful position as a social researcher.

I was also very aware that the list of support agencies I had ready for any participants who needed them did not relate very well to either the needs or the experiences of men. This was an issue I was aware of from the initial stages of the research when the difficulties of contacting male victims of violence were considered. This is not a comment on 'fairness' or 'bias' of victim-support agencies, but a note of the methodological impacts of the largely gendered constructions of the 'victim'.

Although I had no formal intention of interviewing in any particular order, I began with male participants. This I rationalized as a desire to get the more problematic interviews 'over with'. I had anticipated a number of problems specifically associated with women interviewing men, none of which I imagined would be lessened by a focus on gender issues in the research question itself. In constructing the interview schedule I had already encountered the difficulty of using language a diverse range of participants would understand.

Of course, differences and difficulties of understanding can occur as a result of one or many different identifications, from class and upbringing to regional and ethnic backgrounds, age and sexuality. So, whilst understanding and misunderstandings were not merely mediated by gender, the possibility was something of which I strove to remain aware. In this I was helped by the male research participants' willingness to correct my misapprehensions as we discussed events and their significance. The fact that I appeared to misunderstand or be confused by some of the male participants' discussion more frequently than by the female participants' could be an artefact of masculine speech which enables men to contradict or correct authority figures (i.e. the researcher) more easily than women can. It could be a result of the fact that my awareness of *male* attitudes around issues of safety and victimization was initially not as developed as my awareness, as a woman, around female attitudes towards safety and victimization.

Quite apart from a basic level of understanding (Greed 1991), there are problems of talking about certain issues or even talking in particular ways. Hertz in Reinhartz (1992) concluded from her research experience that women are culturally encouraged to talk about feelings, for example, whereas men are not. In this specific instance I anticipated that men might be reluctant to discuss or admit to anxiety about potential victimization, whilst such feelings in women are expected as common sense. I considered that as a woman I at least had more chance than a male interviewer of getting men to discuss such feelings. To a certain extent (although usually within heterosexual relationships) it is more culturally acceptable for a man to discuss such things with a woman than with other men. It was certainly an issue to keep forefronted throughout the interview process. Although in several cases men were reticent to begin with, this did not seem to indicate that any systematic silence or avoidance of issue was involved.

In fact I was surprised at how open and willing to talk most men were. It was the case that many men were *surprised* at having their opinions sought about the experience of violence *as a victim*. The almost universal response from those whom I had contacted but of whom I was unaware of any specific violent event, was 'Do I look violent then?' or 'Who's been telling stories about me?', etc. Their predominantly open response in interviews, however, suggested that perhaps there is less of a reluctance for men to talk about these issues than a lack of opportunity. This is not to deny that certain of the issues were difficult for men to talk about and certainly painful for them to conceptualize in particular ways – issues I will explore later.

This recognition of potential problems was my rationale for interviewing the male participants largely before the female ones. During the interview period however, I began to question this reasoning. I now believe that it was more the result of a desire to 'put off' conducting the interviews that I anticipated would be more painful. Many researchers have noted the difficulties in dealing emotionally with distressing research topics (Thompson 1990; Gordon and Rigier in Reinhartz 1992). As a feminist researching violence, the attempts to achieve a less hierarchical research relationship, and the viewing and valuing of the research subject as a person, can make this more draining still. Kahn and Gozemba (in Reinhartz 1992) acknowledge the strategies they evolved to avoid dealing with the potentially painful research they had done.

Again this can be related to my gendered attitudes towards the interviewing situation. Experience upset my unthinking expectation that the interviews with male participants would necessarily be less traumatic, for them or for me. Undoubtedly several of the men interviewed found the memories they evoked very painful. What I do doubt is that my response to these participants was as sympathetic or as understanding as my response to female participants. The possibility that this could have had an impact on the response I received from male research participants cannot be ignored.

Safety and risk: a gendered concern

To conclude, I will briefly consider some of the themes emerging from the data. I will concentrate mainly on considering some of the issues emerging as a result of including men in this research project. In constructing the research project as a whole, and throughout the research process, I aimed to be sensitive to the differences and similarities between the experiences and descriptions of the men and women I talked to. In recognizing the effect of language upon experience I was concerned to explore questions of definition around the issue of violence and victimization and to consider to what extent, if any, they were shaped by gender. Definitions can be seen to affect the process of becoming a victim in a number of ways. The victim's definition of the event, and themselves in relation to it, can be affected by others' definitions in turn, and by wider public discourses on violence and victimization.

In public discourse, victimization, especially in adulthood, is significantly gendered. Women are the focus of official safety advice. Fear is generated around images of vulnerable women; predominantly women at risk of public violence by unknown men. Men in this study (when not contacted as a result of a specific violent event) were surprised to be asked for their views on experiences of violence *as a victim* and on issues of personal safety and perceptions of risk.

Stanko (1990) notes that talking to men who have recently experienced a serious physical assault is one way of opening a door into discussions of risk and safety. I anticipated this problem, and the majority of my contacts were made through occupational and leisure settings where at least some considerations of personal safety might have been expected. Expanding these context-specific considerations into other areas of their lives proved somewhat problematic.

In contrast, most of the women I talked to, although often not *consciously* aware of the number of precautionary measures against victimization that they took, or of the frequent assessments of risk that they made, were certainly more familiar with discussions around personal safety. The female research participants saw no discrepancy in their being asked about their experiences and opinions on the subject. In considering issues of safety much of the male discussion was framed by constant comparison to the experiences and attitudes of female friends, partners, and co-workers. When asked if they ever talked about safety or risk, and who with, the vast majority of the men who discussed them at all, talked about them with women they knew. Very few discussed safety concerns with other men.

This may be because men find it easier to discuss vulnerability and anxiety with women than with other men. Men's dislike of admitting to weakness or vulnerability is one of the explanations offered to account for men's apparently lower levels of anxiety about violent crime in the face of their apparently greater likelihood of becoming a victim. However, in this study, when men revealed discussions around safety with women, they were talking about discussions about women's safety, not their own.

The male participants were in no way as consciously aware of their safety and of the risk of violence as the female participants were. The women took more precautions than the men, placed greater restrictions on their own movements than the men did, and did so not in hysterical over-reaction, but with an unthinking sense that this behaviour is just common sense, that it is what women do almost automatically. This lack of adaptive behaviour on the part of the male participants is even more marked owing to the fact that many of these men were aware of statistics that rated their risk of experiencing violence as much greater than a woman's. In exploring this issue many of the men and women saw this as partly a result of their perceptions of women's greater vulnerability to attack; i.e. that women are less likely to be able to avoid the attack and more likely to be seriously hurt by it. The majority of participants considered that what they saw as women's especial vulnerability to sexual assault was significant in constructing anxieties about victimization.

Therefore it can be seen that the consequences of indirect victimization are very different for women and for men, and that public discourses around victimization are also in some ways very different for men and women, but in other ways very similar. The immediate consequences of violent victimization, in terms of a range of physical and emotional responses often placed under the umbrella term Post-Traumatic Stress Disorder, can be remarkably similar and painful for both women and men. These most commonly last from the occurrence of the incident over a number of weeks and months, and occasionally for longer periods.

There are indications of gender-differential responses to and consequences of violence. The actual experience of becoming a victim and the negative consequences this can bring can be significantly affected by a previous feeling of unique invulnerability, which can be linked to men's general lack of anxiety about victimization (Stanko and Hobdell 1993). Men often assume a masculine skill in negotiating, avoiding, or winning violent encounters, a notion I will return to later. When victimization occurs, nevertheless, it can be experienced as a challenge to this array of skills, and a threat not simply to the physical self. This can be compared to the assumption that rape is such a significant event for women because of its threat to a sexually inviolable self.

In terms of the actual types of violence experienced, the women and men in this study suffered from a wide range of physical, emotional, and sexual violence; from strangers, family members, friends, co-workers and acquaintances. There were some differences that appeared significant according to gender. More of the men experienced physical assault from unknown men in public places than the women did. More of the women experienced prolonged emotional, sexual and physical abuse from parents as children, and from partners as adults, than the men. Both the women and men experienced sexual threats and unwanted sexual contact and assault. These experiences were very different for the women and the men. To take being flashed at as an example, the majority of the women had experienced this on one or several occasions. Whilst most of them see these experiences as relatively insignificant now, at the time many had been 'really scared' (Karen) or 'anxious . . . [not] know[ing] what was going to happen' (Sarah). The men who had been flashed at (approximately one-quarter of them) on the contrary found it totally unthreatening at the time, and amusing or simply sad in retrospect. This was clearly due to a feeling of relative invulnerability:

> Well that wasn't that serious . . . not really threatening
> . . . again I was amazed really . . . and I knew that he didn't have the physical power to force me into anything. (Rob)
>
> To me that isn't any sort of physical threat. (David)
>
> It isn't any threat to me. (Steve)

Again this is linked to men's belief in their strength or capability to deal with potentially threatening situations successfully.

One issue that I was careful to examine was that of what becomes defined as violent and what does not. Although told that the research was concerned with 'violence' and 'victims', these words were largely avoided in the schedule. When discussing specific incidents it was the participant's own definitions of the 'violence' or of the seriousness of the events that were sought.

Hard men and heroic victimhood: encapsulating and redefining painful experiences

One marked difference between the talk of the women and men I interviewed, was the greater willingness of the men to define their experiences as 'violent' in comparison to the women: and the increased resistance on the men's part to being labelled a 'victim' of their experiences. The men's freer use of the term 'violence' to describe the experiences may be a result of a number of factors. The men suffered more physically injurious violence than the women did.

Both men and women were more likely to view the experience as violent and/or serious the greater the degree of *physical* harm/pain involved. This was also true for those who suffered sexual assaults and rape, but not for those who had been sexually abused as children.

Acknowledging an experience as 'violent' for men did not always appear to mean it was viewed in a totally negative light. When women recalled 'violent' events there was no pleasure involved, and any pride was a result of surviving the incident, coping with the consequences, having 'almost forgotten' it (Karen), or as one woman said, in 'not let[ting] it ruin my life' (Mary). Some of the men, in comparison, had clearly managed to redefine the experience of violence in as almost positive light, and re-cast themselves as heroic moral victors and/or gallant losers.

A significant majority of the men also described the violence they had experienced as neutralized, or encapsulated in some way. The experiences they had had might be relegated to the past: 'when I used to go to clubs a lot' (Terry); 'this was all like, ten, fifteen years ago now' (Simon). Some described violence as unlikely to happen to them now, because they had developed the skills to avoid or negotiate their way out of threatening situations: 'I think I've become reasonably skilled at . . . actually at keeping out of fights' (Rob). Although a number of the women felt they would now recognize and perhaps be able to avoid threatening situations or dangerous people, the important element here for the men was not necessarily avoidance, but an active *choice* not to engage with the situation. Significantly, when the men had become victims despite these skills, perhaps through facing greater numbers or a weapon, the 'unfairness' of such violence, whilst being very traumatic and often having lasting effects, could still be retrospectively mythologized in a way that the violence women experience is not.

Linked to this positive gloss some men place on past experiences of violence is their reluctance to acknowledge themselves as a 'victim'. A number of the men I talked to worked hard to reassure me that although they had experienced violence (bullying, mugging, parental abuse), which they recognized as violent, and as significant, they themselves were not victims: 'I hope you're not going to call me a victim' (Dave). This is not to imply that women unthinkingly accept or are comfortable with victim status, but it was certainly not such an issue with the women I talked to. As Stanko notes: 'These men experience the assault and subsequent feelings of vulnerability as an affront to their masculinity' (Stanko 1990: 128). Male victims of assault view their experience through a male frame of reference, in which being victimized carries implications of weakness and helplessness (Stanko and Hobdell 1993: 413).

The point then is that victimization and its attendant vulnerability is in direct conflict with images of hegemonic masculinity. It is equally central to women's experiences of victimization that models of femininity are rarely in conflict with such constructions of victimhood.

Conclusions

To conclude, I feel it is very important to acknowledge the influences and motivations that inform any researcher's choices of topic and the theoretical and methodological approaches to that topic. Interpretivist and feminist research traditions emphasize this concern with reflexivity, as involving not only a recognition of the socially situated nature of the researcher, but also a recognition of the contextual process of research and, importantly, of the research product. The inclusion of male research participants has underlined the need for such a continuing self-consciousness. This development involved the researcher in negotiation of her own safety, recognition of the potential limits of understanding in interviewing across gender identifications, and acknowledgement of the real and painful nature of many men's experiences of violence. The entangled nature of men's experiences of violence and their experiences of masculinity is one of the primary issues being explored through this research.

References

Acker, J., Esseveld, J., and Barry, K. (1991). 'Objectivity and truth: problems in doing feminist research' in M. M. Fonow and J. A. Cook (eds.), *Beyond Methodology: Feminist Scholarship as Lived Research* (Bloomington, Indiana University Press).

Aldridge, J. (1993) 'The textual disembodiment of knowledge in research account writing in sociology', *Sociology*, 27 No.1, 53–66.

Burgess, R. (1984). *In the Field: An Introduction to Field Research* (London, Allen and Unwin).

Cotterill, P., and Letherby, G. (1993). 'Weaving stories: personal auto/ biography in feminist research', *Sociology* 27 No.1, 67–79.

Finch, J. (1984). ' "It's great to have someone to talk to": the ethics and politics of interviewing women', in C. Bell, and H. Roberts (eds.), *Social Researching: Politics, Problems, Practice* (London, Routledge).

Fonow, M. M., and Cook, J. A. (eds.) (1991). *Beyond Methodology: Feminist Scholarship as Lived Research* (Bloomington, Indiana University Press).

Gelsthorpe, L. (1992). 'Response to Martyn Hammersley's paper "On Feminist Methodology"', *Sociology*, 26 No.2, 213–18.

Greed, C. (1991). 'The professional and the personal: a study of women quantity surveyors', in L. Stanley (ed.), *Feminist Praxis: Research, Theory and Epistemology in Feminist Sociology* (London, Routledge).

Hammersley, M. and Atkinson, P. (1983). *Ethnography: Principles in Practice* (London, Tavistock).

Herbert, C. (1989). *Talking of Silence: The Sexual Harassment of Schoolgirls* (London, The Falmer Press).

Herek, G. M. and Berrill K. T. (eds.) (1992). *Hate Crimes: Confronting Violence against Lesbians and Gay Men* (London, Sage).

Jayaratne, T. E. and Stewart, A. J. (1991). 'Quantitative and qualitative methods in the social sciences: current feminist issues and practical strategies' in M. M. Fonow and J. A. Cook (eds.), *Beyond Methodology: Feminist Scholarship as Lived Research* (Bloomington, Indiana University Press).

Jones, S. (1985) 'Depth Interviewing', in R. Walker (ed.), *Applied Qualitative Research* (Aldershot, Gower).

Kelly, L., Regan, L., and Burton, S. (1992). 'Defending the indefensible? Qualitative methods and feminist research, in H. Hinds, A. Phoenix and J. Stacey (eds.), *Working Out: New Directions for Women's Studies* (London, Falmer).

King, K. (1990) 'Producing sex, theory and culture: gay/straight remappings in contemporary feminism', in M. Hirsch and E. Fox Keller (eds.), *Conflicts in Feminism* (London, Routledge).

Laws, S. (1990). *Issues of Blood: The Politics of Menstruation* (London, Macmillan).

Layland, J. (1991). 'On the conflicts of doing feminist research into masculinity', in L. Stanley (eds.), *Feminist Praxis: Research, Theory and Epistemology in Feminist Sociology* (London, Routledge).

Mies, M. (1991). 'Women's research or feminist research? The debate surrounding feminism, science and methodology', in M. M. Fonow and J. A. Cook (eds.), *Beyond Methodology: Feminist Scholarship as Lived Research* (Bloomington, Indiana University Press).

Morgan, D. H. J. (1990). 'Men, masculinity, and the process of sociological enquiry', in H. Roberts (ed.), *Doing Feminist Research* (6th edn., London, Routledge).

Oakley, A. (1990) 'Interviewing women: a contradiction in terms', in H. Roberts, (ed.), *Doing Feminist Research*, 6th edn. (London, Routledge).

Ramazanolgu, C. (1989). 'Improving sociology: the problems of taking a feminist standpoint', *Sociology,* 23 No.3, 427–42.

Ramazanoglu, C. (1992). 'On feminist methodology: male reason versus female empowerment', *Sociology*, 26 No.2, 207–12.

Reinhartz, S. (1992). *Feminist Methods in Social Research*, (Oxford, Oxford University Press).

Roberts, H. (ed.) (1990). *Doing Feminist Research*, 6th edn. (London, Routledge).

Simmonds, F. N. (1992). 'Difference, power and knowledge: black women in academia', in H. Hinds, A. Phoenix and J. Stacey (eds.), *Working Out: New Directions for Women's Studies* (London, Falmer).

Smith, B. (1989). 'Toward a black feminist criticism', in E. Showalter (ed.), *The New Feminist Criticism: Essays on Women, Literature, and Theory*, 2nd edn. (London, Virago Press).

Stacey, J. (1988). 'Can there be a feminist ethnography?', *Women's Studies International Forum*, 11 No.1, 21–7.

Stanko, E. (1990). *Everyday Violence: How Women and Men Experience Sexual and Physical Danger* (London, Pandora).

Stanko, E. and Hobdell, K. (1993). 'Assault on men: masculinity and male victimisation', *British Journal of Criminology*, Summer 1993, 400–15.

Stanley, L. (1993). 'On auto/biography in sociology', *Sociology*, 27 No.1, 41–52.

Stanley, L. and Wise, S. (1991a). 'Method, methodology and epistemology', in L. Stanley, *Feminist Praxis: Research, Theory and Epistemology in Feminist Sociology* (London, Routledge).

Stanley, L., and Wise, S. (1991b). 'Feminist research, feminist consciousness, and experiences of sexism' in M. M. Fonow and J. A. Cook (eds.), *Beyond Methodology: Feminist Scholarship as Lived Research* (Bloomington, Indiana University Press).

Thompson, B. (1990). 'Raisins and smiles for me and my sister: a feminist theory of eating problems, trauma, and recovery in women's lives' (Ph.D. dissertation, Brandeis University, 1990).

Walker, R. (1985). *Applied Qualitative Research* (Aldershot, Gower).

13

The modelling of threat incidence: Evidence from the British Crime Survey

ANDROMACHI TSELONI

Although crime surveys investigate threats and intimidation as a type of crime against the person, threats have been overlooked in the victimization risk literature. This may be due to their marginal position in definitions of crime by the criminal justice system.

> Only a minority of threats can be prosecuted *qua* 'threats' as indictable offences (and classified as notifiable offences). (Hough 1990: 169)

> Threats, whether verbal or written, are criminal if they menace substantial injury to the recipient or his property. (Scottish Common Law)

A threat may have substantial unpleasant psychological consequences to the victim and his/her immediate environment. It can stimulate anxiety and fear in anticipation of the more serious crime which might have occurred had the threat been carried out. The psychological consequences of a threat differ depending on the victim–offender relation. When a threat is issued by a stranger the initial effect may be greater than when the perpetrator is someone known to the victim. However, the resulting distress is probably more serious, persistent, and upsetting in the latter case. The victim will adjust his/her belief about his/her acquaintances in general and may adopt non-trusting attitudes towards them. In such a case threats may result in depression and isolation of the victim from his/her social environment. It is thus perhaps surprising that threats have been so neglected in analyses of victimization surveys.

To the author's knowledge, the only published research on threats is that of Hough (1990). Hough defines them as follows: 'To threaten someone is to declare one's intention to punish or hurt, or inflict injury to reputation or property which may restrain a person's freedom of action' (Hough 1990: 169). A summary of his results is given in earlier published research on threat prevalence (Tseloni *et al.*, 1994). Hough's data on the upset which threats cause and the seriousness with which they are regarded indicate that the phenomenon merits further research attention.

This study is concerned with the analysis of threat incidence: the average number of threats per respondent as revealed by use of the British Crime Survey. Incidence rates of any type of crime have often been regarded as following similar patterns to the corresponding prevalence rates (proportion of victims per respondent). Sparks *et al.*. (1977) suggested that victimization is better measured via risk likelihoods (i.e., prevalence) rather than the average rates of incidents suffered by individuals (i.e., incidence). The author is unaware of any work on modelling incidence in an attempt to reveal its causal factors and compare them to those associated with prevalence. Incidence analysis may have been neglected owing to the lack of a popular statistical model appropriate for incidence values and the unfamiliarity of most social researchers with the Poisson and its extension the negative binomial model.[1] The only work referring to the latter is by Nelson (1980), who examined victimization rates reported in the National Crime Survey but dealing only with the univariate case. He concluded that '. . .correlates of victimisation are likely to be the same regardless of whether rates or probabilities are used to measure victimisation during a one-year period' (Nelson 1980: 883–4). However, he doubted that strong relations between the number of victimizations and independent variables can be found.

In this chapter, the above assertions are challenged and a formal modelling approach is taken. The average number of threats per respondent is analysed by socio-demographic and life-style attributes of individuals, and their experience of witnessing crime (indirect victimization). The following section presents some introductory information on the data employed here; further sections then discuss the negative binomial model and its interpretation, and the modelling strategy followed here; and the main body of the study then examines the factors associated with threats and their changes over time as revealed in the British Crime Surveys conducted between 1982 and 1988. A concluding section gives some examples of threat rates implied by the models for different types of individuals and suggests some paths for further research.

The data

Definition and profile of threats in the British Crime Survey

The BCS is a national victimization survey carried out in England and Wales in 1982, 1984, 1988 and 1992.[2] Here the first three sweeps are used. More information about the sampling design can be found in the relevant Technical Reports (NOP Market Research 1985; NOP Market Research 1989; and Wood 1984). The classification of victim incidents includes verbal threats and threatening behaviour (intimidation) of which the respondent was either the *recipient* or the *subject*. In most cases (over 90 per cent for the 1982 and 1988 data sets and more than 70 per cent for 1984) the respondent was both the person *to* whom and *against* whom threats were made. Information about threats was obtained in the main questionnaire by asking:

> And [in the period covered by the survey], has anyone threatened to damage things of yours or threatened to use force or violence on you in a way that actually frightened you? How many times? [...] Any non-verbal threatening behaviour (following a person closely, menacing gestures) counts as intimidation.

The BCS combines threats with intimidation and the combined total is reported as one type of *victimization against the person* (Wood 1984). However, if threats or intimidation take place in the course of other offences they are subsumed by these other offences.[3]

Table 1 displays the frequencies of threat victimizations along with the number of respondents (sample size) and number of victims for

Table 1: The distribution of threats

No. of threats per respondent	frequencies 1982	frequencies 1984	frequencies 1988
0	8336	10787	11238
1	153	166	271
2	32	57	49
3	15	21	27
4+	34	42	69
missing values	14	5	10
Sample size	8584	11077	116644
Total no. of victims	234	285	416

Table 2: Threat prevalence and incidence

	1982	1984	1988
Prevalence	2.73	2.57	3.57
Incidence	9.02	7.29	8.80
Modified incidence*	6.89	6.47	8.25

*The number of threats per respondent is truncated for 20 or more to equal 20.

each BCS sweep. The derived threat prevalence (the percentage of respondents who are victims) and incidence (average number of threats per respondent) are given in Table 2. Incidence is also presented in a modified form, where the number of threats for any respondent is truncated at 20 to avoid a few heavily victimized individuals dominating the overall value.[4] All three values are lower for 1984 than for the other two sweeps. The 1984 data may be anomalous, and parsimony would require such an assumption. Comparing 1982 and 1988, threat prevalence increases, but threat incidence decreases marginally. This suggests that incidents of threat (or their recall) became more widespread but less concentrated on particular victims over that period. Incidence for 1982 drops substantially when the number of threats is truncated at 20, supporting the view that the threat victimization reported in the 1982 BCS was heavily concentrated.

In the regression analysis below, only threat *incidence* is modelled. This is done through a variable which takes values of zero for no threat victimization up to seven when the respondent has been a victim of seven or more threats. Seven is chosen as the censoring point because there are only a few isolated cases of victims threatened more than seven times during the reference period of the survey across the three sweeps.[5]

For the purpose of the present work the original data are weighted by the inner-city, the adult and the follow-up weights (see Appendix).

The explanatory variables
Four groups of factors that are strongly related to victimization risk have been featured in the related literature.[6] These are: *1)*.individual socio-demographic characteristics (such as gender, age, marital status, etc.); *2)*. life-style attributes of victims such as nights out, offending, etc.; *3)*. areal exogenous factors (such as residential mobility,

urbanization, etc.); and 4). intervening dimensions of the environment (like unsupervised peer groups and weak local friendship networks). For this study only individual predictors of victimization risk, namely socio-demographic and life-style attributes relevant for *personal* crime, have been employed, together with an indirect victimization indicator. The latter is a concept taken from fear of crime[7] models, which also make use of individual socio-demographic characteristics. Thus, the analysis is kept at the individual level, as appropriate for personal victimization, and is entirely based on BCS data. Employment of any areal and community factors would alter the level of analysis (at a more aggregate one, ward or constituency) and require the use of Census or other statistical sources data (see Osborn *et al.* 1992: 267).

The socio-demographic variables employed here are gender, age, race, marital status, children in the household, employment status, educational level, family income of respondents, inner-city/non-inner-city area and region of residence. They were provided from data collected in the Main and Demographic questionnaires of the BCS. The BCS definition of inner-city area was used, although it was not entirely consistent across sweeps. Region is classified according to the Registrar General's nine standard regions for England and Wales. The Follow-up questionnaire provides information on proxies for life-style factors which may influence the estimated average number of threats. Such variables used here are self-reported offences committed, avoidance of going out or pursuing certain activities due to crime risk, nights out on foot, weekend evenings out, drinking habits, driving after having drunk alcohol, and indirect victimization (whether the respondent has witnessed a crime). However, it is not possible to incorporate the same life-style variables across the three data sets because the questions asked differ substantially. More detailed information about the sources and definitions of the explanatory variables is presented in the Appendix to this chapter.

Modelling threat incidence

The negative binomial model and reference categories for the explanatory variables

The dependent variable of the econometric analysis in this study, threat incidence, is ordinal, that is, it takes on positive integer values from zero to seven. It is plausible that individuals have systematically unequal probabilities of being threatened that are modified by prior victimization. This assumption gives rise to the various 'contagion' models developed in biometrics.[8]

More analytically, considering the univariate case, the probability that victimization occurs may be *pure chance*, a random variable the realizations of which are results of a random experiment. In such a case the employment of the Poisson model is justified. Dependence has, however, been observed in practice, and may arise from various sources. Under the *true contagion* hypothesis, all individuals have initially the same probability of being victimized, but this probability changes after each victimization experience. The *apparent contagion* hypothesis suggests that individuals have constant but unequal probabilities of being victimized. Finally, according to the *spells* assumption, victimization incidents occur in clusters and they are dependent within each spell, but independent across spells, and unrelated to the number of spells. A spell is a period '...of time during which the person's performance is weak' (Xekalaki 1983: 887). The last three hypotheses give rise to the negative binomial distribution. In this model *proneness* and *liability* effects are also present. The former is 'the sum total of the internal factors in the individual, predisposing towards' victimization (Irwin 1968: 224). Liability is defined as 'the sum total of external factors' leading to victimization. (Irwin 1968: 224). In this case it seems realistic to assume true and apparent contagion together.

In a multivariate context, liability may stand for the expected number of threats, and proneness may be proxied by the deviances between the actual and expected number of threats. Thus, two identical individuals (according to their characteristics indicated by the set of explanatory variables) may not experience the same number of threats owing to their different levels of proneness to them.[9]

Data on criminal victimization, threats not excluded, show in practice high over-dispersion, which means that their variance is greater than the mean. Moreover, there are very many individuals with zero occurrence of the event and only a small proportion of the sample had been victimized once, and an even smaller subtotal more than one time. The empirical distribution of times of being victimized is heavily skewed and positively asymmetric, with a long tail compared to the theoretical distribution of a Poisson model. Unlike this, the negative binomial regression model accounts for overdispersion in the data; therefore it is more appropriate for the econometric analysis of crime incidence. In this model, each coefficient relating to a particular explanatory variable gives the estimated change in the natural logarithm of expected occurrences per unit change in the explanatory variable, assuming that all other predictors are constant. The expected occurrences in this case are the average estimated number of threats.

All the explanatory variables except age here are categorical. A categorical variable is expressed by a set of dummy variables in a regression context. Each dummy represents a category, taking the value one when the variable falls in this category and zero otherwise. The different categories are then represented in relation to a selected reference or base category. If certain categories do not show significant effect on the dependent variable then their coefficients are eliminated from the regression model and they are merged with the reference one. The effect of the latter on the dependent variable is incorporated in the constant term (Johnston 1985: 226 and 230). If a variable has n significant categories, there are n-1 dummy variables, with each of the n-1 corresponding coefficients interpreted as the effect on the dependent variable expressed as a contrast to the reference categories. The prediction for the dependent variable corresponding to a particular category is the sum of its coefficient and the constant term.

These comments apply in the case of a negative binomial model, except that the (natural) log of expected occurrences operates as the dependent variable. Since age is a non-categorical predictor, the *constant term* here is the natural logarithm of the average estimated number of threats for an individual who belongs to the reference category for each attribute but is of zero age. To ease interpretation of the results, throughout the discussion the average estimated number of threats is calculated for a hypothetical individual who belongs to the reference category for each characteristic, except (where relevant) the one being explicitly considered, and is of average age (46 years for each of the three BCS sweeps).

This hypothetical individual, for whom the average number of threats can be directly calculated from the constant term of the models, has the following (reference) characteristics. She is a married white female, who lives in a non-inner-city area of East Anglia, without any children under sixteen years, works full-time, has left full-time education at sixteen years old or younger, with an annual family income of £2,000–£14,999 (or £2,500–£14,999 for the 1988

BCS data). The above are the base categories of the total set of socio-demographic variables (see p. 273) employed in the analysis except age. The latter is a discrete variable and takes on integer values of 16 or greater.

The reference categories of the life-style indicators (see p. 273) are: have not drunk any beer or spirits; have not driven after having drunk any alcohol; have not committed any offence in the year preceding the interview; have not seen anything happen which was or may have been a crime in the same period; have not been out last Friday or Saturday night for spare-time activities;[10] have not been out on foot alone after six o'clock at night in the week preceding the interview; and never avoid going out because of crime risk. The reference categories for all the variables were selected in the anticipation that a person belonging to these categories would experience the lowest average number of threats.

To summarize, each of the coefficients of a categorical variable in the negative binomial models below is interpreted as the change in the natural logarithm of the estimated average number of threats, from being in that particular category compared to the reference category(ies) of the attribute under consideration. Positive (negative) coefficients generate larger (smaller) predicted threat incidence and probabilities of being threatened once or more times compared to the reference individual, but smaller (larger) probabilities of no such victimization.

Modelling strategy
Before proceeding to the regression analysis, simple two-way cross-tabulations of the variables listed on p. 273 with the number of threats experienced were conducted. Moreover, some interactions were tested: gender, on the one hand, was used as a control variable for age, area, marital status, and race; and children, on the other, controlled for marital status effects on threat incidence. At this stage of analysis all the variables and their above interactions were significantly related to threats in each of the three data sets (1982, 1984 and 1988) through a Chi-square test statistic.

The initial regression model estimated for each data set incorporated all individual factors and the five aforementioned interactions of gender and children. Then, relying on the p-values of the coefficients, the non-statistically significant variables and categories were removed from this original regression. This is how the models discussed below were formed. Exclusion of some categories of the variables implies that these groups become part of the base category. Only regions are all included in the models regardless of the significance of their coefficients, owing to the particularly exceptional characteristics of economic and social life in East Anglia, the region of reference, compared to the rest of England and Wales.

Results and discussion

For the purposes of this study one set of results of a common negative binomial model on threat incidence across all BCS data sets is presented in Table 3. It includes all individual factors which were statistically significant in at least one model from every BCS. Owing to the different life-style indicators surveyed in each sweep, the common model uses only information collected in the main and demographic questionnaires. It also omits any interaction terms between the demographic variables. These effects (interactions and life-style) are simply discussed, where appropriate, without displaying the full estimated model they came from. As one notices, in 1984 and 1988 there are two models presented. Model 1 excludes data on family annual income because this variable creates a problem of numerous missing values, decreasing substantially the number of observations used. In 1982 this problem does not occur, because information on income was not collected.

In Table 3 the estimated coefficients are displayed with their significance levels shown in brackets. The number of observations is included at the base of each model after the log-likelihood statistic of their overall goodness of fit.

The correlates of threat incidence

As shown in Table 3, the socio-demographic variables which turned out to influence threat incidence significantly are gender, age, area of residence (inner city vs. non-inner city), marital status, children in the household, employment status, family annual income and region. The two interactions of gender with marital status and inner city showed high significance levels. People who encounter *relatively many* threat occurrences are males or divorced females, the young, the poor, the unemployed, parents, and those living in inner cities, particularly in the north-west, the south-east and the south-west.

There seem to be two types of highly threatened individuals, the

Table 3: Common model of threat incidence across all BCS

Explanatory Variables	1982	1984		1988	
		Model 1	Model 2	Model 1	Model 2
Constant	−1.44	−3.46	−3.62	−3.90	−3.79
	(0.01)	(0.00)	(0.00)	(0.00)	(0.00)
Male	0.26	0.47	0.44	0.35	0.20
	(0.21)	(0.01)	(0.04)	(0.01)	(0.27)
Age	−0.039	−0.046	−0.046	−0.024	−0.026
	(0.00)	(0.00)	(0.00)	(0.00)	(0.00)
Inner-city	0.46	0.97	0.88	0.24	0.50
	(0.25)	(0.00)	(0.00)	(0.17)	(0.04)
Single	−0.07	−0.43	−0.35	−0.61	−0.65
	(0.82)	(0.12)	(0.40)	(0.00)	(0.01)
Divorced	1.03	1.23	1.25	1.37	1.26
	(0.02)	(0.00)	(0.01)	(0.00)	(0.00)
Widowed	−0.40	0.69	0.64	−0.35	−0.61
	(0.41)	(0.05)	(0.18)	(0.17)	(1.14)
Working part-time	−0.77	0.08	0.22	−0.43	−0.51
	(0.05)	(0.78)	(0.52)	(0.04)	(0.04)
Unemployed	0.36	−0.25	−0.51	0.66	0,66
	(0.33)	(0.54)	(0.37)	(0.01)	(0.08)
Low family income	–	–	1.01	–	0.82
	–	–	(0.01)	–	(0.02)
Children	0.23	0.19	0.42	−0.01	0.01
	(0.20)	(0.34)	(0.07)	(0.97)	(0.98)
East Midlands	−1.05	1.53	1.45	1.85	1.65
	(0.09)	(0.11)	(0.21)	(0.01)	(0.06)
North	−1.67	1.69	1.78	1.92	1.99
	(0.19)	(0.07)	(0.11)	(0.01)	(0.03)
North-west	0.32	2.61	2.49	1.68	1.68
	(0.54)	(0.00)	(0.02)	(0.02)	(0.06)
South-east	0.02	1.91	1.87	1.69	1.76
	(0.96)	(0.03)	(0.08)	(0.02)	(0.04)
South-west	−0.84	2.18	2.25	1.82	1.89
	(0.08)	(0.02)	(0.04)	(0.01)	(0.03)
West Midlands	0.27	1.17	1.27	1.59	1.42
	(0.62)	(0.20)	(0.24)	(0.03)	(0.11)
Yorkshire/Humberside	−0.34	1.05	1.03	1.83	2.15
	(0.52)	(0.25)	(0.36)	(0.01)	(0.01)
Wales	−0.81	1.82	1.87	1.02	0.26
	(0.20)	(0.05)	(0.09)	(0.19)	(0.79)
a	36.25	34.68	33.74	27.10	28.63
	(0.00)	(0.00)	(0.00)	(0.00)	(0.00)
Log–likelihood	−1260.317	−1576.975	−1122.890	−2189.533	−1506.080
No. of observations	8173	10687	7773	11421	8488

ones who pursue more outgoing lives (such as males, the young and the inner-city residents by choice and not because of financial constraints) and those who are considered socially or physically vulnerable such as divorced women, the poor, the unemployed, etc. The intuition being that the former are threatened by complete strangers but the latter by people with whom they are acquainted and/or intimate. A typical example is a divorced woman, who may be threatened by her present or former spouse. Poor people or unemployed who probably live in deprived areas may be threatened by their next-door neighbour. It seems, thus, that social vulnerability is linked with threats and such victims do not have the means to escape from their threatening environments. Parents, on the other hand, may be threatened as a consequence of the (mis)behaviour of their children or they may be simply more alert and ready to report such incidents because of family responsibilities.

In general, the attributes relevant in victimization risk seem to reappear in this analysis, with some exceptions. Race and educational level do not seem to associate with threat incidence, although the second is an important predictor of threat prevalence. The presence of children in single or divorced adult households does not generate a high estimated average number of threats suffered by these adults, but increases threat risks considerably.

The interaction results suggest that there are differential effects of gender depending on area of residence (inner city vs. non-inner city) and marital status. The first one is only apparent in the 1988 BCS models, where gender, on its own, does not seem to affect threat incidence significantly. This means that both sex groups experience, on average, an identical estimated number of threats. However, in inner-city areas males are more threatened than females. The marital status by gender interaction produces a rates-reversing effect which appears in the 1982 and 1984 BCS regression models. Although single and married men are more threatened than women of the same category, when divorced or separated individuals are considered women suffer the highest average number of threats.

In accordance with the life-style and routine activities theoretical arguments, the presence of indirect victimization experiences – avoidance of going out due to crime risk, self-reported offending, and driving after having drunk alcohol – inflates the average number of threats suffered by the respondent. Nights out alone on foot, drinking behaviour and evenings out do not affect the average number of threats. However, walking alone at night appeared to be a significant predictor in threat risk analysis (Tseloni *et al*. 1994).

The indirect victimization concept was proxied by two dummies: whether respondents have seen a crime in the 1982 and 1988 BCS and whether they have seen a serious fight in the 1988 one. People who live in areas and/or frequent places (and at times) with high likelihood of crime occurrence face a higher risk of being threatened than those who do not come across crime events. The strong indirect victimization effect can be alternatively explained through the personal perceptions of respondents about the event under question. It may be that people who are more sensitive towards actions or events which oppose the order of society are more likely to be able to define and recall threatening behaviour against them.

People who avoid going out owing to fear of crime are also more likely to have experienced threats than those who do not. Their behavioural adaptation to avoid crime may be a result of their direct or indirect victimization experiences.[11] They may, further, have a higher proportion of such experiences because crime occurrences are more concentrated in the areas in which they live and/or the places they frequent. On the other hand, it seems odd that they experience more threats than similar people who go out. The recluse who is a fugitive from crime in the outside world may suffer more threats from neighbours or as a result of their reclusive and perhaps fearful ways.

Self-reported offending was included in the 1982 and 1984 BCS (see Appendix). Taking office supplies, fiddling expenses, failure to pay the exact fare, and using cannabis are the types of offence significantly related with threats for both data sets. People who did any of the above show a higher than average probability of being threatened. People who have taken cannabis are the most threatened among the above categories. This is because they are expected to be in the high-risk socio-demographic groups. In addition, they may associate with those groupings in society in which a disproportionate number of offenders exist.

Those who do not pay the exact fare are probably people in the low-income groups. Their social vulnerability and the fact that they probably live in deprived areas has a positive effect on experiencing threats. The above intuition is supported by the fact that when family annual income is included in the models, self-reported offending loses its statistical significance (in 1984 BCS models where such data are available).

Although these types of offence do not require a 'criminal' to commit them, their interdependence with threats seemed particularly high in the preliminary cross-tabulation analysis. A possible explanation of this effect and the one of driving after having drunk is based on generally deviant life-style patterns and associations.

In the following section a discussion on the estimated threat rates for certain population groups is presented, relying upon the estimates of negative binomial regression models.

Estimating the average number of threats

Having analysed the significant factors affecting threat incidence, I will now demonstrate how the estimates of their corresponding coefficients can be used to calculate the average number of threats. Most of the discussion explores the results of the common model displayed in Table 3. However, when this model is inadequate, additional information is offered based on other models[12] of threat incidence estimated from the same BCS data sets. In what follows, Model 1 from each of the 1984 and 1988 BCS data sets is being considered unless otherwise stated.

As has already been said, the constant term comprises the effects of the missing categories of the variables in the model defining the base individual. Thus, the *reference individual* is a 46-year-old (the average sample age) married female with no children, who works full-time, or has retired, or is a housewife or student, and lives in East Anglia (where there are no inner-city areas). When Model 2 of 1984 and 1988 are examined the reference woman is, additionally, of an average or high annual family income.

Considering for instance the 1982 coefficient of the constant term (which is −1.44), the estimated average number of threats the above individual experiences are calculated as follows: $\exp[-1.44+(-0.039*46)]=0.039$. The component in brackets is the age effect (the age coefficient in the 1982 model is −0.039) for a 46-year-old individual. This should be added to the constant term or any other coefficient under question unless one is interested in the threat incidence faced by a person of zero years old. By using the above formula, threat rates can be estimated for any type of individual defined by the characteristics which are included in the displayed models. Another example will be given later in this section.

Taking into account, over time, the changes for the reference individual, the estimated average threats seem particularly high in

1982 (0.0394) compared to 0.0038 for 1984 and 0.0067 for 1988. This is largely due to the East Anglia effect. If the reference woman moved to the south-east her estimated average threats would be 0.0402, 0.0256 and 0.0354 for the three years respectively. Alternatively, if the reference region was the north-west the constant would imply estimated threat rates equal to 0.0543, 0.0515, and 0.0360 for the 1982, 1984, and 1988 models. But, even when region is controlled, average estimated threats are still the highest in 1982. This may be due to the fact that these incidents seem to be more concentrated on a small number of victims in this year than in the late eighties, as observed in Table 2. However, between 1984 and 1988 estimated threats for the original base individual have almost doubled.

Gender does not seem significant in 1982 and 1988 (Model 2) models. The increase in expected threats from being male compared to being a female with identical characteristics is 30, 60 and 42 per cent in the three data sets, respectively. The above figures were calculated as a simple transformation of the original coefficients. The 1984 increase, for instance, is given by $\{100*[\exp(0.47)-1]\}$ if Model 1 is considered. Although men are threatened more often than women, there seems to be an equalizing tendency of threat rates between sexes in progress which has not been completed yet. However, the estimated average number of threats suffered by a man with identical characteristics with the reference woman increases from 0.0061 in 1984 to 0.0095 in 1988.

The effect of *age* shows that getting older lowers threat incidence and has an increasing 'threat elasticity' for each year under question: the same percentage of years ageing results in a greater decrease of expected threats the older the individual is. Growing one year older gives $100*[1-\exp(0.039)] = 3.82$ per cent reduction of threats in 1982, However, this effect has moderated towards the end of the decade and the decrease in expected threats due to getting older seems to be 4.50 and 2.37 per cent per year, for the 1984 and 1988 data sets, respectively. The above two results are of great interest: being female or elderly no longer constitutes a protection shield from threats. Analogous trends have also been observed for threat prevalence (Tseloni *et al*. 1994).

Similarly, living in the *inner city* seems to contribute less to high threat rates in 1988 than in the earlier years. However, threat rates attained their peak in 1984, when there was 164 per cent increase in the estimated average number of threats suffered by inner-city

Table 4: Estimated average threats by gender and inner city, 1988 BCS

	Males	*Females*
Inner city	0.0132	0.0079
Non–inner city	0.0079	0.0079

residents compared to non-inner-city ones with otherwise identical characteristics. Considering Models 2, the increase in threats attributable to an inner-city area of residence drops by half (141 to 65 per cent) over time. Thus, if the reference woman moved to an inner-city area of the north-west she would suffer an estimated average number of threats equal to 0.0939 in 1984 and 0.0604 in 1988. These figures are calculated by aggregating the effects of the constant term (for a 46-year-old individual), the inner-city and the north-west coefficients; for instance, $\exp[-3.62+(-0.46*46)+0.88+2.49]=0.00939$.

In 1988 models *inner city* showed a significant *interaction with gender*. This implies that threat incidence increases for males within inner-city areas by 97 per cent. Thus, a 46-year-old married man who lives in the inner city, and has all other reference characteristics, suffers an average number of threats equal to 0.0132. However, non-inner-city people (of both sexes) or inner-city females have estimated threat rates equal to 0.0079. Hence, according to that model, estimated threats seem not to differ across gender outside inner cities or across area of residence for females. Table 4 above displays these effects on threat rates.

Going back to Table 3, *divorced* is the only consistently statistically significant and large effect on threat incidence across the three data sets; increasingly so over time. Belonging in this marital-status group results in 180, 242, and 294 per cent increase in expected threats compared to *married*, for the three data sets, respectively (for Models 2 the corresponding figures are 249 and 253). If the reference woman was divorced her estimated average number of threats would equal 0.1104, 0.0130 and 0.0264 in the three years examined. The drop after 1982 is clearly an East Anglia effect. The corresponding figures for a 46-year-old divorced woman with no children, who works full-time, or has retired, or is a housewife or student, and lives in a non-inner-city area of the south-west are 0.0476, 0.1146 and 0.1630 in 1982, 1984 and 1988 respectively. There seems to be something distinguishing about this group of the population which attracts (increasingly so over time) a high concentration of threats, notwithstanding their general pattern of spreading out.

As already mentioned, the *interaction between marital status and gender* seems to influence threat incidence, particularly in 1984 models. If Table 5 is considered, single women show a 68 per cent reduction of expected threats compared to those who are married or widowed, whereas single men show a reduction of only 16 per cent compared to the married. The important result is that more threats occur to divorced females compared to males or other females. Specifically, the sex by marital status interaction effects on the average number of threats experienced by a 46-year-old individual with remaining reference characteristics are shown below. Single men show higher threat incidence than single women, and the same pattern is observed for all row categories other than divorced. The large widowed men rate is hard to interpret criminologically and is probably a sampling error effect.

Between 1982 and 1988 *working part-time* decreases the expected threat rates, yielding 54 and 35 per cent reductions respectively compared to all other employment status categories except unemployed. However, the fact that working part-time is less of a protection against threats over time may be associated with the gender and old-age decreasing differential effects on threats. Indeed, a very high proportion of people working part-time are women (87.5 per cent in 1988) and 67.8 per cent are at least thirty-six years old.

The coefficients for being *unemployed* are statistically insignificant in 1982 and 1984 and show a surprising sign in the latter models. However, in 1988 if the reference woman became unemployed her threat rates would increase 93 per cent, reaching a value of 0.0130. Similar unemployment effects on threat incidence are also observed in models of the 1984 BCS.

The *low family income* category increases threats by 127 per cent in 1988 and 175 per cent in 1984. Married women of forty-six of low income, without children, who do not work part-time or are unemployed and live in non-inner-city areas of East Anglia suffer increasing threat rates from 0.0089 in 1984 to 0.0155 in 1988. This result suggests again that criminal vulnerability resides among socially vulnerable people.

The effects on expected threats of living in particular *regions*, compared to East Anglia, are diverse over time. For instance living in the East Midlands seems to decrease them in 1982 by 65, but increase

Table 5: Estimated average threats by gender and marital status, 1983 BCS

	Male	*Female*
Single	0.0044	0.0014
Divorced	0.0062	0.0193
Widowed	0.0222	0.0043
Married	0.0053	0.0043

them in 1988 by 536 per cent. The north gets slightly worse, from 442 per cent in 1984 to 582 per cent in 1988, but the estimated rates of the reference woman who moved there double from 0.0205 to 0.0458. However, the north-west risk of threat incidence is halved between 1984 and 1988 (1,260 per cent rise in 1984 as opposed to 635 per cent rise in 1988, always in comparison with East Anglia) and the corresponding threat rates are 0.0515 and 0.0360. South-east moves from a 575 per cent increase (and estimated average number of threats for the reference woman of 0.0256) in 1984 to a 442 per cent one (0.0364) in 1988, and south-west from 785 per cent (0.0335) to 517 per cent (0.0414). From the figures in brackets it is obvious that threat concentration per victim increased in the last two regions over time.

The life-style indicator effects from a model of the 1982 BCS, for instance, for the 46-year-old reference woman who has additionally *seen a crime* produce estimated average threats equal to 0.0490 (increasing them by 286 per cent compared to the same woman who has not witnessed any crime). If she *has committed an offence* she shows threat rates of 0.0403 (increased by 217 per cent), and if she *avoids going out due to crime* of 0.0386 (increased by 204 per cent). In 1984 models the average number of threats to the 46-year-old woman who *avoids going to certain activities owing to crime risk* is estimated between 0.0068 and 0.0081. She seems to suffer more threats by 172 to 177 per cent compared to somebody with no restrictions in going out due to crime risk. *Self-reported offenders* show only 36 to 42 per cent higher estimated threats than the general population. In 1988 a 46-year-old reference individual who additionally *witnessed a crime* suffers more than doubled threat rates compared to the one who did not. Similar results come out from the analysis of an indicator on *seen a fight*.

Finally, the *overdispersion coefficient, a,* lowers over time, confirming the amplification of threats among more victims and general population groups with a decrease of the number of incidents suffered per victim. It agrees with the Table 2 results and what has just been discussed about gender, age and inner-city effects, but it does not seem to apply for divorced women.

Concluding thoughts

In contrast to the conclusions drawn by Nelson (1980) some strong relations between threat rates and independent variables (tested by low p-values of their coefficients) have been revealed. Although some differences occurred (which are explored in the next three paragraphs), groups of people with higher risks of being victims of threat also experience threats more frequently than the general population. To restate, these high-risk groups are males or divorced females, the young, the poor, the unemployed, parents, and those living in inner cities. The results for offenders, people who have witnessed crimes and those who avoid going out owing to fear of crime found in threat prevalence analysis (Tseloni *et al.* 1994) are also valid for threat incidence.

Threat prevalence and incidence are not entirely affected by the same factors. One important point to be noticed when comparing the above is that the estimated probabilities of being threatened at least once in the low-risk groups are similar whether logit [13] or negative binomial models are employed. However, the former offer considerably higher likelihoods of risk compared to the latter when the disproportionately threatened groups of the population are under question.

Single parents (divorced or single women with children) and those walking out alone at night are the only groups of people who show high risks of being threatened, but not repetitively. Therefore, they seem to be able to take effective precautions against threats after their first such victimization, as opposed to other high-risk population groups. Perhaps single parents eventually control their children, if threat victimization is a result of the (mis)behaviour of the latter, or manage to get away from threatening environments for the sake of their family. People who walk out alone at nights may prevent themselves from re-experiencing threats by changing route, avoiding passing outside pubs around closing time or places where young men may hang around, and so on.

Inner-city males, on the other hand, seem to suffer more threats compared to inner-city females, although their chances of threat victimization are the same. This may be a result of non-avoidance behaviour, once inner-city men have been threatened, due to their attitudes of machismo and toughness. Such attitudes are not met in women, who would normally try to prevent threats and, generally, any potential danger.

The probabilities quoted in the previous section have always referred to a 46-year-old individual who is a member of the reference group for each qualitative variable, except the one being specifically considered. Here other individuals and their implied threat rates from various of the models are given.

A 30-year-old divorced woman, with children who lives in an inner-city area of the south-east, is unemployed, has the lowest educational level and annual family income, has never committed any offence, but has seen a crime, does not go out on foot alone at night, avoids going out owing to crime risk, and *drinks beer or spirits* shows an average number of threats equal to 0.9231 according to a model from 1982. In 1988 she is expected to be threatened 1.8776 times on average. Similarly to threat prevalence, this high-risk group experiences more threats over time.

On the other hand, a 65-year-old married man, with no children living with him, a non-inner-city resident of the East Midlands, retired, and with medium family annual income seems to be threatened 0.0220 times on average in 1988.

Questions still remain and further research is required. Who threatens and under which circumstances, are two questions which should be answered – and they might be when the BCS Victim Forms are examined. It would also be useful to have specialized surveys conducted for threats, perhaps on the high-risk groups alone, so that more detailed information could be available.

Thus, the psychological and financial consequences of threats for the victim could be established. From the social policy point of view, this would help to support the victims effectively and to incorporate threats adequately in the criminal justice system. Additionally, it would be possible to examine how a threat alters the social behaviour of the victims and, therefore to define its social implications.

The borders between threat victimization and relatively recurrent threat experiences should be clarified. What makes some high-risk groups have low incidence rates, despite the general pattern of uniformity between factors influencing threat prevalence and incidence?

By the same token, why do certain population subgroups experience exceptionally frequent threats, although they face similar risks with others? Such disparity between prevalence and incidence should be further tested and confirmed for threats. These issues also merit investigation with reference to other types of crime victimization.

Notes

This study is based on part of my Ph.D. thesis, which has been financed by the State Scholarship Foundation of Greece. I wish to thank my supervisors Professor Denise R. Osborn and Professor Ken Pease, Dr John Smith from the Computer Support Unit of the Faculty of Economic and Social Studies of the University of Manchester, and my colleagues from the Quantitative Criminology Group at Manchester (namely, the late Cathie Marsh, Dan Ellingworth and Alan Trickett) for their support.

[1] These model the probability that an event occurs a given number of times, in this case the probabilities that an individual is threatened zero to seven or more times. Pages 273–6 of this chapter offer a more thorough discussion on the negative binomial model and its conceptual implications.

[2] The first and third sweep included Scotland as well.

[3] The more serious offence is always the one coded whenever the description of the incident shows that two or more different codes could apply. This implies that threats and intimidation are regarded as always less serious than other offences captured by the survey, and also means that there is an under-counting of threats relative to other offence types. It will also be noted that threats are included only if they induce fear, so that threats to the resilient will be under-counted.

[4] The author recognizes that this procedure is contentious. Crime victimization of all kinds studied (except murder/manslaughter) is heavily skewed, with the same people being repeatedly victimized. It has been contended that victimization surveys incorporate procedures which mask this fact (Farrell 1992), and the approach adopted here is one such.

[5] In the 1982 data set 99.8% of respondents were threatened less than seven, i.e. zero or one to six, times during the survey reference period for both weighted and raw data. For 1984, 99.8% of respondents as unweighted measurements and 99.9% as weighted were threatened seven times or less, included non-victims of threat. For the 1988 BCS the corresponding figures are 99.7% and 99.8%

[6] The life-style (Hindelange *et al.* 1978; Garofalo 1987; Gottfredson 1981), routine activity (Cohen and Felson 1979; Felson and Cohen 1980), victim proneness (Sparks 1981), and community-level theory of social disorganization (Sampson and Wooldredge 1987; and Sampson and Groves 1989) models have been tested by a number of empirical studies

including Cohen (1981); Hough and Sheehy (1986); Gottfredson (1984); Kennedy and Forde (1990); and Maxfield (1987b).

[7] Such as the Physical and Social Disorder, Community Concern, and Indirect Victimization perspectives (Taylor and Hale 1986), and the approaches developed by Garofalo (1981) and Skogan and Maxfield (1981). They have been tested by a number of empirical studies (Box *et al.* 1988; Maxfield 1984, 1987a; Stafford and Galle 1984, etc.).

[8] For more discussion and references to this literature see Cameron and Trivedi (1986) and Xekalaki (1983).

[9] However, if individual and areal characteristics were used in the modelling, the residuals would summarize both types of unexplained factors influencing threats. In this case we may talk about two indistinguishable types of proneness: one linked with the individual and another entailed in his/her environment and affecting everybody living in it.

[10] The alternative category of the variable *weekend evenings out* is 'have not been out on any evening during the week preceding the interview or been out on any one evening from Sunday to Thursday'. This is because simple cross-tabulation analysis showed that people who have been out on each of these five evenings face similar threat prevalence, which is slightly higher than those with no evenings out; and, hence, they were grouped together.

[11] In the first case, if victimization experiences include threats, then 'avoid going out' is a jointly endogenous variable in the analysis. Indeed, it seems to be a problem in knowing the direction of the causality at least in relation to threat prevalence. This is because it showed a significant effect on 'avoid going out' in preliminary regression models where the latter was the dependent variable with demographic characteristics and threat risks of respondents used as the explanatory ones. Both 1982 and 1984 BCS data sets, which contain the relevant information, confirmed the above.

[12] The full estimated models from each BCS have been omitted for the purposes of simplification.

[13] Logit models are commonly used for the analysis of crime prevalence, number of victims per respondent. They model the probability of being victimized at least once, which is directly comparable with the sum of all probabilities obtained by the negative binomial model except that of zero victimizations.

References

Box, S., Hale, C. and Andrews, G. (1988). 'Explaining fear of crime', *British Journal of Criminology*, vol. 28, no. 3, 340–56.

Cameron, C. A. and Trivedi, P. K. (1986). 'Econometric models based on count data: comparisons and applications of some estimators and tests', *Journal of Applied Econometrics*, vol. 1, 29–53.

Cohen, L. E. and Felson, M. (1979). 'Social change and crime rates trends: a routine activity approach', *American Sociological Review*, vol. 22, 588–608.

Cohen, L. E. (1981). 'Modeling crime trends: A criminal opportunity perspective', *Journal of Research in Crime and Delinquency*, vol. 18, no. 1, 138–62.

Davidson, R. and MacKinnon, J. G. (1984). 'Convenient Specification Tests for Logit and Probit Models', *Journal of Econometrics*, vol. 25, 241–61.

Farrell G. (1992). 'Multiple Victimisation: Its extent and significance', *International Review of Victimology*, vol. 2, no. 2, 85–102.

Felson, M. (1986). 'Linking criminal choices, routine activities, informal control, and criminal outcomes', in D. B. Cornish and R. V. Clarke (eds.), *The Reasoning Criminal: Rational Choice Perspectives on Offending* (Springer-Verlag), 119–28.

Felson, M. and Cohen, L. E. (1980). 'Human ecology and crime: A routine activity approach', *Human Ecology*, vol. 8, no. 4, 389–406.

Fridstrom, L. and Ingebrigtsen, S. (1991). 'An aggregate accident model based on pooled, regional time-series data', *Accident Analysis and Prevention*, vol. 23, 363–78.

Garofalo, J. (1987) 'The fear of crime: Causes and consequences', *Journal of Criminal Law and Criminology*, vol. 72, no. 1, 839

Garofalo, J. (1987). 'Reassessing the lifestyle model of criminal victimisation', in M. R. Gottfredson and T. Hirschi (eds.), *Positive Criminology*. (Sage).

Godfrey, L. G. (1988). *Misspecification Tests in Econometrics: The Lagrange Multiplier Principle and Other Approaches*, Econometric Society Monographs, No. 16 (Cambridge, Cambridge University Press).

Gottfredson, M. R. (1981). 'On the etiology of criminal victimisation', *Journal of Criminal Law and Criminology*, vol. 72, no. 1., 714–26.

Gottfredson, M. R. (1984). *Victims of Crime: The Dimensions of Risk*, Home Office Research and Planning Unit, Report, no. 81.

Hindelang, M. J., Gottfredson, M. R. and Garofalo, J. (1978). *Victims of Personal Crime: An Empirical Foundation for a Theory of Personal Victimisation* (Ballinger Publishing Company, Cambridge Mass).

Hough, M. (1985), 'The impact of victimisation: findings from the British Crime Survey', *Victimology*, vol.10, no. 1–4, 488–97.

Hough, M. (1990). 'Threats: findings from the British Crime Survey', *International Review of Victimology*, vol. 1, 169–80.

Hough, M. and Sheehy, K. (1986). *Incidents of Violence: Findings from the British Crime Survey* (Home Office Research and Planning Unit, Research Bulletin no. 20).

Irwin, J. O. (1968) 'The generalized Waring distribution applied to accident theory', *Journal of Royal Statistical Society*, 131, series A, 205–25.

Johnston, J. (1985). *Econometric Methods* (International Student Edition, McGraw–Hill).

Kennedy, L. W. and Forde, D.R. (1990). 'Routine activities and crime: An analysis of victimisation in Canada', *Criminology*, vol. 28, no. 1, 137–52.

Maxfield, M. G. (1984). *Fear of Crime in England and Wales*, (Home Office Research and Planning Unit, Report No. 78).

Maxfield, M. G. (1987a). *Explaining Fear of Crime: Evidence from the 1984 British Crime Survey* (Home Office Research and Planning Unit, Paper No. 43).

Maxfield, M. G. (1987b). 'Household composition, routine activity, and victimisation: a comparative analysis', *Journal of Quantitative Criminology*, vol. 3, no. 4, 301–20.

Nelson, J. F. (1980), 'Multiple victimization in American cities: a statistical analysis of rare events', *American Journal of Sociology*, vol. 85, no. 4, 870–91.

NOP Market Research Limited (1985). *1984 British Crime Survey Technical Report*. (NOP, Southampton).

NOP Market Research Limited and Social and Community Planning Research (1989). *1988 British Crime Survey (England and Wales) Technical Report* (NOP, Southampton).

Osborn, D. R., Trickett, A. and Elder, R. (1992). 'Area characteristics and regional variates as determinants of area property crime levels', *Journal of Quantitative Criminology*, vol. 8, no. 3, 265–85.

Sampson, R. J. and Groves, B. W. (1989). 'Community structure and crime: Testing social disorganisation theory', *American Journal of Sociology*, vol. 94, no. 4, 774–802.

Sampson, R. J. and Wooldredge, J. D. (1987) 'Linking the micro- and macro-level dimensions of lifestyle – routine activity and opportunity models of predatory victimisation', *Journal of Quantitative Criminology*, vol. 3, no. 4, 371–93.

Skogan, W. G. and Maxfield, M. G. (1981). *Coping with Crime: Individual and Neighbourhood Reactions*, Sage Library of Social Research, vol. 124 (Beverly Hills and London, Sage).

Sparks, R. F. (1981). 'Multiple victimisation: Evidence, theory, and future research', *Journal of Criminal Law and Criminology*, vol. 72, no. 1, 762–78.

Sparks, R. F., Genn, H. J. and Dodd, D. J. (1977). *Surveying victims: A study of the measurement of criminal victimization* (New York, Wiley).

Stafford, M. C. and Galle, O. R. (1984). 'Testing alternative models of fear of crime', *Journal of Criminal Law and Criminology*, vol. 77, no. 1, 151–190.

Taylor, R. B. and Hale, M. (1986). 'Testing alternative models of fear of crime', *Journal of Criminal Law and Criminology*, vol. 77, no. 1, 151–90.

Tseloni, A., Osborn, D. R. and Pease, K. (1994). 'The modelling of threats: evidence from the British Crime Survey', *International Review of Victimology*, vol. 3, no. 3, forthcoming.

Wood, D. (1984). *British Crime Survey, 1982 Technical Report* (Home Office).

Xekalaki, E. (1983). 'The univariate generalized Waring distribution in relation to accident theory: proneness, spells or contagion?', *Biometrics*, vol. 39, 887–95.

Appendix

Explanatory variables, data sources and definitions

In the first sweep of the BCS there was not a separate Demographic questionnaire, the equivalent information being incorporated in the Main questionnaire. No information about income was collected. Both questionnaires were completed for all respondents. A number of weights have been calculated and are provided with the BSC data for correcting biases which derive from its sampling design. For this study the inner-city and the adult weight were applied to data from Main and Demographic questionnaires. The former redresses the imbalance of over-sampling inner-city areas. The latter counteracts the imbalances between the number of electors on the register relevant to the selected household and the number of adults actually living in it. For more information on the weighting methods of BCS consult the BCS Technical Reports (1982, 1984, and 1988).

In 1982 and 1984 the Follow-up questionnaires were completed for all victims and 2 in 5 non-victim respondents. The BCS gives the appropriate weighting for counteracting this disproportionate number of victims in the sample of Follow-up questionnaires, and these weights have been employed in the analysis here. In the 1988 BCS the Follow-up questionnaire was completed for all respondents in the sample, but the information has not been used here (see Note 9).

The definitions of the explanatory variables employed are as follows. Area is classified as inner-city or non-inner-city. It is, however, not exactly comparable between the 1982 and the remaining BCS, owing to the different definition of 'inner-city' which was used.

Parliamentary constituencies were employed for the construction of Region. In the 1984 and 1988 sweeps of BCS the same classification of sampling points by regions was used, based on the 1983 constituency boundaries. In 1982 their classification is slightly different to the aforementioned: it made use of the parliamentary constituency boundaries defined prior to the 1982 Boundary Commission Report. As a result, this variable in the 1982 data set is not completely comparable to the same one in 1984 and 1988. The Registrar General's Standard Regions – widely used for statistical analysis in Britain – are: East Anglia, East Midlands, North, North West, South West, West Midlands, Yorkshire & Humberside, Wales, and South East, which incorporates Greater London.

Offence is a composite variable of self-reported offensive behaviour of respondents in the reference period preceding the interview. The types of offences were:

'Taken office supplies from work (such as stationery, envelopes and pens) when not supposed to';

'Taken things other than office supplies from work (such as tools, money or other goods) when not supposed to';
'Fiddled expenses';
'Deliberately travelled without a ticket or paid too low a fare';
'Failed to declare something at the customs on which duty was payable';
'Cheated on income tax';
'Taken pot, cannabis or marijuana';
'Not bought a television licence when should have done';
'Defaced a wall by spraying paint or writing on it';
'Deliberately damaged property such as a phone box, a car, a window or a street light (but without stealing anything)';
'Bought or accepted things thought to be stolen from someone else';
'Taken things from shops, stores, supermarkets or market stalls without paying';
'Broken and entered someone else's premises and stolen something';
'Been involved in a physical fight with someone outside the family since the age of 16';
'Started a physical fight with someone outside the family since the age of 16';
'Deliberately injured someone outside the family'; and
'Carried a weapon for self-protection or in case it was needed in a fight'.

This information is available in the 1982 BCS. In the 1984 one, respondents were asked only about the first seven types of offences from the above list and 'driving after having drunk'.

Information about adjustments to behaviour in order to avoid potential victimization is available in the 1982 and 1984 BCS. In the former the question was: 'Do you *ever* avoid going out on foot by yourself in this area because of the risk that you might be a victim of crime?'. The question asked in 1984 differs, however, from that asked in 1982: 'Are there any events and activities which you would like to go to but do not because of crime or violence?'

Information about nights out alone is requested only in the first sweep of BCS. The question asked is: 'On how many nights in the past week have you been out on foot *by yourself* at all after 6 o'clock at night?'

Evenings out in the week preceding interview is the only Follow-up information common across the three data sets. The question in the first and second sweeps is: 'In the past seven days, have you spent any evenings outside your home on leisure, social or other spare-time activities?' If 'yes', 'Which evenings in the past seven days? Any others?'. In the third BCS the question is slightly different: 'In the last seven days, have you spent any evenings outside your home for any reason?' If yes, 'Which? Any others?', allowing for the inclusion of being out for work.

The question about drinking behaviour in the 1982 questionnaire is: 'Which of these have you drunk at all in the months since the first of January,

1981?' The categories are 'Beer, lager or cider', 'Wine – including sherry, port and martini', and 'spirits – gin, whisky, rum, vodka, brandy, etc.'. The second of these did not show any significant influence on threat prevalence, and was excluded from the aggregate variable 'drinking'. Similar information is available in the 1988 BCS, version A, but is not employed in this study.

In the 1982 BCS respondents were asked: 'Apart from anything you have mentioned already, since the first of January, 1981, have you seen anything happen which was or may have been a crime?'. Indirect victimization proxies are also available in both versions of the 1988 BCS, but they are not used here.

14

Fear of crime:
Children and gendered socialization

JO GOODEY

> I mean you know these things won't happen all the time. You know it's not
> going to happen every time you walk past someone, but it's a possibility in
> it. It's always there in your mind. (Boy, aged twelve)

Upon first glance even the trained victimologist's eye could interpret
the above quote as the sadly typical comment of a young woman
fearful of harassment or sexual assault on the street, a quote that may
be extracted from any adult victimization survey (such as the
Islington Crime Survey: Jones, MacLean and Young 1986). As the
comment came from a discussion on concepts of fear and crime with
a group of boys aged 12–13, the reader is forced to reconsider certain
assumptions concerning gender, age and fear of crime.

The purpose of this chapter is to introduce the child into
victimology and the investigation of influential processes of gendered
socialization upon childhood leading to the resultant exhibition of a
differential fear of crime between adult men and women. Theories
and established concepts of gendered fear are examined and from an
on-going piece of research are discussed. From a feminist perspective
the research findings and the words of the children are allowed to
speak for themselves, viewed as the documentation of hitherto
'invisible' findings which so far have led to further questions rather
than concrete 'answers'. At the same time it is hoped that the reader is
left with a set of questions regarding fear of crime rather than a sense
of confusion or the 'set text' of gendered responses found in much
criminological work on fear.

There is a continuing debate concerning the location of fear in
public places (Imray and Middleton 1983; Mazey and Lee 1983;

Stanko 1990; and Valentine 1989 – to name but a few). Emphasis on public space may exacerbate the false public/private divide whilst negating the real extent of women's experience of male violence. Despite media coverage of domestic violence and the rape of wives, women continue to fear the public domain, as exemplified by the crime survey work of Painter (1991). The research outlined here ultimately aims to ask not only why male/female fear of the outside is different, but why women's fear *is* positioned outside. The paper cannot incorporate the range of theories of patriarchy, power and knowledge with regard to the fear dilemma, but the fears of children angle is introduced in relation to established work.

The basic premiss for inclusion of research on and *for* children within victimology is so that children's voices may be heard and utilized for comprehension of their own and adult fears. As to the means by which information is gained, the power relationship between researched and researcher is noted and reflected in the resultant methodology. Employing both quantitative and qualitative methods is viewed not as a compromise but as the way forward for holistic and balanced research. While methodology and results are discussed later, the background from which they are approached is briefly considered.

Rethinking fear

Victimization surveys have revealed the extent of adult women's fear of crime, allowing the researcher to examine findings and conclusions in which women's fears have been regarded as irrational. Location alters the nature and extent of fear, but women's fear is firmly placed in the realms of a rational fear stemming from the patriarchal roots of female avoidance of incivilities, sexual harassment/assault and ultimately rape from men to women (as documented in Brownmiller's 1975 classic text). Television advertisements can play on this recognized fear (note the RAC advert about the lone female whose car has broken down in the dark, forbidding alleyway). Having established that a 'justifiable' female fear exists and armed with the statistics to 'prove' this on innumerable occasions, the researchers and policy-makers progress from this point to suggest policy to address gendered fear. Measures range from advice in the newspapers, such as Emma Wilkins's report in the *Daily Telegraph* which reviewed driving courses for women dealing with aggressive male drivers and potential attackers on the road, to the official handbook approach of the police. Good advice may be established, but alongside this are alarmist tendencies which easily surface (simply note public reaction to sex crimes in the news as highlighted by Soothill and Walby 1991).

If crime is a disease (as UK Conservative policy suggests it is) and if fear of crime is a symptom of this disease, then the measures women are supposed to adopt are basic curative attempts against a well-established plague. Prevention is better than cure, and at the heart of the fear-of-crime dilemma (the prevention dilemma) is crime itself, but if challenged to address fear at this its root (crime) the government may balk at the concept. This is an attempt to address fear of crime within the realms of accepted victimology research while leaving the causes of crime to one side. There is a gap in crime survey work that needs to be filled in order for research to progress beyond the reiteration of accepted facts regarding adult women's fear of crime. It is at this juncture that I turn back to the original quote and the reader is asked to comprehend the emerging criminological niche of children's fear of crime.

Introducing children

Those aged eighteen and under can provide information to enable the researcher to look beyond the confines of work on adult fear of victimization. Working with children allows an insight into earlier life factors influencing adult fear (Kelly 1987). Focusing on adults means the emphasis is directed at curative measures, or rather the containing and stabilizing influences intended to affect fear of crime. This approach may sound somewhat defeatist, implying that adult fear is essentially the inevitable 'end process', but in many ways it is. It could be argued that adult fear arises as the conclusion to a developmental process of fear beginning in childhood. Therefore it is to childhood that research needs to turn if we wish fully to comprehend adult fear, and particularly the influences upon its gendered nature.

There is a growing body of work on children as victims (Feyerherm and Hindelang 1974; Garofalo 1979; Mawby 1979; Morgan 1988; Foster 1990; Anderson *et al.* 1990; and the latest British Crime Survey incorporates questions for adolescents); but much of victimology continues to concentrate on the child as offender rather than the child as victim. Just as the majority members of society are likely to be the victims of crime rather than its perpetrators, so too are children.

Where criminology appears somewhat ill-equipped to research children, sociology has long been addressing the child's view. Concepts of childhood are now being referred to as the new 'paradigm shift' by sociologists and anthropologists alike (James and Prout 1990). Feminist criminologists are realizing the need to broach the notion of masculinity when examining criminality and victimization, and through this to re-think established gender constructs of aggressive male/submissive female; alongside this the route through childhood towards the stage of expected gender norms must be interpreted. To appreciate and comprehend women's fear accurately we must also reflect on men's fear and, at the same time, go beyond the present to look at life history and the period and processes by which fear was *learned* or allowed to surface. To know the meanings behind the actions of a fearful adult women, one may need to know the child behind the adult.

In accepting a heightened adult female fear of crime the victimologist can ask him/herself when and how this phenomenon emerges. From its first months a child may exhibit fear of spiders and sudden noises and progressive fear of unwanted attention, strangers and the notion of a 'big bad world'. Fear focused on sexual assault and rape needs to be assessed regarding the emergence of gendered fear. Much of value can be extracted from the much used (and abused) nature-versus-nurture debate to suggest that (a) as a result of nature women are physically weaker than men, and (b) as a result of nurture women can be raped. Rape is both biologically and socially determined. However, society functions in such a way that sexual violence against women is curtailed and placed (literally) behind closed doors. As societal structuring does confine the worst excesses of sexual violence against women, then it is to gendered socialization processes that the victimologist must turn to appreciate not only that female fear is reducible to physical differences but that it is part of a sophisticated learning process.

Initial theorization into method

Central to gender-specific fear is the realization that individuals *are* different and that one gender (male) has the advantage of strength and society's patriarchal structuring, whereas the other gender (female) does not. Difference is initially formalized upon the key recognition of oneself as permanently male or female around the ages of four to six (Piaget and Inhelder 1969). This knowledge establishes gender, but fear does not necessarily follow. As women display a fear of crime with apparently overt or covert sexual implications, and men are fearful of other threats, then it is the sexuality of difference that is at the core of emergent gendered fear.

Puberty is the period in which sexuality and gender differences develop. Equally it is a time for adjustment to and recognition of one's role in society. The centrality of gendered socialization processes (Maccoby and Jacklin 1975) during the adolescent years leads to the unconscious adoption of certain masculine and/or feminine traits. So one encounters the emergence of the individual as 'sexual being' which differs according to gender (boys learning an aggressive sexuality, girls learning one of passivity). Burt and Estep (1981) uphold the central importance of the teenage years to propose that women's fear of sexual assault develops in adolescence rather than childhood.

The means by which gender roles are learned are diverse. The researcher often relies on the tools of speculation and theorization to establish the importance of one influence over another when developing gender constructs. Children are the voice by which the reality of the developmental process of the fear of crime is articulated. By puberty, subjects are capable of correcting the researcher's often misplaced assumptions about the influences of peers, parents, school, the media and their own personal experiences regarding their fear of crime. The child informant does not simply provide a back-up to the theories of socialization and fear of crime, but *is* the source from which established theory can be challenged and modified.

Through repeated reference and direct inference, children reveal the importance of one influence over another in shaping their personal fear of crime. By 'cataloguing' children's statements about fear they can be defined as predominantly 'internally' (fear of spiders) or 'externally' (fear stemming from TV watching) based. External or socially structured fears can be noted and assessed alongside personal or psychological fears. In turn each influence is partitioned and compared according to age and gender.

Methodological considerations and setting

The school, youth club, street-corner hang-out and the home are all potential sites for studying adolescents. For purposes of a fixed,

attentive population of eleven- to sixteen-year-old girls and boys, a
school was regarded as the most appropriate site for this study.

As the research partly stems from a feminist perspective, it carries
with it specific methodological considerations. Gill Valentine (1989)
outlines 'eight principles of power ethics' for her methods employed
in assessing adult female fear. Maria Mies (1983) also suggests
methodological guidelines for feminist research which reject the
quantitative, positivist outlook of the traditionalists. She considers
the process by which research may progress through the adoption of
feminist criteria. In comparison with Mies, Toby Jayoratne (1983)
argues for the value of quantitative methodology in feminist research.
Jayoratne acknowledges the criticisms that Mies directs at
quantitative research, but concludes her own work through the
suggestion that if social scientists wish to combat sexist quantitative
research then they must adopt and make use of quantitative research
for feminism's benefit.

Although the prescriptive discussions of research may outline the
inherent pitfalls of biased methods, the resultant methodology often
simply reinforces the stereotypes as feminine/masculine questions are
asked so that differences rather than the similarities between the sexes
are highlighted. Attempting to avoid this bias the research reported
here employed a number of methods, for example: discussion groups
and role play. The research goes some way towards adoption and
adaptation of methods from various disciplines. While attempting to
open up the framework of methods within victimology, the dangers of
this process have had to be accounted for. Use of methods from
numerous disciplines can become over-complex with the creation of a
'super-methodology'. There is also the question of implementing new
methods with little prior testing. Working within a feminist mould
can exacerbate the problems of language associated with much
academic work: accessible gender research needs to avoid jargon, with
the emphasis being on plain language.

Research can only benefit from the use of both quantitative and
qualitative work. Rather than allow the two to be viewed as opposed
methodological bases with the implication that to use both is
something of an ethical compromise, research can move forwards if
methods are employed from various disciplines.

The research methodology employed here involved quantitative
methods such as the questionnaire, and a 'mixed bag' of qualitative
approaches. An intense, in-depth multi-method analysis of both sexes

in one school was considered the best approach for examining the gendered socialization of fear. Research was conducted in a large comprehensive school in one of Europe's most extensive edge-of-town council estates in a northern British city. The study does not and cannot claim to speak for a broad cross-section of British youth aged 11–16, as it only refers to the adolescent boys and girls of one school, in one place and at one time. One could argue that the work suffers from important limitations in terms of its generalizability, but such an argument could be said of research involving two or more schools. What the research does do is to present the results of an intensive investigation of fear of crime among a group of working-class, white youth from a single estate.

This is a report on the findings arising from the use of one method in a multi-method project – the questionnaire. The results of the discussion groups and other qualitative methods have yet to be fully interpreted, but will ultimately complement the questionnaire findings. The results are to be viewed as 'pointers' towards later theoretical formalization.

Questions

Attempting to address the process to be termed 'The Socialization of Gendered Fear', the questionnaire was designed to investigate: What is fear to children and what is it attributable to? Are girls demonstrating a greater fear of crime in the public domain than boys? Are girls' fears focused on males as potential harassers/sex attackers? With age do gendered fears become progressively polarized and is this illustrated either by girls' expression of increased fear or does gendered fear become the accepted 'norm' by the late teens, with fear of *men* by girls viewed as a non-verbalized 'fact of life'? The main hypothesis was: 'Heightened adult female fear of crime develops during adolescence as a result of gendered socialization processes and the emergence of the "sexual being".' The basic research question – Is there a significant difference in the responses of boys and girls? – is assessed through the use of chi-square, with significance noted at 0.05 or above.

Results

Questionnaires were completed by 318 boys (48% of the sample) and

Table 1: Has something made you feel 'on edge' when outside?

Age	Per cent 'Yes'	
	Boys	*Girls*
11	72.1	57.9
12	62.5	70.8
13	53.4	77.5 **
14	41.2	80.2 ***
15	30.4	63.9 ***
16	29.7	68.3 **

** differences significant at the 99% confidence level
*** differences significant at the 99.9% confidence level

345 girls (52% of the sample). In an attempt to assess the degree of general apprehensions in girls and boys they were asked: 'Have you been worried or has something made you feel "on edge" recently when outside (for example, walking home from school)?' The results indicate that there is a significant difference in response by gender with 46.5 per cent of boys and 72.2 per cent of girls responding 'Yes'. A fuller examination of the relationship between gender and age is presented in Table 1; it reveals considerable and statistically significant differences in the responses of boys and girls at age fourteen. Overall there is a steady decline with each year of age in the percentage of boys expressing feelings of fear when outside, while the fears of girls remain consistently high in all age groups (ranging between 57.9% and 80.2% aged 11–16). What is of particular interest is the high level of fear that boys reveal at age eleven. At this age a higher proportion of boys (72%) than girls (58%) are responding 'Yes' to the question 'Do you feel "on edge" when outside', but from age twelve onwards girls are consistently showing statistically significant higher levels of fear than boys.

Those responding 'Yes' to the above question were asked 'what' makes you feel worried, the options being: people, traffic, noise, stray dogs and badly lit areas. None of the options proved significant in terms of gender-differentiated response (see Table 2) with comparable proportions of boys and girls noting people, badly lit areas and stray dogs as main sources of worry. It is interesting to reflect here (though not statistically significant) that whilst 10.5% more girls than boys recorded 'people' as fear-evoking, 9.8% more boys than girls specified 'stray dogs'. (Numbers attributing worries to traffic and noise were

Table 2: If you have felt 'on edge' outside, what made you feel that way?

Options	Per cent 'Yes'	
	Boys	Girls
People	53.4	63.9
Traffic	16.2	14.5
Noise	10.1	7.2
Stray dogs	47.3	37.5
Badly lit areas	63.1	59.8

Not significant at the 95% confidence level

too low to be noted as an important source of fear.) These data suggest that children's general fears focus on people and badly lit areas when outside, with stray dogs also generating apprehension. At ages eleven to sixteen fears are revealed which mirror adult concerns to a large extent. One can take the analogy a stage further with fear of people possibly revealing itself via indirect means as fear of badly lit areas. In other words, one is not simply afraid of the dark but afraid of what could be there in the dark, that is people and 'things' such as dogs.

Boys' fear of badly lit areas and stray dogs may reflect a number of wider, more diffuse reasons, one being that people are regarded as less of a threat than more abstract fears. Alternatively, boys more than girls may regularly encounter fearful situations in relation to darkened areas and stray dogs (a much berated problem on the estate). Another factor could relate to boys' growing machismo and their sense of being disallowed the ownership of 'direct' fears; this phenomenon translating itself to an inability or avoidance towards directly stating 'I'm afraid of people', particularly when alternative options are provided. Indirect or abstract fears are the means by which boys can legitimately express fear among their peers (a potential factor to consider even in the completion of an anonymous, self-report questionnaire). One could simply conclude with the statement that girls are more fearful of others than boys, as illustrated by the higher percentage of fearful girls for each year of age. Although analysis of fear-evoking options proved non-significant by gender, it is interesting to note some of the 'patterns' that emerge from an overview of option selection with increased respondent age. Of the five possible options to explain levels of respondent fear, four are cited less often with increased respondent age (remaining proportional by gender) while

Table 3: When outside do some people make you feel worried or 'on edge'?

	Per cent 'Yes'	
Age	Boys	Girls
11	72.2	94.7
12	81.3	88.9
13	82.2	88.7
14	72.1	96.3 ***
15	70.7	83.6
16	56.8	75.6

*** differences significant at 99.9% confidence level

the fifth option 'badly lit areas' is specified slightly more with age and more so with boys. Having somewhat extrapolated the evidence to date, the researcher can move on to test the assumptions further with other questionnaire results.

In order to further explore 'fear' in young people and to identify the reasons for such apprehensions they were asked 'When you're outside do some people make you feel worried or "on edge"?' Table 3 shows the results. Overall, 74 per cent of boys and 88 per cent of girls responded 'Yes', to this question. Further, a comparison of age and gender reveals a consistent pattern: girls of all ages are more likely than boys to report that some people make them feel worried; but the only significant gender differential occurred at age fourteen with 72.1 per cent of boys and 96.3 per cent of girls responding 'Yes' (see Table 3). Why is age fourteen of recurrent significance? One explanation could be that girls' fears 'peak' as they drop their final 'childish' or 'tomboy-like' attributes upon entering the conflictual mid-teen years where gender differences, particularly in relation to emerging sexuality, are enhanced and played upon. In line with certain psychology arguments, as highlighted by Robson-Scott (1992), for girls, the 'conflict' years of gender identity and loss of self-esteem emerge from age twelve onwards (boys already having gone through this stage with the rejection of the Mother figure at ages 5/6). This process could be reflected in the data presented in Tables 1 and 3 which show that, on average, girls are most fearful at age fourteen, but by the age of fifteen and sixteen this has apparently dissipated.

The research also investigated *of whom* the girls and boys are afraid at different ages in an attempt to clarify any emergent 'trends'.

Table 4: Which of these groups make you feel worried?

	Per cent 'Yes'	
Groups	Boys	Girls
Boys your age	6.8	5.2
Girls your age	1.3	6.2 **
Older boys	48.3	28.5 ***
Older girls	4.2	20.0 ***
Drunks	71.3	83.0 **
Men	21.2	42.6 ***
Women	3.4	2.6
Old people	2.1	3.9
Druggies	76.5	76.7

** differences significant at the 99% confidence level
*** differences significant at the 99.9% confidence level

Table 5: Fear of older boys when outside

	Per cent 'Yes'	
Age	Boys	Girls
11	46.2	33.3
12	38.5	37.5
13	55.7	33.3 *
14	63.8	25.6 ***
15	46.3	21.6 *
16	Test not possible	

* differences significant at the 95% confidence level
*** differences significant at the 99.9% confidence level

The options as to 'who' they might be fearful of are: boys your age, girls your age, older boys, older girls, drunks, men, women, old people and druggies.

For both boys and girls fear of someone the respondent's own age was negligible. For the category 'older boys,' male respondents voiced greater fear at all ages than female respondents (see Table 4). The most significant age for variation in response to fear of older boys by gender was at fourteen (see Table 5). This result invites the question 'why' are boys demonstrating heightened fear of older boys at this age and 'why' are girls failing to mirror this fear. The explanation could lie with the other categories of 'people', as girls have consistently higher levels of fear for all groups at all ages in comparison with boys; coupled with this are the highly conflictual mid-teen years for boys, where same-sex rivalries can often take the form of aggressive behaviour from older boy to younger boy, as male egos are tested. Boys' fear of older boys declines from age fourteen as growing machismo may be emerging. At the same time the enhancement and adoption of feminine traits by teenage girls may remove them from much of the direct, aggressive contact they encountered with boys in their early and pre-teen years. It must be remembered that physical strength is an important element running throughout the emergent patterns of gendered fear. Boys' later pubertal development around fourteen could instil and exacerbate conflict as a result of their growing strength, while girls learn to shun physical conflict at this time as a reflection of their physical and socially constructed 'weakness'.

As Tables 4 and 6 show, boys expressed almost no fear of girls and women, regardless of age. Fear of 'older girls' is however important for girls. A reasonable proportion of girls, 16–31 per cent, express a fear of older girls, with the highest levels being apparent at twelve years of age. There is a highly significant gendered response regarding the fear of 'men'. As Table 7 shows, a considerable proportion of girls of all ages express a fear of men when outside and this is especially marked at the ages of eleven and twelve, where 67 per cent of girls express such a fear. Although boys of all ages express a fear, the proportions of boys expressing fear never surpasses the reports of girls and significant differences are noted at ages twelve and fourteen. A common trend, however, is that as both boys and girls grow up there is a reduction of fear of men. The two categories that produce a consistently high level of fear among both sexes are 'drunks' and 'druggies' (see Table 4). Fear of 'women' and 'old people' remains at a negligible 3.9 per cent or lower across both genders and all ages.

The research needs also to consider other influences on childhood, particularly fear-inducing incidents. In order to investigate potentially important incidents, children were asked: 'Has anyone in the last few weeks done or said something to worry or scare you when you've been outside?' This question is broken down to ask whether the last incident happened when the child was alone/in a group, was it dark, where did it take place, was the 'aggressor' or 'aggressors' alone/in a group, and the relationship of aggressor(s) to respondent in terms of friend/stranger, age and gender. Responses to the question proved

Table 6: Fear of older girls when outside

	Per cent 'Yes'	
Age	Boys	Girls
11	Test not possible	
12	3.8	31.3 ***
13	8.3	15.9
14	4.1	20.5 *
15	0.0	15.7 *
16	Test not possible	

* differences significant at the 95% confidence level
*** differences significant at the 99.9% confidence level

Table 7: Fear of men when outside

	Per cent 'Yes'	
Age	Boys	Girls
11	23.1	66.7 *
12	34.6	67.2 ***
13	21.7	34.9
14	12.2	34.6 **
15	17.1	35.3
16	Test not possible	

* differences significant at the 95% confidence level
** differences significant at the 99% confidence level
*** differences significant at the 99.9% confidence level

highly significant with regard to the gender of respondents overall, with 21.4 per cent of boys and 34.2 per cent of girls worried by what someone said or did to them outside in the last few weeks. Given controlling for age (see Table 8) the only significant gender differential occurs at age fourteen, with 14.7 per cent of boys and 37.0 per cent of girls responding 'Yes'. At each year of age the number of girls worried by someone when outside is higher than the number of boys, but for both sexes, with increased age, the numbers reporting fear-evoking encounters when outside gradually decreases.

Roughly half the children had been approached when alone and during darkness; a feature named by both girls and boys. The primary place for incidents to have occurred was on the street: 37.3 per cent of boys and 40.9 per cent of girls mentioned this location. Non-specified

Table 8: Has anyone in the last few weeks done or said something to
worry or scare you when you've been outside?

Age	Per cent 'Yes'	
	Boys	Girls
11	16.7	47.4
12	29.7	38.9
13	30.1	35.2
14	14.7	37.0 **
15	15.5	31.1
16	13.5	17.1

** differences significant at the 99% confidence level
*** differences significant at the 99.9% confidence level

locations accounted for 29.7 per cent of boys and 23.5 per cent of
girls, and school locations for 13.4 per cent of boys and 16.5 per cent
of girls. Playing-fields were as important as the school location for
male respondents, but only 6.1 per cent of females attributed an
incident to such a location. (Incident locations were too numerous to
allow a meaningful breakdown of differential response by age and
gender.) As to the aggressors being alone or in a group, again the
evidence was not significant in terms of age or gender differentials.
The percentages do indicate that for both sexes with increased age the
focus of incidents changes from the likelihood of approach by group
or lone person, to approach by group. For example, at age 11–13, 53.5
per cent of boys and 54.4 per cent of girls are made to feel worried by
a lone person, with the figures falling to 36 per cent of boys and 32.1
per cent of girls at age 14–16; while fear-evoking incidents stemming
from groups increase from 46.5 per cent of boys aged 11–13, to 64 per
cent of boys and 67.9 per cent of girls age 14–16. This could reflect,
on the one hand, vulnerability of younger children to approaches by
strangers, and on the other, the potential for inter-group conflict in
the mid-teen years.

The question also generated evidence regarding the relationship of
respondents to the lone person or group who scared them. Statistical
tests as to whether the aggressor(s) was a friend, stranger, family
member or girl/boyfriend of the respondent, along with a comparison
of aggressor(s) age to respondent age, proved non-significant when
tested against respondent sex; however some interesting findings did
emerge. The majority of respondents claimed to have been

approached by a stranger, or a group containing a stranger (64.8 per cent of boys and 50 per cent of girls), with most of the remainder having been involved in an incident with a 'friend' or 'friends' (29.4 per cent of boys and 39 per cent of girls). Already a gendered response can be interpreted, with more girls than boys citing 'friends' as the aggressors, and more boys citing strangers. Although non-significant, it appears that with age more boys may experience problems with 'friends', whilst the inverse could be happening to girls; at age 11–13, 25 per cent of boys and 41.9 per cent of girls have been worried by a so-called 'friend' when outside, whereas at age 14–16 the figures are 37.5 per cent of boys and 35.7 per cent of girls. Perhaps the adolescent definition of 'friend' needs further examination.

The findings for the age relationship were mirrored between genders: 40.8 per cent of boys and 40.7 per cent of girls having been approached by an older child or a group containing an older child; 36.2 per cent of boys and 35.6 per cent of girls by an adult or adults; and 27.5 per cent of boys and 25.4 per cent of girls by someone or a group their own age. Although the figures do not prove significant in terms of any gender differential, extrapolating them by age suggests that as boys grow older they may experience increasing problems from peers and adults. In comparison, girls suffer continued victimization from older children. Analysis of aggressor sex could aid understanding of the above.

The data further show that the gender of the aggressor is highly differentiated. Males feature most prominently in the accounts of girls and boys; 94.3 per cent of boys and 55.9 per cent of girls were scared by a lone male or a male member of a group. Only 8.7 per cent of boys but 45.8 per cent of girls said they were scared by at least one female. With an age breakdown one is able to see a 'peak' at age thirteen. Male aggressor incidents 'peak' around the same period. Inter-male conflict remains high through ages eleven to sixteen (although the expected frequencies disallowed for statistical testing). By contrast, the number of girls and boys worried by a female 'aggressor' decreases with age.

Fundamentally what these data may reflect is the abstractness of the notion of 'men' (that is all men, encompassing drunks and druggies) as potential attackers. The popular scenario of the rapist is that of the atypical male monster who prowls darkened alleys. The media and other sources 'educate' us to the reality of the atypical attacker – the stranger who assaults the unknown victim. The statistically more typical male attacker of women – the husband who beats his wife and the father who sexually abuses his child – is usually invisible. The idea of fearing male intimates is a concept which most of us (including children) do not want to take on board. What may be on view here is a high sense of vulnerability revealed by both sexes when young, translating itself into the everyday normality of expected and particularly gendered fears when older.

It would seem that both girls' and boys' fears centre on the early teen years and decline with increasing age. Evidence is inconclusive regarding the relationship of respondent to aggressor. Initial findings reveal that amongst the population sampled, both sexes had been approached by a stranger more often than by someone known to them (a significant percentage of girls were involved in an incident with a 'friend'). Aggressor age was mirrored between respondent sexes, with approaches (in declining order of frequency) by older children, adults, and someone the respondent's own age. There could be an argument for division of incident interpretation into four categories: that of (1) male (2) female victim, and aggressor as either (3) other child or (4) adult. The teenage years produce a great deal of 'in-fighting' within and between the sexes. Although girls' heightened fear of other girls may highlight female aggressiveness and/or increased female sensitivity towards situations, we may simply be witnessing reluctance on the part of young males to reveal feelings of fear in certain situations and/or an absence (real or learned) of any concrete fear. As girls leave the teen years and aggressive group interaction is reduced, movement to adulthood may reveal higher levels of fear of adult males than that displayed by boys.

Concluding remarks

Having examined a number of issues, it must be acknowledged that a comprehensive understanding of gendered fear has to incorporate the other influences of peer group pressure, knowledge of other people's experiences, media influences, etc., as outlined in the remainder of the questionnaire. One cannot attempt to begin to provide comprehensive answers to the fear dilemma only with the above results, as numerous factors have yet to be incorporated in the equation. What *has* been established is that fear amongst eleven- to sixteen-year-olds is gendered, with girls expressing greater fear when outside, greater fear of 'people' and more specifically greater fear of *men* and with more girls than boys having been worried by 'someone' when outside.

If a research question were to ask women 'Are you fearful of men?', it is not unreasonable to imagine the response of many would be 'No'. It is also reasonable to assume that if women were asked 'Are you fearful of rapists?', many would answer 'Yes'. This illustrates somewhat crudely the dilemma of the researcher attempting to tap the reality of gendered fear. The questionnaire is an excellent tool for quick, large-scale analysis, but may fail through its directness and the nature of its formatting to deal with 'delicate' subjects such as fear of sexual assault. It is to the qualitative methods of discussion and drama groups that the research initiative outlined above must turn if wishing to comprehend the full expression of children's fears.

Ultimately these fears will have to be contextualized through categorization into understandable sources of fear such as 'internal' (psychological, private space) and 'external' (socially constructed, public space). The nature/nurture argument is an umbrella that overshadows both spheres, but one that is itself over-arched by the suggestion of a process to be termed 'The Socialization of Gendered Fear', 'Why is it gendered?', and 'What is gendered fear attributable to?' I would suggest that children are the key to this holistic approach towards fear of crime.

Bibliography

Anderson, S., Kinsey, R., Loader, I. and Smith, C. (1990). *Cautionary Tales: A Study of Young People and Crime in Edinburgh* (Edinburgh, Edinburgh University Centre for Criminology).

Bowles, G. and Duelli Klein, R. (eds.) (1983). *Theories of Women's Studies* (London, Routledge and Kegan Paul).

Burt, M. and Estep, R. (1981). 'Apprehension and fear: learning a sense of sexual vulnerability', *Sex Roles*, 5, 511–22.

Brownmiller, S. (1975). *Against Our Will: Men, Women and Rape* (London, Penguin Books).

Feyerherm, W. and Hindelang, M. (1974). 'On the victimisation of juveniles: some preliminary results', *Journal of Research in Crime and Delinquency*, 11, 40–50.

Foster, J. (1990). *Orchard Park: A View from the Youth* (London, Department of Sociology, London School of Economics),

Garofalo, J. (1979). 'Victimisation and the fear of crime', *Journal of Research in Crime and Delinquency*, 16, 80–97.

Home Office Research and Planning Unit (1982, 1984, 1988). *British Crime Survey* (London, Home Office).

Imray, L. and Middleton, A. (1983). 'Public and private: marking the boundaries', in E. Gamarnikov, D. Morgan, J. Purvis and D. Taylorson (eds.), *The Public and the Private* (London, Heinemann), 12–27.

James, A. and Prout, A. (1990). 'A new paradigm for the sociology of childhood? provenance, promise and problems', in A. James and A. Prout (eds.), *Constructing and Reconstructing Childhood: Contemporary Issues in the Sociological Study of Childhood* (London, The Falmer Press), 7–35.

Jayoratne, T. (1983). 'The value of quantitative methodology for feminist research', in G. Bowles and R. Duelli Klein (eds.), *Theories of Women's Studies* (London, Routledge and Kegan Paul), 140–61.

Jones, T., MacLean, B. and Young, A. (1986). *The Islington Crime Survey, Victimisation and Policing in Inner-City London* (London, Gower).

Kelly L. (1987). 'The continuum of sexual violence', in J. Hanmer and M. Maynard (eds.), *Women, Violence and Social Control* (London, Macmillan), 46–60.

Lacey, C. (1970). *Hightown Grammar* (Manchester, Manchester University Press).

Maccoby, E. and Jacklin, C. (1975). *The Psychology of Sex Differences* (Oxford, Oxford University Press).

Mawby, R. (1979). 'The victimisation of juveniles: a comparative study of three areas of publicly owned housing in Sheffield', *Journal of Research in Crime and Delinquency*, 16, 98–110.

Maxfield, M. (1984). *Fear of Crime in England and Wales*, Home Office Research Study No. 78 (London, HMSO).

Mazey, M. and Lee, D. (1983). *Her Space, Her Place – A Geography of Women*, (USA, Association of American Geographers), 37–50.

Mies, M. (1983). 'Towards a methodology for feminist research', in G. Bowles and R. Duelli Klein (eds.), *Theories of Women's Studies* (London, Routledge & Kegan Paul), 117–39.

Morgan, J. (1988). 'Children as victims', in M. Maguire and J. Pointing (eds.), *Victims of Crime* (Milton Keynes, Open University Press), 74–82.

Open University Press (1979). *Block 3B – Research Design* (Milton Keynes, Open University Press).

Painter, K. (1991). *An Evaluation of Public Lighting as a Crime Prevention Strategy with Special Focus on Women and the Elderly* (Manchester, Faculty of Economic and Social Studies, University of Manchester).

Piaget, J. and Inhelder, B. (1969). *The Psychology of the Child* (London, Routledge & Kegan Paul).

Robson-Scott, M. (1992). 'The growing pains of teenage girls', *Guardian*, 15/1/92.

Soothill, K. and Walby, S. (1991). *Sex Crime in the News* (London and New York, Routledge).

Stanko, E. (1990). *Everyday Violence – How Women and Men Experience Sexual and Physical Danger* (London, Pandora).

Valentine, G. (1989). 'Women's Fear of Male Violence in Public Space: A Spatial Expression of Patriarchy' (Department of Geography, University of Reading, Ph.D. thesis).

Wilkins, E. (1993), 'He pulled up alongside and I could feel his eyes peering into my car', *Daily Telegraph*, 4/6/93.

15

Child sexual abuse and age of consent laws: A response to some libertarian arguments for 'sexual liberty'

A. MARK LIDDLE

In the last two decades, issues surrounding adult–child sexual interaction have received increasing attention both in academic literature and in the media, and a body of new empirical research concerning such things as prevalence and sequelae has also accumulated during this period. The latter research has in turn given rise to controversial debates about causation and the possible impact on children of sexual activities with adults, and in the light of some of the more recent prevalence data, difficult questions have also arisen concerning how the criminal justice system or state agents should respond to adult–child sex. More specifically with regard to the question of 'official response', professionals in a number of countries and from a variety of disciplines have pointed to the negative impact on children of some of the more blunt forms of state intervention into the arena of childhood or family sexuality. This debate concerning appropriate forms for state intervention into cases of adult–child sex has also not simply been confined to practical questions about suitable court procedures for such cases, or about improvements to techniques for interviewing child victims. The debate has also focused attention on some rather more fundamental questions concerning sexual development and desire, consent, parental authority, and individual human rights.

It is with questions of the latter sort that the present paper is concerned, and the discussion to follow will focus on a set of claims that has been offered by some writers of a libertarian persuasion, in support of arguments against blanket criminalization of adult–child sexual activity. While the case for decriminalization of such activity and for the relaxation of age-of-consent laws more generally has been argued by a variety of writers, consideration will here be given to a particular body of work within which arguments for decriminalization have been linked to calls for children's 'emancipation' from legal and other restrictions on their 'sexual liberty'. In work adopting this perspective, the vocabulary of child protection is regarded to some extent as being a smoke-screen for practices which are 'ageist' and oppressive to children and young people, and age-of-consent laws specifically are felt to be rooted in simple prejudice or unenlightened moralism.[1]

More specific reference to individual writers in this tradition will be made throughout the discussion to follow, but the general claims to be found in this work are worth noting at the outset. Aside from some differences in emphasis and presentation, libertarian arguments for decriminalization of adult–child sex usually involve the following, interrelated claims:

1. The available evidence suggests considerable historical and cultural diversity in societal reaction to sexual activities involving adults and children.
2. The application of 'abuse' labels to adult–child sex is often based on nothing more than subjective feeling of outrage or revulsion, and the wish to see paedophiles punished is often similarly motivated.
3. Contrary to a common assumption that children are 'asexual', children do have sexual responses and desires of their own, and they are in many cases fully able to invite and understand sexual activities with adults.
4. While some adult–child sex can be harmful to children, available evidence suggests that in many individual cases such activity has been either neutral or beneficial in its outcome.
5. Some cases of adult–child sexual activity involve both a loving adult and a willing, consenting child, and the criminal law should not be invoked to prohibit consensual sexual behaviours of this sort, where evidence of harm cannot be demonstrated.

These claims will be further detailed in what follows, and it will be argued in response that adult–child sexual activity is almost always non-consensual, in that child participants are precluded from offering informed consent to such activity, and secondly, that adult–child sex is a species of non-consensual activity which cannot be justified by reference to the needs of children, and is therefore ethically indefensible. It will also be suggested that although the research does indicate that evidence concerning harm is equivocal (though far less equivocal than suggested by libertarians), demonstrable harm does not supply the sole ground for intervention in cases of adult–child sex. Most interactions of the latter sort are a form of injustice whether or not subsequent harm can be demonstrated; they involve a type of rights-violation which arguably requires state response quite independently of any clear resolution of the debate on impact. Finally, it will be noted that evidence concerning the 'secondary victimization' caused by official intervention into cases of sexual assault generally does not tip the scales in favour of decriminalization of adult–child sex. The presence of secondary victimization of this kind suggests rather that forms of intervention themselves need to be further humanized and tailored to the unique needs of children and their experience as victims, as they have been in some jurisdictions with respect to sexual crimes against women.[2]

Some preliminaries

The literature on adult–child sex presents a number of definitional and other difficulties, which warrant some mention at the outset. Variations in 'abuse' definitions are notorious, first of all, and I have therefore opted for the term 'adult–child sex', instead of 'child sexual abuse', 'child sexual victimization', 'sexual misuse of children', or any of the other terms currently in use. The term 'sex' itself also gives rise to problems of interpretation, especially in the literature on incidence and prevalence, where it is not always clear which behaviours are the object of discussion. Summit and Kryso (1978) have highlighted some of the difficulties in specifying whether a particular interaction is a sexual one or not, but I have construed the term 'sex' as used in the phrase 'adult–child sex', as referring to adult–child interactions involving direct sexual contact such as sexual intercourse, masturbation, or manual, oral or other manipulation of the genitals, breasts or anus, where the purpose of the interaction is the sexual gratification of one or more of the participants. This characterization is therefore virtually identical to most definitions of 'contact child sexual abuse' employed in the literature, as contrasted with 'non-contact' abuse (e.g. sexual threats or invitations, exposure, etc.). In keeping with most other writers in the field, I do not use the term to refer to incidents where a child is not a *direct* participant in the interaction.

I will use the term 'child' to refer to a pre-pubertal young person, and the term 'adult' to refer to a sexually mature person aged eighteen years or older, although greater specificity will be offered where it is relevant to the arguments given.

Adult–child sex and cultural/historical diversity

The fact of cultural and historical variations both in sexual practice generally and in societal reaction to adult–child sex specifically is a prominent plank in the libertarian position, and presentations made by the writers referred to often begin with references to the literature on 'sexual diversity'. This literature is now vast, and examples of wide variations in sexual practice and official response to it are quite easily found. General surveys offered by writers such as Bullough (1976), Ford and Beach (1952), or Marshall and Suggs (1971) abound with descriptions of particular cultures or periods in history where various sexual behaviours involving adults and children have been regarded as being healthy, humorous, or simply a pleasurable pastime. Examples of this kind have led libertarians such as Edward Brongersma to claim that:

> . . . all forms of sexual activity have been admired in certain places at certain times. There is not a single act from marital intercourse to mother–son incest, from masturbation to bestiality, that has not been considered praiseworthy in some cultures, or beneficial to health, just as it has been thought objectionable, sinful or unhealthy in other cultural environments. (Brongersma 1988: 32)

Middleton (1986: 157) similarly notes that:

> . . . there is no universally accepted definition of what constitutes normal sexual behaviour. Instead, we find that such definitions are historically and culturally variable, so that behaviour which one society views as normal might not be considered so normal in another.

Comments of this sort are also frequently made in other fields (such as ethics, for instance), but their use in libertarian arguments is clearly designed to pre-empt efforts to ascribe any universality to 'abuse' labels, and more generally, to place moral assessments of sexual practice on a less secure footing. Libertarian writers employ a familiar chain of reasoning in this context – if adults in Siriono or Hopi society regularly masturbate their children (as Ford and Beach

(1952), for example suggest), and if it is at least unclear whether 'abuse' labels are applicable to such behaviour, then why should similar behaviour be so vociferously condemned in some Western countries? If clear answers to such questions do not seem readily available, then readers are invited to consider whether negative judgements about adult–child sex more generally might be rooted in a kind of ethnocentrism.

Evidence of diversity in sexual practice does raise some crucial questions about how we might distinguish between 'abusive' and 'non-abusive' adult–child interactions in a way which is sensitive to socio-cultural differences, and questions of this kind will be addressed more directly in the discussion of 'needs assessments' to follow. However, it is worth noting at the outset that nothing whatever *follows* from the mere fact of sexual or other diversity, although such diversity is sometimes taken to support relativist conclusions of one sort or another. Moreover, the examples of diversity offered by libertarians are often highly selective, falling if anything at the benign end of the scale of adult–child interactions, and ignoring cases involving extreme brutality for example. Practices such as child rape and sexual mutilation have also flourished during certain historical periods according to Radbill (1968) and others (Aries, 1962; De Mause, 1974, 1975),[3] and as Schultz has concluded more generally, 'the history of sex and children is an unpleasant walk through a house of horrors, a disgusting heritage that, even so, cannot be disowned' (1980: 3). This kind of diversity seems far removed from the (often quaint) examples employed by 'child liberationists', and does just as little to call current practice into question as the past popularity of Paris cat-burnings or racist lynch mobs.

In any case, evidence of diverse sexual practice is often difficult to utilize for purposes of comparison with our own society, as Plummer (1984) has pointed out. The difficulty of course is that 'sex acts' themselves cannot simply be extracted from the constellation of beliefs or practices in which they are lodged within particular societies, in order to support a relativist conclusion about societal reactions to these. To anticipate some of the arguments offered below, a particular form of adult–child sex as practised in one culture may differ fundamentally from an apparently similar form practised elsewhere, in the sense that its social significance and the motivations for engaging in it may differ widely. Related to the last point, many of the examples of *cross-cultural* sexual diversity taken up by libertarians are also drawn from studies of tribal or other pre-state societies, and social structure in these societies differs fundamentally from that in state societies such as our own. Pre-state societies are characterized by extensive kin-based networks and their attendant clusters of rights, statuses, and obligations, and sexual behaviour itself is both informed and contained by these networks. Sexuality within some of these cultures is in a sense interpolated more widely, and is woven into a different field of meaning within which stages of life and so on are uniquely invested with ritual and significance. State-formation necessarily erodes some of these wider ties, and arguably leads to a radically different emotional and psychological landscape for the individual. Even the concept of 'the individual' itself takes on new significance in state-societies, especially in circumstances of modernity, and there is a real sense in which the sexual practices of relatively self-contained pre-state cultures are not even possible within our own.[4]

Adult–child sex, ethics, and consent

Issues concerning consent are obviously of central importance both to judgements about the moral status of particular sexual practices, and to efforts to specify the conditions under which state intervention might be warranted. These issues also continue to generate sometimes heated debate in a number of disciplines, both in work focusing on specific forms of sexual interaction (such as rape, most notably, or sexual assaults against women),[5] and more generally, in connection with proposals concerning reform of criminal laws covering sexual behaviour. However, debates tend to centre on the question of how the presence or absence of consent can be *recognized* as such, rather than on whether consent itself is worthy of consideration in this context, and there appears to be a general consensus that non-consensual sexual interactions are both morally indefensible, and worthy of some form of official intervention.[6] A detailed discussion of these general issues surrounding consent cannot be offered here, but it seems to be generally accepted that a participant in a sexual encounter can be judged to have consented to the latter, if he or she was willing for the encounter to take place, and:

1. the participant generally understood the nature of the encounter itself and the conditions under which it was to take place, and was not misled about either of these;

2. the participant was not threatened, forced, or coerced into participating in the encounter, and
3. the participant was not in a position with respect to the other participant(s) which limited or precluded the former's scope for refusing to participate in the encounter.

Concerning adult–child sex specifically, most writers on the topic appear to operate with a similar notion of consent, although assumptions about the nature of consent itself are not usually addressed directly in such work. Connections between consent and the moral status of sexual interactions are also not always spelled out in this literature – that is, it is not always clear why the presence or absence of consent is thought to be relevant to the moral status of adult–child sex. I will return to this issue at the end of the section.

Libertarians also appear to accept the general claim that non-consensual sexual interactions should be proscribed (legally or otherwise), although some have argued that the term 'consent' itself tends to mislead the debate.[7] Writers adopting the perspective in question usually make specific mention of the central importance of consent to an understanding of adult–child sex (although most of these writers also define consent in a way which differs markedly from definitions offered in more mainstream accounts, as will be seen in following paragraphs). Warren Middleton, for example, suggests that '[paedophiles'] own literature constantly emphasizes that the child's consent is of paramount importance' (1986: 147), and he notes more generally that 'refusal to recognize consent is a refusal to recognize the person' (1986: 150–51).[8]

For the most part, consent is strongly linked in libertarian work (perhaps not surprisingly) with notions like 'willingness' and desire; that is, a particular adult–child sexual encounter is regarded as being consensual if the older party does not use force or coercion, and if the child is 'willing' to have the encounter take place. The child's 'understanding' of the encounter is construed in terms of the child's awareness of the encounter's potential for producing sexual pleasure, and 'willingness' is in turn described in terms of the child's desire to have the encounter take place.

Examples of this characterization of consent can be readily found in libertarian writing; Brongersma notes that 'the question of a child's ability to give sexual consent is a relatively recent one' (1988: 34), for example, and he goes on to suggest that in medieval times adult–child sexual encounters were fairly common, and that they were engaged in '*because* children evidently liked this' (1988: 34; my emphasis). There as been a 'repressive trend' since that time, however, and this trend:

> eventually resulted in a wholly new concept which appears quite bewildering in the light of later research: a vision of the child as an asexual being and, on that account, 'innocent'. The asexual child could not, himself, desire contact. If he did have such contact it was entirely because of the indecent man who imposed on the innocent child, and for this crime, fatal to a favourable upbringing, he deserved punishment. (Brongersma, 1988: 34)

The more or less direct equation between consent and desire is drawn quite clearly in passages of this sort, and the relegation of non-consent to the realm of 'asexuality' is also tied conceptually to this equation. In short, the libertarian argument here is that sexual pleasure and willingness are the operative considerations for judging the presence or absence of consent, and although there may be difficulties in determining whether a child participant really is willing for an encounter to take place (as in the case of very young children, for example, who may not have mastered the language sufficiently to be able to verbalize their own wishes), age differences between participants in adult–child sex are otherwise not especially relevant. As O'Carroll expresses the latter point, 'For those who feel that consensual sex is a harmless and pleasant activity, the question of age is irrelevant' (O'Carroll, 1980: 58).

As noted earlier, this account of consent differs considerably from accounts offered by most writers in this field, and almost all of the prevailing 'abuse' definitions rest on assumptions concerning restrictions on children's capacity to consent to sexual activities with adults. The perspective adopted in much of the literature[9] is that children are unable to consent to sex with adults, first of all because their limited cognitive, emotional and social maturation would preclude their grasping either the social meanings or the consequences of sexual activities in general. Human sexuality is a complex and multi-faceted phenomenon, and plays a significant role in a myriad of human interactions which children have simply not experienced. For this reason, children are unlikely, as Finkelhor puts it:

> . . . to be aware of the rules and regulations surrounding sexual intimacy, and what it is supposed to signify. They are probably uninformed and inexperienced about what criteria to use in judging the acceptability of a

sexual partner. They probably do not know much about the 'natural history' of sexual relationships, what course they will take. And, finally, they have little way of knowing how other people are likely to react to the experience they are about to undertake, what likely consequences it will have for them in the future (Finkelhor 1979: 403).

Given these kinds of developmentally imposed limitations, then, it is often argued that children are not in a position to make an informed decision about having sex with an adult. This lack of knowledge and experience on the child's part, however, is coupled with a glaring asymmetry in the degree of power held by the participants in adult–child sexual encounters. Children are dependent on adults for the very necessities of life, as well as for emotional support and affection. Given this kind of deep-rooted dependency, the pressure not to refuse adult sexual advances must be considerable for the child, and genuine consent would therefore seem to be precluded by it. To be meaningful, consent must surely be given in circumstances where there is more than one real option for the person making the choice, and given the social position and perceptions of the child, these circumstances do not obtain in cases of adult–child sexual activity.[10] Hence, in terms of the general account of consent offered above, adult–child sex could be judged to be non-consensual because the first and third conditions cannot be satisfied where children are participants.

Libertarians have responded to these claims in a number of ways, as some of the above remarks should already suggest. Concerning children's 'developmental limitations', first of all, since libertarians usually define consent in terms of willingness to engage in pleasurable activity, it does seem to follow that children could in certain circumstances consent to sex with adults, and most of the libertarian effort in this context is therefore simply directed to offering examples which cast doubt on the view that children are 'asexual'. In response to the claim that a child's immaturity might compromise his or her ability to consent, Brongersma, for example, suggests that:

> it was obvious as soon as the matter was investigated in a scientific manner, that these a priori opinions [i.e. concerning the asexuality of children] were untenable. It is now known that children have sexual feelings from birth and that at a very young age they spontaneously begin sexual play. Thus they know very well whether they want a particular kind

of sexual contact with a specific person and whether they want it here and now. In other words, the concept that below a certain age a child can have no will or desire of his own in these matters or, if he did that it would be judicially irrelevant is not based upon fact. (1988: 35)

Again, the equation 'consent = expressed desire for pleasure' is clearly made in this passage,[11] and the use of the term 'thus' (which is, after all, a *logical* connective used to assert that flanking propositions stand in a relation of implication) makes this conceptual connection very strong indeed. Given this characterization of consent, the developmental factors referred to above simply have far less relevance within libertarian work; as O'Carroll remarks with regard to one of these developmental aspects:

There is nothing about sexuality for which one *needs* a competent rationality. It is completely harmless, unlike many of the things children want to do and claim a right to do; theoretically, sexuality is one area in which there should be no finely balanced claims as to what is in 'the best interests of the child'. (1980: 145; O'Carroll's emphasis.)

The point is also made by libertarians that many *adults* are unaware of what the consequences of a particular sexual encounter will be, and yet the claim that adults can consent to have sex with one another is not usually thought to be controversial.

Finally, the latter point is related to the issue of power and its relevance to consent, and libertarians have strongly criticized arguments such as those quoted above by Finkelhor. If the power asymmetry between adults and children precludes the possibility of consensual adult–child sex, then to be consistent we will have to conclude that consensual sexual interaction is almost always impossible. After all, as writers such as Middleton and O'Carroll argue, there are similar power differentials between men and women, between whites and ethnic minority groups, and so on – how can it be claimed that individuals from these groups are able to consent to sex with one another, while children are unable to do so?

The general point to be made in response to many of the above remarks concerning 'differences between adults and children', is that when taken together, the experiential, developmental and power factors add up to a fairly unique set of impediments to consensual adult–child sex – a set which does not obtain for relations between any of the other groups referred to (men and women, whites and blacks, and so on). Some brief remarks on the notion of dependence can serve to illustrate this general point. In contemporary state societies in the West, children are dependent on adults not only economically and structurally, as noted above (in the sense that they are entirely outside structures of labour and power), but also emotionally and psychologically, in a way which differs from forms of dependence in traditional societies, to return to some of the comparisons drawn earlier. Characterizations of children's dependence such as that offered above by Finkelhor are already persuasive, but they can be further strengthened by reference to recent contributions in social theory. The account of childhood development offered by Giddens, for example (which also draws on work by Erikson and Garfinkel), is especially useful in this regard, since it links social processes in modern state-societies to the development and structuring of individual character. The development of trust during childhood in this account is prerequisite to the development of personality structures which are sufficiently resilient to maintain the individual's future ontological security. Trust relations which develop between the child and significant adults provide an anchor for resolution of crucial dilemmas which the child must surmount during its psychological development – presence and absence, invasiveness and zones of bodily control, boundaries of the self, and so on – and the development of trust in this way provides what Giddens calls an *'emotional inoculation* against existential anxieties' (1991: 39; his emphasis). An important point to make here is that anxieties surrounding maintenance and control of the *body* are of key significance to the early determinants of individual character, and connections between autonomy, trust, and bodily integrity are therefore very deeply rooted. It is at least partly for this reason that consent in *sexual* matters is deemed to be so important, and that sexuality more generally is invested with an emotional significance which does not always obtain in other spheres of human activity.

To return to the connections between power, consent and childhood development again, the general point is simply that, as a result of factors such as those referred to above, adult–child sexual interaction can never take place on a level playing-field. These factors should allow us to distinguish between power differentials which nullify a capacity to consent and those which do not; in the case of children, their ability to understand (and not just in a cognitive sense) sexuality and what sexual behaviour signifies is compromised for developmental reasons, and their multi-faceted dependence makes for a significant power imbalance in relationships with adults (especially sexual relationships). Finally, the question of harm is obviously of some relevance here as well, especially if we consider cases of adult–child sex where the adult participant is also a parent or significant caretaker.

Even if the above arguments are convincing, however, it does not follow that adult–child sex is ethically indefensible, since the relevance of a child's non-consent varies according to the type of activity being assessed. Libertarians have I think been correct in noting that while arguments concerning a child's inability to consent are quickly offered as part of an assessment of sexual behaviour, the same logic is not often applied to activities in other spheres, where it might also be applicable. As Middleton has noted, for example, the same argument could be pressed into service in order to support the claim that parents should not hug their children, since the child's ability to consent to this (and many other activities) is by no means clear (1986: 170). In response to objections of this kind, it needs to be argued that adult–child sex is a *species* of non-consensual activity which cannot be justified by reference to the needs of children. Some non-consensual activities *can* be justified in this manner – if I physically restrain my children from playing out in the traffic, for example, the exchange in question is a non-consensual one, or might be. Perhaps my children do not see any traffic at the time, and are not cognizant of future danger in the way that I am, but my actions can be justified after the fact by reference to their own needs. Their 'needs' in this case seem pretty obvious, since they have to do with direct physical protection from death or injury, but many 'needs assessments' cannot be made without reference to socio-cultural factors. If reference to needs assessments does not provide any obvious justification for a particular kind of non-consensual adult–child interaction, then the motivations of individual adult participants move more clearly into the foreground, and a prima-facie case for moral unacceptability is suggested (especially, to anticipate the remarks to follow, if the interaction is a sexual one).

Returning to the issue of cross-cultural differences in sexual practice, when we look at sexual practices that are engaged in by members of tribal societies, and so on, we can often see how these practices are woven into clusters of beliefs which lend credence or provide justification for them. Sometimes these beliefs are themselves false beliefs about the facts of reproductive biology (such as that particular bodily fluids hold magical powers, or are toxic, for instance); but they form part of the context in which the activities of interest take place. These beliefs impact not only on the question of consent, but also on the 'needs assessments' that we might make in order to specify the conditions under which adult–child sexual activity would qualify as abuse. In societies where mothers regularly masturbate their young sons, this activity might be justified by reference to strongly held beliefs about the toxicity of retained seminal fluids, and so on, where these beliefs might alone provide justification for the non-consensual adult–child sexual activity (although, to repeat, the question of whether the activity *is* non-consensual will also need to make reference to this background of socio-cultural factors).[12]

Things are rather different here in the West, however, and instead of allowing for needs assessments which might justify non-consensual adult–child sexual activity, reference to socio-cultural factors seems to require us to shift the focus on to the motivations of individual participants. That is, since there is no obvious socio-cultural justification for adult–child sexual activity, no apparent justification in terms of 'the needs of children', we have to look elsewhere for it, and the only place to look seems to be at the motivations of individual adult participants. Some libertarians do claim that adult–child sex *does* (ideally) address the 'needs of children', of course, and I will return to this issue in the following section on harm, but the general conclusion to be drawn here, to recap a bit, is that adult–child sex is morally indefensible not because it is non-consensual (although it is, for the reasons given above), but because it is a species of non-consensual behaviour which cannot be justified by reference to the needs of children.

The question of harm

What the impact of adult–child sex might be on child participants is a question that is still subject to some argument in the literature, even though a multitude of studies have focused on the matter. There are now literally hundreds of written works dealing solely with either short- or long-term effects of adult–child sex, and reviews of the literature offer increasingly comprehensive bibliographies on the subject (Augoustinos 1987; Browne and Finkelhor 1986; Conte and

Berliner 1987; Lusk and Waterman 1986 and Sheldrick 1991). Mrazek and Mrazek (1981) summarize over sixty effects most commonly reported by writers in the field, and although most authorities argue that such effects are negative or damaging to the child, it has been claimed that adult–child sexual interaction can have a positive impact (Rosenfeld, Nadelson, Krieger and Backman 1977; Farrell, in Dunwoody 1982), or that such interaction may be neutral in terms of impact (Baurmann 1983, cited in Brongersma 1988; Bender and Blau 1937; Bender and Grugett 1952; Yorukoglu and Kemph 1966). It is usually agreed that, in the short term at least, a child's reaction to a sexual experience with an adult will vary, depending on a number of factors such as the child's age and maturity, the child's relationship with the adult, the degree of coercion used, the existence of 'family pathology', and the reactions of the family and society to the incident (De Vine 1980; Schultz 1972). The Kinsey study found that out of 4,441 females, 1,075 had had sexual contact with adults in childhood, and that 80 per cent of these individuals had found the experience to be frightening or emotionally upsetting (cited in Badgley 1984: 210). Landis (1956) found that about one half of the victims he surveyed recalled the experience as being shocking, emotionally upsetting, or frightening.[13] De Francis (1969) discovered that of the victims he interviewed shortly after experiences of this kind, two-thirds had some identifiable emotional disturbance, while 14 per cent were severely disturbed.

A variety of longer-term negative effects have also been correlated with adult–child sex; Hyde (1984) has grouped reported adverse long-term effects into categories of physical effects, sexual dysfunction, and psycho-social effects, and she lists a number of specific effects within each category (e.g. psychosomatic disorders, abdominal pains, and eating disorders in the first; arousal dysfunction, promiscuity, and various orgasmic difficulties in the second, and depression, negative self-image, guilt complexes in the third). Lusk and Waterman (1986) have offered a broader categorization of effects into affective, physical, cognitive, behavioural, self-destructive, psychopathological, and sexual (as well as a residual category), and conclude that although recent work seems to confirm the generally negative impact of adult–child sex, there is a clear need for more controlled and rigorous research. Some studies even link multi-personality disorders with adult–child sex (Summit, 1983; Putman, cited in Whitman 1982: 3), while connections between child sexual abuse and character disorders have been asserted by Rist (1979), and between abuse and psychosis by Peters (1973), Summit (1983), and Westermeyer (1978).

Taken as a whole this body of evidence is difficult to interpret, not least because of wide differences in methodology, sampling techniques, and even definitions of key concepts such as 'sexual behaviour' (concepts which in some studies have remained extremely vague or even unspecified). Many of the available studies on impact have also had the considerable disadvantage of being based on clinical or volunteer samples, although some of the more recent non-clinical studies on adults offer a much more reliable base for theorizing. Some of the latter studies have involved large random community samples (e.g. Bradgley 1984; Russell 1986), and have been much more rigorously implemented than several of those referred to above. In their own analysis of the evidence on harm (which included consideration of some of the more recent random sample studies) Browne and Finkelhor concluded that:

> from studies of clinical and nonclinical populations, the findings concerning the trauma of child sexual abuse appear to be as follows: In the immediate aftermath of sexual abuse, from one-fifth to two-fifths of abused children seen by clinicians manifest some noticeable disturbance . . . When studied as adults, victims as a group demonstrate more impairment than their non-victimized counterparts (about twice as much), but less than one-fifth evidence serious psychopathology. (1986: 164)

More recently, Glaser and Frosh have offered a similar conclusion on the basis of their own survey of the available evidence, that:

> although there is considerable variation in the response to sexual abuse shown by different children, there is no doubt that abuse acts as a significant stressor and substantially raises the risk of childhood or later adult psychological difficulties. The sources of this raised risk probably lie in the mixture of the specific sexual content of the abuse and the general context of betrayal of trust, secrecy and powerlessness. (Glaser and Frosh 1993: 25)

The libertarian response to this accumulated evidence, and to the question of sexuality and harm more generally, has tended to take several forms. First, reference to the evidence in libertarian work has usually been highly selective, and the studies that are referred to in the course of arguments for decriminalization of adult–child sex have tended to be those which have suggested a positive or neutral impact on child participants. Hence, Brongersma (1988) Middleton (1986), and O'Carroll (1980) refer to studies such as Landis (1956), Bender and Blau (1937), or Bender and Grugett (1952), which for a number of reasons (e.g. the samples employed) can hardly allow for reliable extrapolation to the general population, or to studies such as Baurmann (1983), Tindall (1978), or Sandfort (1982), which tend to focus on sexual interactions involving adult males and adolescent boys, which are unrepresentative of adult–child sex in general, and also associated with the lowest levels of subsequent trauma or adverse effect.[14]

Secondly, where evidence is referred to which seems to indicate that children have been harmed by sexual encounters with adults, libertarians have tended to argue that such damage has been caused largely (or even solely) by societal response to the interaction subsequent to the child's disclosure, rather than by the sexual interaction itself. As Middleton puts it, for example:

> we already know that many studies agree that children are not usually damaged or 'corrupted' by enjoyable acts with friendly adults. We may safely conclude, therefore, that it is not the sex itself which is most often harmful, but the societal reactions upon discovery. (1986: 148)

When discussing the 'repressive' background against which a young person's disclosure of sexual involvement with an adult usually takes place, he moves on to suggest that some child 'partners' in adult–child sex

> will almost certainly grow up damaged, not so much . . . by the sex itself, but because of unjust laws, insensitive police and police surgeons, gruelling court cases, and hysterical adults who treat the child as if he/she had been contaminated. Put together, such behaviour can only teach children two things: to distrust all adults, and to fear sex, for such children will soon convince themselves that sex must surely be the filthiest thing on earth. (Middleton 1986: 173)

Again, a virtually identical position is also argued both by Brongersma (1988) and O'Carroll (1980), and similar remarks concerning children and consent to adult–child sex more generally are offered by Gough (1981: 68–9), Presland (1981, 1986), and Tatchell (1986).

Finally, in libertarian discussions of harm more generally, it is usually claimed that more extensive damage is caused to children when their right to sexual freedom is repressed by adults, and evidence concerning such damage is sometimes referred to, to supplement the claim that age-of-consent laws should be revised or eliminated. Middleton's remarks are again representative, if more detailed than most:

> Let us be quite clear about the consequences of the systematic inculcation of sex-negative values and the deprivation of sex/sensuality in childhood. It causes paralysing feelings of guilt and shame, sexual dysfunctions, neuroses, depression, and numerous other mental/nervous disorders. The equation often runs as follows: oppression entails repression, and repression, requiring some outlet, frequently manifests itself in psychological disturbance, aggression, crime, and other antisocial behaviour. In addition, it can also lead to unhealthy obsessions, and the only sure way to cure these is to satisfy the desire whose repression caused them in the first place. (1986: 181)

These libertarian claims concerning harm warrant two general criticisms. First, it does seem clear that most of the writers referred to have adopted a double standard for assessing the available research on the impact of adult–child sex. In assessing the accumulated evidence on harm, libertarians are quick to point out some of the methodological and other difficulties which seem to exemplify some of the available studies. This critical stance is then softened when claims are being made about the impact on children of a 'sex-negative' culture; the evidence cited for impact of this kind is purely anecdotal, and suggestions that the presence of harm established in some studies is *really* caused by various facets of societal response, amounts to nothing more than bald assertion. In fact, it is extremely difficult to disentangle some of these alternative sources of adverse effect within an impact study, and perhaps the most that a critic of these studies could say about this issue is that the precise source of documented harm is in many cases unclear.[15]

Secondly, the concept of 'harm' *itself* is not employed consistently within libertarian work, since a broad characterization of harm is employed in discussions of the impact of sexual repression (in the above quote from Middleton, for example, everything from guilt to criminality is attributed to such repression), and a rather narrower one where the possible negative effects of adult–child sex itself are being discussed (as in O'Carroll's remark about the 'complete harmlessness' of much adult–child sex). The latter construal is perhaps consistent with the notion of harm which the courts have traditionally employed in cases of rape or other crimes against women, where evidence of direct and demonstrable physical harm or extreme psychological trauma have often been deemed necessary to legitimize state intervention.

It might also be pointed out that if it really is the case that child participants in adult–child sex are damaged by negative or repressive societal reactions to disclosure, then those adults who claim to act from a concern about reducing children's suffering would surely seek to avoid sexual contact with them, since this contact carries a potential to generate this kind of reaction even if the other evidence suggesting adverse effects is thought to be irrelevant. In other words, it is arguable that in their own terms paedophiles should refrain from having sex with children, in order to shield them from some of these damaging potential consequences. It is also naïve in the extreme in this regard to think that children who have themselves been socialized in the sort of society which libertarians criticize will not have begun to internalize some of the very same attitudes which underlie societal response to adult–child sex. Some *ambivalence* is surely characteristic of human attitudes and emotional correlates to sexual interaction in modern state-societies, and the sort of hydraulic purity of sexual desire as conceived of in libertarian work probably has little contact with reality even in traditional societies. In any case, as noted above, we are quite far removed in fundamental respects from societies of this sort, and it is difficult to take seriously arguments which suggest that children might extricate themselves from the social and intra-psychic complexities of sexual development by engaging in liberatory sex with adults.

Finally, while some of the libertarian claims detailed above concerning the potentially negative effects of 'repressive' attitudes toward sexuality and sexual expression may have merit, it has not been demonstrated by any of the writers referred to that children have in any way suffered damage because they have been denied the right to engage in sex *with adults*. Libertarians do argue that undue prudery in family life can damage young people, by making them uncomfortable or anxious about subjects which can be difficult at the best of times, and with which they will need to come to terms in the course of their own maturation. This seems to be another equivocation in the libertarian platform; from the undoubted fact that many families are too restrictive of sexual expression, and so on, it certainly does not follow that sexual activity between adults and children ought to be encouraged as a remedy. The 'sexual liberty' gloss to libertarian arguments for decriminalization of adult–child sex perhaps seems at its thinnest at this point, and the arguments for the 'sexual empowerment of young people' begin to sound more like efforts to afford greater scope to adult males who wish to exercise their own desires without fear of legal censure.

Some concluding comments on intervention and 'secondary victimization'

Of course, even if it is true that adult–child sex is morally indefensible, as I have argued above, it does not follow either that official intervention is warranted, or that this intervention should involve the criminal justice system; this issue is worthy of some brief final remarks.

On the question of intervention, first of all, it is arguable that adult–child sex involves a type of violation which warrants state response quite independently of any clear resolution of the debate on impact. The question of harm is not *irrelevant* in this context, of course – and given the clear potential for harm that such behaviour appears to pose for children, it seems prudent to protect them from it unless some other justification for the behaviour can be found (which it apparently cannot be) – but it is arguable that the state should in any case proscribe adult–child sex simply because it is a kind of injustice which denies personhood to the child 'participant'. More specifically, it is a type of interaction which involves an erosion of individual autonomy, and a violation of perceived rights to bodily integrity and control. To stand opposed to practices which involve the use of others for personal sexual satisfaction where the route to such satisfaction involves ignoring another's lack of consent, is to stand opposed to a particular form of victimization whether or not the victimization causes 'harm'. Similar arguments are perhaps applicable to cases of rape, where few would argue that we should hold official response in abeyance until the evidence concerning harm has had time to come in. The matter of potential harm is simply icing on the cake for the anti-libertarian.

It is also inappropriate to claim, as some have done in response to libertarian arguments about secondary victimization, that victimization of the latter sort must itself justify decriminalization of adult–child sex. As already noted above, libertarians themselves have been quick to point out some of the adverse effects on children which criminal justice procedures can have. Brongersma, for example, argues in an earlier paper that 'only contact brought about through violence, threats, compulsion or abuse of authority should continue to be punishable', and he goes on to suggest that:

> contacts which are only slightly objectionable, distasteful, ridiculous or mildly frightening to the child should be prevented as far as possible but should never be the basis of criminal procedure, since the child is usually more traumatised by being questioned as a witness by police and prosecutors than by the sexual acts themselves. (1980: 20)

Arguments to this effect have also been offered by more mainstream writers; Donald West (1980) has suggested, for example, that criminalization is simply the wrong course to take in response to the phenomenon, in light of the suffering experienced by children when they are dragged through an insensitive criminal justice system. He suggests that:

> the trauma of the criminal justice process is worse for the child than the sexual incident itself. Consensual sexual behaviour of children, however inconvenient or inappropriate, is better controlled by education and welfare measures than by the criminal law. (1980: 33–4)

It is worth noting, on the one hand, that each of these claims involves question-begging references to 'consent', and on the other, that they frame their descriptions of possible state responses to adult–child sex solely in terms of the potential consequences for the child victim under currently existing legal and investigative procedures. If it is accepted that there are sufficient grounds for state intervention of some kind, however, an alternative course of action must surely be to ensure that legal and other procedures are tailored to meet the needs of children more closely, as they have been in other jurisdictions. To refer again to official response to rape, nobody would now argue that since women victims of rape have traditionally been poorly treated by the criminal justice system, we should argue for the decriminalization of rape or sexual assault.

That criminal processing of sexual abuse cases can be damaging both to children and their families is of course now well documented, and the prosecution of such cases in England and Wales has in the past often seemed to produce results which inconvenience everyone and satisfy no one. More importantly, although state interventions are supposed to be animated in large part by an official concern to protect the interests of children, investigative and other procedures have tended *in practice* to compromise these same interests, and to compound or extend the child victim's trauma, as numerous writers (including those referred to above) have suggested.

The most notable problems of this kind have been associated with evidence-gathering techniques and court-room procedures, which have until very recently been ill-suited to the needs of child victims and/or witnesses. Efforts have been made to change these procedures in the wake of the Cleveland Report (Butler Sloss 1988) and the report of the Advisory Group on Video Evidence (Pigot 1989), but progress has been quite patchy across the country, even though the Criminal Justice Bill 1991 incorporated many of the recommendations made in them (NACRO 1992). More specifically, these and other recent reports have suggested that special procedures be established for the presentation of children's testimony, that agencies involved in abuse investigations co-ordinate their activities in order to avoid multiple questioning of children, that court cases involving child victims be processed more quickly, and that 'the welfare of the child is recognized as the overriding concern of all the professional agencies' involved in the investigation of abuse cases (Home Office 1988). While some of these recommendations appear to have led to positive changes in the field (e.g. an apparent increase in multi-agency arrangements), approaches taken to abuse cases in England and Wales do not always compare well with practice elsewhere in Europe, where alternatives to prosecution, for example, have been more widely explored and implemented (Cornwell and Arendsen 1991).

As already hinted in the latter remark, efforts to improve official responses to adult–child sex need not be limited *only* to procedural or other changes to 'humanize' the criminal justice system to accommodate child victims or witnesses (although such changes are clearly necessary). Ideally, forms of non-judicial intervention could also be designed which, although they would have final backing from the criminal courts if necessary, could in many cases bypass those processes which have proved so difficult to adapt to abuse cases. That alternatives of this kind have been developed in other jurisdictions (e.g. the Netherlands) suggests that humane and workable forms of official intervention are not out of reach.

Notes

1   The sort of position focused on here has been advanced by specific groups such as NAMBLA (the North American Man–Boy Love Association) in the United States, PIE (Paedophile Information Exchange) here in Great Britain prior to its demise in 1985, and also by a number of similar groups in Europe (see O'Carroll 1980 for a description of some of these groups and Smith 1986 for a history of PIE). Also in North America, Dunwoody (1982) and others have referred more generally to the activities of the 'pro incest lobby', a loose confederation of groups who wish to see legislative changes in sexual offence legislation. Among the individual writers adopting a 'libertarian' perspective are Edward Brongersma, Tom O'Carroll, Warren Middleton, and David Tsang. Age-of-consent laws have of course also been questioned by a variety of more 'mainstream' writers; see Walmsley and White (1979), for example, for some brief remarks on consent, conviction rates, and sexual offences more generally.

2   I will not focus on the specific details of libertarian proposals for the reform of age-of-consent laws in this country, but on the general arguments which libertarians have employed in defence of their claims for decriminalization of adult–child sex. If readers are interested in further details on the proposals themselves, more detailed discussion is offered in O'Carroll (1980), and in papers both in Middleton (1986), and in Tsang (ed., 1981); see especially North American Man–Boy Love Association (1981) in the latter work.

3   The latter examples are from the historical literature, but current practices such as clitoridectomy could also be mentioned in this context. Also concerning historical diversity in sexual practices, the recent debate sparked by the release of Kincaid's (1992) book *Child Loving – The Erotic Child and Victorian Culture* is worthy of mention in this context; for some representative responses see Barrie (1992), and Carey (1993).

4   This is because modernity involves the emergence of what Anthony Giddens calls an 'internally referential system of knowledge and power' which in turn marks the origin of the 'reflexive project of the self'. The way in which individual experience is organized in modern state societies becomes increasingly de-localized and mediated by abstract systems, and these changes have profound implications for the way in which experience of such things as sexuality, death, and criminality is related to everyday routines (Giddens 1984, 1991).

5   More recently, these issues have also come to the fore in legal deliberations concerning rape within marriage, and in media attention paid to the phenomenon of 'date rape'.

6   Although there are wide differences of opinion about what form these 'official' interventions should take; the most notable division here seems to be between those who recommend a criminal justice response, and those who argue for 'softer' forms of state intervention.

7   Presland (1986), for example, prefers that the term be dropped altogether

and he argues instead for a focus on 'awareness of significance', or the ability to 'put oneself in another's shoes'. As he puts it: 'Consent is something given by the powerless to the powerful in order to placate . . . Indeed, the concept of consent is at best misleading, and at worst, irrelevant' (Presland, 1986: 87).

8 O'Carroll expresses a similar view: 'Murder, and rape, and all non-consensual acts, can of course only be condemned in the strongest terms . . . [but] all *consensual* sexual activity is acceptable' (1980: 101; O'Carroll's emphasis).

9 See De Vine (1980), Glaser and Frosh (1993), Finkelhor (1979, 1984), or Nelson (1987), for some representative accounts of this sort.

10 Similar considerations of power have resulted in courts of law pronouncing that prisoners cannot give informed consent to experimental medical treatments.

11 Such an equation is also offered in Brongersma (1984).

12 Herdt's (1981) fascinating (and much referred to) account of sexual practices involving adult men and boys within Sambian society provides a useful illustration of how complex socio-cultural factors might impact on these judgements about consent, needs, and adult–child sexual activity.

13 In spite of figures suggesting that the child participants in the relevant incidents recalled them negatively in adulthood, the Landis study is referred to by Brongersma (1988) as supporting the claim that adult–child sex can be neutral in its effects on children.

14 Prevalence studies clearly suggest that girls are much more commonly involved in sexual incidents with adults, and even sexual encounters between adult males and boys tend to take place with known family members (fathers, stepfathers, uncles, etc.) rather than within paedophilic relationships. See Peters *et al.* (1986) for a comprehensive analysis of the prevalence research. The prevalence data also underline the fact that the overwhelming number of adult participants in sexual interactions with children are male, although this issue is not always referred to within libertarian work. I have assessed this data in Liddle (1993a), and offered a theoretical account of the 'male majority' in child sexual abuse in Liddle (1993b). It is also worth noting that libertarian arguments are offered almost exclusively by male writers (and, as Plummer (1981) has observed, the membership of paedophile groups is also almost entirely male).

15 It is also clear from the self-report data on adult–child sex that in a significant number of cases the incident in question never *was* officially reported by the child, and there could therefore not have been such a societal reaction to the incident. In many cases even memory of the incident becomes subject to later repression in adulthood, and the victim only becomes aware of it much later in life (e.g. during therapy). Of course, it is open to the libertarian to respond that harm in such cases could have resulted from the child's internalization of prevailing sex-negative attitudes, but this claim would be inconsistent both with the

libertarian position on the general benefits for children of having 'sexua outlets', and on the uncluttered descriptions of hydraulic 'childhoo sexual desire'.

References

Aires, Philip (1962). *Centuries of Childhood* (New York, Basic Books).

Augoustinos, Martha (1987). 'Developmental effects of child abuse: recen findings', *Child Abuse and Neglect*, 11 (1), 15–27.

Badgley, Robin F. (chair) (1984). *Report of the Committee on Sexual Offence. Against Children and Youths* (Ottawa, Canadian Government Publishin Centre).

Barrie, Edward (1992). 'Speak of the wolf – see his tail', *New Statesman an Society*, 21 August 1992, 22.

Baurmann, M. C. (1983). *Sexualität, Gewalt und Psychische Folger* (Wiesbaden, Bundeskriminalamt).

Bender, L., and Blau, A. (1937). 'The reaction of children to sexual relation: with adults', *American Journal of Orthopsychiatry*, 7, 500–18.

Bender, L., and Grugett, A. E. (1952). 'A follow-up report on children whe had atypical sex experiences', *American Journal of Orthopsychiatry*, 22 825–37.

Brongersma, Edward (1980). 'The meaning of "Indeceny" with respect tc moral offences involving children', *British Journal of Criminology*, 2((1):20–31.

Brongersma, Edward (1984). 'Are children fit for sex?', *NAMBLA Bulletin – Voice of the North American Man–Boy Love Association*, 5 (7), 11–12.

Brongersma, Edward (1988). 'A defence of sexual liberty for all age groups', *The Howard Journal*, 27 (1), 32–43.

Browne, Angela and Finkelhor, David (1986). 'Initial and long- term effects: A review of the research', in Finkelhor *et al.* (1986) 143–79.

Bullough, V. (1976). *Sexual Variance in Society and History* (New York, John Wiley & Sons).

Butler Sloss, Lord Justice (1988). *Report of the Inquiry into Child Abuse in Cleveland 1987* (London, HMSO).

Carey, John (1993). 'The Age of Innocents', *The Sunday Times*, 7 March 1993, 7.8–7.9

Conte and Berliner (1987). 'The impact of sexual abuse on children: clinical findings', in L. Walker (ed.) *Handbook on Sexual Abuse of Children: Assessment and Treatment Issues* (New York, Springer).

Cook, M. and Howells, K. (eds.) (1981). *Adult Sexual Interest in Children* (London, Academic Press).

Cornwell, G. and Arendsen, E. (1991). 'The Prosecution and Post-Conviction Disposal of Serious Child Sexual Abusers in England and Wales and the Netherlands: an International Comparison of Philosophies and Outcomes', Paper presented to the British Criminology Conference 24–27 July 1991.

De Francis, V. (1969). *Protecting the Child Victim of Sex Crimes Committed by Adults* (Denver, American Humane Society).

De Mause, L. (1974). *The History of Childhood* (New York, Harper & Row).

De Mause, L. (1975). 'Our forebears made childhood a nightmare', *Psychology Today*, 8 (April) 85–8.

De Vine, R. (1980). 'Developmental sexuality' in Barbara McComb Jones, Linda Jenstrom and Kee MacFarlane (eds.), *Sexual Abuse of Children: Selected Readings* (Washington, DC, National Centre on Child Abuse and Neglect, 1980), 3–8.

Dunwoody, Ellen (1982). 'Sexual abuse of children: a serious, widespread problem', *Response*, vol. 5, no. 4.

Finkelhor, David (1979). 'What's wrong with sex between adults and children? – ethics and the problem of sexual abuse', *American Journal of Orthopsychiatry*, 49 (4), October, 1692–7.

Finkelhor, David (1984). *Child Sexual Abuse: New Theory and Research* (New York, Free Press).

Finkelhor, David, and associates (1986). *A Sourcebook on Child Sexual Abuse* (London, Sage).

Ford, C. S. and Beach, F. A. (1952). *Patterns of Sexual Behaviour* (London, Methuen).

Giddens, Anthony (1984). *The Constitution of Society: Outline of the Theory of Structuration* (Cambridge, Polity Press).

Giddens, Anthony (1991). *Modernity and Self-Identity: Self and Society in the Late Modern Age* (Cambridge, Polity Press).

Glaser, Danya and Frosh, Stephen (1993). *Child Sexual Abuse,* 2nd edn. (Basingstoke, Macmillan).

Gough, Jamie (1981). 'Childhood sexuality and paedophilia' in Tsang (ed.), (1981) 65–71.

Herdt, G.H. (1981). *Guardians of the Flute: Idioms of Masculinity* (London, McGraw-Hill).

Home Office (1988). *The Investigation of Child Sexual Abuse*, Home Office Circular 52 (London, HMSO).

Howells, Kevin (ed.) (1984). *The Psychology of Sexual Diversity* (Oxford, Basil Blackwell).

Hyde, Naida (1984). 'Long-term effects of childhood sexual abuse', *British Columbia Medical Journal*, 26 (7), 448–9.

Kincaid, James R. (1992). *Child-Loving: The Erotic Child and Victorian Culture* (London, Routledge).

Landis, J. (1956). 'Experience of 500 children with adult sexual deviants', *Psychiatric Quarterly*, 30, 91–109.

Leaman, Karen (1980). 'Sexual abuse: the reactions of child and family', in Barbara McComb Jones, Linda Jenstrom, and Kee MacFarlane (eds.), *Sexual Abuse of Children: Selected Readings* (Washington DC, National Center on Child Abuse and Neglect) 21–4.

Liddle, A. Mark (1993a). 'Describing the Male Majority in Child Sexual Abuse: Some Comments on the Empirical Evidence, and a Review of

Explanatory Accounts' (Cambridge, Institute of Criminology, being prepared for separate publication).

Liddle, A. Mark (1993b). 'Gender, desire and child sexual abuse: accounting for the male majority', *Theory, Culture and Society*, 10 (4), 103–26.

Lusk, Rob, and Waterman, Jill (1986). 'Effects of sexual abuse on children', in Kee MacFarlane and Jill Waterman, *et al.*, *Sexual Abuse of Young Children: Evaluation and Treatment* (London, Holt, Rinehart and Winston) 101–18.

Marshall, Donald S. and Suggs, Robert C. (eds.) (1971). *Human Sexual Behaviour: Variations in the Ethnographic Spectrum* (Englewood Cliffs New Jersey, Prentice-Hall).

Middleton, Warren (ed.) (1986). *The Betrayal of Youth: Radical Perspectives on Childhood Sexuality, Intergenerational Sex, and the Social Oppression of Children and Young People* (London, CL Publications).

Middleton, Warren (1986). 'Childhood sexuality and paedophilia: some questions answered', in Middleton (ed.) (1986), 141–88.

Mrazek, P. B. and Mrazek, D. A. (1981). 'The effects of child sexual abuse methodological considerations', in P. B. Mrazek and C. H. Kempe (eds.) *Sexually Abused Children and their Families* (New York, Pergamon Press).

NACRO (1992). *Criminal Justice and the Prevention of Child Sexual Abuse* (London, National Association for the Care and Resettlement of Offenders).

Nelson, S. (1987). *Incest: Fact and Myth* (Edinburgh, Strathmullion).

North American Man–Boy Love Association (1981). 'The case for abolishing age of consent laws', in Tsang (ed.) (1981), 92–106.

O'Carroll, Tom (1980). *Pedophilia: The Radical Case* (London, Peter Owen).

Peters, J. J. (1973). 'Child rape: defusing a psychological time bomb', *Hospital Physician*, 9, 46–9.

Peters, Stephanie, Wyatt, Gail and Finkelhor, David (1986). 'Prevalence', in Finkelhor *et al.* (1986), 15–59.

Pigot (His Honour Judge) (1989). *Report of the Advisory Group on Video Evidence* (London, HMSO).

Plummer, Kenneth (1981). 'Paedophilia: constructing a sociological baseline' in Cook and Howells (eds.), (1981), 221–50.

Plummer, Kenneth (1984). 'Sexual diversity: a sociological perspective', in Howells (ed.) (1984), 219–53.

Presland, Eric (1981). 'Whose power? Whose consent?' in Tsang (ed., (1981), 72–9.

Presland, Eric (1986). 'Power and consent', in Middleton (ed.) (1986), 62–92.

Radbill, Samuel (1968). 'Children in a world of violence: a history of child abuse', in Henry Kempe and Ray Helfer (eds.), *The Battered Child* (Chicago, University of Chicago Press), 1980, 13–20.

Rist, Kate (1979). 'Incest: theoretical and clinical views', *American Journal of Orthopsychiatry*, 49, 680–91.

Rosenfeld, A. A., Nadelson, C. C., Krieger, M., and Backman, J. J. (1977).

'Incest and sexual abuse of children', *Journal of the American Academy of Child Psychiatry*, 16, 327–39.

Russell, D. (1986). *The Secret Trauma: Incest in the Lives of Girls and Young Women* (New York, Basic Books).

Sandfort, T. (1982). *The Sexual Aspect of Paedophile Relations* (Amsterdam, Pan/Spartacus).

Schultz, Leroy (1972). 'Psychotherapeutic and legal approaches to the sexually victimized child', *International Journal of Child Psychotherapy*, 1, 115–28.

Schultz, Leroy (1980). *The Sexual Victimology of Youth* (Springfield, Illinois, Charles C. Thomas).

Sheldrick, C. (1991). 'Adult sequelae of child sexual abuse', *British Journal of Psychiatry*, 158 (supplement 10), 55–62.

Smith, Steven A. (1986). 'PIE: from 1980 until its demise in 1985' in Middleton (ed.) (1986), 215–45.

Summit, Roland (1983). 'The child sexual abuse accommodation syndrome', *Child Abuse and Neglect*, 7, 177–93.

Summit, R. and Kryso, J. (1978). 'Sexual abuse of children: a clinical spectrum', *American Journal of Orthopsychiatry*, 48, 237–51.

Tatchell, Peter (1986). 'Questioning ages of majority and ages of consent' in Middleton (ed.) (1986), 117–19.

Tindall, R. H. (1978). 'The male adolescent involved with a pederast becomes an adult', *Journal of Homosexuality*, 3, 373–82.

Tsang, D. (ed.) (1981). *The Age Taboo: Gay Male Sexuality, Power and Consent* (London, Gay Men's Press).

Walmsley, R. and White K. (1979). *Sexual Offences, Consent and Sentencing*, Home Office Research Study No. 54 (London, HMSO).

West, D. J. (1980). 'A commentary', *British Journal of Criminology*, 32–4.

Westermeyer, J. (1978). 'Incest in psychiatric practice: a description of patients and incestuous relationships', *Journal of Clinical Psychiatry*, 39, 643–8.

Whitman, Grace (1982). 'Research links multi-personality disorders to child sexual abuse', *Response*, 5 (5), 3–4.

Yorukoglu, A., and Kemph, J. (1966). 'Children not severely damaged by incest with a parent' in Schultz (1980), 125–39.

16

Re-orienting *the criminal justice system:*
Towards a consideration of victims' rights

ROB MAWBY AND SANDRA WALKLATE

As Maguire and Shapland (1990) have observed, it appears that concern for the victims of crime is here to stay. Indeed, the last fifteen years have seen a remarkable rate of activity in the UK and elsewhere related to the crime victim. It is now commonplace to comment on the rapid growth and development of Victim Support as a marker of that activity. Moreover, the production of the Victim's Charter (1990) and the Citizen's Charter (1991) stands as recent testimony to the broadly based concern which the victim of crime has attracted.

Of course, the underlying motivations for these developments are mixed. What is clear is that focusing on the crime victim has offered both ideological and political support to a criminal justice system which has faced increasing difficulties in dealing with and responding to crime. Indeed, how the victim of crime responds to the criminal justice system has increasingly become the focus for evaluating the effectiveness and efficiency of that system as the crime victim has been recast as the 'consumer of the criminal justice system' (Jefferson, Sim and Walklate 1992). The question remains, however, as to how effective such developments have been in actually representing the interests of the crime victim *per se*.

It is the view of this chapter that there is certainly more that could be done in re-orienting the criminal justice system in the UK towards representing the interests of the crime victim. Looking to existing practices within the United States and continental Europe we shall offer practical suggestions for policy implementation which could succeed in the UK. These suggestions stem from a position which has as one of its starting-points a particular view on the relationship between victims' needs and victims' rights. It is to a summary of that relationship that we shall turn to first of all.

Victims' needs or victims' rights?

The needs/rights debate is emotive and fraught with difficulties in every area of policy implementation. This is also the case with the question of whether or not crime victims have needs or rights. Research has established that victims do have substantive needs (see for example, Shapland, Willmore and Duff 1985; Maguire 1985). These needs range from the need for information from the criminal justice system to the (variable) need for emotional support. Matching needs with service delivery is, however, neither an easy nor a straightforward process. What is clear is that an approach solely based on needs is likely to reproduce the individualized discretionary response of earlier charitable eras, rooted in distinctions between deserving and undeserving victims (see Mawby and Walklate 1994: Chapter three). Such an approach would result in a good many victims of crime not having their needs met and would potentially exclude or marginalize those victims who fail to match the stereotypical expectations of such a discretionary process. A rights-based approach may overcome some of these problems. However, there are also difficulties to be faced here.

There are a number of problems associated with the question of victims' rights. For example, the criminal justice system deals with defendants and complainants, not offenders and victims (McBarnett 1983). This structural relationship usefully reminds us that offenders also have rights, but additionally draws our attention to the inherent problems associated with the term 'victim' itself.

The term 'victim' (or complainant) is generic; it suggests a certain neutrality. The neutrality of the term is, of course, not without its uses. It has certainly served the interests of Victim Support without diminishing the potential emotional and political impact that the victim imagery might effect (Bottoms 1983, Walklate 1993). This implied neutrality, however, served to gloss over who the victims of crime are. Feminist research in particular has shown that when the concept of crime is broadened from crime of the streets to crime behind closed doors, then women, children, and the elderly are a significant if not predominant dimension of criminal victimization. In other words crime victims comprise individuals who share a certain socio-structural location. They are individuals who, in reality, constitute collectivities which certainly do not represent a neutral standpoint when it comes to the political or policy process.

From this point of view, then, it can be argued that it makes more sense for a policy position focusing on crime victims to be constructed on the basis of a claim to rights emanating from structural inequalities rather than the experience of criminal victimization. In developing such a position, as Smart (1989) has cogently argued in respect of a feminist rights-based approach rooted in the law, there are difficulties. Such rights can be used to serve the interests of those for whom they were not intended. On occasion this has resulted in the strengthening of the position of men, in respect of parental rights in relation to the unborn child, for example. It is important therefore not to separate the question of legal rights from the questions associated with social citizenship. It is by combining these issues that a position on the question of victims' right can be constructed. It is such a position which we offer for consideration.

Mawby (1988: 133) argues for a justice-based approach to the question of victims' rights in which 'the state is obliged to acknowledge the rights of citizens with regard to welfare'. He goes on to suggest that three principles flow from this position for the victim of crime: that victims have rights irrespective of need; that such rights should be substantive; and that in constructing such rights attention should be paid to public opinion. It is perhaps worth clarifying a number of issues associated with this view.

First of all, it is important not to assume that all victims possess the same personal or collective power to claim such rights. As stated earlier, recognition of who the victims of crime are and who, in particular, are the *vulnerable* victims of crime, involves recognizing the power relationships structured around sexism, ageism, and racism. Therefore, for example, children as victims of crime and individuals as victims of corporate crime also require claimable rights if such a principle as that suggested by Mawby is to be translatable into a notion of justice.

Second, the incorporation of public opinion into the policy-making process may be considered problematic. It raises the question of which 'publics', whose views, and how to consult. Again, the structural powerlessness of certain groups could render this problematic. There are, however, ways of engaging in such a consultation process which can overcome these problems; in the case of women by ensuring that the full range of venues in which women operate were contacted (from pre-school playgroups to women's refuges). Moreover, public opinion may not be such a variable phenomenon as is often supposed: it clearly depends on the issue for which opinion is being canvassed. For example, there is evidence of some consensus and constancy with respect to public opinion on service delivery (on the National Health Service) despite major policy changes in this area. The constancy of those views, despite attempted political manipulation, suggests that in areas where the policy agenda is seen to be crucial then public opinion might well be reasonably incorporated into the debate regarding the provision of rights. The extent to which the issue of victims' rights has reached this point is, of course, open to debate.

So whilst there are a number of difficulties and dangers in translating a rights stance into policy provision, it is the view of these authors that this certainly represents a more meaningful starting-point from which to advance a range of more particularistic concerns. In practical terms, if we accept victims' perceived needs as a basis for service provision, then following Wilson (1977) we might argue that victims' rights should be practicable (i.e. we should be able to guarantee them); they should be of paramount importance (i.e. deprivation of them should be accepted as a grave affront to justice); and they should be universal (i.e. possessed by everyone). Such a position is clearly predicated on particular assumptions concerning the notions of citizen and state which have been developed more fully elsewhere (see Mawby and Walklate 1994).

This returns us to the current British context of the Citizen's Charter and the Victim's Charter. The position adopted here agrees with the view that the Victims' Charter will 'continue to cast the victim in a subservient role, as the recipient of service' (Miers 1991) unless a critical examination of the policy possibilities of representing the interests of the crime victim are more fully and seriously explored. And whilst individual organizations may or may not have responded more or less positively to the increasing presence of the 'charter culture', such processes do not, in and of themselves, guarantee an understanding of who the victims of crime are and how that understanding clearly connects with the issue of structural powerlessness. A rights-based approach might make some inroads into these issues.

Earlier Mawby and Gill (1987) argued that there were at least four areas in which victims' rights required strengthening: the right to play an active part in the criminal justice system; the right to knowledge; the right to financial help; and the right to advice and support. Here we shall reconsider these four areas in the light of policy changes over recent years, paying particular attention to the role of the police, the courts and support services in these areas and assessing the extent to which a rights-based approach might be considered progressive.

The right to play an active role in the criminal justice system

The fundamental question in this context is whether or not victims experience the criminal justice system as a form of secondary victimization which further distresses or disillusions them. It is clearly the case that women and children as 'victims' of various kinds of violence have certainly experienced it in this way; but so too do many more 'ordinary' victims of crime when their needs are not being met. This reminds us that policy here should not only address questions of principle but should also be concerned to deliver a quality service.

Of course, the right to play an active role in the criminal justice system has been epitomized in the extreme by US initiatives towards mandatory victim impact statements (VIS). Whilst the current British government appears to have toyed with the idea of similar developments it is unlikely that any new initiatives of this kind will emerge, nor would we welcome any. If VIS influence sentences then a further inequity is introduced to the system; that is, where the likely impact on the victim was unknown to the offender prior to the offence and the different experiences and attitudes of crime victims lead to different sentences. If VIS do not influence sentences, then asking victims' opinions and not acting on them increases victims' feelings of frustration and injustice. There are, however, other ways in which victim involvement can be facilitated; in their relationship with the police, by reconsidering their formal role in the court, and through their involvement in mediation or reparation schemes. We shall consider each of these in turn.

Concerns to improve the ways in which the police respond to crime victims have been expressed in a number of international and national policy documents. Among the first of these were the Council of Europe recommendations adopted by the Committee of Ministers, and whilst less explicit the United Nations resolution also recommends that the police and other relevant agencies 'should receive training to sensitize them to the needs of victims, and guidelines to ensure proper and prompt aid' (Joutsen 1987: 325–6, 297). Similarly the International Association of Chiefs of Police

(ACP) advises forces to provide information on social and financial services for victims on the progress of their case (Waller 1990: 39–40).

Within this broad international context there has been an interesting twist to the developments with respect to policing in this area in England and Wales. Since the 1980s, police forces in England and Wales have endeavoured to respond more positively to women who report incidents of rape or sexual assault to them and latterly have attempted also to improve their service response to women experiencing violence from their partners. This emphasis on quality of service was foregrounded in the Victim's Charter. Part III of the Victim's Charter on 'Standards for the Criminal Justice Services' includes a checklist by which one might evaluate the treatment victims receive. Regarding the police this includes: whether or not victims feel empathetically treated; whether and how follow-up visits are arranged; whether victims are given an information leaflet; how victim details are recorded; what information is fed back to victims on the case proceedings; whether or not the victim is given a contact name at the police station; and whether police decisions on the case are fed back and explained to the victim. Some of these issues overlap with the question of the right to information which will be dealt with below; but they are also issues which have been given an added impetus from central government.

Following government concern to improve the effectiveness and efficiency of the police and to monitor and evaluate police performance more rigorously (Home Office 1983; Horton 1989) a number of central government bodies have recommended the expansion of police performance indicators to include perceptions of police response (Audit Commission 1990). It would thus become the responsibility of the police to monitor victims' reactions, perhaps through interviewing samples of complainants about the service they received. Some forces are moving in this direction with the establishment of Quality of Service Units (Bunt and Mawby 1993). This is a welcome move, though we note that the police should seek the views of victims in general (including the more contentious areas of 'domestic' violence and not merely the relatively safe cases of burglary) and the results of such surveys and any practice changes should be made available to the public. These developments certainly provide an obvious mechanism for victims to play an active role in the criminal justice system, and the formation of local policy, which might prove to be more effective than simply relying on police training and the dissemination of 'good practice', both of which have been shown to be ineffective elsewhere.

A second way of securing the involvement of victims in the criminal justice system is by examining their formal role in the court process. A number of countries, for example, identify circumstances in which the onus of prosecution falls on the victim or may identify a role for the victim as joint or subsidiary prosecutor. Of more significance, however, is those countries where the legal system is based on Roman law and provides the possibility of the victim's acting as a civil claimant in the criminal courts: the *partie civile*.

Since Schafer's (1960) early account of the *partie civile* or adhesion process, a number of victimologists have looked to Europe as providing a 'better deal' for victims. However, as many European commentators have more recently acknowledged, the system, while promising much in abstract, in practice appears of little benefit to victims. This is partly due to cost, both in monetary and time and effort terms, and partly because, as with other forms of compensation from the offender, its success depends on the offender's being able to pay. In this context, d'Hautville and Bertrand (1989) note that in France, since the victim and not the government is responsible for collecting the award from the offender, in most cases it remains unpaid. The same authors also point out that less than a third of victims actually appear in court, and most of these are required to attend as witnesses. Active participation by the victim is not therefore very great!

Evidence indicates that in Europe, at least, the move has been towards enhancing access to the right to compensation as a way of improving the formal status of the victim in the court decision making process. In recent years in the UK the use of compensation to the victim has also been enhanced and strengthened. The 1988 Criminal Justice Act made it a requirement that any losses suffered by the victim should be brought to the attention of the court, and required courts to justify not giving compensation, though it is a process which still appears to be highly dependent on the quality of the information received by the court and the victim. Nevertheless, there is some evidence from official sources which suggests that improvements are occuring. Figures for 1989 (Home Office 1991) show an increase in the use of orders, especially for offences of violence.

The likelihood of the impact of the crime being formally recognized and the victim receiving compensation in this way is, of course, dependent on the offender appearing before the court. This consequently excludes the victim from being considered in an increasingly significant area of criminal justice activity – the caution. The use of cautioning of both adult and juvenile offenders has increased in recent years. We are concerned that many victims are effectively becoming 'disenfranchised' where a decision to caution is taken, since this eliminates the possibility of their claiming compensation in the court. We recommend that, where appropriate, compensation be made a condition of caution. This brings us to the possibility for out-of-court settlements using mediation and reparation.

Compensation can be made to victims by offenders in ways other than the financial. Repairing the 'harm done' covers a much broader range of possibilities for policy development. Whilst many European countries operate a sentence similar to community service as a way of 'paying back' the community, historically Britain and North America have been distinctly different in making compensation part of the criminal sanction and in developing reparation initiatives using the principle of mediation.

The Victim/Offender Reconciliation Programme (VORP) in Ontario 1974 is commonly acknowledged as the forerunner to such initiatives (Peachey 1989). By the mid-1980s the VORP model had been applied across a wide variety of areas in both Canada and the US. In the UK, early discussions were provoked by Chinkin and Griffiths (1980) following visits to a number of North American schemes, and gathered momentum in the early 1980s, notably through the writings of Wright (1981) and Harding (1982). In 1984, FIRM, the Forum for Initiatives in Reparation and Mediation (later renamed Mediation UK), was founded and given government support (Rock 1990). Consequently, major changes might have been anticipated. The government funded projects in Cumbria, Leeds, Wolverhampton and Coventry which were extensively evaluated (Marshall and Merry 1990).

However, by the late 1980s it had become apparent that the government's priorities were shifting towards backing for victim support rather than reparation, and the Home Office White Paper on the Criminal Justice System and subsequent Act of Parliament offered little future for mediation and reparation. In contrast, however, we would recommend the extension of such initiatives and would wish to see Mediation UK develop with government backing. The possibility of mediation not only provides the victim with a means of becoming involved in the process (should they wish to) but also allows for more constructive solutions than are available in the courts. It may also be of value to explore projects where known offenders (rather than sentenced offenders) meet with victims of their offence. Such projects would be more oriented to the needs of the victim rather than the needs of the offender, and there is some evidence that some victims benefit from such meetings. Who, and under what circumstances, however, is also likely to be informed by the structural variables commented on above, which suggest that gender and age need to be taken into account in formulating such responses.

All such active participation in the criminal justice system is to a large degree dependent not only upon victims wanting to participate, but also on their having knowledge of services and procedures. It is to improvements in these areas that we now turn.

The right to information

Lack of available information has been a consistent complaint made of the criminal justice system both by victims of crime and by researchers in the area alike, though it is on this issue perhaps that most changes have occurred in recent years. Thus the police are now more likely to provide victims with information on available services and to feed back progress (or otherwise) on their case. Indeed, the provision of information in terms of the range and variety of leaflets available in police stations for victims of different crimes has certainly increased. This has clearly been the case in formulating response to 'domestic violence' for example. In addition, the growth and development of Victim Support, in and of itself, has had an impact on levels of awareness amongst victims in general and with respect to criminal injuries compensation claims in particular.

On the other hand, the introduction of the Crown Prosecution Service in England and Wales has created a void resulting in no single agency's accepting responsibility for providing information on cases going to court. Moreover, whilst providing information may be seen as good practice (as represented in the Victim's Charter), no sanctions are attached to failure to provide such information. We would therefore recommend that police forces be required to:

1. provide all victims with written details of services available in their area, including state compensation;
2. send all complainants a letter after six weeks outlining progress on the case, and a further letter should there be any subsequent developments.
3. inform all victims where they intend to issue a caution to an offender rather than prosecute; and
4. not caution any offender unconditionally where to do so would inhibit the victims' right to compensation.

We would further recommend that where cases are proceeding to court the CPS be required to:

1. inform all victims, irrespective of their being required as court witnesses, of court dates;
2. provide all victims with details of their rights to claim compensation from the offender.

In addition, as practice has shown, considerable work still needs to be done in the context of the CPS's role in relation to decisions to prosecute which particularly pertain to women pursuing criminal charges against violent partners. Greater awareness of the nature and impact of violence in a relationship, alongside greater awareness of the legal options available, would significantly improve women's experiences of the criminal justice system, might encourage their greater participation, and would certainly contribute to their right and access to information.

Such proposals are scarcely original and echo the spirit of the Victim's Charter. However, given the difficulty of monitoring discretion and ensuring consistency, and mindful of the Dutch experience, we would make them the subject of a 'victims' charter' given to all victims when they report their crime, specifying their right to claim compensation should the terms of the charter not be met. Such a charter would indeed be quite consistent with the government's current stance on citizens' rights to redress where public services prove inefficient or ineffective.

The right to financial help

Whereas compensation from the offender is dependent upon the identification of an offender with the ability to pay compensation, state compensation, where compensation is paid to the victim by the state, appears preferable from the viewpoint of the victim of crime. It also provides one way in which governments can get their message across that they are concerned to help victims, and since 1960 this has been espoused in a variety of countries. In this respect though, the system in England and Wales is often considered to be a 'trail blazer' (Waller 1988) in the establishment of the Criminal Injustice Compensation Board in 1964.

The core principles of the CICB work on the notion that the state should make an award in recognition of the damage done, but victims have no right to compensation; it enshrines the notion of the 'innocent' victim; compensation is restricted to physical or psychological harm as a result of offences of violence; and, whilst there is no limit to the maximum award, there has always been a minimum level set. This minimum level was set at £1,000 in 1991. (It is important to note that the decision to raise the minimum standard is an administrative one, taken by the government in consultation with the Board, and is not made subject to a parliamentary debate.) It is also important to recognize that the amount of compensation awarded is in relation to the impact of the offence, not the financial circumstances of the victim. However, because for social security purposes payment by the Board is counted as additional income rather than compensation for a loss suffered, those victims who are dependent upon state benefits may actually get their benefits cut by the amount of the reward.

A wider issue of access concerns the way in which the Board is structured to make it more or less 'consumer-friendly'. Criticism of the CICB as a bureaucratic monster led the Home Affairs Committee (1990) to carry out its 1989 review, which resulted in a highly critical report. Pointing to poor management practices, the report noted that increasing numbers of applications had resulted in a log-jam; in 1988–9 there were 43,385 applications, but 38,830 resolved cases with 82,520 applications outstanding; a majority (73%) of cases had taken over a year from the time of the application to be submitted to a Single Member, much less resolved (Home Affairs Committee 1990: v 21). Additional staff helped the CICB to deal with more claims than it received in 1990–91, though 75 per cent of cases took over twelve months to resolve, and where an applicant appealed two-thirds of appellants waited over a year before an oral hearing was arranged (Home Office 1991b: 4–7). While interim payments may be made, for most it appears that application to the CICB results at best in an award some considerable time after the event, and at worst rejection.

This overview of the operation of state compensation is clearly suggestive of areas for policy activity. First, victims' ability to claim compensation has been drastically reduced as the government has raised the minimum award. Yet much crime is an irritant rather than a disaster and impacts differentially on the poor, under-insured or non-insured individual (Mawby and Walklate 1993, Chapter 2). To deny victims compensation in such cases is unjust. We would therefore reduce the minimum award to £200.

Second, state compensation only covers crimes of violence. There are no good grounds, other than cost, why other offences should not be incorporated. The cost burden would however be considerable, even if it were only extended to traffic crimes, as in many states in the US. We would therefore reiterate the earlier recommendations of Mawby and Gill (1987: 231) that a comprehensive state insurance scheme be formed to provide adequate coverage for all crime victims.

Third, it is clearly unfair that state compensation is counted, for social security purposes, as income. We would change the rules to ensure that victims received compensation proportional to the harm done, not relative to income support. Finally, mindful of the backlog of cases and the inefficiency of a centralized system, and in the light of the French (and US) experience, we would decentralize the system and operate state compensation within police boundaries.

Finally, it is clear that the nature of the claims handled by the CICB has changed since its original inception. In its early days there was a common presumption that the CICB functioned primarily to meet the needs of police officers injured in the course of duty. Public awareness of the more general availability of the CICB has clearly changed since then. Indeed, the kinds of cases in which compensation is awarded have broadened. For example, Morgan and Zedner (1992) report that there has been a significant increase in the number of applications made on behalf of abused children towards the end of the 1980s. There is, however, still contention around the kinds of awards made and the question of eligibility, given the board's continued brief to identify the deserving.

The right to advice and support

Broadly, this need falls within three time-periods; the immediate response received by the victim, the kind of early support offered and support at court. It has already been noted that there is a key role for the police, as stated in the Victim's Charter, in setting the tone for the way in which victims subsequently deal with their experience. The increasing emphasis on involving victims in the evaluation of police performance will undoubtedly serve to remind police forces that they have a duty to serve victims, not merely to detect crime.

Early support is also dependent on efficient policing, in that it requires that cases are passed on by the police (or otherwise collated by other agencies) promptly and effectively. The nature of the early support offered can, however, vary considerably. Essentially we might identify four broad areas within which to describe the key features of support services. First is the organizational structure of the agency; second is its location *vis-à-vis* other organizations, that is its relationship with other agencies; third is the nature of the services provided; fourth is the nature of the victim population targeted, or prioritized, by the organization. What is self-evident is that much of this kind of support comes from volunteers.

The implications of this are wide. For example, in most cases funding is on a short-term basis and may be withdrawn with a change of political climate, or it may be provided for a limited period on the expectation that the agency becomes self-financing in the long term. Voluntary bodies may therefore spend considerable time fund-raising rather than providing services. Equally important, the dependence on volunteers means that services may be competing with rival agencies to recruit from a far-from-bottomless pit, and lack of availability of volunteers may restrict the provision of services in some areas (Gill and Mawby 1990).

As has been clearly documented elsewhere, Victim Support came to be seen as the support agency in the UK during the 1980s (Rock 1990; Mawby and Walklate 1994). The rapid expansion of this organization has also seen an extension of its brief in the process. This now includes involvement with families of murder victims, rape, victim/witnesses, etc. The extension of Victim Support in this way has led to other agencies suffering in some areas – particularly support agencies emanating from the feminist movement. Given the specific expertise offered by the different emphases within both types of organization we would recommend the establishment of an umbrella group, rather like NOVA in the United States, whose role would be to represent and sustain the diversity of groups whose focus falls within the remit of criminal victimization. Such a development might provide one way in which different and competing voices debate the questions of policy and practice with needs of different victim groups in mind and with a view to ensuring that those needs are met as of right.

As was stated earlier, reliance on voluntary organizations and volunteers for advice and support poses its own practical and financial difficulties, and Victim Support has clearly and continuously faced these difficulties despite its receipt of funding from central government. Such constraints act as significant delimiters of the service that Victim Support can offer. Whilst Victim Support in the UK is inevitably going to remain a voluntary organization, we would see it shifting its form of organizational provision (Gill and Mawby 1990) from a reliance on volunteers to an increased reliance on paid workers (co-ordinators, deputies and aides). It seems incontestable that if Victim Support nationally is going to meet the needs of an increasing number of crime victims it cannot do so by relying on volunteers to the same extent. Volunteers may be sufficient in many rural areas, but in other areas greater flexibility is required to equate provision with need. Only then can victims' rights to help and support be fully addressed.

But of course Victim Support is not the only answer to service provision, and as we have argued elsewhere (Mawby and Walklate 1994) there is a need for additional funds for other agencies to provide different types of service or services for specific categories of victim. It is patently unfair that those initiatives designed to support women, in particular, should struggle in a hand-to-mouth existence, often in competition for scarce local resources with many other kinds of local voluntary groups. The need for many more refuges, for example, has long been established. Yet government funding appears to play one agency off against another. To fund Victim Support and not its more radical cousins is clearly unjust.

There is one further area in relation to offering advice and support where there is room for further development; that is in relation to court services. In this context it is clear that US provisions are a model for the level of services required in the UK. US provision for supporting witnesses in court developed in the 1970s, partly as a means of securing support for an ailing criminal justice system by encouraging people to appear as witnesses. The provision subsequently became tied to the provision of Victim Impact Statements and, as Roberts (1990) reports, there is now almost complete coverage of support services for victim/witnesses, with 90 per cent of projects being funded at federal level. Recognition of the needs of victim/witnesses developed much later in the UK.

Whilst feminist work had long commented on the particular experiences of women as rape 'victims' in the court room, it took a working party of Victim Support chaired by Lady Ralphs (1988) to recognize the more generic difficulties faced by those called to give evidence in the criminal courts. The report from that working group made a number of recommendations, and, following on from it and the fact that at grass-roots level *ad hoc* court-based initiatives were emerging, Victim Support secured funding for and established seven projects offering support in crown courts to prosecution witnesses. These projects were evaluated by Raine and Smith (1991), and some central funding was secured for the continuation and expansion of such services. There is a certain illogicality to the current situation. Either victim/witnesses need help in all crown courts and possibly all magistrates' courts, or they do not. Either all witnesses (as opposed to prosecution witnesses) need the opportunity to gain advice and support, or they do not. In addition the victim-support-based model creates difficulties in respect of relations with schemes outside the court and with professional actors inside the court system. Some clarification of areas of responsibility is required. We would therefore recommend that the prosecution service and the court bodies themselves take responsibility for provision in this area in two ways:

1. by providing details of case progress and giving relevant information to help witnesses attend court with the minimum of inconvenience to all witnesses; and
2. by providing facilities and services to be made available separately to prosecution and defence witnesses to allow justice to be felt to be done.

In each case, support services might be provided through liaison with Victim Support, who should be funded appropriately to deliver such support. Whilst there is some provision along these lines in the 1994 Criminal Justice and Public Order Bill, we feel that these should be statutory responsibilities and a feature of public-sector provision.

The suggestions for policy development outlined above in some instances address the gaps in existing provision and in others tighten that provision. However, it is also necessary to ensure that the victim's experience of the criminal justice system is seen as a whole and that agencies within that system are encouraged to co-ordinate and develop their policies in concert with one another. In this respect we recommend the establishment of Criminal Justice Forums. These would include in their membership all those who have a responsibility for and an ability to respond to the victim of crime: the police, the magistracy, the CPS, the judiciary and voluntary organizations of all kinds. Such forums would have the specific remit to ensure the prioritization of quality of service delivery in an accountable framework, and consequently might offer some real prospect of change in relation to how victims experience the criminal justice process.

Conclusion

The proposals for reform we have listed above cover three main areas. First, some are based on a change in the organizational structure through which victim services are provided. Second, others are related to the specification of services to which victims are entitled and, most importantly, identification of redress where services prove inadequate. The third area of reform, however, quite clearly posits an expansion of state provision: by the police, the crown prosecution service, and the voluntary sector – all of which carry financial implications.

It will obviously be argued that increases in expenditure are unwarranted, or at least impossible in the current economic climate. On the contrary, we would argue that the recognition of the victim as citizen requires that the cost of crime be borne by the community, not by crime victims who are frequently among the most disadvantaged in the community. To put it bluntly, *crime costs*, both in a personal and a financial sense. At the moment too much of that cost is borne by the victim of crime. In a just system it is appropriate for the state, through its citizens, to take over that burden.

References

Audit Commission (1990). *Effective Policing – performance review in police forces* (Police Papers) (London, HMSO).

Bottoms, A. F. (1983). 'Neglected features of the contemporary penal system', in D. Garland and P. Young (eds.), *The Power to Punish* (London, Heinemann) 166–202.

Chinkin, C. and Griffiths, R. (1980). 'Resolving conflict by mediation', *New Law Journal*, 130, 6–8.

d'Hautville, A. and Bertrand, B. (1989). 'A better position for victims of crime – legislation and guidelines', in First European Conference of Victim Support Workers, Utrecht, The Netherlands (VLOS) 64–9.

Dijk, J. J. M. van (1985). 'Research and the Victim Movement in Europe', in *European Committee on Crime Problems, Research on Crime Victims* (Strasburg: Council of Europe), 143–64.

Dijk, J. J. M. van (1988). 'Ideological trends within the victims movement: an international perspective', in M. Maguire and J. Pointing (eds.), *Victims of Crime: A New Deal?* (Milton Keynes, Open University Press), 115–26.

Gill, M. L. and Mawby, R. I. (1990). *Volunteers in the Criminal Justice System* (Milton Keynes, Open University Press).

Harding, J. (1982). 'Victims and offenders', NVCO *Occasional Paper Two* (London, NVCO).

Home Affairs Committee (1990). *Compensating Victims Quickly: the Administration of the Criminal Injuries Compensation Board* (London, HMSO).

Home Office (1983). *Manpower, Effectiveness and Efficiency in the Police Service*, HO Circular 114 (London, HMSO).

Home Office (1991a). *Crime and Justice in England and Wales* (London, HMSO).

Home Office (1991b). *Criminal Injuries Compensation Board 27th Report* (London, HMSO).

Horton, C. (1989). 'Good practice and evaluating policing', in R. Morgan and D. J. Smith (eds.), *Coming to Terms with Policing* (London, Routledge), 31–48.

Jefferson, T., Sim, J., and Walklate S. (1992). 'Europe, the Left and criminology in the 1990s: accountability, control and the social construction of the consumer', in D. Farrington and S. Walklate (eds.), *Offenders and Victims: Theory and Policy* (British Society for Criminology, ISTD).

Joutsen, M. (1987). *The Role of the Victim of Crime in European Criminal Justice Systems* (Helsinki, Finland, HEUNI).

Joutsen, M. and Shapland, J. (1989). *Changing Victim Policy: The United Nations Declaration and Recent Developments in Europe* (Helsinki, Finland, HEUNI).

Lurigio, A. J., Skogan, W. G., and Davis, R. C. (eds.) (1990). *Victims of Crime: Problems, Policies and Programs* (Newbury Park, CA, Sage).

Maguire, M. (1985). 'Victims' needs and victims' services', *Victimology*, vol. 10, 539–59.

Maguire, M. and Pointing, J. (1988). *Victims of Crime: A New Deal?* (Milton Keynes, Open University Press).

Maguire, M. and Shapland, J. (1990). 'The "Victims Movement" in Europe', in A. J. Lurigio, W. G. Skogan and R. C. Davis (eds.), *Victims of Crime: Problems, Policies and Programs* (Newbury Park, CA, Sage).

Marshall, T. and Merry, S. (1990). *Crime and Accountability: Victim/Offender Mediation and Practice* (London, HMSO).

Mawby, R. I. (1988). 'Victims' needs or victims' rights: alternative approaches to policy making', in M. Maguire and J. Pointing (eds.), *Victims of Crime: A New Deal?* (Milton Keynes, Open University Press), 127–37.

Mawby, R. I. and Gil, M. (1987). *Crime Victims: Needs, Services and the Voluntary Sector* (London, Tavistock).

Mawby, R. I. and Walklate, S. (1994). *Critical Victimology: The Victim in International Perspective* (London, Sage).

McBarnett, D. (1983). 'Victim in the witness box – confronting victimology's stereotype', *Contemporary Crises*, 7, 279–303.

Miers, D. (1991). 'The responsibilities and rights of victims of crime', paper to the British Criminology Conference, York.

Peachy, D. E. (1989). 'The Kitchener experiment', in M. Wright and B. Galaway (eds.), *Mediation and Criminal Justice* (London, Sage), 14–26.

Raine, J. W. and Smith, R. E. (1991). *The Victim/Witness in Court Project: Report of the Research Programme* (London, Victim Support).

Ralphs, Lady (1988). *The Victim In Court: Report of the Working Party* (London, Victim Support).

Rock, P. (1990). *Helping Victims of Crime* (Oxford, Clarendon).

Schafer, S. (1960). *Restitution to Victims of Crime* (London, Stevens and Son).

Shapland, J., Willmore, J., and Duff, P. (1985). *Victims in the Criminal Justice System* (Aldershot, Gower).

Smart, C. (1989). *Feminism and the Power of Law* (London, Routledge).

Walklate, S. (1993). 'Responding to women as consumers of a police service' in J. Vigh (ed.), *Police Crimes and Social Change* (Budapest, Eötvös Lorand University Press).

Waller, I. (1988). 'International standards, national trail blazing and the next steps', in M. Maguire and J. Pointing (eds.) (1988), 195–203.

Waller, I. (1990). 'The police: first aid', in Lurigio, Skogan and Davis (eds.) (1990) 139–56.

Wilson, E. (1977). *Women and the Welfare State* (London, Tavistock).

Wright, M. (1981). 'Crime and reparation: breaking the legal logjam', *New Society*, 10 December.

17

Evaluating criminal justice programmes for violent men

RUSSELL P. DOBASH, R. EMERSON DOBASH,
KATE CAVANAGH AND RUTH LEWIS

In the past two decades domestic violence has been the focus of a number of criminal justice innovations. In this paper we describe the methods employed in a unique British evaluation of two innovative programmes in the context of previous evaluations of the criminal justice response to domestic violence. We analyse the problems confronting attempts to evaluate criminal justice interventions in this area and describe how the research design adopted in this study was intended to extend and improve upon existing approaches. The design and content of the current evaluation are considered in detail and the completed research is described.

The research described in this paper involved a comparative evaluation of two programmes for men who had been convicted of a violent offence against their female partner. CHANGE and the Lothian Domestic Violence Probation Project (LDVPP) are modelled on American programmes for violent men, particularly the Domestic Abuse Intervention Project (DAIP) created in Duluth, Minnesota in 1980 (Pence and Paymar 1993). CHANGE, the first British criminal justice community-based programme for abusers, was established in Stirling, Scotland in 1989. It is an independent programme funded through the Urban Programme which operates an intensive three-month group programme for men who are placed on probation by the Scottish courts. The LDVPP, established in 1990, is located within a statutory, local authority, social work department which carries out work with all offenders placed on probation. Unlike CHANGE, the LDVPP does not carry out community-wide programmes of education and training, the commitment is to an intensive group programme. Both projects describe themselves as broadly 'pro-feminist', conceptualizing the violence of men as methods of power and control. Psycho-dynamic work is rejected; cognitive–behavioural methods, re-education and a focus on the offending behaviour are stressed in group work.

Background to the Present Evaluation

Criminal justice innovations in Great Britain have included: enhanced police awareness of domestic violence through improved training; strengthening of civil injunctions (interdicts in Scotland) through the addition of the powers of exclusion and arrest; improved support for the victims of violence in the home, sometimes through the creation of specialized Domestic Violence or Women and Children units in the police, and in a few locations an increasing emphasis on arrest and a greater commitment to prosecution (Dobash and Dobash 1992). Developments of this nature have occurred elsewhere, particularly in Canada, the United States, Australia and New Zealand, where there has been a growing awareness of the need to improve criminal justice response by supporting the victim and arresting the offender. In some jurisdictions in the United States a strong pro- or mandatory arrest policy has been introduced, whereby the police are required to arrest under the presumption of 'probable cause' in situations where secondary evidence indicates an assault has occurred. In Canada and the United States these innovations are often linked to programmes dedicated to altering the behaviours and beliefs of the men who perpetrate this violence. Ostensibly, innovations such as these have altered criminal justice practices, brought greater protection to victims and their children and deterred offenders from perpetrating subsequent abuse.

Research evaluations of arrest and injunctions

In North America, researchers have attempted to assess the impact of improved training, civil injunctions, arrest, prosecution and programmes for violent men (Fagan and Browne 1994). In the United States, the National Institute of Justice sponsored a series of interconnected studies on the impact of arrest. In the early 1980s Sherman and Berk, using an experimental field model, compared the impact of arrest to other means of dealing with domestic violence. Police officers using a system of random assignment when responding to an incident of domestic violence allocated cases to three types of disposition: arrest, offering advice and asking either the man or women to leave the household (Sherman and Berk 1984; Sherman 1992). Police officers were not allowed to use their judgement or discretion; the specific reaction was dictated by random processes. The results of this study offered strong support for the assumption that, all things being equal, arrest of a man who was violent toward his partner was more likely to reduce subsequent violence than other responses. Using interviews with victims and official arrest records in a subsequent six-month period of follow-up, the researchers found that arrest reduced violence by 50 per cent compared to non-arrest. Sherman and Berk (1984) argued that men who were arrested for incidents of domestic violence were deterred from committing subsequent acts of violence because of the fear of re-arrest. They implied that fear of arrest was a significant means of protecting women from future assault.

Once completed, the Minneapolis study provoked a rash of interest, receiving national prominence when its pro-arrest strategy was endorsed by the Attorney General's Task Force on Family Violence. According to one of the researchers who conducted the study, the research resulted in the introduction of a pro-arrest strategy in several police jurisdictions in the United States (Sherman 1992). Claims such as these ignored the efforts of women's organizations who had successfully lobbied for improved police reactions, including pro-arrest strategies, in several states and cities long before the results of the Minneapolis experiment were known (see Dobash and Dobash 1992).

The research community responded with scepticism to the claims of the Minnesota arrest study. The effectiveness of specific and general deterrence on crime was not widely accepted and many observers, including the researchers themselves, identified numerous flaws in the initial research. A range of problems were identified: the 'experiment' excluded other than simple assaults – 'cases of life-threatening or severe injury, usually labelled as a felony' were excluded from the design; the specific effects of arrest were not actually assessed because all arrested men were also detained – therefore the experiment investigated the impact of arrest *and* detention; offenders who left the scene were excluded; the randomized design was compromised by the discretion of police officers in the field; and a handful of critics voiced concern about the ethical problems associated with the failure to obtain informed consent from those who participated in the randomized procedures and the denial of potential services to women at risk (Fagan 1992; Dobash 1993 on ethical issues).

Apparently ignoring the potential ethical issues involved in such research and in an attempt to overcome the technical limitations of the initial arrest experiment, the National Institute of Justice embarked on a massive research programme aimed at replicating the Minneapolis study. Studies using a similar, though not identical, experimental design were carried out in Kansas City, Missouri; Colorado Springs, Colorado; Dade County, Florida; Charlotte, North Carolina; Atlanta, Georgia; and Milwaukee, Wisconsin (see for example Dunford, Huisinga and Elliot 1990). Results of these investigations have been less clear-cut than those of the initial study. In three locations conclusions similar to those drawn in Minneapolis seemed appropriate – arrest appeared to have a modest effect on the incidence and rate of domestic violence to a greater degree than other responses. In two cities arrest seemed no more effective than the other interventions, and in one location arrest was the *least* effective response in reducing subsequent incidents of domestic violence. Equivocal results such as these across a range of locations provoked considerable debate among researchers and criminal justice policy-makers and practitioners. Apparently some commentators urged, counter-intuitively, that those offenders who were least responsive to arrest because they were the most criminalistic should not be arrested for violence against their partner (Sherman 1992). On balance, North American observers appear to agree that in most cases of domestic violence arrest is an appropriate and effective method for deterring subsequent incidents of domestic violence, not least because of the wider societal message conveyed by a criminal justice response that such violence is a criminal offence (Berk 1993). Comparable research on arrest has not been carried out in Britain. Whatever the outcome of attempts to assess arrest, such research provides no indication of the potential benefits of civil procedures and various criminal justice sanctions, such as fines, probation, prison and treatment programmes.

Arrest remains an infrequent response to domestic violence in Britain; recent research indicates that despite new policies and practices only a small proportion of call-outs (2 per cent in one study) result in arrest and prosecution (Edwards 1986). The most frequently employed justice intervention in this area is the use of civil injunctions

(Dobash and Dobash 1992). Beginning in the early 1980s – when they were first emphasized as an appropriate response – the number of injunctions has risen annually (Edwards 1989). A number of studies have investigated the use of these measures and while not, strictly speaking, evaluation studies they have nonetheless provided insight into the 'effectiveness' of injunctions (see Barron 1990). Research conducted in Britain reveals that enforcement of injunctions and the use of the powers of arrest are often inconsistent and inefficient. In some forces officers fail to serve injunctions on the abusive man and continue to tell women that their problems are purely private, not associated with the justice system. Other research shows that even where the powers of arrest are attached to an injunction and the police have evidence of a breach – such as injuries – they are reluctant to act. Women report that their partners do not take injunctions seriously, ignore the provisions for exclusion and non-molestation and continue to intimidate and use violence against them. It appears from these research reports that injunctions are often ineffective; only a minority of women judged them as useful. Research and experience in the United States indicates that under certain conditions injunctions can be useful (Finn and Colson 1990). In jurisdictions where the judiciary provide clear and explicit admonitions regarding the violence and harassment, and other justice personnel are prepared to enforce these messages, injunctions can be effective. Willingness to apply sanctions when violent men breach the civil order is also important. While British investigations of the use and effectiveness of injunctions provide important evidence, these studies could have been strengthened if comparison groups had been included in the research design. As the evidence suggests, most women do not find injunctions very useful, but it is important to know how they compare with doing nothing or arresting the man. Comparisons such as these would have enhanced the validity of these investigations.

Research evaluations of programmes for violent men

To date, no substantial research has been conducted on programmes for violent men operating in Britain. By contrast, considerable research has been carried out in the United States and Canada on similar interventions. Investigations into men's programmes have not, somewhat surprisingly, been extensive and many suffer from serious limitations in design and implementation. In some cases evaluations have been conducted by programme staff and/or through anecdotal assessments, such as phoning directors of programmes who provide estimates of rates of success (Pirog-Good and Stets 1986). More commonly investigations of the impact of programmes, for violent men involve direct attempts to determine changes in men's reported behaviours and attitudes as a result of programme participation. Evaluations are frequently based on officially recorded arrests during a follow-up period after completion of a men's programme. Measures of success are also obtained by asking men about their violent behaviour through telephone interviews, paper–pencil questionnaires and occasionally face-to-face interviews. Evaluation research of this nature indicates high rates of success for those men who complete programmes: using arrest records and men's reports, researchers and professionals claim that while participating in treatment programmes most men do not use violence, and after programme completion 70–80 per cent of these men remain violence-free for up to one year or more (Dutton 1986; Saunders and Hanusa 1986; Gondolf 1988; Bersani *et al.* 1988; Edelson and Grusznski 1988; Chen 1989; Eisikovits and Edelson 1989; Burns, Meredith and Paquette 1991; Hamm and Kite 1991). These are impressive results. However, it is important to treat such claims with caution; there are serious limitations in many of these studies.

The most important limitations of extant research evaluations of programmes for violent men are small sample sizes, the lack of comparison groups and inadequate methods of measuring outcome. Samples as small as nine have been used as supposedly valid bases of generalization, with the largest samples being around 150. A recent review of these studies estimated the average sample size as fifty-seven (Hamm and Kite 1991). The results of studies based on such generally small samples, while possibly providing useful indicative results, do not constitute an adequate basis for generalization. Studies which indicate impressive levels of success but do not employ comparison groups are suspect because similar rates might have been achieved through other criminal justice interventions or as a result of doing nothing. Without comparison groups the achieved results lack validity because other methods might have been just as successful or men might have improved without intervention as a result of other experiences. The classic solution to this problem (as employed in the arrest studies) is to compare a number of interventions to which subjects are randomly assigned and assessed over a comparable period of time using valid, standardized measurements. None of the existing evaluation studies of programmes for violent men have been designed to assess these innovations relative to other types of criminal justice sanctions. Relying on police or participants' reports of subsequent violence is now seen as a notoriously unreliable method of assessing outcomes because many incidents of domestic violence go unreported and men persistently underestimate their use of violence. Police records usually under-represent the incidence of violence and introduce reporting biases that reflect police reactions rather than the 'true' incidence of violence. This in turn can raise the apparent success rate of programme participants. Increasingly, evaluators are proposing the use of the accounts of victims to corroborate police reports and the reports of men. Unfortunately, existing evaluations of men's programmes do not routinely include the reports of the women who have been victimized by violent men.

Other design and implementation problems are apparent. Existing evaluations generally fail to use adequate baseline measures of relevant behaviours and beliefs. In addition, very abbreviated and inadequate assessments are made at the first and subsequent stages of research. Often a limited and narrow range of violent acts is assessed and other forms of coercive and abusive behaviour and attendant orientations are not investigated. The most widely used measurement instrument in these evaluations is the consistently criticized Conflict Tactics Scale, which severely limits the range and type of abusive behaviours assessed (see Dobash *et al.* 1992; Dobash and Dobash 1992; Yllo 1993). Employing inadequate uni-dimensional measures means that investigations fail to attend to the complexities of the offending behaviour, and subsequent follow-up assessments will incorporate these limitations. Valid investigations will employ a multi-baseline approach involving the measurement of a range of violent, coercive and intimidating acts, thus constituting a meaningful starting-point for assessing change over time.

Meaningful assessments should also employ standardized measurements and reasonably lengthy periods of follow-up. While qualitative materials are certainly useful and valid, indeed essential in certain types of evaluations, assessment over several time-periods requires standardized, controlled forms of measurement. Periods of follow-up should also be as long as practicable and standardized within and across treatments. A considerable proportion of extant studies employed no follow-up periods, and many assessed men only a few months after programme completion. An often noted dditional problem is variation in the period of time that subjects are t risk of failure; some men are interviewed after a few months, others after several months. A reasonable standardized period of ollow-up is necessary for valid assessment; a few commentators ndicate three years, most indicate nine months to a year as a valid eriod of time. A recent meta-analysis of existing evaluations of rogrammes for violent men indicates that follow-up periods of more han a year may not be necessary, since results show that when men ail, abuse usually occurs reasonably soon after programme ompletion and generally does not increase thereafter (Burns, Meredith and Paquette 1991).

A problem that plagues all longitudinal evaluation studies – articularly those with long periods of follow-up – is the loss of ubjects over time. Longitudinal evaluation studies must retain a easonable proportion of those who have completed treatment in the eriods of follow-up in order to count as valid comparisons. In this esearch, high rates of attrition are not unusual, even in short periods f follow-up. High rates of attrition may introduce systematic biases n results if, for example, it is only the most co-operative and uccessful who participate in the follow-up. Exclusion of those who re least co-operative and possibly less successful in reducing their iolence introduces serious distortions in the completed evaluation.

Where randomized designs are not employed it is important to be lert to the possibility of selection bias in the choice of programme articipants. Programmes based on voluntary or socially mandated articipation accept only those men who are highly motivated to rogramme completion and change (even if only temporarily). election bias is also a potential problem in criminal justice valuations and can occur at several points in the criminal justice rocess. In programmes based on diversion from criminal justice, rosecutors may divert to men's programmes only those cases they onsider to have a high probability of success. When sentencing, idges, magistrates, sheriffs, may refer only men judged less violent nd more amenable to change. Similar biases may be introduced if rogramme participation is based on the recommendations of robation officers. Comparative designs must be attuned to the reats to validity these procedures introduce and attempt to vercome them by using *post hoc* matching procedures where otentially relevant variables – e.g., background characteristics, istories of domestic violence, arrest and prosecution – are explored for all participants and attempts are made to discover and deal with the potential selection biases. Ideally, the men in all comparison groups should be broadly similar.

Most evaluation studies in this arena fail to include men who do not complete programmes in their assessment. Another source of bias is a failure to consider the impact of divorce and separation on assessments of violence at follow-up. If a man separates or is divorced from the woman to whom he has been violent, the risk of subsequent violence may be reduced. Existing evaluations frequently fail to account for separation and may therefore count as successes cases that should more properly be excluded from the analysis. It should not be assumed, however, that separation or divorce means lack of contact and the cessation of violence; research indicates that the risk of assault and homicide is often elevated for women who are in the process of separating or divorcing and that this risk continues after divorce or separation (Daly and Wilson 1988; Fagan and Brown 1994). Evaluation researchers should thus be attuned to the residential circumstances of the men being evaluated, not assume that separation/divorce necessarily means there is no subsequent contact and an absence of the risk of violence; and assess the amount of contact during the periods of follow-up.

Creating adequate and practical evaluation designs is only one of the significant problems facing researchers. Other problems are associated with the implementation and operation of the programmes being investigated. Monitoring programme integrity and evolution must be an integral aspect of all evaluations. Energetic dedicated staff, efficient referral procedures, apparently useful programmes and ambitious treatment targets may come to nothing. Well-designed programmes may fail not because of internal problems associated with the projects but because the programme does not fit its external environment and, for example, does not appear to meet the needs of those who might use it. If the programme does not receive clients or if it exists in a malevolent or indifferent environment, this will have a significant pernicious effect on its operation. Evaluators should be alert to this possibility because it may have an important impact on programme delivery. Evaluation researchers should initially assess and continuously monitor the precise nature of the programme being scrutinized. In this way it is possible to provide at least a characterization of the nature of treatment on offer and to carry out a more precise investigation of the elements of the programme that produce an effect. Internal change within a project, such as high staff turn-over and radical shifts in philosophy, may seriously effect the nature of the 'treatment' on offer. If, for example, a programme starts its life with staff dedicated to a certain form of intervention – psycho-educational – and half-way through changes in staff and philosophy bring about a shift to a more cognitive–behavioural approach this will mean that the research is evaluating two different and distinct programmes or that the supposed comparison between distinct types of treatments has not occurred. Continuous contact and monitoring of the programme(s) under investigation should form an integral aspect of all evaluations.

After considering this litany of problems associated with conducting valid evaluation studies in this area, it might be assumed that it is impossible to carry out meaningful research. The lessons to be drawn from the above review are: indeed, it is impossible to conduct the perfect, evaluation study, but careful attention to the following problems will increase the validity of research in this area:

— significant changes in the programme during the time of evaluation
— failures to implement fully the programme being investigated
— lack of randomized or comparative designs
— small sample sizes
— the use of faulty or weak measures of outcome, e.g., self-reports and/or records of arrest
— the use of uni-dimensional, abbreviated assessments of violence
— short, non-standardized periods of follow-up
— lack of comparison groups of men who have not experienced intervention or who were involved in other, more orthodox, forms of intervention
— a failure to include the reports of women who were the victims of the offender's violence
— biases in selection of programme participants
— failure to include/evaluate programme participants who fail to complete
— failure to attend to separation effects

Research evaluation of British programmes for violent men

The evaluation study of the two British programmes for violent men reported here has been designed to limit, avoid and overcome the problems outlined above. In designing the study we sought to compare the effects of the two innovative programmes to the impact of other criminal justice sanctions. The principal research question was: are the experimental men's programmes more likely than other criminal justice sanctions to inhibit and eliminate violence and enhance the well-being of the women who have been victimized? As well as attempting to assess differential outcomes, the research was designed to explore *why* men changed. By considering men's and women's interpretations of the specific and general impact of programme participation or of a fine, for example, we sought to unravel the pathways and mechanisms associated with change. Straightforwardly, we sought to uncover the specifics of change and to explore what it was about programme participation that generated change, if and when it was apparent. In its broadest sense the study was designed to assess the impact of a range of criminal justice sanctions on subsequent violent behaviour. A comparative longitudinal approach was proposed wherein the impact of a number of sanctions was assessed at three periods of time: immediately after the imposition of a criminal justice sanction, three months after the initial assessment and nine months after the initial assessment. The study was designed to last three years, as this would make it possible to accumulate a reasonable number of cases in the recently created programme groups and to assure meaningful periods of follow-up.

Sample populations were drawn from the cases of all men who were sanctioned for an offence involving violence against their partner in Edinburgh and Central Region, Scotland during the course of the fieldwork. In the initial design, four criminal justice comparison groups were identified: 1. CHANGE; 2. LDVPP; 3. other court sanctions – fines, admonishments, and compensation orders; and 4. probation. Based on the assumption that a woman's stay in a refuge may have important consequences for subsequent violence and the well-being of a woman, a fifth comparison group composed of women who spent time in a refuge was included in the initial design. A sixth comparison group composed of men who were imprisoned for assaulting their partners was subsequently added in the field when was recognized that it was, indeed, possible to obtain a small sample of men experiencing this sanction.

Assessments of a number of important indicators were to be conducted at three points in time: immediately following the criminal justice sanction (a stay in a refuge) and at the beginning of programme participation, three months after the initial contact and nine months after the initial contact. At time one, men and women were to be involved in separate face-to-face interviews covering a wide range of issues focusing on the violence and criminal justice sanctions (see below). In this way the researchers sought to establish a multi-dimensional baseline for assessing change over time. At the second time-period – after three months – men and women were to be sent a postal questionnaire which included questions aimed at assessing changes in the criterion behaviours and orientations assessed in the first stage. Nine months after the interview, at time three, men and women were to be sent a second postal questionnaire aimed at assessing changes in the baseline measures over this extended period of time. Face-to-face interviews at times two and three would have been the preferred method, but this was deemed to be too costly and time-consuming. Telephone interviews at times two and three – an often-employed method in North America – were ruled out because we rightly assumed that many of the couples would not have telephones. In this quasi-experimental study the proposed method of assessing outcomes was to be interviews and questionnaires with men and women at three points in time. An additional and orthodox method was also envisaged, the use of arrest records subsequent to the initial sanction and adjudication. The research design is set out in Table 1 below.

Table 1: Evaluating programmes for violent men – initial design

Intervention	Time 1 Interview		Time 2 PQ-3Mos.		Time 3 PQ-9Mos.	
	M	W	M	W	M	W
Men's Programmes	∞	∞	a	a	•	•
Other court (fines, etc.)	∞	∞	a	a	•	•
Prisons	∞	∞	a	a	•	•
Probation	∞	∞	a	a	•	•
Refuges (for women)	∞	∞	a	a	•	•
TOTAL	∞	∞	a	a	•	•

North American researchers are suspicious of quasi-experimental studies and urge the use of randomized designs as the only means of conducting valid evaluations (Sherman 1992). In this study a randomized design was rejected because such procedures were considered unethical and impractical. Assigning cases of domestic violence to selected criminal justice sanctions as a result of random procedures, in contrast to basing outcome on the considered judgement of the sentencers, eliminates the judgement of sentencers and potentially denies women important benefits. Furthermore, it is doubtful that the Scottish judiciary would have endorsed and consented to the use of such procedures in their courts. It is important, however, to consider the potential biases introduced in the sample through judicial processes. It may be that Scottish sheriffs (magistrates) only sentence men to CHANGE and the LDVPP who have committed minor offences and who have histories of perpetrating minimal violence and/or that the projects only accept men with such histories.

The approach used here was to obtain a reasonably robust sample of men who were arrested, prosecuted and sentenced for an offence involving a violent act against their intimate female partner. Establishing a comparative baseline on a range of relevant issues was to be achieved by asking a series of questions in the initial interviews (e.g., history of violence and criminal offences) which facilitated a comparison of the samples on a number of potentially significant variables and in order to measure change over time. The significant threat to the validity of the comparison is that men sentenced to one of the innovative programmes are vastly different to men in the other sample groups. *Post hoc* matching was proposed as the method to overcome potential biases introduced through sentencing practices. If men in the various sample groups could be shown to be relatively similar on a range of significant variables, the comparison of outcomes at times two and three could be deemed to be more valid because potential selection bias had been dealt with. Basically this means that it is possible to be reasonably confident that the men sentenced to and selected for the innovative programmes are not different from men sentenced to other sanctions.

A number of strategies were employed to monitor and assess programme integrity over time. Significantly, two of the researchers had considerable contact with both innovative projects while they were being established and this provided important background knowledge about the structure, content and early operation of the two projects. Throughout the duration of the evaluation research, the researchers maintained near-continuous contact with the two projects, enabling them to monitor their evolution during this period. Four formal group interviews were conducted with project staff during the course of the evaluation, in which philosophy, aims and programme content were explored. Procedures such as these have provided a wealth of information, and although they chart changes in programme content, staffing and procedures, they show that throughout the conduct of the research the programmes maintained their original goals, content and philosophy.

Obtaining samples of men and women for the distinct categories of offenders usually involved time-consuming and lengthy negotiations with several agencies and the creation of complex procedures for contacting potential participants. Samples of men sentenced to one of the programmes, probation, other court sanctions, and prison were obtained through systematic monthly scrutiny of pending criminal cases in the sheriffs' courts (equivalent of magistrates' courts in England and Wales) of Central Region and Edinburgh during the course of the evaluation. As there is no offence category 'domestic assault', all pending criminal cases had to be examined and cases involving violence in marital and marital-like relationships were identified from information such as names and addresses of offenders and victims, charges and details of the offence. Charges in these cases ranged from attempted murder and assault to severe injury to breach of the peace. Using these procedures, approximately 938 cases were identified as involving some form of domestic violence during the course of the fieldwork, from October 1991 to June 1994. The aim of the researchers was not to obtain a sample of comparable proportions of men from each of these categories but to gain a sample which reflected sentencing practices. Given the focus of the research the main aim was to obtain as many programme men as possible in order to accumulate a reasonable and representative number of cases in this group.

For a variety of reasons a number of cases were eliminated from this initially identified group of 938: no address was recorded for the couple or one of the partners, the researchers were unable to trace the man and/or woman, the man was considered too dangerous (only one man was so defined) and the death of the man (two men). This resulted in a sampling universe of 313 cases from which to draw the four criminal justice groups – programme, other court, probation and prison. Table 2 provides a summary of the numbers of initially identified cases and the sampling universes for each of the four criminal justice groups. The results show that a considerable number of cases (938) involving violence against women are being processed through these two jurisdictions. As column two of Table 2 reveals, 75 per cent of men involved in offences of violence against their partners are fined, admonished or given some other non-restrictive type of sanction. Only in 10 per cent of these cases were men sentenced to one of the innovative re-education programmes.

Table 2: Identified cases and sampling universes of cases

Groups	No. of Initially identified cases	Per cent of all ID cases	No. of Valid cases
Programme	97	10	84
Other court	700	75	138
Probation	84	9	57
Prison	51	6	34
Total	932	100	313

During the course of the fieldwork we contacted all those women and men it was possible to contact within each of the target groups and set about achieving their co-operation. Men who had been fined or otherwise given a non-restrictive sentence were contacted directly. Obtaining cases in the probation, prison and programme groups required, at least in the first instance, protracted procedures for obtaining access.

Time One: depth interviews
The depth interviews conducted at time one of the study included a range of issues that would enable the researchers to assess, among other things, the backgrounds of men and women, levels of violence and other aggressive and controlling forms of behaviour, and broader aspects of the relationships such as quality of interaction. Given the focus of the evaluation, obtaining valid estimates of levels of violence at time one and in the subsequent follow-ups was crucial. Past research by Dobash and Dobash (1979; 1983; 1984) employed a combination of qualitative and quantitative methods to explore violence with women who had been the victims of assaults from their

male partners. Focusing on specific violent events – the first, the worst and last before a woman went to a refuge – a contextual form of event analysis yielded a wealth of quantitative and qualitative data. Systematic, open-ended, depth forms of interviewing proved particularly useful and sensitive in obtaining detailed accounts of violence. Experience has shown that this is the most valid method for obtaining meaningful information about violent incidents. The present study required a method that would yield comprehensive accounts and valid and comparable data from both men and women over three periods of time.

An obvious option would have been to employ one of the widely used measures for assessing domestic violence. The most widely used scale, the Conflict Tactics Scale or CTS, while readily available, has been criticized because, among other things, it attempts to measure a narrow range of violence, fails to assess injuries and ignores the context of violence, and thus produces unreliable results when used to measure violence between men and women in the family (see Pagelow 1985; Dobash *et al.* 1992; Yllo 1993). We opted for the use of event analysis involving systematic questioning and open-ended answers in combination with more standardized, quantitative forms of data collection. In the initial depth interview, through systematic questioning, women and men were asked to discuss the first violent event and the one that resulted in criminal justice intervention. They were also asked to describe the nature, prevalence and severity of the violence occurring during the relationship. The series of questions pertaining to any particular violent event began with a question such as 'Can you tell me what happened during the incident which led to the court case?'. When interviewing women a question such as this would usually, though not always, illicit a wealth of information regarding the nature of the argument preceding the violence, the violence itself, the injuries sustained, the responses of the man and woman, and subsequent patterns of help-seeking behaviour. Most men were rather less forthcoming.

In designing this study we opted for an approach incorporating the strengths of qualitative and quantitative methods. The chosen method for interview was to ask a series of systematic questions about the first and last violent event and any violence ever experienced as a means of obtaining general descriptions and interpretations. In order to assure the collection of systematic data and to facilitate the disclosures of men, men and women were also asked to respond to

A	Restrained her from moving or leaving the room
B	Choked her or held your hand over her mouth
C	Punched her in the face
D	Forced her to do something against her will
E	Slapped her on the face, body, arms or legs
F	Pushed, grabbed or shoved her
G	Threatened to kill yourself
H	Punched her on the body, arms or legs
I	Used an object to hurt her
J	Kicked or punched her in stomach when pregnant
K	Threw things at her or about the room
L	Demanded sex when she didn't want it
M	Punched or kicked the walls or furniture
N	Threatened to hit the kids
O	Shouted at or threatened the kids
P	Forced her to have sex or some kind of sexual activity
Q	Tried to strangle, burn, smother or drown her
R	Kicked her on the body, arms or legs
S	Shouted and screamed at her
T	Threatened her with an object or weapon
U	Kicked her in the face
V	Swore at her or called her names
W	Threatened to kill her
X	Twisted her arm
Y	Dragged her or pulled her by her hair
Z	Threatened her with your fist, hand or foot

Figure 1: Violence assessment index

pre-prepared indices of violent acts and injuries developed for this research.

The Violence Assessment Index (VAI) included acts ranging from aggressive threats and acts of restraint to punching and kicking and the use of a weapon. The VAI included twenty-six separate and distinct acts. In contrast to most existing approaches we attempted to 'connect' specific violent acts to the objects and/or parts of the body to which they were directed, reasoning that a punch in the face (item C) would be experienced rather differently than a punch to the body (item H). Men and women were asked to indicate how often during a specific attack they had used or experienced any particular act. Figure 1 shows the range of behaviours included.

A significant problem with many existing scales, particularly the

A	Cut/s on her face
B	Bruise/s on her body
C	Burn/s anywhere
D	Lost hair
E	Broken arm or leg
F	Cut/s on her arms or legs
G	Bruise/s on her face
H	Miscarriage
I	Blackout or unconsciousness
J	Bruise/s on her arms or legs
K	Cut/s anywhere on her body
L	Black eyes
M	Internal injury
N	Lost or broken teeth
O	Sickness or vomiting
P	Bleeding on any part of face
Q	Broken ribs
R	Bleeding on body, arms or legs
S	Split lip
T	Sprained wrist or ankle
U	Broken nose, jaw or cheekbone

Figure 2: Injury assessment index

CTS, is a failure to assess the consequences of violent acts. Injuries and the responses of victims are rarely assessed in most studies of violence against women in the home. We were particularly keen to rectify this omission by assessing injuries in a direct way. The Injury Assessment Index (Figure 2), like the VAI, attempts to deal with injuries and consequences in a specific way. For example, cuts to the face (item A) are likely to be experienced and perceived as more serious than are cuts on the body or limbs (items F and K); of course this depends on the severity of such injuries. Using the Injury Assessment Index (IAI), men and women are asked to provide information about the nature and extent of any specific injuries sustained by the women during the life of the relationship and as a consequence of the first and last violent event. Figure 2 shows the twenty-one separate injuries that might be sustained as a result of a violent attack. These injuries ranged from bruising of the body to lost hair, fractures, cuts and internal injuries.

At interview the Injury Assessment Index (IAI) and the Violence Assessment Index (VAI) were used after men and women were asked specific open-ended questions about the violence and its consequences. In this way women and men were able to tell their story in their own way before providing specific and comparable details. The IAI and the VAI were used in a systematic manner during the course of the interviews. Rather than directly asking men if they had, for example, punched their partner in the face, item C on the IAI, they were given a card and the interviewer read out the letter corresponding to a particular violent act and asked the respondent if he had committed that act. In this way respondents and the interviewers avoided having to use the words associated with a particular type of violence. The results of the interviews showed that such a method enabled men to admit to certain acts that were not recounted in their general description – exactly what we expected. More surprising was the way this method jogged the memories of women, who would usually recount more violence through the use of this method. In particular, women were likely to describe spontaneously the 'more severe' types of violence; the VAI jogged their memories in terms of, for example, threats of violence. In contrast, men more often spontaneously described the 'less severe' types of violence; the VAI enabled them to admit to, for example, punching and kicking their partner. The use of the 'cue' cards turned out to be an excellent way of enhancing disclosure and jogging memories. The VAI and the IAI enabled us to gather comparable data about violence and injuries from men and women in all sample groups across three periods of time.

Men who perpetrate violence against their female partners usually engage in a range of other aggressive, controlling and coercive acts and the two innovative programmes aim to reduce these behaviours and address the values and beliefs that generate and rationalize violence. In order to assess these acts the researchers developed the Controlling Behaviours Index (CBI). The CBI includes: acts involving direct forms of physical aggression such as 'making to hit'; verbal forms of intimidation and coercion such as 'swear at you' and 'question you about your activities'; and more indirect acts such as 'put you down in front of others'. Figure 3 reproduces the twenty-two distinct forms of behaviour included in the CBI. Women and men were asked about these behaviours within the context of potential and actual violence. Women were asked 'Does he ever do any of the following in a way which you know means you have to be careful?'

Can you tell me how often you do any of the following things to your partner in a way which means she has to be careful?

Threaten her
Shout at her
Swear at her
Shout at the children
Threaten to hurt the children
Call her names
Question her about her activities
Check her movements
Have a certain look/mood
Try to provoke an argument
Criticize her
Criticize her family/friends
Put her down in front of friends/family
Deliberately keep her short of money
Make her feel sexually inadequate
Point at her
Make to hit without doing so
Restrict her social life
Use kids in argument against her
Threaten to hurt the pet
Nag her

Figure 3: Controlling behaviours index questions for men

The Violence Assessment Index, Injury Assessment Index and Controlling Behaviours Index provided the primary baselines for assessing changes across the three periods of time. We also explored other behaviours and orientations that were intended to constitute additional baseline measurements (see Figure 4). Men who are violent usually lack empathy toward others and insight into their concerns. It is argued that their relationship with and attitudes toward women, particularly the women they abuse, are often negative. In particular they tend to deny the abuse, minimize its impact and deflect responsibility for the violence on to others. Researchers and commentators have also noted that these men are often isolated, except from other men who hold similarly aggressive and antagonistic views of women. Women who experience prolonged systematic abuse

(VAI) Violence Assessment Inventory
(IAI) Injury Assessment Index
(CBI) Controlling Behaviours Index
Empathy: knowledge of partner's background and attitudes
toward partner
Denial, minimization and deflection
Quality of the relationship
Social networks
Help-seeking behaviour
Orientation toward criminal justice intervention
Potential for change

Figure 4: Baseline assessments

are also described as isolated. Networks of relations and friends that might offer alternative attitudes, challenge violent men and support them in altering their violence are weak or non-existent. Weak networks and attitudes supporting violence make it unlikely that men will engage in help-seeking behaviour to find informal and/or professional support for changing their behaviours and attitudes. Men who are violent toward their female partners generally reject the intrusion of others in what they see as a 'private matter' between themselves and their partner. Yet all of the men in this study have experienced at least one such intrusion, they have all been arrested and convicted of an offence involving a violent incident. The research question is: what is their orientation to this intervention, and has it prompted a new attitude toward the violence; has the intervention increased the potential for change? These areas, like violent and controlling acts, were also considered significant to this study and were used as baseline measures at time one.

At interview, men and women participating in this study provided other pertinent information: biographical details, including violence in the family of origin; history of alcohol/drug dependency and abuse; family activities and routines; nature and levels of conflict; reactions to conflict and violence; attributions of responsibility associated with conflict and violence in the relationship; women's efforts to avoid or reduce the violence and men's prior attempts to stop; women's physical reactions to the violence of men; history of the man's violence toward others; criminal and penal history of the men; previous criminal justice interventions regarding violence against the woman; the sequence of events leading to criminal justice intervention; patterns and reactions associated with the legal intervention; behaviour of men toward partners during the court process; immediate impact of intervention; the use and perceived impact of civil restraints; men and women's assessment of the impact of specific sanctions. All interviews were tape-recorded and a representative sample of approximately 40 per cent were either fully or partially transcribed.

The men and women interviewed at time one were initially contacted by post and asked if they would be willing to participate in the study. If they responded and agreed to participate an appointment was made for an interview. Relatively few responded immediately, however, and evolved procedures involved one of the researchers visiting each person at their home after the initial letter. At this stage many who had not responded to the letter agreed to participate in the research after this more personal, face-to-face contact with a member of the research team. At initial contact some were very receptive, interested and keen to be interviewed; others were not so sure or so keen but were willing to be persuaded; some were definitely not interested and not open to persuasion ('it's private', 'not interested in talking', 'too traumatic, upsetting to talk about'); and a few (particularly men) were angry, even aggressive at being approached. In order to enhance the likelihood of participation, men and women were paid a nominal fee of £5 at this and each subsequent stage of the research.

There appeared to be a strong gender difference in the motivations to participate in the research. Women were often keen to tell their stories and to discuss the violence they experienced from their partner. They spoke openly and spontaneously about the positive aspects of being able to tell their 'story' in their own way to a non-judgemental outsider. We learned that it was particularly important not to be judgemental about male partners lest it jeopardized rapport with women. Men agreed to participate in the study for a variety of reasons: they wanted to tell their side of the story, many feeling that they had been dealt with unjustly by the courts; some wanted to 'set the record straight'; some appeared to need to 'confess'; and others wanted to castigate those involved in their court case, e.g., social workers, probation officers, police, women and judges. Still others wanted to use the interview as a vehicle for denial, minimization and deflection of responsibility. Men often demonstrated considerable skill when proffering such positions: the language of denial and minimization was often sophisticated and, at times, convincing Interviews with women provided powerful antidotes to these accounts.

Interviews were usually lengthy, typically lasting one to one-and-a half hours for men and two to three hours for women. Interviews with women would sometimes extend over two days, lasting upwards of seven hours. All interviews were conducted individually by a member of the research team, and all but a handful were carried out in the homes of the participants. When arranging interviews we always sought to interview men and women separately when partners were not at home. Occasionally this proved impossible and a few interviews were held when partners were present in the residence. In all situations we sought to be sensitive to a woman's sense of safety and security and if she felt uneasy about the time and location of the interview it was rearranged. If a woman indicated that she felt an interview would threaten her security, we withdrew. Fortunately women did not usually feel threatened by the prospect of an interview. When asked we offered counsel and advice within the limits of our expertise.

Sensitive approaches, persuasion and persistence have paid off; 264 interviews were conducted at time one and, as Table 3.8 shows, robust numbers of men and women have been achieved in the distinct comparison groups. The achieved sample includes 122 men convicted of and 142 women who had been the victims in an incident involving domestic violence. Of these 122 men and 142 women there were 95 couples. The Programme group includes 51 men and 47 women and the Other CJ group is composed of 71 men and 97 women. Unfortunately the numbers of women and particularly men in the Refuge group were so small that meaningful comparisons were impossible; therefore this group was dropped from subsequent analysis. Importantly, the numbers of men and women involved in this study surpass those included in most research evaluations conducted in North America.

Times Two and Three: postal questionnaires
The two postal questionnaires were intended to assess any changes in the behaviour and orientations of men and the predicament of women at two periods of time. A fundamental issue was the extent and nature of contact with the violent man. Women were asked to provide details of their living arrangements and if they were separated

Table 3: Interviews at time one

Comparison Groups	Men No.	%	Women No.	%	Total
Programme					
LDVPP	22	18.0	21	14.8	41
CHANGE	29	23.7	26	18.2	57
Other CJ					
Probation	19	15.6	16	11.2	35
Court	41	33.7	64	45.0	105
Prison	11	9.0	7	4.9	18
Women's Aid					
Refuge	0	0.0	9	6.3	8
Total	122	100.0	142	100.0	264

from the man who had assaulted them to indicate how much contact there had been during the two follow-up periods. Collection of this sort of information was crucial in establishing whether a particular woman had actually been at risk of violence from the man who had assaulted her during the period of follow-up. Importantly, as indicated above, it could not be assumed that separation or divorce meant no subsequent contact.

Once it was established that a woman was living with or had contact with her partner, it was then important to assess the current levels of violence, injury, and intimidation. Women and men were asked how many incidents of violence had occurred in the period under scrutiny and to provide details of the violence and coercive behaviours they had experienced by filling out the three indices used at time one: the Violence Assessment Index, the Injury Assessment Index, and the Controlling Behaviour Index. All three of the measurement devices were included in the questionnaires used at times two and three. The indices would provide direct quantifiable assessments of the violence and other types of controlling behaviour, but it was important to gauge the subjective judgement of women and men: did they think these behaviours had increased and in their opinion was the violence more or less serious than before the criminal justice intervention? They were also asked to give their views on *why* the violence had increased or decreased and to consider how the particular criminal justice sanction experienced by the man had affected subsequent levels of violence. Assessing specific changes in the level and type of violence was of course crucial to the evaluation; of equal importance was an evaluation of changes in the relationship and the level and seriousness of conflict between the men and women.

The basic question was how, if at all, had the criminal justice intervention altered the relationship. At both follow-up stages, women and men were asked to indicate the current levels of conflict in their relationship and to assess how well they were 'getting on' with their partners – had the relationship deteriorated or improved during the follow-up period? As violence against women in the home is often preceded by aggressive conflicts and arguments, it follows that interventions should aim to alter the nature and intensity of these conflicts. It seems that all intimate relationships involve conflict and cessation of conflict is an unrealistic, indeed possibly undesirable, goal. It could be argued that successful programmes might increase women's ability to argue; if men are less violent and learn new methods of communication they may be better equipped to argue safely and women will feel more secure when disagreeing with their partners. If the innovative programmes are effective, a reduction in violence should be associated with a diminution of the intensity and seriousness of conflicts and aggression within the relationships under investigation.

Questionnaires used at times two and three were nearly identical. At time three, however, men and women were asked to respond to a unique list of questions regarding how their quality of life had changed since the initial interview. Figures 6 and 7 detail the distinct and identical items used in the Quality of Life Index (QLI) for men and women. Specific questions aimed to assess changes in the respondent's sense of well-being, 'I am happy'; the perceived well-being of their partner, 'My partner is happy'; improvements in the quality of their relationship, 'I like spending time with my partner'; changes in their partner's awareness of their needs, 'My partner is able to see things from my point of view'; and changes in their partner's ability to control his violence and associated behaviours, 'My partner wants to stop his violence' and 'My partner controls his temper'. By asking whether these behaviours had increased, remained the same or diminished during the period of follow-up, it was possible to make direct assessment of changes during the twelve-month period. The Quality of Life Index proved an especially useful way of assessing women's sense of well-being and their views of the quality of the relationship at the end of the period of evaluation.

Listed below are a number of things about you and your partner which might have changed *since I interviewed you about a year ago*. Please read them and tick one box for each statement.

	More	Less	Same
I am happy			
I do housework			
I am aware of my partner's feelings			
I understand my partner			
I am relaxed			
I feel angry with my partner			
My partner understands me			
I enjoy the company of my children			
I am possessive/jealous of my partner			
I understand myself			
I discuss things with my partner			

	More	Less	Same
I am interested in my partner's life			
I am able to see things from my partner's point of view			
My partner is frightened of me			
I restrict my partner's life			
My partner and I can laugh together			
I am likely to use physical violence against my partner			
My partner is happy			
I look after the children			
I like spending time with my partner			
My partner feels able to argue with me			

	More	Less	Same
I get on with other people			
I take responsibility for my violence towards my partner			
I am selfish			
I control my temper			
I see violence as a solution to problems with my partner			
I control my drinking			
I respect myself			
I think about my violent and abusive behaviour			
I want to stop my violence			
I threaten my partner			
I use physical violence against my partner			

Figure 6: Quality of life index – men

Listed below are a number of things about you and your partner which might have changed *since I interviewed you about a year ago*. Please read them and tick one box for each statement.

	More	Less	Same
I am happy			
My partner is aware of my feelings			
My partner understands me			
I am relaxed			
I feel angry with my partner			
I discuss things with my partner			
My partner is able to see things from my point of view			
I am frightened of my partner			

	More	Less	Same
My partner restricts my life			
My partner and I can laugh together			
My partner is likely to use physical violence against me			
My partner is happy			
I like spending time with my partner			
My partner respects me			
I am likely to use physical violence towards my partner			
My partner is selfish			
I feel able to argue with my partner			

	More	Less	Same
My partner takes responsibility for his violence towards me			
My partner controls his temper			
My partner wants to stop his violence			
My partner controls his drinking			
I respect myself			
My partner sees violence as a solution to problems with me			
My partner uses physical violence against me			

Figure 7: Quality of life index – women

The final section of the postal questionnaires dealt with the intervention of the police and criminal justice system in the violent incidents reported at times two and three. We were interested in collecting information from men and women on police action – was the man arrested, charged and detained – and any subsequent court disposition regarding violence since the initial sanction. Respondents were also asked to indicate how these interventions affected them, the violence and their relationship.

In the initial research design the researchers intended to send follow-up postal questionnaires three and nine months after interview. In the actual research it was possible to extend the third time-period and, in the main, respondents completed postal questionnaires three months after the initial interview, as initially proposed, and twelve months after the initial interview. This was a fortuitous development as it extended the period of time of assessment, thus providing a longer period to test the impact of the programmes and other CJ sanctions.

A well-developed and thoroughly tested method for administering postal questionnaires was used at times two and three. At time two, men and women were sent a letter reminding them of the research and the initial interview and were asked to return the questionnaire in the pre-paid envelope. The letter also indicated that, as with the interviews, they would receive £5 for their time upon receipt of the completed questionnaire. If the questionnaire had not been returned after a fortnight they were sent a reminder urging them to complete and return the questionnaire. After an additional fortnight, a second questionnaire was sent repeating the earlier requests. In our correspondence we sought to be sensitive to the difficulties our request might pose for women.

It was usually possible to trace respondents at times two and three, although a few could not be found because they had moved or otherwise could not be contacted. At time two, 5 per cent of Programme men and 2 per cent of Programme women who had been interviewed could not be traced. Ten per cent of Other CJ men and 8 per cent of Other CJ women could not be found at time two. Considering only those individuals who were sent a questionnaire at time three – some were excluded because it became clear at time two that they could not be traced – 14 per cent of Programme men and 3 per cent of Programme women could not be traced. Of the Other CJ group, 21 per cent of men and 15 per cent of women could not be located at time three. In comparison to other longitudinal evaluation studies in this area, this study did not encounter profound problems in tracing respondents, although there was a diminution in the number of study participants, particularly at time three for the men in both groups and for the women in the Other CJ group.

Table 4: Return of postal questionnaires at times two and three

	Follow-up periods			
	Time 2		Time 3	
	No.	%	No.	%
Groups		time 1		time 1
Programme				
Men	38	75	25	50
Women	38	81	27	58
Other CJ				
Men	51	72	35	54
Women	67	71	51	54

The results presented in Table 4 show that the rates of return of questionnaires at times two and three were very robust. At time two, 75 per cent (calculated as a proportion of those interviewed at time one) of men and 81 per cent of women in the Programme group and 72 per cent of men and 71 per cent of women in the Other CJ group returned a questionnaire (these results include non-returns and those we were unable to trace). These are excellent rates of return for postal questionnaires, particularly in a longitudinal study examining such a sensitive subject. The rates of return at time three, while lower, are still respectable. Fifty-eight per cent of women in the Programme group and 54 per cent of women in the Other CJ group returned questionnaires one year after they were interviewed. The rates for men in both groups are lower: 50 per cent of men in both groups returned a questionnaire at time three. These good rates of return reflect the excellent rapport established through interview at time one and possibly the small financial inducements offered at each state of the research.

Using both extensive and intensive methods, a comparative, quasi-experimental evaluation of programmes for violent men has been completed. Interviews conducted with men and women at time one immediately following the imposition of a court sanction were extensive and intensive, allowing for the collection of a multiplicity of data that can be used to establish baselines for assessing change over time. Standardized follow-ups were conducted at similar periods of time – three and twelve months after initial interview – across all comparison groups. Follow-up questionnaires enabled us to assess levels of failure in both groups at two periods of time and to assess the nature and extent of positive changes over time. Questionnaires used at the follow-up periods, while not as intensive as the depth interviews, were extensive enough to provide equivalent data on the significant baseline measurements. As with all longitudinal studies there was some attrition of participants at follow-up, but the rates encountered in this study are well within acceptable levels. Throughout the period of research the two innovative programmes for violent men have successfully operated within their respective locations, and, while changes have occurred in programmes and staff, in the main their philosophies, orientations and techniques have remained stable.

The results of the research show a strong effect (for a fuller account of results see Dobash *et al.* 1995). A comparative analysis of the backgrounds, criminal histories and patterns of violence of the men in the two groups – Programme and Other CJ – reveals considerable symmetry. There are differences, but these are not significant, and we judge the men in the two groups to be very similar on most of the important comparisons. On the basis of the data gathered at interview and court records it appears that there has been no systematic selection bias skewing membership in the two groups. Comparisons made at times one, two and three demonstrate strong and significant differences in the two groups. In the first instance there is an effect for both groups: arrest, prosecution and the imposition of a sanction appears to reduce the prevalence of subsequent offending for both groups. Using the reports of women, the findings further indicate that the men who have been through one of the innovative programmes, either CHANGE or the Lothian Domestic Violence Probation Project, are much less likely to have committed a subsequent violent act and, if they have perpetrated violence, their partners report fewer incidents during the period of follow-up. Furthermore, women whose partners have been on one of the innovative programmes report a reduction in the prevalence and incidence of a range of controlling behaviours and are more likely to indicate that their quality of life and the relationship with their partner has improved. By contrast, women whose partners have not been on one of the innovative programmes report about the same level of controlling behaviours at interview and follow-up and are likely to indicate that their quality of life and the relationship has either remained the same or actually worsened.

References

Barron, J. (1990). *Not Worth the Paper* . . . ? (Bristol, Women's Aid Federation, England).

Berk, R. A. (1993). 'We can do no better than arrest', in R. Gelles and D. R. Loseke (eds.), *Current Controversies on Family Violence* (London, Sage).

Bersani, C., Chen, H. T. and Denton, R. (1988). 'Spouse abuser and court-mandated treatment', *Crime and Justice*, 11, 43–59.

Burns, N., Meredith, C. and Paquette, C. (1991). *Treatment Programs for Men Who Batter: A Review of the Evidence of Their Success* (Abt Associates of Canada).

Chen, H. T., Bersani, C., Myers, S. C. and Denton, R. (1989). 'Evaluating the effectiveness of a court-sponsored abuser treatment programme', *Journal of Family Violence*, 4, 309–22.

Daly, M. and Wilson, M. (1988). *Homicide* (New York, Aldine de Gruyter).

Dobash, R. E. and Dobash, R. P. (1979). *Violence Against Wives* (New York, Free Press).

Dobash, R. E. and Dobash, R. P. (198 3). 'The context specific approach', in D. Finkelhor, *et al.* (eds.), *The Dark Side of Families* (Beverly Hills, CA, Sage).

Dobash, R. E. and Dobash, R. P. (1984). 'The nature and antecedents of violent events', *British Journal of Criminology*, 24, 269–88.

Dobash, R. E. and Dobash, R. P. (1992). *Women, Violence and Social Change* (New York, Routledge).

Dobash, R. P. (1993). 'Ethical and methodological issues in researching the effects of arrest in domestic violence', paper presented at the American Sociological Association Meetings, Miami, August.

Dobash, R. P., Dobash, R. E., Wilson, M. and Daly, M. (1992). 'The myth of sexual symmetry in marital violence', *Social Problems*, 39, 402–32.

Dobash, R. P., Dobash, R. E., Cavanagh, K. and Lewis, R. (1995). 'Research Evaluation of Programmes for Violent Men', report for the Scottish Office and Home Office, Edinburgh.

Dunford, F. W., Huizinga, D. and Elliott, D. (1990). 'The role of arrest in domestic assault', *Criminology*, 28, 183–206.

Dutton, D. G. (1986). 'The outcome of court-mandated treatment for wife assault: a quasi-experimental evaluation', *Violence and Victims*, 1, 163–75.

Edleson, J. L. and Grusznski, R. J. (1988). 'Treating men who batter: four years of outcome data from a domestic abuse project', *Journal of Social Service Research*, 12, 3–22.

Edwards, S. S. M. (1986). 'Police attitudes and dispositions in domestic disputes: the London study', *Police Journal*, July, 230–41.

Edwards, S. S. M. (ed.) (1989). *Policing 'Domestic' Violence* (London, Sage).

Eisikovits, Z. C. and Edleson, J. L. (1989). 'Intervening with men who batter: a critical review of the literature', *Social Service Review*, Winter, 414.

Fagan, J. (1992). 'The social control of spouse assault', in F. Adler and W. Laufer (eds.), *Advances in Criminological Theory*, Vol. 4 (New Brunswick, NJ, Transaction Publishers).

Fagan, J. and Browne, A. (1994). 'Violence between spouses and intimates: physical aggression between women and men in relationships', in A. J. Reiss and J. A. Roth (eds.), *The Understanding and Control of Violent Behaviour* (Washington, DC, National Academy Press).

Finn, P. and Colson, R. (1990). *Civil Protection Orders: Legislation, Current Court Practice and Enforcement* (Washington, DC, National Institute of Justice, US Department of Justice).

Gondolf, E. W. (1988). 'The effects of batterer counselling on shelter outcome', *Journal of Interpersonal Violence*, 3, 275–89.

Hamm, M. S. and Kite, J. C. (1991). 'The role of offender rehabilitation in family violence policy: the batterers anonymous experiment', *Criminal Justice Review*, 16, 227–48.

Meredith, C. and Burns, N. (1990). *Evaluation of Batterer's Treatment Programmes* (Abt Associates of Canada).

Pagelow, M. (1985). 'The "battered husband syndrome": social problem or much ado about little', in N. Johnson (ed.), *Marital Violence* (London, Routledge).

Pence, E. and Paymar, M. (1993). *Education Groups for Men Who Batter: The Duluth Model* (New York, Springer Publishing).

Pirog-Good, M. A. and Stets, J. (1986). 'Program for abusers: who drops out and what can be done', *Response*, 9, 17–19.

Saunders, D. G. and Hanusa, D. (1986). 'Cognitive–behavioral treatment for men who batter: the short-term effects of group therapy', *Journal of Family Violence*, 1, 357–72.

Sherman, L. W. (1992), *Policing Domestic Violence: Experiments and Dilemmas* (New York, Free Press).

Sherman, L. W. and Berk, B. A. (1984). 'The specific deterrent effects of arrest for domestic assault', *American Sociological Review*, 49, 261–72.

Yllo, K. (1993). 'Feminist: gender, power and violence', in R. J. Gelles and D. R. Loseke, *Current Controversies on Family Violence* (London, Sage).

18

An overview of community-based intervention programmes for men who are violent or abusive in the home

RUTH FRANCES

Although it is difficult to ascertain the real incidence of domestic violence in Australia, there is growing concern about what is considered to be an unacceptably high level of violence in the home. Some indication of the level of concern is that family violence was the most common topic of submissions made to the 1989 National Committee on Violence Inquiry. A recent telephone survey estimated that 321,000 people in Victoria (resident population 4,465,200) are direct victims of domestic violence, and more than half a million people interviewed said that they knew someone in their immediate family who was a victim (Saulwick Poll, June 1993). The definition of violence used in that survey involved physical violence only.

Thirteen per cent of the women surveyed and 17 per cent of the men believed that such violence was justified if a partner was having an affair. Nine per cent of women and 8 per cent of men thought that violence was justified if the partner refused to have sex. Seven per cent of the women and 5 per cent of the men believed that violence was justified if the partner failed to fulfil household duties (Saulwick 1993).

Victoria's response to family violence

At the present time, a wide range of services and resources are available to support victims of family violence in Victoria. They include specialist services, such as the Domestic Violence and Incest Resource Centre, Women's Refuge Referral Service, women's refuges, Domestic Violence Outreach Services, and Ethnic Refuge Workers programme. Support is also available from Community Police Crisis Support Units; Community Legal Centres; Court Welfare nformation Network; telephone counselling services; and Citizens' Advice Bureaux; together with a range of other health and welfare agencies, both government and non-government funded. These services are almost all available in the metropolitan and urban areas; however, they are markedly less available in rural areas of the state. During 1993 the Victorian Department of Health and Community Services alone spent $8.25 million on the provision of services to victims of domestic violence. The same department spent approximately $33,000 during one year (1992) on direct intervention programmes for abusive men.

Development of group programmes for violent men in Victoria first occurred in 1985, in response to initiatives in legal reform, and following public meetings on the topic of what to do about family violence. Initially, this work was considered to be somewhat contentious; however, there is evidence in recent times to suggest a considerable shift of opinion. Since their first appearance in Victoria, groups for men have evolved considerably in terms of ideology, process, structure and content. There has been a significant amount of collective effort and developmental work around issues of standards of practice, agency accountability, professional safeguards, partner safety and quality assurance.

Programmes for violent men are now available throughout the state. They are mainly provided by community-based health and welfare services, and are conducted by generalist workers at the agency. Group leaders are usually social workers or psychologists. In most agencies, groups for men have been established as a direct consequence of staff involvement in working with women and children victims, and in response to community demand. It is important to stress that the men presently attending Victorian services are mainly voluntary clients, and are not being referred by the courts.

Group programmes use a mixture of educational and psychological strategies to facilitate attitude and behaviour change. Programme staff believe that men are confronted with the criminality of their behaviour, and encouraged to take full responsibility for what has occurred. Within the group, the men consider how society and culture impact on the individual, and covertly support a wide range of attitudes and behaviours which collectively become known as family or domestic violence. Men are taught various techniques and strategies to cope with frustration and anger, and to identify correctly what is going on in their relationships. There are fairly rigorous intake and selection processes at most agencies, before men are admitted to the group.

To date, there has been little evaluation of programmes for batterers in Australia; however, studies which do exist have suggested that groups can have significant success in preventing physical violence. The findings are less clear about the effectiveness of groups in the area of attitude change. This may be partly due to the very small numbers in most Australian studies, and is probably also due to the inadequacy of most measurement instruments to deal with the complexities of family violence (Follingstad 1990; Dobash and Dobash 1990; Yllo and Bograd 1988). There are enormous difficulties in conducting research in this area, as most previous researchers have discovered (Follingstad 1990).

One study of male programmes in South Australia reported evidence to suggest that '60–80% of violent men prepared to engage in group counselling can achieve very substantial reductions in their level of abuse' (Wehner 1985). Poynter (1989) found that groups were successful in realizing nearly all of their goals and objectives; however the most significant result was the reduction in men's physical and non-physical abusive behaviours (Poynter 1989). Another study at the Melton Community Health Centre found that the group was successful in significantly reducing physically abusive behaviours, and in reducing the level of conflict experienced in the family environment (Hughes 1991).

The underlying beliefs about working with men are similar to the idea of re-integrative shaming, described by Braithwaite (1989). Braithwaite maintains that 'a society which shames an offender without stigmatising him will be a less violent society'. He suggests that shaming which is 'reintegrative . . . followed by re-acceptance of the offender into the community of law-abiding citizens, can have a rehabilitative effect' (Braithwaite 1989). However, what Braithwaite seems to suggest is that, if men are *only* receiving messages to the effect that violence and abuse in the home are criminal acts, *without any accompanying information, or alternative strategies being taught*, then this will only serve to stigmatize, and will 'reinforce and perpetuate offending'. According to this theory, any strong intervention about the criminality of family violence should also be accompanied by measures which serve to re-educate, and re-integrate men as acceptable persons in the community. This is consistent with learning theory and other behaviour modification techniques, which also maintain that while getting rid of undesirable behaviours is possible, unless they are replaced by alternative behaviours and strategies, the individual is likely to return to former tactics as soon as the intervention terminates (Bandura 1973; Bandura and MacDonald 1963; Bandura and Walter 1959; Walker 1984).

In the context of violence in the home, Braithwaite's theory is only useful provided that working with men is not necessarily about their acceptance back into the home, or family. It is not about men working on their marriages or relationships. It is *only* about working on men's violence and abusive behaviour and attitudes, which may then impact on their interaction with *anyone* in the community who comes into contact with them, adult or child, either in the present or the future. Taking responsibility for what has occurred, and commitment to long-term work towards change, would be seen as leading to eventual re-integration *in the community*. In Victoria, community education messages, via electronic and print media, are now being given to men that violence and abusive behaviour in the home is wrong, illegal, and unacceptable to the community. Most of these messages also include contact phone numbers for the Men's Referral Service, or places where men can get help. These messages targeting men have only appeared in recent times; earlier campaigns have almost exclusively targeted women, with messages about their rights to legal protection, that abusive behaviour is wrong, and that they don't have to put up with it, and can get help from a variety of sources.

The work now taking place in Victorian groups for men traverses the disciplines of social psychology, education, sociology, and feminist theory; particularly the area known as group dynamics and what are described as experiential learning techniques (Lewin, Lippitt and White 1939; Bavelas 1942). Largely owing to the professional qualifications, training and experience of some workers in this area, this work has also borrowed a combination of techniques more often used in therapeutic settings, such as stress management,[1] behaviour modification,[2] or cognitive restructuring processes.[3] It is well documented in the fields of education and psychology that almost any behaviour which is learned can also be 'unlearned' (Bandura and Walter 1959) in certain circumstances. The basic principles and processes involved in education or 're-education' can be observed in daily application in any classroom, as well as in the training of military personnel, in the recruitment process and practices of evangelistic religious groups, or in political prison camps in various parts of the world.

In many instances, abusive men have themselves been severely physically, sexually and psychologically abused as children, or have witnessed violence at a formative stage in their understandings about interpersonal relationships. Workers say that in these circumstances, it is sometimes necessary to use therapeutic techniques in order to assist men who have been almost 'frozen' into a state of flattened affective response: an inability to 'feel' or experience emotional states. They believe it is not always possible to clear the way towards effective new learning without this taking place. Sometimes, it is suggested that men deal with this situation in one-to-one counselling sessions outside the group setting, or when the group has finished.

The groupwork approach

If Braithwaite's notion of reintegrative shaming fairly accurately describes *what* groups for men set out to achieve, the work of Lewin and others in the area of group dynamics and experiential learning illustrates exactly *how* this is to be achieved.

Group work is a common way of bringing about attitude change. The field of group dynamics and experiential learning was mainly derived from the work of Kurt Lewin (1945) and others, looking at how the experience of being in a particular group can help bring about changes of attitude and acceptance of new social norms which are different to those originally held by individual group members. Lewin's research drew attention to the importance of 'active participation in groups in order to learn new skills, develop new attitudes, and obtain new knowledge'. Lewin's work revealed that 'learning is achieved most productively in groups whose members can interact, and then reflect on their mutual experiences . . . behaving democratically in structured learning situations'.

Working in this way generally involves creating exercises or learning situations where the group is involved in some task or discussion which simulates or recreates some problematic real-life situation. Actively participating in discovering more productive ways or comparing different ways of dealing with situations leads to more rapid learning and understanding of the dynamics of what is occurring. In addition, working in the group provides an environment conducive to learning new ways of thinking about or doing things, and practising newly learned skills. These experiential learning techniques are well known to teachers and other educators.

eminist perspectives

eminist theory has provided the central framework for nderstanding the nature of family violence. This body of knowledge as provided explanations of how it has come about that men and omen's unequal status in society and interpersonal relationships, nd the differential socialization of male and female children, have erpetuated violence and abuse in the home. Within this structural nalysis of gender relations, most Victorian groups use a combination f the techniques described above in order to assist men to move away om undesirable behaviours, and towards ways of thinking and cting which are more consistent with peaceful and egalitarian elationships with others.

However, there has been a certain amount of mistrust in Victoria out the credibility of groups for men who say they have adopted a eminist perspective'. There are differing views among workers about hat that means, in terms of working with the men. However, there is reason to suppose that professionals working directly with violent usive men, who regularly come into contact with victims in the ormal course of their work, meet often with other family violence orkers, attend conferences, seminars, and are involved in ongoing aining, etc., are any more or less likely to adopt a feminist rspective than others in the community. It is surely a matter of the gree to which feminist theory informs practice. Womens' Studies e alive and well in Victoria, and the understanding of the impact of nder in social relations is now present in some shape or form in ost social sciences at the tertiary level, and in the policy-making ea in most welfare organizations or government departments.

he context of development of programmes for men in Victoria

is sometimes suggested that groups for men are 'rapidly oliferating, in a policy vacuum'. However, in Victoria, a series of ents and enquiries have led to the establishment of programmes for olent men. Whilst policy-makers have not exactly been keen to ake public statements about their departments' policies, there has en a very definite trend which can be seen by examining the llowing documents and recommendations:

i.) Womens' Policy Co-ordination Unit, Department of Premier d Cabinet, Victoria 1985: 'Criminal Assault in the Home: Social d Legal Responses to Domestic Violence' 13.3, 13.4:

There are many women who, whilst not wishing to leave either their home or their partner, want the violence to stop. For these women, their partner's involvement in a counselling program may be the answer.

One of the major problems is that there is a dearth of such counselling programs in Victoria . . .

The document went on to recommend that funding be made available to a working party to ensure that pilot programs be established.

ii.) Social Development Committee, Parliament of Victoria, 1988 (p. 137):

Whilst it is important to provide support services for the victims of family violence, unless the perpetrators of the violence change their behaviour, the violence will continue.

This was followed by several specific recommendations about the type of services that should be made available, including calls that:

Detailed funding proposals be developed specifically for counselling services for violent men and that provision of such funds should be available throughout the state . . .

Counselling services for violent men should be provided by a variety of models using methods that are appropriate to the clients . . .

State-funded counselling programs for violent men be required to maintain a proportion of places in such programs for court referrals . . .

The Office of Corrections develop counselling services for violent men placed on Community Based Orders in circumstances where community programs are unavailable or unsuitable.

(Social Development Committee Report 1988)

iii.) National Committee on Violence, 1990 (p. 135) in the report 'Violence: Directions for Australia':

The recent development of preventative programs, such as counselling for violent men, is commendable . . .

These programs should be encouraged by Federal, State and Territory authorities, subject to systematic, controlled evaluation.

iv.) Victorian Community Council Against Violence, Inquiry into Services for those affected by family violence, Report No. 3, 1991:

The Community Council is generally supportive of the notion of perpetrator programs as a part of an integrated strategy to reduce and prevent violence against women and children . . .

Again, this was followed by a comprehensive series of recommendations, including many which are specific to the conduct of group programmes for men.

Concerns about groups for violent and abusive men

Workers in some of the strongly feminist-based women's services oppose the idea of programmes for violent men, and have suggested that:

> Counselling groups for men fit comfortably within a right wing capitalist ideology which uses and accepts patriarchy as an appropriate model for social organisation. The concept endorses the institution of the family as the most suitable unit of social cohesion. The family is the private arm of a public commitment to the values and aspirations of patriarchy. (Lazarus and McCarthy 1990)

This is not now reflective of general feeling in the community. A great many family violence workers are not opposed to the existence of groups for men, and support the method, provided that programmes meet with various criteria relating to the safety of women, and men take full responsibility for their violence. It is interesting that within agencies that are publicly opposed to this work, there are still many women who will privately indicate that they support male programmes in principle.

Family violence workers (those who work with men, as well as those who work with women and children) have expressed specific concerns about the development of group programmes for violent men. These concerns are:

— that programmes may not prioritize the safety of women, or that women may be unsafe if they make the decision to stay with a violent man, just because he is attending a group (McFerran, 1989);
— that scarce funds and resources will be diverted from victim support services if state or federal governments fund programmes for violent men (Dankert 1990; McCarthy 1990; Federation of Community Legal Centres 1992);
— that group programmes may be ineffective, or might make men worse;
— that courts might use such programmes as a diversionary

strategy (and thereby decriminalize and privatize the violence)
(McCarthy 1990), or that attendance at programmes might be
used as a way of obtaining favour in court, for the purposes of
obtaining bail, or continuing access to their partner's home, or
children;

— that the use of words such as 'therapy', 'counselling', 'support
programme', 'anger management' distracts the community's
attention from the criminality of family violence, and use of
these words in programmes allows men to deny or minimize
their violence (McCarthy 1990);

— that treatment programmes are 'an unworkable strategy given
the high drop-out and recidivism rates' (Lazarus and
McCarthy 1990; McFerran 1989);

— that by locating the problem with the individual offender, they
do not address or change the power relationship between
women and men (McCarthy 1990), and that if groups focus on
the development of stress and anger-management skills, they
evade the issue of abuse of power (Lazarus and McCarthy
1990);

— that programmes might be conducted by unskilled or
inappropriate persons, or former perpetrators;

— that whilst programmes might be effective in reducing physical
violence, they might at the same time actually increase the
amount of verbal or emotional violence;

— that programmes might be conducted by persons who do not
have an understanding of the centrality of gender issues in
social relations, and the imbalance of power between men and
women in our society and culture.

The Victorian Family Violence Prevention Committee, in its 1989
discussion paper *Programs for Violent Men* states:

the criminal nature of family violence must be dealt with accordingly and
programs for violent men should not provide an avenue whereby violent
behaviour can be excused if the aggressor is attending counselling, or
'program' in anger management. (FVPC Discussion Paper, 1989)

It then goes on to make a number of recommendations to the effect
that if programmes for violent men do exist, then they should abide
by certain principles. This discussion paper also recommended that
'an evaluation of services for violent men be undertaken to help shape
policy guidelines for future service development' (FVPC Discussion

per 1989). Whilst most of these concerns are perfectly reasonable, me have been grounded in the absence of accurate information out what actually takes place in group programmes, and of the perience of men or their partners attending these programmes.

It is now widely believed in Victoria that there is a need to explore osely the future development of groups for men, disseminate more curate information about the nature, processes, and content of oups, and evaluate not only in terms of how the programmes pact on men, but also how they impact on women and children. It considered essential to know how men's groups impact on other zencies supporting victims and where and how they fit into the erall, long-term strategy to prevent violence and abuse in the home.

ypes of service available for men in Victoria

recent years, there have been several different initiatives in the velopment of intervention with violent and abusive men in ustralia. To some extent, workers have had something of an lvantage, in that they have been aware of the overseas experience id aware of the concerns of women's services, and have been able to iggy-back' on the research and developmental work inter-state and erseas. There have been five significant stages or events in the ovision of intervention programmes for men in Victoria:

— The development of attitude/behaviour-change programmes
— The development of ongoing men's discussion/'support' groups
— The establishment of residential facilities for men
— The establishment of a Men's Telephone Referral Service (Australian Red Cross)
— The establishment of VICNET: a men's programme providers' network

ttitude/behaviour-change groups

he main stated aim or purpose of attitude/behaviour-change groups
: *i.)* to stop physical violence; *ii.)* to commence work towards anging other forms of abusive and controlling behaviour. In ictoria, these groups are mainly located at Community Health entres, which are funded by the state government. These centres ovide a wide range of other health and welfare services, in addition one-to-one counselling support and other services for women and ildren victims of violence. Group leaders are normally generalist

workers. Other groups are located in non-government agencies, such as church-based welfare agencies.

Groups are also conducted by private practitioners; some being retained by the Department of Justice to conduct groups for Office of Corrections clients. In Victoria, it is possible for any private individuals to set themselves up as 'counsellors' or 'therapists', provided they do not describe themselves as psychologists, doctors or other regulated professionals.

Attitude/behaviour-change groups have a limited life of somewhere between 12 and 16 weeks, and a set of specific aims and objectives connected with stopping or preventing further violence. There is usually a fairly rigorous intake-screening process, before men are admitted to the group. There is a specific content, structure or programme which aims to re-educate men. In contrast, 'support' or discussion groups are generally an ongoing affair, and do not have any particular format, although there may well be recurring themes which reflect the similarity of men's experiences.

Ongoing discussion or 'support' groups

Men attend these groups as and when they choose to attend. Such groups are frequently established as an adjunct to an attitude/behaviour-change group, as described above. The stated aim and purpose of this type of group is to provide encouragement and support to men who have decided they wish to change:

1.   while waiting for the next attitude/behaviour change group to begin;
2.   after attending a behaviour-change group, as a means of maintaining or continuing work commenced there, or as a stepping-stone to some other form of personal development course;
3.   during the time they are attending a behaviour-change group, if they would like more support in between meetings of that group.

Such groups are often located in the same agency as attitude/behaviour-change groups, or at nearby community centres. Usually they are conducted by the same generalist workers from the men's group, or men who are considered suitable 'graduates' from nearby attitude/behaviour-change programmes. They are often used as a

olding bay, where it can be ascertained whether or not men are
ufficiently motivated to work on changing attitudes and behaviour.

esidential facilities: 'Men's House'

Vhere men are physically violent, they are encouraged to move out of
ome, and live in at a men's house while attending an attitude/
ehaviour-change group. Edward Gondolf, who is regarded as a
eading figure in the field of working with abusive men, speaks of
ree practical advantages of residential men's centres:

> They can provide an atmosphere that more decisively challenges the
> abuser's sense of isolation and more comprehensively monitors his
> behaviour . . . a residential men's centre offers a place to 'cool off' for men
> encountered by police on domestic violence calls . . . such centres present
> an alternative to battered women being uprooted from the convenience of
> their homes and children being removed from their friends and school.
> (Gondolf 1985; 180)

he underlying belief at the Victorian mens' houses is that: *i.)* men
ould take responsibility for their violence and its consequences, and
.) that women and children should not have to move out of their own
ome, on account of men's violence/abuse. These houses require that
en living there attend a men's attitude/behaviour-change group, and
re supervised by a committee of management for the house.
Vomen's refuge workers and female family violence workers have
ngoing input into the conduct of these houses, and have significantly
ontributed to their existence. At present there are two such houses in
ictoria, with a third being planned for the future. In both existing
tuations, the residential facility is only one component of a total
ackage' of family violence services provided by the agency or centre
volved.

elephone referral service

he most recent initiative in working with men in Victoria is a state-
ide telephone referral service, staffed by trained male volunteers,
hich is on-line Monday to Friday from 6.00 to 9.00 p.m. This service
an initiative of Australian Red Cross. It aims to provide confidential
formation and referral to appropriate services for men who want to
ange violence or abuse. In its first year of operation, the Men's
eferral Service has received over 1,500 calls from men seeking help to
ange violent and abusive behaviour. There is a known 'success' rate

of 70 per cent – success being defined as the man subsequentl
presenting himself to a men's group or private practitioner fo
assistance.

VICNET: the men's programme providers' network
VICNET (Victorian Network for the Prevention of Male Famil
Violence) presently consists of some sixty-two individuals an
agencies, within the health, welfare or corrections system, who ar
presently working with violent men towards changing their attitude
and behaviour. The network liaises with government departments an
other family violence networks in the community. Members mee
monthly and are concerned with working on issues of accountabilit
standards of practice and supervision and training of workers. Th
network conducts ongoing in-service training workshops/seminars fo
workers in this area. In 1994 the network received government fundin
to provide a full-time project worker, who will develop a policy an
procedures manual, and training modules.VICNET liaises wit
tertiary institutions, assists in the placement of tertiary students
assists researchers, and generally acts as a clearing house for th
exchange of information between workers in Victoria and inter-state.

The Melbourne University study

During 1992–3, the Criminology Department at Melbourne
University obtained funds to conduct an independent study of eigh
Victorian attitude/behaviour-change groups for violent or abusive
men. The study has operated within a feminist research paradigm,
using a series of guiding principles based on the work of Mies (1983).
Within these guidelines, the researchers adopted something of a
'stakeholders' approach, in that the concerns of all interested partie
were identified and incorporated into the framework of the research
The study has attempted to provide a detailed descriptive analysis o
the groups, their history, philosophy, source of funding, structure an
practice.

The research included examination of programme documentation
interviews with programme staff, survey questionnaires administere
pre- and post-attendance to participants, and interviews with mal
participants and female partners. Demographic information has now
been obtained from 116 male participants (including pilot studies)
and pre–post measures were attempted with a sample of eighty-seve

men. Fourteen programme staff were interviewed; twenty-nine women and thirty-two men volunteered to be interviewed. A number of important methodological problems were encountered. However, qualitatively rich information has been obtained, and a substantial amount of demographic information hitherto unavailable in Australia has been collected.

Some preliminary findings of the Victorian study

Who attends the groups?

It is important to state that there appears to be a certain amount of self-selection in the type of men who make it as far as attending a men's group in Victoria. There is a fairly rigorous process of screening out of men who are not thought to be sufficiently motivated to work towards change, or have unaddressed alcohol/drug abuse problems, psychiatric problems, or an intellectual disability. The question being asked here is whether or not this selection bias is any reason to downgrade the quality of the work being done, when there is a clearly demonstrable need in the community.

Whilst Victorian groups are attended by those from a diverse range of socio-economic circumstances, there is a distinct bias toward older, less well-educated working-class men. The largest proportion of men who attended were in the 25–34 years age group, 70 per cent had not completed their secondary education, and 46 per cent listed trade/labour as their employment. Twenty-four per cent listed their occupation as white-collar. Seventy-seven per cent said they used alcohol, but mainly described themselves as 'occasional' drinkers. Just over half of the men (51 per cent) were not living with partners at the time they attended the groups.

While the men who participated in the study were not referred by the criminal justice system, this could potentially occur. Thirty-four per cent of participants had been referred to groups by social workers, 16 per cent by telephone counselling services, and 16 per cent had been told about the group by their wife or partner. Many said they had responded to community education campaigns targeting men.

Half of the men (50 per cent) said police had never been called on account of their violence, while 47 per cent said police had been called. Thirty-three per cent said their wife/partner had taken out intervention orders against them. Sixty-two per cent of the men said they had been victims of violence or abuse as children, and 67 per cent said they had witnessed violence between their parents or care-givers as children. Seventy-six per cent of the men said they had been physically violent towards their partners, and 84 per cent said they were also abusive in other ways. Twenty-eight per cent said their partners had needed treatment for physical injuries, 16 per cent said their partners had needed treatment for depression on account of the violence, and 29 per cent said their partners had needed treatment for other psychological or emotional distress as a result of the violence.

Drop out
Twenty-seven per cent of men who attended the first session did not complete, or did not attend on the last night when the final survey questionnaire was administered. Men who dropped out were no different in age distribution to the other men, but were more likely not to have completed secondary education (87 per cent, compared to 65 per cent of stayers), less likely to be employed, and less likely to be living with a partner than the other men. The level of alcohol use among men who dropped out was somewhat heavier, and men who left programmes scored higher on self-reported measures of violence than those who stayed.

Women partners' beliefs
Of the women partners interviewed, 45 per cent thought there were differences in the way their partner behaved towards children since attending. Forty-eight per cent of the women said his attendance had made a real difference to her life, regardless of whether or not they were living together. Sixty-six per cent of the women said her partner's attendance had been a worthwhile experience from her point of view.

Men's beliefs about the groups
Of the men interviewed, 78 per cent believed they had learned something about male socialization and the roles of men and women in society. Eighty-four per cent reported they had learned something specific which had been helpful to them personally. Over half (59 per cent) vividly remembered experiential learning exercises. Three-quarters of the men (75 per cent) interviewed said their attitudes or behaviours had been challenged or confronted by programme staff Thirty-one per cent said programme staff had suggested that they

:rsonally should move out. Eighty-four per cent believed that
tending the group had been of practical use and had made a
fference to their lives. Ninety-four per cent believed the group had
:en effective in helping them to change their behaviour. Sixty-seven
:r cent said they had definite plans to continue with the work stated
. the group.

onclusions

— There are fewer differences between groups and programmes
than we would have expected, based on a reading of the
literature. We believe this may be partly attributable to the
community development model which has emerged in
Victoria, and the existence of VICNET, which has encouraged
more uniform standards of practice and accountability.

— Victorian groups are not at this time being used as a
diversionary strategy or an alternative to sentencing.

— There is no evidence to suggest that the provision of such
groups in community health centres in any way undermines
the agencies' capacity to provide support services to women.

— There is evidence to suggest that men in Victoria are
responding to community education campaigns targeting
violent and abusive men.

sues for policy-makers and research

istralian policy-makers have been in the unenviable situation of
iving to attempt to provide direction for appropriate government
sponses in the area of programmes for violent men, on the basis of
ry limited information about the groups. In the number of men
esenting themselves, and the number of enquiries about pro-
ammes for men, there is now evidence that the community is
:pressing a need for some process by which violent and abusive men
n be assisted to change. It appears that most of the men who attend
oups believe the process to be helpful and conducive to change. A
gnificant proportion of women partners also find the existence of
oups for men helpful.

Programmes for men represent only one part of the community's
tal response to family violence. Long-term community education is
:en as the primary means of bringing about a significant reduction
family violence and violence towards women in Australia. Another

critical component of the overall strategy is appropriate action and response by the police and the criminal justice system. The community must be able to respond quickly to support victims, and to provide emergency accommodation and crisis response. However programmes for violent men are now in place as part of the total community response to family violence in Victoria, and further research is needed in order to determine the most effective format and procedures.

There has been much public debate about custodial sentences as a response to family violence. The view expressed here is that perpetrators of family violence must be subject to the same application of the criminal law as others in society. If a custodial sentence is appropriate, then it must be used. However, there are situations where gaol sentences are not considered to be an appropriate legal option. It is possible that in these situations group programmes for men could offer an additional opportunity for attitude or behavioural change to occur. However, it seems likely that men who might be referred in this way could be considered unsuitable to attend the type of community-based group presently seen in Victoria. It also seems likely that the apparent 'success' of groups in Victoria may have a lot to do with the make-up of the groups, and the voluntary nature of participation. If existing community-based group programmes experienced increased numbers of referrals from courts or correctional systems the authors of the present study believe that it might well undermine the work being done.

Those working in the justice and correctional system, and programme staff of male groups, need to enter into some dialogue around this process, and explore whether there needs to be a different type of group for men who are referred by the courts. The expertise and skills of community-based workers are surely a valuable source of information for the development of any new corrections-based programme. Those in the difficult position of having to make referrals must now have clear, detailed information available to them concerning the nature, quality and efficacy of groups for men. It is essential they are able to make referrals based upon a clear understanding of which men will or will not be accepted into such a group, and whether or not the group is appropriate for the man being referred.

It is also essential that workers supporting women, whether they are still living with abusive partners or not, can also have a clear derstanding of what these groups actually do, and about women rtners' beliefs on this issue. Everyone needs to know what impact oup attendance might potentially have in facilitating a more aceful separation; what impact it might have on men's behaviour wards children, and the consequences for children; or on men's elihood of being abusive towards future partners or children. We ed to know what combination of strategies will give us the most fective, long-lasting result of bringing about a reduction in the cidence of family violence, and in bringing about positive changes the community's thinking and response to family violence.

The present discussion is occurring at a time of more holistic proaches to health and welfare in Australia, and multi-faceted lutions to social problems, rather than specialized responses dealing ith only one aspect of the problem. Effective response to family olence crosses all professional boundaries, and needs the active pport and participation of all sectors of the community.

Gondolf (1993) suggests that we should be asking whether oviding groups for men is better than doing nothing at all, when tions are few and resources are limited. He goes on to suggest that ther than continually attempting to 'prove the unprovable' we ould be more concerned with looking towards the conduct of oups and with developing appropriate standards of practice and ntent. We would concur with this position, and suggest that orkers and researchers continue to address these questions. We also rongly suggest that the provision of groups for men only takes place an agency context where a full range of support options are ailable for women partners and children.

otes

In particular, recognition of physiological indicators of arousal, stress, anger. This is important, as men often believe that they 'fly off the handle' in a matter of a couple of seconds. Men are taught that the process actually takes a lot longer than that; there are many physiological warning signs and indicators of arousal and accompanying emotional states that need to be accurately identified.

Usually involving the 'shaping' of behaviour, and intermittent reinforcement of moves towards more acceptable ways of thinking and doing things. See Walker (1984) for a thorough description of this process. Also involving vicarious learning through observing other men's changes in attitudes and behaviour. See Bandura (1973); Bandura and MacDonald (1963); Bandura and Walter (1959).

[3] This is a term used by psychologists to describe a specific process, which is often aimed for in a therapeutic setting. However, within the analysis above, this simply means bringing about men's understanding of what are patriarchal or unacceptable ways of thinking about things, and learning non-patriarchal, egalitarian ways of thinking about things. While the technical definition of this process is a psychological term, it is difficult to decide whether this activity in working with men can be accurately described as 'therapeutic' in the usual sense. If this were so, then any act of changing one's mind could be described as therapeutic – which may or may not be the case.

References

Bandura, A. (1973). *Aggression: a social learning analysis* (Englewood Cliffs NJ, Prentice-Hall).

Bandura A. and MacDonald, F. J. (1963). 'Influence of social reinforcement and the behaviour of models in shaping children's moral judgements' *Journal of Abnormal and Social Psychology*, 67, 274–81.

Bandura, A. and Walter, R. H. (1959). *Adolescent Aggression* (New York Ronald Press).

Bavelas, A. (1942). 'Morale and training of leaders', in G. Watson (ed.) *Civilian Morale* (Boston, Houghton Mifflin).

Braithwaite, J. (1989). *Crime, Shame and Reintegration* (Cambridge, Cambridge University Press).

Dankert, M. (1990). 'The seductive power of men's counselling', *Women's Liberation Newsletter*, September.

Dobash, R. E. and Dobash, R. P. (1990). 'How theoretical definitions and perspectives affect research and policy', in D. J. Besharov (ed.), *Family Violence: Research and Public Policy Issues* (Washington, DC, The AEI Press).

Follingstad, D. (1990). 'Methodological issues and new directions for research on violence in relationships', in D. J. Besharov (ed.), *Family Violence: Research and Public Policy Issues* (Washington, DC, The AEI Press).

Gondolf, E. W. (1985). *Men Who Batter: An Integrated Approach for Stopping Wife Abuse* (Florida, Learning Publications Inc.).

Gondolf, E. W. (1993). 'Reconceptualising Batterer Program Evaluation', paper presented at the Third National Conference for Professionals Working with Men Who Batter, Minneapolis, MN, 14–17 April, 1993.

Hughes, B. (1991). 'An Evaluation of a Group Programme for Perpetrators of Domestic Violence', unpublished thesis, School of Social Sciences, Monash University College, Gippsland.

Lazarus, S., and McCarthy, K. (1990). 'Panacea for social issues', *Legal Service Bulletin*, 15(1), 30–1.

Lewin, K., Lippitt, R. and White, R. (1939). 'Patterns of aggressive behaviour in experimentally created "social climates"', *Journal of Social Psychology* 10, 271–99.

McCarthy, K. (1990). 'Therapy or social change? What to do about men who are violent to women and children', paper presented at the 'Family Violence Working for Change' Conference, 27 October 1990, University of Melbourne.

McFerran, L. (1989). *Report to the NSW Domestic Violence Committee on Batterer's Programs*, June.

Mies, M. (1983). 'Towards a methodology for feminist research', in G. Bowles and R. Duelli-Klein (eds.), *Theories of Womens' Studies.*

Poynter, T. (1989). 'An evaluation of a group programme for male perpetrators of domestic violence', *Australian Journal of Sex, Marriage and Family*, 10(3), 133–42.

National Committee on Violence (1990). *Violence: Directions for Australia* (ACT: Australian Institute of Criminology).

Social Development Committee, Victorian Parliament (1988). *Inquiry Into Strategies to Deal with the Issue of Community Violence: Second Report of the Inquiry, with Particular Reference to Children, Young People and Families* (Government Printing Service).

Victorian Community Council Against Violence (1991). *Treatment and Counselling of Perpetrators* (Victoria: VCCAV).

Victorian Family Violence Prevention Committee (1989). 'Programs for Violent Men' (discussion paper).

Walker, S. (1984). *Learning Theory and Behaviour Modification* (London, Methuen).

Women's Policy Co-ordination Unit (1985). *Criminal Assault in the Home: Social and Legal Responses to Domestic Violence* (Victoria Department of Premier and Cabinet).

Yllo, K. and Bograd, M. (1988). *Feminist Perspectives on Wife Abuse* (London, Sage).

19

The role of the police in combating domestic violence

SAM WRIGHT

This chapter reports on the interim findings of an empirical study into the policing of domestic violence in the Nottinghamshire Constabulary, focusing on a single police division.[1] The study forms one part of a three-year research project investigating the legal and economic dynamics of domestic violence. There are many different definitions of domestic violence, but the one used in this research programme has been developed by Nottinghamshire Domestic Violence Forum, and includes: 'all emotional, sexual, physical, psychological and economic abuse of a woman by a man . . . with whom she has, or has had a relationship'.[2] In contrast, the police see domestic violence as being suffered by both men and women, although they acknowledge that more women report violence. Moreover, the term 'relationship' is certainly narrower for the police than it is for the Forum,[3] and is restricted to close personal relationships; yet this does include extended family members, girlfriends and boyfriends, and relationships which have ended.

The aim of the police study as a whole is to analyse policing policy as formed by police ideologies and official statistics, and to contrast this with the real and perceived needs of women, as revealed by in-depth interviews with a small sample of women survivors of domestic violence. However, this chapter is limited to a descriptive analysis of the nature and scope of domestic violence reported to one police subdivision in Nottingham over a period of twenty-three months, and the range of police responses that are made. This initial appraisal suggests that police statistics may merely *reflect* police attitudes rather than being an accurate source from which to develop policy. This is of particular concern given the recent Home Affairs Select Committee (1993: para 10) recommendation that 'the Home Office upgrade the quality of national statistics on domestic violence which come to the attention of the criminal justice system'.

The first section of this chapter reviews police powers, and previous research into the policing of domestic violence, contrasting two main themes: women's needs or motivations for calling the police, and police attitudes towards domestic violence. In the second section there is a discussion of the field study, and an examination of the findings from an analysis of police statistics from that sub-division. The conclusion presents suggestions for the future development of policing practices.

Policing practices

The criminal law

The law with respect to the criminal dimension of domestic violence is mainly covered by the Offences Against the Person Act (1861). This encompasses offences ranging from common assault to murder. Common assault is the only offence which is not arrestable, yet under the Police and Criminal Evidence Act (1984) arrests can be made where an offence has not actually been committed, if it is deemed necessary to prevent physical injury to vulnerable persons (section 25), or if the constable suspects that an arrestable offence has been, or is about to be committed (section 24). In addition, a constable may enter any premises for the purpose of arresting a person for an arrestable offence, in order to save life or limb or to prevent serious damage to property, or, under common law, to prevent a breach of the peace. Arrests can also be made under the common law to prevent a breach of the peace, or in response to a breach of an injunction which has a power of arrest attached.

However, the discretion of individual police officers to define a crime is absolute, as is their decision of how to dispose of the case. Obviously, one important issue when considering policy changes is the extent to which initiatives are adopted by the police in action. Stanko (1989) notes that the police on the ground are reluctant to change their methods in line with new initiatives from policy-makers, in order to maintain a sense of control over their work. This is in line with anecdotal evidence from Nottingham, where the individual officer's discretion to deal with cases is seen as a fundamental aspect of police work, and anything seeking to remove that power is defined as undermining the position of the officer.

Thus, the police have very wide statutory and common-law powers to intervene in any violent incident, or in response to any threatening behaviour. Nevertheless, the degree of discretion which is available to the police means that their response is not uniform, and may vary for a whole host of reasons which have been examined by researchers on police attitudes towards domestic violence.

Recent research on policing domestic violence

Traditionally, domestic violence has not been seen to be the preserve of the police. Owing to notions surrounding the privacy of family relations, and the perceived rights of husbands to chastise their wives, the criminal element of interpersonal violence has been largely ignored, apart from exceptional cases (Faragher 1985; Freeman 1985). The dominant ideology that domestic violence was a private matter, due largely to the inadequate personality traits of both parties, only increased this tendency for the police to be reluctant to intervene.

Thus, the police have been one of the most highly criticized professional bodies, owing to their attitudes to both domestic violence, and women in general (Dobash and Dobash 1979; Dunhill 1989; Edwards 1989). Their status as one of the most patriarchal institutions in a patriarchal society appears to have been the source of one of their major problems. Trying to maintain the status quo in an ever-changing social arena places the police at the forefront of political upheaval. This inertia against social change has been well documented, particularly as it forms the basis of their victim-blaming attitudes, and of their problems in dealing with the ethnic minority community (Edwards 1989; Hanmer, Radford and Stanko 1989; Smith and Gray 1983).

In 1986, however, there appeared to be a watershed in the area of domestic violence, as it began to be recognized and treated as a serious social problem. The Home Office (1986a) produced a circular for the police which emphasized that when dealing with domestic violence, there was an 'overriding concern to reduce the risk of further violence . . . after the departure of the police from the scene'. In the same year, however, lesson notes were published by the Home Office (1986b) for the guidance of officers on the initial police training course. These stated:

1) A domestic dispute is generally a breakdown in day to day domestic family relationships, which have reached a stage where police attendance is required.

2) There is usually no criminal offence involved and although the dispute may be an isolated occasion, it is common for some disputes to occur regularly over a long period.

Police Objectives: The object of police attendance at the scene of a domestic dispute is to restore the peace.

These lesson notes remained in use until July 1989 (Bourlet 1990).

Such conflicting messages, advocating an increased concern about domestic violence, but in practical terms minimizing the role of the police, can be found in the very structure of the criminal justice system. Section 39 of the Criminal Justice Act (1988) made the offence of common assault and battery a summary one, triable only in the magistrates' courts, and increased the maximum penalty to six months imprisonment. The magistrates' courts may be preferable to Crown courts because they tend to hear cases more quickly, there is only one hearing, and the defence is not entitled to advance disclosure of the prosecution's case. However, as Edwards and Halpern (1992) argue, this opportunity to use a common assault trivializes the severity of domestic violence. Thus, despite the discourse surrounding the seriousness of domestic violence, for example, the 1990 Home Office Guidelines for Chief Officers of Police, there is a definite incentive to 'down-crime' assaults to common assault so that cases can proceed speedily through the criminal justice system, with less chance of the victim's withdrawing evidence (Edwards and Halpern 1991).

In looking at women's decisions to call the police, Pahl (1985) found that women normally only turn to the police after suffering a sequence of violent attacks, and after seeking help from a variety of other informal and formal sources. Once women do involve the police they generally need 'to be believed, to be taken seriously and to be helped by stopping the violent man from continuing the violence' (Bourlet 1990: 93), although any positive action or sympathetic approach made by the police is welcomed.

In contrast, the police, in the face of increasing pressure to improve arrest and charge rates, become easily disillusioned with problems which they see as being largely irresolvable, preferring 'decisions to be clear cut and problems to have a solution' (Victim Support 1992: 11). They view domestic violence as more of a private issue, to be addressed within the relationship, or through the civil courts (Borkowski *et al.* 1983; Pahl 1982), and categorize domestic violence as an aspect of 'soft' policing, which includes community policing and support work, resulting in a more lenient and non-interventionist approach towards domestic violence (Faragher 1985).

In minimizing the severity of domestic violence, the police provide several 'mitigating factors' to explain violence in the home. One of the common police conceptions is that violence is linked to alcohol consumption, especially amongst the 'working class', and in particular with the unemployed members of the working class. Thus the police anticipate more violence over the weekend when people tend to drink more, and on a Thursday when unemployment benefit and income support payments are made available. Other common 'mitigating factors' include the end of the relationship, the relationship being known as 'violent', or judgements about women provoking violence.

It is this general reluctance to act in cases of domestic violence, and the belittling of the damage that emotional and physical abuse cause, which are still the main problems with the police. Whilst they view such abuse as 'six of one and half a dozen of the other', and as a normal occurrence within an intimate relationship (Edwards 1986), it is hard for them to make a positive contribution against domestic violence. There seems to be a great divide between women's motivations for calling the police, and the resulting police action. Women call the police in an emergency, wanting direct intervention, and above all needing to be believed and helped. The police, on the other hand, interpret domestic violence as an argument which has got out of hand. They try to act as a calming influence, sometimes offering advice on civil protection. Where the police do consider a prosecution they require evidence and the commitment of the woman to the criminal justice process. It can be suggested therefore that the change in policy will not result in the police being more pro-active because the two bases of understanding about domestic violence have not converged, and attitudes towards domestic violence remain largely the same. Thus, it could still be anticipated that the police will 'down-crime' domestic violence, producing low arrest and charge rates, and that they will continue to divert cases through civil proceedings. This chapter is thus intended to provide an initial indication of the extent and scope of domestic violence that comes to the attention of the police, and their decisions concerning the disposition of the case.

The field study

Nottinghamshire Constabulary has a specially trained Family Support Unit which deals with the physical and sexual abuse of children and with domestic violence, working closely with Nottinghamshire Social Services. However, the police have a statutory duty to deal with child abuse, and given the great demands that such work makes on resources, the Family Support Unit only deals with very serious cases of domestic violence. Nevertheless, the police acknowledge the prevalence of domestic violence and the consequences that this has for their work, and have representatives on the County Council Domestic Violence Forum.

In 1992, Nottinghamshire Constabulary issued its own Domestic Violence Policy document, as a result of which all Nottinghamshire police subdivisions now keep a domestic violence register. This records personal details relating to both parties, the nature of the offence, and police action. In addition, domestic violence incidents are recorded on a card index, listing all the victims of domestic violence, their home address, the history of police call-outs, and the existence of any injunction. The information is recorded in a handwritten incident log which is kept at the station, and is not transferred to computer.

In May 1992 contact was established, initially with the chief constable, and then with Police Headquarters. The constabulary are willingly co-operating with this research programme, granting access to a police station for the collation of data from police files and message logs, and interviews with both officers and policy-makers. The overall aim of this project is an assessment of the extent to which the official policy changes have been adopted by the police on the ground.

The socio-economic context of the Radford Road Police subdivision

Nottinghamshire has the highest reported rate of violent crime in the country. Home Office criminal statistics for 1992 show that there were 315 reported cases of violence against the person per 100,000 of the population (in comparison with the national average of 395). Furthermore, Nottinghamshire has the highest rate of reported sexual offences, at 106 per 100,000 of the population (the national average being 58). The subdivision under study contains just over a quarter of the population of Nottingham, with 60,932 individuals being maintained within approximately 25,000 households. This part of

Nottingham in particular is notorious for its high crime levels, mainly burglary, car theft, and drug abuse. Crack is a growing problem in this area of Nottingham, threatening the area with ever-spiralling crime rates.

Nottinghamshire County Council (1991) reveals that household tenure in the area is: 46.8 per cent owner-occupier, 7.5 per cent privately rented, 5.2 per cent housing association rented, and 40.5 per cent council rented. The ethnic distribution of the population varies within the study area, but averages out at 8.45 per cent of the population being from the black and ethnic minority communities. Within the ethnic minority population, 47 per cent are identified as being Afro-Caribbean (4 per cent of the total population), and 40 per cent are Indian, Pakistani or Bangladeshi (3.4 per cent of the total population).

Nottinghamshire County Council estimates that the average unemployment rate for the study area is 12.8 per cent. However, the Nottingham City Council District Profile estimates that in the period March 1991–March 1992, the unemployment rate for the area rose by 25.5 per cent, meaning that approximately 16 per cent of the active population are unemployed. This compares with the national average of 9.56 per cent (Employment Gazette 1992: Table 7.1) In addition, 1.9 per cent of the population of the sample area is retired, 5.7 per cent are permanently sick, and 5.3 per cent are either students, or are on a government training scheme.

Radford Road Police statistics

Not all the cases of domestic violence are entered in the register; only the more violent ones get recorded. This screening occurs when individual officers judge that an incident was not 'serious' enough, or they forget to record the case in the register. The decision about whether a case warrants mention in the register depends not only on the attending officer, but also the shift to which he/she belongs, as different duty inspectors have different attitudes to domestic violence. It was, therefore, necessary to compare the information held in the register with the message logs which record all telephone calls made to the control room. Owing to the volume of calls that come into the station every day, it was necessary to take a sample of the log rather than reviewing all the calls, analysing the messages for a random week of every month. There did not appear to be any systematic bias in this sample.

To date there have been three volumes of the Domestic Violence Register at the station, but only the two most recent books can be found. The first register (February–May 1992) contained information about 126 cases of domestic violence (approximately 32 per month). Since May 1992 the rate of recording incidents in the register has fallen dramatically, in line with the informal screening of cases recorded in the register, so that the rate now averages out at twelve cases per month. Despite this, detailed information was available for the cases from June 1992 onwards, and this has been analysed.

During the period June 1992 to the end of April 1994, 279 domestic violence calls were registered in the station, with at least thirty-eight of them being repeat calls from women. Taking the estimate of 241 individual women calling the police, and county council figures for the number of households in the police subdivision (roughly 25,000 households), this accounts for almost 1 per cent of households in the area. An analysis of the police telephone message logs, however, suggests that there are approximately eight times as many domestic violence calls as the number entered in the register. Multiplying the figures for a 23-month period suggests that Radford Road actually received 2,470 reports of domestic violence. Discounting for the same rate of repeat calls (i.e., roughly 14 per cent),[4] it can be approximated that there have been 2,167 households reporting cases of domestic violence in that period. Thus, 8.7 per cent of households in the area *reported* domestic violence to the police in the period of twenty-three months.

An analysis of the nature of domestic violence calls recorded on the *message pad* was calculated for a random sample of weeks drawn from November 1992 to October 1993. Table 1 classifies all domestic violence calls that came into the control room, including those that were finally entered in the register. There are approximately twenty-four reports of domestic violence made to the station every week. On average, only three of these cases will be recorded in the domestic violence register, one-eighth of the true number of calls. As Table 1 shows, whilst the non-registered cases generally did not involve violence, or were cases where the victim later declined assistance, there were cases of Actual Bodily Harm, cases where a weapon was used threateningly, breaches of bail or injunctions, and reports from women already registered as victims of domestic violence.

All the tables use the classifications defined by the attending police officers, and where mere descriptions of the injuries were recorded the

Table 1: Message-pad statistics relation to domestic violence
November 1992–October 1993)

	Average no. of calls per week	Percentage	Estimated number of calls for a 23-month period
Argument	6	24.3	600
Harassment	6.1	24.7	610
Threatened or forced entry	1.6	6.5	160
Abuse of property	3.1	12.6	310
Child kidnapped	0.6	2.4	60
Assault	4.3	17.4	430
ABH	2.1	8.5	210
Use/threat of weapon	0.9	3.6	90
Totals	24.7	100	2470

Source: Nottingham Domestic Violence Study.

Table 2: Classification of registered violence (June 1992–April 1994)

	no.	%
Verbal dispute	50	17.9
Abuse of property	30	10.8
Assault	95	34.1
ABH	77	27.6
Beating up	12	4.4
Rape	1	0.4
Use of weapon	14	5.0
Total	279	100

Source: Nottingham Domestic Violence Study.

case was subsumed under one of the above categories. In Table 2, the categories of 'Argument' and 'Harassment' correlate to the description 'Verbal dispute', whilst 'Threatened/forced entry' and 'Abuse of property' are combined into one category.

The distribution of incidents recorded on the *register*, as Table 2 shows, is clearly skewed to physical violence, although the physical abuse of property features quite strongly in the registered cases. Such an analysis of the distribution of violent offences has been undertaken several times over the 23-month study period. The distribution has remained stable throughout this 23-month period, suggesting that decisions to record incidents in the register have been more or less consistent throughout the study period.

Table 3 shows the relationship between the severity of violence and the outcome of police action, and reveals that over 60 per cent of registered calls concerned an assault or ABH. However, only 23 per cent of cases involved the police pressing charges for assault or ABH. The most common police response was to decide that no action was required, or to issue advice or a warning, and this occurred in fifty cases of assault or ABH, and five cases of more severe violence.

In 40 per cent of cases no police action was taken, or only advice or cautions were issued. This is slightly higher than the proportion found after one year (32 per cent), and may indicate a decrease in the incentive to take action since the policy change first came into being. In 30 per cent of cases the police charged the perpetrator (compared with a rate of 43 per cent found in May 1993), with 59 per cent of the charges being of ABH (compared with 48 per cent last year). Given that the actual distribution of the severity of violence reported has remained more or less constant, the fall in the rate of arrests and charges reflects a decline in the propensity of the police to invoke the criminal justice system.

Of these 279 reports, only nine cases involved circumstances where the women had been violent. In two cases the woman's behaviour was in direct response to an attack, but both parties were nevertheless arrested and charged. One other case involved a woman being violent who had reported violence from her partner to the police in the past. The other three incidents did not record the preceding events. Six out of the nine women were arrested (66 per cent), and two women were charged with GBH. (See Dobash *et al.* 1992 for a full discussion of the sexual asymmetry of domestic violence.)

There does not seem to be much difference between these results in comparison with research findings on police action prior to the 1990 Home Office guidelines. The report of the Commissioner of the Metropolitan Police Force (1989) reported that 40 per cent of all recorded violent assaults resulted from domestic violence (13,119 cases out of 32,255) and, of those, 70 per cent resulted in an arrest. The subdivision in this research produced an arrest rate of 66 per cent out of the 199 registered violent assaults.

Edwards (1986b) described the tendency of the police to

Table 3: Police response by classification of violence

Outcome	Severity of Violence				
	Verbal dispute	Abuse of property	Assault or ABH	Severe violence	Row total (%)
Evidence refused	4	1	17	3	25 (8.9)
No police action, advice, or caution	40	16	50	5	111 (39.8)
Circulated but unfound	0	0	7	5	12 (4.3)
Arrest	6	6	34	2	48 (17.2)
Criminal damage/ public order charge	0	5	7	0	12 (4.3)
Assault charge	0	0	14	1	15 (5.4)
ABH	0	2	42	5	49 (17.6)
GBH charge	0	0	1	6	7 (2.5)
Column total (Percentage)	50 (17.9)	30 (10.8)	172 (61.6)	27 (9.7)	279 100

Source: Nottingham Domestic Violence Study.

downgrade the seriousness of the injuries, and rely on public order charges such as public drunkenness, public nuisance, breach of the peace. In her 1984/5 study of two London police stations she found that of the 773 domestic incidents which were reported, 93 (12 per cent) were recorded as crimes, and 16 (2 per cent) resulted in a charge (Edwards 1986a). In comparison, findings from the Radford Road Police station reveal that a charge was made in 20 per cent of the *registered* cases of domestic crimes. This figure has dropped

Table 4: Relationships of women to the aggressor

Relationship	no.	Valid percentage
Married	80	30.8
Cohabitants	74	28.5
Girlfriend	33	12.7
Past relationship	58	24.0
Other family member	6	2.3
Total	260	100

Source: Nottingham Domestic Violence Study.
Note: missing cases: 19.

substantially from the 39 per cent discovered in May 1992. One reason for this may be the decline in interest in enforcing the policy once it was no longer a new initiative. Moreover, given that there are approximately eight times as many domestic violence reports as entries in the register, this suggests that roughly 4 per cent of all domestic violence reports result in a charge.

The next three tables provide descriptive information about the nature of the relationship, the ethnicity of the women, and the geographical ward from which the call to the police came.

Table 4 reveals the complexity of the relationships in which domestic violence occurs, and indeed, relationships that have ended accounted for 24 per cent of registered incidents. Out of the 'past relationship' category, a total of 31 (11.9 per cent) were ex-girlfriends. Furthermore, of the calls regarding on-going relationships, 12 per cent were from 'girlfriends', which may also include 'visiting relationships' as described by Mama (1989a). This is of great concern, because women in these relationships are largely ignored by civil statute law relating to domestic violence and thus have little protection other than recourse to the criminal law.

Similarly, Mooney's 1993 study of 1,000 men and women in north London found the distribution of relationships to be: husband or cohabitant, 54 per cent; current boyfriend, 3 per cent; former husband or cohabitant, 23 per cent; former boyfriend, 7 per cent. Thus, 10 per cent of cases involved men who had apparently never lived with the women they assaulted, and 6.2 per cent of the violence occurred after the break-up of the relationship. The relevance of this information to

Table 5: Ethnic origin of women

	no.	Valid percentage	Proportion of study area population
Black	33	13.5	9.1
White	211	86.5	90.9
Total	244	100	100

Source: Nottingham Domestic Violence Study.
Note: missing cases: 35.

any analysis of police practice is suggested by Pahl (1982), who proposes that a cohabiting, rather than a marital relationship, and separation, rather than an on-going relationship, lead to an increased likelihood of police action. This is linked not only to notions of the continuance of marital relations, and the privacy of the family home, but also tied to predictions of the likelihood of the woman withdrawing evidence.

At the beginning of 1993, the Home Office changed the requirement for recording the ethnicity of the victim, and so now, instead of the categories being 'black' and 'white', the distinction is made between 'white', 'black', 'Asian' and 'other'. However, owing to the small total number of black women noted in the register, these categories have been combined. It appears that black women are disproportionately represented in these data. This may be accounted for by the fact that the ethnicity of black women is more likely to be recorded in the register than that of white women; thus the vast majority of the thirty-five missing values are more likely to be white women. Even accounting for this, the relative proportion of black women reporting domestic violence is higher than that expected given the potential racism which deters black women from reporting violence to the police (Mama 1989 a and b). This most probably reflects the paucity of alternative options for black women, and the difficulties faced in trying to obtain assistance from other agencies.

Smith and Gray (1983) report how police officers are often reluctant to act assertively within the Asian community because they see it as a 'closed community'. Yet, black women fear not only a lack of positive assistance from police, but also that if their partner is black he may face worse treatment from the criminal justice system than white

Table 6: Ward percentages

	no.	Valid percentages	Ward population ratio
Bilborough	11	4.7	12.2
Beechdale	9	3.8	14.8
Strelley	51	21.6	15.3
Aspley	58	24.6	17.9
Robin Hood	25	10.6	9.4
Radford	66	28.0	14.2
Basford	16	6.8	16.2
Total	236	100	100

Source: Nottingham Domestic Violence Study
Note: Missing cases: 43.

offenders. The Commission for Racial Equality (1992), for example, reported that Afro-Caribbean men have a 17 per-cent greater chance of custodial sentencing than white men convicted of similar offences. In addition, many women fear that involving the police may put them under the scrutiny of organizations dealing with child welfare and immigration, thereby putting them at risk from child care orders or deportation (Mama 1989a). Black women's groups are concerned that the information held on police domestic violence registers may be used by the Home Office to check up on the immigration status of black victims of domestic violence (Roshni 1992).

Table 6 indicates the spatial distribution of registered calls by ward. A distinctive pattern emerges which has been maintained throughout the study period. Clusters of registered calls are apparent in the areas of Strelley, Aspley and Radford, which cannot be explained by the differences in population ratio. Unfortunately, time constraints have meant that the police telephone message logs could not be completely analysed, so there is no direct evidence of the geographical mapping for all domestic violence calls. However, the pattern of distribution for registered calls suggests that the police interpret calls more seriously when they come from areas which are reputedly more violent. The distribution of police decisions about whether or not to charge the aggressor will indicate whether a more serious attitude is taken in certain areas, when controlling for the level of violence.

On a more critical level, the growing intervention of the police into the arena of domestic violence is not welcomed by all. Whilst it serves an important symbolic role in society, stating that violence against women is unacceptable to the community, and emphasizing that it is a crime, is it merely a transfer of the control of women from individual men to the public sphere? Hanmer *et al.* (1989) argue that the patriarchal nature of the police force and the criminal justice system just provides another form of social control that women must face. As Morley and Mullender (1991) point out, compelling a woman to testify against her partner, and punishing her for contempt if she refuses, could be seen as being just one more form of abuse. Moreover, the motivation for the sudden interest in women's rights has been questioned; for example, Southall Black Sisters (1989) suggest that this response was a feature of the hidden agenda of re-establishing police credibility, and reasserting surveillance and control amongst inner-city communities.

Research in Canada suggests that women are sometimes forced into co-operating with the criminal justice system in order to receive assistance from other agencies (Macleod 1989). This coercion can arise from other agencies refusing to provide help without police evidence of violence, or from the police withholding information about other support agencies unless women co-operate with their enquiries. Indeed this has emerged from my interviews with women about their experiences of police from other areas. This issue needs to be carefully addressed alongside the question about what we can realistically expect the police to achieve, and how far the structure of the criminal justice system can be used to meet women's real needs. Until there is a closely defined role for the police in domestic violence, incorporating an acknowledgement of what the police cannot be expected to achieve, it will remain extremely hard to use police statistics as a basis for policy development or resource appraisal.

Concluding comments

The timidity of the police in intervening in domestic violence does not arise from inadequate police powers, as those granted by the Police and Criminal Evidence Act (1984) are extremely wide. Rather, it would seem that police discretion in dealing with the abuse of women allows an enormous amount of crime to be ignored. The Women's National Commission (1985: 9) recognized the fundamental problem of trying to ensure arrest, and advised that when dealing with domestic violence, police officers 'should not use their own discretion'. Bourlet (1990) warns against this, arguing that owing to the police officers' original authority to perform their duty, any restriction on their discretion lays them open to being sued through the civil law. However, it seems very unlikely that, if implemented properly, the position of police officers would be compromised at all by a comprehensively enforced pro-active policy.

The interim findings from Nottinghamshire suggest that, given the wide discretionary powers of the individual officers, policy change in itself is not very useful. Domestic violence cases are now being screened to decide whether to log them in the register, and both arrest and charge rates remain low. It is this inertia of the police, particularly with relation to aspects of their duties which are seen as not being 'proper' police work, that raises concern for the benefit of policy change. The emphasis should not be so much on changes in police procedure, but rather focus on the re-education of officers at every level so that they see domestic violence for the crime that it is.

This study of the police responses to domestic violence in Nottingham reveals that police statistics derived from domestic violence registers seriously underestimate the extent of the abuse that the police work with because of the screening of calls. Calls are screened for two reasons. Firstly, the police do not regard the vast majority as being serious enough to merit recording. Secondly, because of the sheer volume of calls, they do not feel able to record them all, and only the most 'violent' calls are registered. If domestic violence registers are used to inform and direct policy development, then the whole domestic violence picture will not be uncovered, leading to serious resourcing deficiencies.

Whilst the police are continuing to be criticized for their work in this area, we must remember that they are placing an increasing emphasis on domestic violence work, and this is an important step forward. Unfortunately, resource constraints mean that this is unlikely to be developed further. One of the most important issues is the training of officers to ensure that domestic violence issues are understood. It must be asked whether police work pertaining to domestic violence needs to be restructured. In particular, it must be recognized that traditional evaluations of police work, such as arrest and conviction rates, cannot be applied to domestic violence cases in a meaningful way when the most important factor is working in a flexible manner with the injured party.

Notes

[1] I wish to thank Nottinghamshire Police Constabulary for their complete co-operation in this research programme.

[2] Nottinghamshire Domestic Violence Forum, Nottinghamshire County Council, 17 September 1992.

[3] The Forum's definition of 'relationship' extends it to any association of 'an economic, emotional or sexual nature, for example partners, friends, male family members, ex-partners, lodgers or landlords'.

[4] As registered calls are generally more violent cases, and domestic violence tends to escalate in both severity and frequency (Dobash and Dobash 1979), it can be assumed that they are more likely to be repeated in a shorter time-span; therefore, using the same repeat-call rate for non-registered cases is probably an underestimate of the true number of calls.

References

Binney V., Harkell G. and Nixon J. (1981). *Leaving Violent Men: a Study of Refuges and Housing for Battered Women* (London, Women's Aid Federation, England).

Borkowski, M., Murch M. and Walker V. (1983). *Marital Violence. The Community Response* (London, Tavistock Publishers).

Bourlet, A. (1990). *Police Intervention in Marital Disputes* (Milton Keynes, Open University Press).

Commission for Racial Equality (1992). *The Hood Report* (Oxford, Clarendon Press).

Department of Employment (1992). *Employment Gazette*, October 1992, table 7.1, s.64 (London, HMSO).

Dobash, R. E. and Dobash, R. P. (1979). *Violence Against Wives* (New York, The Free Press).

Dobash, R. P., Dobash, R. E., Wilson M. and Daly M. (1992). 'The myth of sexual symmetry in marital violence', *Social Problems*, 39, 1 February, 71–91.

Dunhill, C. (ed.) (1989). *The Boys in Blue: Women's Challenge to the Police* (London, Virago).

Edwards, S. S. M. (1986a). 'Police attitudes and dispositions in domestic disputes: the London study', *Police Journal*, July, 230–41.

Edwards, S. S. M. (1986b). *The Police Response to Domestic Violence in London* (London, Central London Polytechnic).

Edwards, S. S. M. (1989). *Policing 'Domestic' Violence. Women, the Law and the State* (London, Sage).

Edwards, S. S. M. and Halpern, A. (1991). 'Protection for the victim of domestic violence: time for radical revision?', *Journal of Social Welfare and Family Law*, No. 2, 94–109.

Edwards, S. S. M. and Halpern, A. (1992). 'The progress towards protection', *New Law Journal*, 5 June, 798–800.

aragher, T. (1985). 'The police response to violence against women in the home' in J. Pahl (ed.), *Private Violence and Public Policy* (London, Routledge & Kegan Paul).

reeman, M. D. A. (1985). 'Towards a critical theory of family law', *Current Legal Problems*, 38, 153–85.

lanmer, J., Radford, J. and Stanko, E. A. (1989). *Women, Policing and Male Violence: International Perspectives* (London, Routledge).

lanmer, J., Radford, J. and Stanko, E. A. (1989). 'Improving policing for women', in J. Hanmer, J. Radford, and E. A. Stanko (eds.), *Women, Policing and Male Violence: International Perspectives* (London, Routledge).

lanmer, J. and Stanko E. A. (1985). 'Stripping away the rhetoric of protection: women, law and the state', *International Journal of the Sociology of Law*, November.

lome Affairs Committee (1993). *Domestic Violence*, third report, Volume 1. (London, HMSO), Para 10.

lome Office (1986). *Home Office Circular 69/1986* (London, HMSO).

lome Office (1986). *Police Initial Training Notes* (London, HMSO).

lome Office (1990). *Home Office Circular 60/1990*, 31 July (London, HMSO).

lome Office (1992). *Criminal Statistics: England and Wales (1992)*, Cm. 2410 (London, HMSO).

lacleod, L. (1989). *Preventing Wife Battering: Towards a New Understanding* (Ottawa, Ontario, Canadian Advisory Council on the Status of Women).

lama, A. (1989a). *The Hidden Struggle* (London, London Race and Housing Research Unit).

lama, A. (1989b). 'Violence against black women: gender, race and state responses', *Feminist Review*, No. 32, Summer.

looney, J. (1993). 'Researching domestic violence: the North London domestic violence survey', paper given at the British Sociological Conference.

lorley, R. and Mullender, A. (1991). 'Hype or hope: the importation of pro-arrest policies and batterers' programmes from North America to Britain as key measures for preventing violence against women in the home', Law and Society Association and Research Committee, International Sociological Association Joint Meetings, University of Amsterdam, 26–29 June 1991.

lottingham City Council (1991). *Nottingham City District Profile* (Nottingham City Council, Development Department).

ottinghamshire County Council (1991). *1991 Census, Area Profile* (Nottinghamshire County Council, Planning Policy Group, Department of Planning and Economic Development).

ahl, J. (1982). 'Police response to battered women', *Journal of Social Welfare Law*, November, 337–43.

ahl, J. (1985). *Private Violence and Public Policy: The Needs of Battered Women and the Response of the Public Services* (London, Routledge).

Report of The Commissioner of Police of The Metropolis (1989). (London, Metropolitan Police).

Roshni (Nottingham Asian Women's Aid) (1992). *Forwarding the Struggle* (Conference Report, April 1992) (Nottingham, Roshni).

Smith, D. J. and Fray, J. (1983). *Police and People in London* (Policy Studies Institute) (London, Gower).

Smith, L. (1989). *Domestic Violence: An Overview of the Literature*, Research Study 107 (London, HMSO).

Southall Black Sisters (1989). 'Two struggles: challenging male violence and the police', in C. Dunhill (ed.), *The Boys in Blue: Women's Challenge to the Police* (London, Virago).

Stanko, E. A. (1989). 'Missing the mark? Policing battering', in J. Hanmer, J Radford, and E. A. Stanko (eds.), *Women Policing and Male Violence International Perspectives* (London, Routledge),

Victim Support (1992). *Domestic Violence: Report of an Inter-agency Working Party* (London, Victim Support).

Women's National Commission (1985). *Violence Against Women – Report of an Ad-Hoc Working Group* (London, Cabinet Office), Recommendation 18(iv) p. 9.

ndex